Fielding transnationalism

The Sociological Review Monographs

Since 1958, *The Sociological Review* has established a tradition of publishing one or two Monographs a year on issues of general sociological interest. TheMonograph is an edited book length collection of refereed research papers which is published and distributed in association with Wiley Blackwell. We are keen to receive innovative collections of work in sociology and related disciplines with a particular emphasis on exploring empirical materials and theoretical frameworks which are currently under-developed.

If you wish to discuss ideas for a Monograph then please contact the Monographs Editor, Steve Brown, Professor of Social and Organisational Psychology, School of Management, University of Leicester, Leicester, LE1 7RH, UK. e-mail: s.d.brown@le.ac.uk

Our latest Monographs include:

Biosocial Matters: Rethinking Sociology-Biology Relations in the Twenty-First Century (edited by Maurizio Meloni, Simon Williams and Paul Martin)
Radical Futures? Youth, Politics and Activism in Contemporary Europe (edited by Hilary Pilkington and Gary Pollock)
Gender and Creative Labour (edited by Bridget Conor, Rosalind Gill & Stephanie Taylor)
Violence and Society: Toward a New Sociology (edited by Jane Kilby and Larry Ray)
Disasters and Politics: Materials, Experiments, Preparedness (edited by Manuel Tironi, Israel Rodriguez-Giralt and Michael Guggenheim)
Urban Rhythms: Mobilities, Space and Interation in the Contemporary City (edited by Robin James Smith and Kevin Hetherington)
Waste Matters (edited by David Evans, Hugh Campbell and Anne Murcott)
Live Methods (edited by Les Back and Nirmal Puwar)
Measure and Value (edited by Lisa Adkins and Celia Lury)
Norbert Elias and Figurational Research: Processual Thinking in Sociology (edited by Norman Gabriel and Stephen Mennell)
Sociological Routes and Political Roots (edited by Michaela Benson and Rolland Munro)
Nature, Society and Environmental Crisis (edited by Bob Carter and Nickie Charles)
Space Travel & Culture: From Apollo to Space Tourism (edited by David Bell and Martin Parker)
Un/Knowing Bodies (edited by Joanna Latimer and Michael Schillmeier)
Remembering Elites (edited by Mike Savage and Karel Williams)
Market Devices (edited by Michel Callon, Yuval Millo and Fabian Muniesa)
Embodying Sociology: Retrospect, Progress and Prospects (edited by Chris Shilling)
Sports Mega-Events: Social Scientific Analyses of a Global Phenomenon (edited by John Horne and Wolfram Manzenreiter)

Other Monographs have been published on consumption; museums; culture and computing; death; gender and bureaucracy; sport plus many other areas. For further information about the Monograph Series, please visit: www.sociologicalreviewmonographs.com

Fielding Transnationalism

Edited by Julian Go and Monika Krause

Wiley Blackwell/The Sociological Review

This edition first published 2016

ISBN 9781119237877 and The Sociological Review Monographs, 64:2.

All articles published within this monograph are included within
the ISI Journal Citation Reports® Social Science Citation Index.
Please quote the article DOI when citing monograph content.

Registered Office
John Wiley & Sons Ltd, The Atrium, Southern Gate, Chichester, West Sussex, PO19 8SQ, UK

Editorial Offices
350 Main Street, Malden, MA 02148-5020, USA
9600 Garsington Road, Oxford, OX4 2DQ, UK
The Atrium, Southern Gate, Chichester, West Sussex, PO19 8SQ, UK

For details of our global editorial offices, for customer services, and for information about how to apply for permission to reuse the copyright material in this book please see our website at www.wiley.com/wiley-blackwell.

First published in 2016 by John Wiley & Sons

Library of Congress Cataloging-in-Publication Data

Names: Go, Julian, 1970- editor. | Krause, Monika, 1978- editor.

Title: Fielding transnationalism / edited by Julian Go and Monika Krause.

Description: Chichester, West Sussex, UK : John Wiley & Sons, 2016. | Series: The sociological review monographs | Includes bibliographical references and index.

Identifiers: LCCN 2016011547 | ISBN 9781119237877 (alk. paper)

Subjects: LCSH: Transnationalism--Social aspects. | Field theory (Social psychology)

Classification: LCC JZ1320 .F54 2016 | DDC 320.54--dc23 LC record available at http://lccn.loc.gov/2016011547

A catalogue record for this title is available from the British Library

Set in TimesNRMT 10/12pt by Aptara Inc.

Printed and bound in the United Kingdom

1 2016

Contents

Fielding transnationalism: an introduction

Julian Go and Monika Krause

The new interest in transnational phenomena since the 1990s has produced a wide range of studies across the social sciences. In the discipline of history, Akira Iriye (1989: 2) has called for historians to 'search for historical themes and conceptions that are meaningful across national boundaries', a call echoed by the new global and transnational history. In sociology, agendas for a 'global sociology' have come from former President of the American Sociological Association, Michael Burawoy (2000, 2008) and prominent European theorist Ulrich Beck (2006), among others. Meanwhile, Immanuel Wallerstein has long urged social scientists to 'unthink' state-centrism and theorize on a more global scale (Wallerstein, 2001).

The intellectual space constituted by this work has been interdisciplinary. It has also sometimes been 'undisciplined' in its use of diverse concepts, theories and literatures. Rather than overarching theoretically guided research programmes, we find disparate areas of research: studies of immigration, global cities, neoliberalism, neoimperialism, the global diffusion of organizational forms, and so on. The interdisciplinary and undisciplined nature of this space has had its advantages. It has led, for example, to surprising dialogues across the boundaries that sometimes separate theoretical schools within disciplines. It also brings with it potential disadvantages: It might mean, among other things, that the full potential of any one theoretical approach is not fully explored. Each of these empirical areas are rich but they have yielded, and engage with, separated theories of the middle-range: for example, theories of immigration, theories of global cities, theories of global culture, and so on. Besides a few exceptions, to be discussed below, shared theoretical frameworks or concepts on transnational processes across the subfields are comparably lacking.

The papers in this collection specifically explore the potential of the concept of the 'field' in the Bourdieusian tradition for analysing transnational processes. Throughout his career, but especially in his latter half, Bourdieu theorized 'field' as an important part of his overarching theoretical corpus, alongside and part of concepts like practice, habitus, and capital (Swartz, 1997). He explored a

The Sociological Review Monographs, 64:2, pp. 6–30 (2016), DOI: 10.1111/2059-7932.12000

Published by John Wiley & Sons Ltd, 9600 Garsington Road, Oxford OX4 2DQ, UK and 350 Main Street, Malden, MA 02148, USA

diversity of fields, starting from the religious field (Bourdieu, 1991b) and then to the political, artistic and literary fields (Bourdieu, 1993), and the intellectual and academic fields (Bourdieu, 1984a), among others (Bourdieu, 2005). Bourdieu did not systematically examine field dynamics or processes on non-national scales. Early in his career (Bourdieu, 1959), he was prompted by his work in Algeria to theorize cross-cultural relations wrought by colonialism, but he did not employ the field concept. His latest work only alluded to a global economic field of neo-liberal capitalism (Bourdieu *et al.*, 2000; Bourdieu, 2003). In between, he wrote about the transnational circulation of ideas (Bourdieu, 2002), the 'possibility of a field of world sociology' (1991a), and briefly referred to globalization and culture in his book on television (1999). But in these instances he focused on intellectual fields rather than other types of fields, and he did not identify transnational or global logics. He argued instead that, for the time being at least, national fields were impeding the construction of transnational or world intellectual fields. A full systematic consideration of transnational and global fields in the work of Bourdieu eludes us.

As we will develop in more detail below, we suggest that field theory offers a set of concepts especially generative for analysing transnational processes and relations. It gives us a lens through which we can inquire about patterns and institutions in the social world in a way that does not privilege the national state a priori, and in a way that transcends the opposition between 'national order' on the one hand and 'global flows' on the other hand. This project of 'fielding transnationalism' – and 'transnationalizing fields' – is a collective one. This volume builds on recent work in sociology, international relations (IR) and history by some of our authors and others.[1] *Fielding Transnationalism* is a work in progress and one that we hope will be sustained in the future. Together the papers in this volume show the strengths of field theory for apprehending transnational processes and relations, even as they also raise questions for future work. In the spirit of Bourdieu's own work, the papers are grounded in fine-grained empirical research, and the empirical range is wide. Some speak to institutions that are or could be central to discussions of the transnational in political science – such as the European Central Bank (Mudge and Vauchez), the US government (Stampnitzky), and the British and the German empire (Wilson; Steinmetz). Others show their sociological heritage by also paying attention to cultural production (Buchholz), to academic disciplines (Steinmetz; Krause), and to journalism (Christin). Empirically, of course, there are many further areas of inquiry that could benefit from a field analysis. We could learn from a wide range of historical and contemporary cases. These papers offer a starting point.[2]

There is also more work to do theoretically. One motivation for bringing these papers together is that they are all deeply engaged with a similar set of theoretical resources, organized around Bourdieu's thinking, which we think are very useful. Precisely because of this, the work also shows productive tensions, fault lines and building sites for future theoretical work. There is more work to be done, for example, concerning the implications of different versions of field-theoretical approaches and concerning the way field theory can be used while also dealing with issues that have traditionally been outside its focus, such as technologies and territory. Still, we hope this volume is a fruitful beginning.

In what follows, we will first briefly outline field theory and then discuss some of the advantages of the approach in dialogue with other approaches to the transnational, including world-systems theory, world society/neoinstitutionalism, and global governmentality. We will highlight field theory's specific version of going beyond methodological transnationalism, and we will highlight why, in the context of discussions about transnationalism, field theory's efforts to go beyond the dualism of meanings and interests, and its focus on differentiated spaces and practices, might be of value. We will discuss the distinctive emphasis that field theory brings to discussions of world culture, and the ways in which field theory raises questions about change. Lastly we will provide a glimpse into the papers comprising this volume.

Bourdieu's field theory

Field theory does not start with Bourdieu. Field theory first arises from physics and philosophers who then extended the concept 'field' for various purposes (Martin, 2003; Hilgers and Mangez, 2014). Kurt Lewin (1975) is generally cited as the first social scientist to have used the term. Today, scholars in a number of areas within sociology, such as especially organizations and social movements, have employed the 'fields' concept (eg Dimaggio and Powell, 1991; Fligstein, 2001; Fligstein and McAdam, 2012; Thornton *et al.*, 2012). However, not all of these theories are directly indebted to Bourdieu. For example, as Wilson in this volume notes, Fligstein and McAdam's (2012) concept of 'strategic action fields' has a different emphasis and set of concerns than Bourdieu's field theory. This is part of a larger pattern. In organizational studies or social movement studies, 'fields' often refer to any meso-level social relation (Emirbayer and Johnson, 2008; cf. Fligstein and McAdam, 2012). Alternatively, Bourdieu's field theory is much more specific.

So what is a 'field' in Bourdieu's sense? Bourdieu's conceptualization is initially straightforward enough: a field is *not* just any meso-level relation, it is a social space of relations or social configuration defined by struggle over capitals. That is, it is an arena of struggle in which actors compete for a variety of valued resources. Bourdieu refers to these resources as different species of 'capital' that are potentially convertible to each other. Fields, then, consist of two related but analytically separable dimensions: (1) the objective configuration of actor-positions and (2) the subjective meanings guiding actors in the struggle; that is, the 'rules of the game' and particular types of cultural or symbolic capital (Bourdieu and Wacquant, 1992: 97). The actors can be individuals or corporate actors; the 'capitals' pursued by any particular actor in the field might be multiple (eg economic capital, political capital or symbolic capital); and the 'rules of the game' can vary across fields or across time (Bourdieu and Wacquant, 1992: 232). In brief, fields are multidimensional spaces of social action and struggle. They are not 'structures' or 'systems' – entities with stable and

The Sociological Review Monographs, 64:2, pp. 6–30 (2016), DOI: 10.1111/2059-7932.12000

essential identities. They are collections of fluid and dynamic *relations*. 'To think in terms of fields is to think relationally' (Bourdieu and Wacquant, 1992: 96).

There are many other aspects to Bourdieu's field theory, and the essays in this volume each offer their own elaborations and highlight different aspects of it. Here we register five additional points. First, what actors in fields compete for is capital but, in any given field, there might be multiple forms of capital: economic, political, cultural, symbolic, or whatever the particular field in question may valorize (Bourdieu, 1986). In some fields, economic capital dominates; in others, cultural capital reigns (Swartz, 1997: 66). And there can be different forms of different types of capital, such as different kinds of symbolic capital, depending upon the field: 'academic capital' (Bourdieu, 1984a) or 'juridical capital' (Bourdieu, 1994), for instance (see also Desan, 2013). 'It is in fact impossible to account for the structure and functioning of the social world unless one reintroduces capital in all its forms and not solely in the one form recognized by economic theory' (Bourdieu, 1986: 242). In other words, there is always the possibility that there may be more than one form of capital, and field theory is attentive to this possibility. Furthermore, there is also the potential of convertibility. A field may valorize economic capital more than cultural capital but this does not mean cultural capital is not important or fought over; it just means that its value is less, in that particular field, than economic capital. Cultural capital, in such cases, may indeed convert to economic capital, which is why actors might still seek it in the first place; or other types of capital might be at play in the field. In any case, the point is to recognize the possibility of multiple forms of capital.

The multiplicity of capitals in fields brings us to the second point: fields, like capitals themselves, cannot be analytically reduced to either their 'objective' or 'subjective' dimensions. Rather than stressing either the material or cultural dimensions of social life, a fields approach incorporates both. The concept field refers to the configuration of actors (the multidimensional 'field of forces') *and* the classificatory schemes and rules of the game which actors use as they strategize and struggle for position (ie the 'rules of the game') (Bourdieu and Wacquant, 1992: 97). Field is an inclusive concept orienting analysts to both objective positions and cultural meaning, to both objective positions and cultural stances (Bourdieu and Wacquant, 1992).

Third, fields are typically characterized by dominant and subordinate positions; or 'dominants' and 'pretenders' (Bourdieu, 1996: 206). In any given field, at any given time, one group of actors will likely wield most of the capital (whichever form of capital is most highly valued) while others will have less (Bourdieu, 1971: 161). This establishes some of the key logics to fields. Actors compete for capital, which means subordinate actors compete with dominant actors even if they might compete with each other. The 'rules of the game' are most often set, and protected, by the dominant actors, while subordinate actors eventually come to challenge those rules and impose new ones. The latter become 'heretics': they challenge the existing rules, or 'orthodoxy' of the dominant players who cling to their privileges through their 'conservation' strategies in the face of the 'subversion' strategies of challengers (Bourdieu, 1991b; Swartz, 1997). Thus challengers

The Sociological Review Monographs, 64:2, pp. 6–30 (2016), DOI: 10.1111/2059-7932.12000

or subordinate actors might try to make some forms of capital more valuable than others – that is, the types of capital that they might happen to have access to – and they might engage in 'classification struggles' (see also Barman, 2013). In short, struggle and hierarchy are not only characteristic of fields, they also form the basis for many of the processes and logics of fields themselves.

Fourth, fields exhibit certain logics (of competition for capital; of particular capitals being valued more than others; of which form of capital transfers to another form and their conversion rates, etc.) that are not entirely reducible to other social logics. Bourdieu thus speaks of fields as 'relatively autonomous' in the Althusserian sense of autonomous – following their own inherent logics – but also connected with or related to other fields. As Steinmetz and Buccholz in this volume point out, fields are only 'relatively' autonomous because they are often 'influenced by external causal chains or mechanisms'. Therefore, there are often several fields that intersect or relate, but they are each relatively distinct (see also Hess and Frickel, 2014). The field of universities in France may connect with or be adjacent with the field of finance, but they each follow their own distinct rules and principles (Bourdieu, 1984a; Bourdieu and Passeron, 1977). One field may subsume another field into it; or one field may break off from another. The struggles in one field may correspond with and depend upon struggles in another field – as Bourdieu (1996) argues in discussing the literary field; and agents in a field may appropriate resources from other fields to deploy as capital in their own field – following the 'heteronomous principle' (Bourdieu, 1996).

Finally, the *degree* of autonomy of any given field can vary over time. And we can differentiate between different types of autonomy (Benson, 2005, 2013; Krause n.d., Buchholz this volume). Thus the dynamics of field autonomization, articulation, convergence, subsumption, or separation are exactly the sort of processes susceptible to empirical analysis and further theorization. Also susceptible are the *spatialization* of fields. This brings us to the possible utility of field analysis for transnational and global analysis, to which we now finally turn.

Fields beyond the nation state

The field approach has been used to answer many different questions, concerning cases from different time periods and geographical areas. But we are interested not just in field theory per se but in how it might be fruitfully deployed for thinking about social relations beyond the nation-state. We are interested in spatially extending or 'scaling' up field analysis – or 'scaling' down – in order to understand social struggles across, between, and through conventional national boundaries. In short, we are interested in *transnational and global fields,* which Bourdieu himself did not pursue. What, then, are the premises, possibilities and promises of extending the field concept in this way?

Boundaries: beyond methodological nationalism

An important aspect of transnational and global analysis has long been the scale or unit of research and theorizing. This rethinking of scales or units

 The Sociological Review Monographs, 64:2, pp. 6–30 (2016), DOI: 10.1111/2059-7932.12000

has been pioneered by dependency theory (Frank, 1967), world systems theory (Wallerstein, 1974, 2004), world society/neoinstititutional theory (Meyer *et al.*, 1997; Meyer, 2010) and a range of approaches in international relations (Holsti, 1985; Slaughter, 2011). Within the terms of its own theoretical logic, field theory can be rightfully deployed to join the existing scholarship critiquing and reaching beyond methodological nationalism. As has been noted, much of Bourdieu's work analyses fields that align with the national state. But theoretically, for Bourdieu, fields are not predetermined, given or static. The starting point of field-analysis are relationships, not any pre-given unit of analysis. The boundaries of fields are always open to redefinition and fields can extend or contract (Sapiro, 2013).

This relational feature of social fields – that their boundaries are never settled or preordained but contingent and open to expansion or contraction – is one of the features that make it particularly amenable to transnational and global analysis, equipping scholars with a conceptual apparatus that is not intrinsically tied to methodological nationalism. Fields do not necessarily overlap with the boundaries of the nation-state. Bourdieu himself notes that the boundaries of fields do not typically correspond with geographic and political boundaries. When it does, it 'is a *special* case of a field where the limit in the mathematical sense is a border in the geographical and political sense' (Bourdieu as quoted in Sapiro, 2013: 71–72, emphasis added). Therefore, as social relations of competition bleed across or through national boundaries – as they often do – the concept 'fields' captures transnational relations and offers categories for analysing their dynamics and outcomes.

Indeed, field analysis helps overcome attempts to privilege *any* one social scale a priori. World systems theory (Wallerstein, 2004) insists that the appropriate unit of analysis is the world system. Others privilege the 'local' or 'micro' as a privileged window into all scales of relations. Recent works in micro-sociology and actor-network theory, for instance, claim that they have transcended the issue of scale, but in many ways they still privilege the micro because of their very narrow conception of what is observable (Knorr-Cetina, 2007; Hilbert, 1990; Latour, 2005; Latour *et al.*, 2012). Alternatively, from a field perspective, we should treat the question of scale as an object of empirical inquiry. We can ask, which other actors are important to a given group of actors? On what scale are stakes that are relevant to actors articulated? What are the range of responses to scale-relevant stakes? How do these change?

We can learn about empiricizing scale by looking at the history of the national: the national as a scale is itself the result of specific struggles. State-formation as a project is successful when stakes are constructed on the national scale; that is, when elites become actors on the national level (eg Bourdieu, 1994; Loveman, 2005). This was not always so: the aristocracy, for example, was not traditionally oriented towards national stakes. Norbert Elias (2000 [1939]) describes the European's aristocracy's *international* outlook: aristocrats were oriented towards other aristocrats, holidaying in the same resorts, using French as their shared language. They were also to some extent interested in the fields of their own locality, comprising tenants, clergy and local competitors. In France, the king's court was one step towards producing a national field. In Germany and in many other contexts, it was ultimately a bourgeois project to restrict relevant competitors to those tied to language and territory. Some aristocrats started buying into the stakes of the emerging national fields. This did not mean that the international aristocratic field, or that local fields ceased to exist, but they lost in relative importance via-à-vis national fields.

We see here that in some cases transnational fields precede national fields. But in some contemporary fields, we see global fields emerge from national fields, such as with the globalization of art (Buchholz, 2008; Buchholz, this volume) or science (Gingras, 2002; Heilbron, 2014; Fourcade, 2006). This is what Buchholz, in her contribution to this volume, calls the 'vertical' autonomization of transnational fields. Or we can see how some new, genuinely global fields emerge that were never national. This is the creation of entirely new fields: arguably, the first is the system of states itself after 1648. International law is another, studied by Yves Dezalay and Bryan Garth (1998, 2002a, 2002b, 2011). Humanitarianism, defined as cross-border neutral relief, is another genuinely transnational field, though organizations may at the same time be embedded in national fields of charities (Krause, 2014; see Dromi, this volume; also Stamatov 2013).

Considering fields beyond but including the national levels invites students of fields to ask new questions about their object of analysis. To give one example, we can try to analyse how the question of scale itself becomes a stake within fields of struggles. For a field of any given scale, we can ask to what extent access to resources from fields on other scales play a role in the symbolic oppositions that differentiate positions. National fields, for example, may be divided between globalizers and their opponents. Scale here becomes a stake in the competition within a field. Marion Fourcade (2006), for instance, reveals how international links have played a role in national fields of economists in peripheral countries, and international influence also plays some role in structuring national fields in core countries (see also Bockman and Eyal, 2002). Adopting a different analytical starting point, we could inquire about whether resources from national fields create symbolic divisions within global fields, and whether links to local or regional fields create symbolic divisions within national fields. National and transnational fields interact in complex ways (see also the contributions by Dromi, Buccholz and Christin to this volume).

Finally, related to this question of scale is the question of who the 'actors' or 'players' are in the field. In Bourdieu's standard analyses of fields, the actors are individuals: priests in a religious field, state officials in a state bureaucratic field, artists and curators in artistic fields, sociologists or literary scholars in the academic field, and so on. Analysing fields at the international, transnational or global level surely offers promise for examining individuals as actors: think, for instance, of experts and professionals in the global humanitarian field, international union organizers in a global field of labour, or European diplomats in a regional political field (eg Neumann, 2002). But, following the lead of the sociology of organizations, we can also think of organizations themselves as actors

 The Sociological Review Monographs, 64:2, pp. 6–30 (2016), DOI: 10.1111/2059-7932.12000

in a wider field (assuming, of course, their terrain of action is 'fielded' already in Bourdieusian terms). In such cases, an organization itself might constitute a field while also being embedded in larger transnational fields external to it, and its actions would then follow the principles of field action laid out by Bourdieu. We could then think of national states as actors in a wider international field (eg Go, 2008); or humanitarian organizations as actors in a global humanitarian field (Krause, 2014). These organizations would be seen as competitors for capital in fields that transcend national boundaries, and their actions could be analysed in those terms.

Global culture beyond world culture

Field theory thus offers a novel way to conceptualize and analyse social relations at multiple scales, not just the national or the purely 'world-systemic' scale. In doing so, field theory also opens a new perspective and new questions regarding transnational or global cultures. Existing theories of global space often fail to treat culture as a distinct arena of production. World society/world polity approaches to culture analyse it only in terms of cultural models or forms that spread throughout the globe. The only logic is diffusion. Other studies follow the cultural imperialism thesis, insisting on culture as merely a vehicle for Western ideologies and the spread of consumerism (Tomlinson, 1991). By contrast, studying global or transnational fields urges us to examine struggles between cultural producers, relations of power within cultural fields, the different types of capital at play, and the activities and practices of various cultural agents.

The global field of contemporary visual art, as analysed by Buchholz (2008, 2013), is a case in point. Contemporary visual art operates on a global scale. And it constitutes a field in its own right – 'a competitive arena that revolves primarily around acquiring international artistic legitimacy or obtaining the monopoly for determining the criteria of international artistic legitimacy itself' (Buchholz, 2008: 213). In this global field, a variety of actors strive for 'international artistic legitimacy' from artists, curators and museums. And they are not all equal partners in a flat world. Buchholz's analysis finds hierarchization between dominant players monopolizing 'Western symbolic capital' and pretenders. This is similar to what Christin finds in her discussion of US and French journalism in this volume; the only difference is that the opposition is not between 'Western' and 'non-Western' but rather between 'US/Anglophone' and 'non-US/non-Anglophone'. In short, a fields approach illuminates such relations, conflicts and power relations that are otherwise elided in theories of diffusion or one-way imposition (ie 'Westernization').

Not only does Bourdieusian field theory offer an alternative to world society theory's implicit dualism between meaning and economic system, it also offers an alternative to its emphasis upon functional cohesion. World society theory sees global culture as cultural templates or models to which all societies and organizations adhere and which they support and so reproduce. The image projected is of a consensual world society (Finnemore, 1996). In contrast, as discussed,

Bourdieu's very definition of field theory incorporates conflict: fields are spaces of struggle or competition for capitals. As Krause's paper in this volume suggests, the sciences are not only a sphere of rational truth-seeking that gradually spreads throughout the world, or only a unified hegemonic ideology that subjugates other forms of knowledge, but an arena for struggle among positions that are intertwined with struggles about the kind of knowledge that is valued. As Petzke's contribution to this volume shows, religious fields also involve such competition. In fact, it is part of the *nomos* of the Christian missionary field that is imposed upon India in the nineteenth century. Field theory also emphasizes inequality and power relations along with competition. Fields are structured in terms of dominant and dominated positions. We might think, for instance, of the distribution of different capitals across nations in the global political or economic field. When states participate in the United Nations, they clearly not only have different economic resources but also different amounts of political capital, with dominant states monopolizing such capital from others. A field approach thereby illuminates these aspects of the world polity that world polity theory categorically brackets (see Go, 2008). Whereas other approaches do not, a field approach enables us to analyse global culture as an autonomous realm, not fully reducible to economic systems – and one that is contested and conflicted, shot through with power relations.

Meanings and interests, differentiated spaces and practices

While helping us reconceptualize and analyse culture on transnational scales, field theory also helps us overcome the dualism that often arises when studying culture – or when ignoring it. This is the dualism between interests and values that is evident in many theories and empirical studies of transnational phenomena. The theoretical debates in IR scholarship is one manifestation of this dualism. In classical realist IR theory, for instance, the key actors are states who presumably always strive to maximize their resources, and hence their power, due to the anarchic nature of the international system (Waltz, 1979). In reaction to this, a range of theories, from regime theory (Krasner, 1983; Hasenclever *et al.*, 1993; Breitmeier *et al.*, 2007) to neo-institutionalist work (Keohane and Martin, 1995) has emphasized the role of norms and values. And some recent scholarship has focused on the power of human rights and human rights actors to constrain and shape states' behaviour (Risse, 2002; Keck and Sikkink, 1998). The analysis thus shifts from material resources to values or norms, and the analytic opposition between them is reproduced. Sociological theories of the global also manifest this dualism between the material and the symbolic. Consider, for instance, the materialist emphasis of world-systems theory as compared with the culturalist analysis of world society/world culture theory – the latter often directly pitched as an alternative to the material focus of world-systems theory (Boli and Thomas, 1997, 1999; Meyer, 1980; Meyer *et al.*, 1997; Thomas, 2007).

When Bourdieu developed his version of field-theory, he confronted a different version of the same dualism. Debates about art, science and religion in

 The Sociological Review Monographs, 64:2, pp. 6–30 (2016), DOI: 10.1111/2059-7932.12000

domestic contexts are shaped by a similar opposition between values and interests, though the historical succession of the two emphases is usually reversed. In discussions of art, for example, some observers assume art is guided by its inherent values – beauty, inherent aesthetic qualities – while others point out that actors and institutions associated with the arts engage in self-interested behaviour or explain how these values serve the reproduction of some unfair state of affairs (Bourdieu, 1996). Bourdieu sees his sociological approach as a departure from this opposition, trying to give an account of specific arenas of action that go beyond celebrating stated values, while acknowledging that actors' interpretations matter (Bourdieu, 1977). In other words, Bourdieu's field theory tries to absorb both the material and cultural dimensions of social life into the same logically integrated conceptual apparatus. Bourdieu directs us to inquire how interests are interpreted and how values get articulated through mediating spaces, such as fields. Meso level sets of relationships shape how actors perceive and interpret their interests. But values also get entangled in games and symbolic values can become a kind of resource. Fields are shaped by competition for resources, but relationships within the field constitute their own interests, which also include symbolic interests. Bourdieu stresses, for instance, that the power of those who monopolize economic capital is not only due to economic resources but also to symbolic domination, which reflects the successful use of all capitals in the field (Bourdieu, 1977; Swartz, 1997). A field-theoretic approach thus insists upon analysing multiple resources – that is, capitals – that may or may not be purely 'material'. For example, states may seek prestige or honour, which is potentially convertible to other forms of capital (eg material wealth) but can also be an end in itself (Go, 2008). And the pursuit of these resources or capitals is not intrinsic to the actor/state: the 'interests' are not given but shaped by the distinctiveness of the field at play. The field of art, for example, constitutes its own stakes – a field-specific capital – and so actors in this field will be interested in that particular capital form rather than another (Bourdieu, 1993, 1996; see also Buchholz, 2008). Field theory, in short, goes beyond the opposition between values and interests by inviting us to pay attention to the way meanings and interests are constituted within specific social spaces.[3]

Global governance and fields

Field theory's emphasis on the complex interrelation of meaning and interests, as well as its attention to power, brings us to questions of global governance. Owing to a tradition in IR that linked states to power and power to states, and moreover emphasized a state's quest for power as a result of anarchy and distrust, international cooperation and the increasing role of non-state actors were initially conceived as opposed to the exercise of power (Keck and Sikkink, 1998; Wapner, 1996; Willetts, 1996). Since then, it has become clear that transnational processes are part of how order is reproduced and power is exercised. Field theory here opens up new sets of questions about how power is mediated through specific logics of practices, specific forms of symbolic capital, and different kinds of actors.

This contrasts with two critical approaches that have been particularly influential. One diagnoses the present situation as a new form of imperialism; another emphasizes the novel features of governance through networks. In the first approach, the new order is seen as the result of the direct outward projection of the power of certain key states (Furedi, 1994; Chomsky, 1999; Chandler, 2001, 2002, 2004). Commentators point out that NGOs and states are very close (Hulme and Edwards, 1997; Brand *et al.*, 2001) and portray NGOs as tools of interested governments. The other approach sees global power through the lens of 'governmentality' (Duffield, 2001; Larner and Walters, 2004; Hardt and Negri, 2000), inspired by the work of Michel Foucault *et al.*, (1991). Accounts either emphasize NGOs as sites of disciplinary power themselves, such as in micro-credit programs (Rankin, 2001), or refugee settlement (Lippert, 1998). Or they imagine NGOs as integrated into a 'strategic complex of liberal governance' (Duffield, 2001), governmentality (Sending and Neumann, 2006) or empire (Hardt and Negri, 2000).

Each of these approaches has its specific strengths. The imperialism thesis uniquely draws attention to the amount of power that some actors accumulate in the new world order. The governmentality approach usefully points at new aspects of power that are not visible through the lens of the new imperialism, such as the non-territorial and multilateral nature of new forms of governing and the possibly dispersed nature of power. But both also overemphasize the coherence and totalization of global power. Even Foucauldian approaches, despite Foucault's explicit statements to the contrary, risk overestimating the coherence of governmentality (as O'Malley *et al.*, 1997, have also argued). As a consequence, it is difficult to understand the mechanisms of reproduction, the mobilization of actors and their specific forms of resistance. A field approach can provide a theoretical framework for asking these questions. Krause's (2014) study of humanitarian relief NGOs is a good example. Krause argues that neither a focus on stated values nor a focus on state's interests can fully explain what these organizations do and do not do; or the role these organizations play. Rather, since the late 1960s a relatively autonomous field of relief organizations has emerged which mediates the relationship between Western publics and Western states on the one hand and distant suffering on the other hand. This shared social space produces the sorts of assumptions that are common across agencies. It also produces the debates that agencies have with each other over what it means to be a 'humanitarian'.

Field-theoretical accounts of other areas also offer generative perspectives on global power. The wager is that if we are to understand power on a global level we need to pay attention to the specific logics of mediating fields of practice. The European Central Bank, for example, could be described as an expression of neoliberal ideology or a tool of German hegemony. But as Mudge and Vauchez show in this volume, we can better understand its role if we also inquire into the specific ways in which it is and is not integrated into the field of professional economists and if we also consider it as an actor in the European political field competing for capital (Mudge and Vauchez, this volume; see also Lebaron, 2008, 2010; Fourcade, 2006). And as Stampnitzky's contribution to this volume shows,

The Sociological Review Monographs, 64:2, pp. 6–30 (2016), DOI: 10.1111/2059-7932.12000

fields have effects, not only on actors within it, but also beyond it. In her account, the relatively new field of human rights has an effect on states, even if it is not always the effect intended by actors within it.

We might even try to retheorize political globalization from a field perspective. This remains perhaps the more audacious promise of a field approach. For Bourdieu, a properly global political field would require, at minimum, actors who recognize each other and compete for capital. And we could say that, since the Second World War, we have such a political field. The main actors are nation-states competing for economic resources, raw materials and legitimacy. On the other hand, if there is such a global political field, it is weak in Bourdieusian terms. The autonomization of the field is not complete: there is no single authority that fully sets all the 'rules of the game'. The UN, international law, and International Criminal Courts can all be seen as attempts to establish those rules of the game, but it is unclear how successful they will be. The rising field of non-governmental organizations and the economic field populated by transnational corporations pose further complications, impinging upon the full autonomy of the global political field. So how far will autonomization in the global political field go? And is this field of nation-states and international organizations going to be fully subsumed or undermined by the field of global capitalism? Might global capitalism create unique conditions for the global field, making economic capital dominant over global political or cultural capital – something Bourdieu (2003) alluded to but did not systematically address?

These sorts of questions raise the larger problem of globalization and meta-capital. For Bourdieu, the ideal-typical national state is a state with the capacity to regulate and define other forms of capital in its territorial domain. This is the state's 'meta-capital': a form of power which, by regulating and defining what counts as capital, also carries the ability to regulate relations between fields. But since Bourdieu's analyses have remained at the level of national states, he never addressed the question as to whether or how such 'meta-capital' might exist at the *global* level. Since the international organizations like the United Nations or the International Criminal Court have some but not full power over countries in the international system, it would be untenable to point to those institutions as exercising meta-capital. What about an organization like the World Bank or International Monetary Fund? It might be that there is no meta-capital at the transnational or global level, and that processes associated with globalization unfold differently than they would if there were meta-capital. Maybe the end point of globalization is exactly the institution of global meta-capital, once and for all.

Change: the role of struggles

These questions of globalization as a historical process involving autonomization bring us to the contribution of field theory for transnational and global analysis: it can help us analyse social transformation on extensive spatial scales. An important if not obvious task for the analysis of global processes is the analysis of change: how to conceptualize and analyse transformations on transnational or global scales. How does change occur? What forms does it take? What explains transformation? Existing theoretical approaches have different answers – when they answer them at all. In world society/world polity approaches, change in global culture is treated as a matter of diffusion: change in this sense is really just expanded reproduction on a new spatial scale (ie one model spreads throughout the system) (cf. Chorev, 2012). In conventional world systems theory, change in the global system does not actually happen at all: the capitalist system retains its basic core-periphery structure. At most, exactly which countries occupy which positions change; but the slots themselves are never moved around (Wallerstein, 2004). Other variants of world-systems theory see change as mostly cyclical: the system oscillates between hegemonic periods and competitive periods, and between periods of productive and financial expansion (Arrighi, 1994). Finally, Luhmann systems (cf. Holzer *et al.*, 2014) analyses offers a vocabulary for different forms of differentiation and includes also more recently a focus on dedifferentiation. But it rarely goes beyond description to discuss mechanisms of change (Holzer *et al.*, 2014).

While Bourdieu has once been criticized for overemphasizing social reproduction, his corpus in fact includes at least two models of transformation (Gartman, 2002; Swartz, 1997; Steinmetz, 2011; see also Gorski, 2013a, 2013b). One model refers to changes in social actors' habituses and associated social transformations. In this model, changes in habitus occur when there is a disjuncture between the habitus and the field of its application. This disjuncture can happen either because the field faces novel elements (ie economic crisis or the installation of wage labour into subsistence economies) or because social actors are put into an entirely new or foreign field (ie migrants move to a new country) (Bourdieu, 1961 [1958]). Change thus happens due to some kind of external disruption, in which case the habitus forged in one field confronts an entirely different field and undergoes 'hysteresis' (Bourdieu, 1990: 108).

The other model of change emerges from factors endogenous to the field rather than from an external disruption. It occurs through competition and struggle. Fields are typically structured between dominant and dominated positions – the former monopolizing not only capital but also the definition of capital and the 'rules of the game' itself. Conflict and struggle unfolds between the dominant and dominated, as the dominated challenge the definitions of capital and rules which benefit the dominant but keep the dominated at bay. This basic structure sets the basis for various types of change to follow, depending upon the nature of the field and contingent events. In cultural fields, for instance, both the dominant and challenging groups compete with each other but also different class fractions *within* the dominant class compete for distinction. The highest class seeks to differentiate itself from other classes by adopting a distinct 'taste' for 'high art', but then the petty bourgeoisie seeks to distinguish itself from the lower classes by imitating the highest classes. New struggles by the different class fractions ensue, and as these struggles unfold the content of culture itself changes (Bourdieu, 1984b). In other fields, such as the religious field, challengers to the dominant groups emerge as 'heretics' to the defenders of the 'orthodoxy' and struggle to question the dominant groups' legitimacy to define the fields' standards and rules. Bourdieu calls this a 'subversion' strategy of challengers, as opposed to the 'conservation' strategy of the orthodox defenders, and it can ultimately lead to a redefinition of the fields' rules for the distribution or definition of capital (Bourdieu, 1991b). In brief, the type of struggles in fields can vary, and the outcomes are contingent rather than predetermined. But the overarching model remains the same: changes in fields or relations within fields result from competition over capital between subordinated groups challenging the dominant groups' control over the distribution and definition of capital; or among class fractions competing for distinction (symbolic capital).

We believe that such a field theoretic framework on change can also be extended to transnational and global scales. Existing work intimates the possibilities. For instance, Go (2008) uses Bourdieusian field theory to show how the mechanism of struggle between dominant groups and challengers led to changes in the global political field of empires. In the nineteenth century, colonial empires were the norm – the orthodoxy – but by the mid-twentieth century, direct colonization was no longer acceptable, so much that dominant powers like the US ceased annexing new territory as colonies and instead turned to 'informal' imperialism. Colonies today are nearly non-existent: it is part of the *doxa* of global political culture that direct colonization is unacceptable. In Bourdieusian fashion, Go (2008) argues that this change occurred as a result of struggle among dominant powers and between them and revolutionary nationalists in the colonial world, ultimately making anti-colonial nationalism itself a new form of capital. The struggles changed 'the rules of the game', such that competition between great powers could no longer take the form of colonial scrambles.

Another promising example comes from Berling (2012), who analyses the changing field of European security. In the 1980s, the orthodox view on European security, pushed by NATO, European states, and security experts saw 'security' as a matter of external material threats and therefore emphasized military balancing as the main strategy for maintaining security. It valorized military power as capital. The heterodox view, promoted by a small group of peace researchers, emphasized detente, dialogue and common security and thereby downplayed military power and emphasized democratic values. By the 1990s, the field had changed: the orthodox view now emphasized democratic values and the emphasis upon military power was downplayed. The fall of the Soviet Union, Berling explains, was key for this change, but only because the fall articulated with experts' competition with each other to define the legitimate security logic in Europe. Again, we see here how Bourdieusian field concepts help illuminate critical processes of change at transnational and global scales.

The papers in this volume

The contributions to this volume exploit this potential and expand upon and elaborate the issues regarding the rescaling of field theory, although they each do so in different ways, and each hit upon distinct themes. Together they address questions and problems that have been raised in the nascent interdisciplinary scholarship that rescales Bourdieusian concepts but which, as yet, have not been fully addressed. For example: if fields can be transnational rather than only national, what is the process by which such transnational fields are created? Or, what about field extension, that is, when the social agents and relations in fields from one geographical locale are stretched across or enter into new social spaces? What are the modalities, either historical or contemporary, by which transnational fields are created or extended? If fields are indeed transnational or global, what role do national spaces or dynamics still play if any at all? And when or why do fields fail to become transnational or global? What are the limits of extending national fields or creating transnational ones? How can an analysis of the dynamics within and across fields be combined with attention to the material objects of practice?

Field emergence

The first papers address the question of field *emergence* or how fields are created. One criteria, as noted earlier in this introduction, is autonomy. This is the concept explored in Buchholz's essay. She argues that 'autonomy' is a useful concept but that it must be differentiated into 'vertical' as opposed to 'horizontal' autonomy. Horizontal autonomy is the sort of process of field creation that Bourdieu himself refers to in his analysis of the emergence of the literary field in France. It means the differentiation of a social space from existing spaces to the point where it develops its own unique *nomos* and a new practice – a social logic that is distinct from other adjacent fields. It can thus be seen as part of the larger social process of field proliferation through social differentiation. Vertical autonomy is different: it involves the autonomization of a social space not from social fields adjacent to it but from fields 'below' it. It is an extension upwards. It is about 'scalar differentiation' rather than functional differentiation, and it does not mean an entirely distinct field of practice but rather a rescaling upwards of the same sphere of practice. In the case of the literary field in France, a domain of practice – literature – is differentiated from other domains of practice, like politics. But vertical autonomy means the same domain of practice – in Buchholz's case, the visual arts – already differentiated from other fields is maintained, it just becomes autonomous from its previous national-level spatiality. Globalization in this light can be thought of as this rescaling upwards of existing domains as opposed to the mere geographical extension or differentiation of social spaces into new domains.

Wilson's essay shifts gears to trace how the emergence of the East India Company as a territorial power in India after 1765 came with a distinct imperial administrative field structured around the rule of colonial difference. How exactly did this field form? Wilson suggests that Bourdieu's field theory is helpful for identifying a key logic of this field and its emergence, especially Bourdieu's concept of 'interest in disinterest'. A distinctively imperial field of

 The Sociological Review Monographs, 64:2, pp. 6–30 (2016), DOI: 10.1111/2059-7932.12000

administrative vision emerges when officials struggling with one another for metropolitan recognition provided moral accounts of themselves which, on the one hand, explained their behaviour in terms drawn from abstract, purportedly universal social spaces, and, on the other hand, claimed credibility through a personal 'interest in disinterest'. But to fully account for historical emergence, Wilson suggests that concepts from Fligstein and McAdam's theory of 'strategic action field' and Padgett and Powell's network approach need to be employed.

Dromi's paper also shows how transnational fields are created, but additionally shows how national-level dynamics in themselves shape the emergence of transnational fields. Drawing on Bourdieu's work on the international spread of ideas, Dromi points to the role of intercultural translation processes in the expansion of field structures beyond national boundaries. His case is the nascent humanitarian field of the late nineteenth century, and in particular the international Red Cross movement. The International Committee of the Red Cross (ICRC) was a key organization in laying down the organizational and cultural infrastructure upon which a transnational humanitarian field would later be mounted. But the processes that led to the eventual establishment of the transnational humanitarian field initially deployed rather than transcended nationalism and national-level social relations. National Red Cross societies drew upon the transnational humanitarian language of the ICRC as they did their work but also articulated it with discourses promoting national identities. Nationalism, ironically, had a 'generative effect' upon the emergence of a transnational field.

Field extension

Once fields are formed, there is always the possibility that they might extend outwards and be articulated with, or encompass, new previously foreign actors and relations. The next essays explore this possibility of field *extension*. Historically, we could point to particular modalities by which fields have been extended in the early modern or modern era, not least imperialism or religious diasporas or missions, and both of these are addressed here.

Steinmetz's paper considers the extension of fields through imperialism. What happens as the social relations constituting a field in one site are extended elsewhere? Steinmetz shows, imperial 'fielding' is a complex process. It is not a mere extension of fields. As he points out, not all social spaces take on the logic of fields, and there are different dynamics to the extension of social relations to new scales. Some relations that have already formed as fields are extended into the colonies from their metropolitan origin and undergo little change, but they might also end up as subfields of other fields or end up as entirely new separate fields. He shows the former with the example of the field of French sociology; the latter with the 'colonial state' which becomes a new distinct field of its own. With the development of colonial states, metropolitan colonial offices and overseas colonial states were organized around completely different forms of symbolic capital. This is the creation of a new field. By contrast, the development in subfields is an internal differentiation of an already existing field, not the breaking off into a new field. Steinmetz shows this with French colonial sociology. As sociologists went to the overseas colonies they remained attuned to the struggles and capitals of metropolitan sociology; at most they distinguished themselves from metropolitan sociology by trying to turn ethnography or non-Western research into a valued resource and strived to distinguish themselves from other adjacent disciplines. But unlike the colonial state, they did not organize themselves internally around completely different forms of capital.

Petzke's paper also discusses field extension, though his historical medium of expansion is religion: specifically, nineteenth-century Christian missionaries who penetrated pre-existing religious dynamics in India. The essay reveals a different outcome from the two outcomes sketched in Steinmetz's essay. While Steinmetz points to field autonomization or subfield creation as a result of extension, Petzke's story is one of field colonization or full replacement. The work of the Christian missionaries in India ended up not only penetrating but also supplanting local religious fields, compelling pre-existing religious groups in the region to do religion according to new 'rules of the game' imposed by Christian missionaries. Religious competition centred upon religious affiliation and individual conversion became the new logic. Petzke also illuminates *how* this happened: through the census, a technology of quantification. The census classified different spiritual practices into distinct 'religions' with numbers of adherents, presenting them implicitly as converts to be targeted or defended. Pre-existing religious groups in India thus became roped into a competitive religious game of conversion, reproducing thereby 'Western' religious field dynamics. The new *nomos* became a matter of the 'numerical preponderance' of the religious group.

Field effects

Stephanie Mudge and Antoine Vauchez and Lisa Stampnitzky explore transnational fields through their effects. Mudge and Vauchez examine the European Central Bank (ECB) and the specific kind of authority the institution exercises – a form of authority that combines charismatic and scientific authority, which the authors call 'hyper-scientization'. The authors argue that this construction of the bank's authority cannot be explained with German hegemonic influence or some underlying essence of (independent) central banks but is best understood as an effect of its field position. The ECB's is positioned both in the European political order and in professional economics: the ECB uses academic production as a means to bureaucratic authority, and its heavy investment in scientific prestige expresses the scientization of the economic profession along with the less central position of European (versus American) economics within it. Both are made possible by the ECB's oddly non-European research capacity, established on the model of the American Federal Reserve. The result is an institution that produces a unique sort of historical figure: the scientific, yet European, yet technocratic central banker.

 The Sociological Review Monographs, 64:2, pp. 6–30 (2016), DOI: 10.1111/2059-7932.12000

Stampnitzky's essay takes us from Europe to the United States. She deftly deploys field theory to explain why the United States has openly acknowledged torture during the 'War on Terror' following 9/11. Stampnitzky notes that the war on terror has been characterized by the development of a legal infrastructure to support the use of 'forbidden' practices such as torture and assassination, along with varying degrees of open defence of such tactics. So why does the United States admit and justify torture in this way, rather than conduct it under the cloak of plausible deniability? Drawing on first-order accounts presented in published memoirs, she argues that the Bush administration developed such openness as a purposeful strategy, in response to the rise of a transnational field of human rights. Stampnitzky challenges theories that presume that the spread of human rights norms means that states will increasingly adhere to such norms in their rhetoric, if not always in practice. She suggests that a more robust theory of state action can help to better explain the ways that transnational norms and institutions affect states, and suggests that such a theory is best formulated through the use of field concepts.

The limits of fields

While the preceding essays reveal the complex effects of fields, the concluding essays by Monika Krause and Angèle Christin explore the *limits* of fields. Krause brings together field-theoretical hypotheses with attention to the material objects of study inspired by science and technology studies in her discussion of inequalities among field positions and among research 'objects' or 'topics' in transnational social science. She argues that conventions surrounding privileged research objects (model systems) shape the way attention is distributed in the discipline of sociology, and the way knowledge travels across borders. The 'West', and certain countries and cases within it, receive a disproportionate amount of attention in social scientific research. Krause suggests that conventions around model systems interact with processes of hierarchization and symbolic differentiation in national, regional and transnational disciplinary fields. Direct access to model systems, such as certain Western countries and certain cities, can be a source of capital within national fields of sociology and within the transnational field of sociology; in second-hand references, knowledge about model systems can provide a shortcut to field-specific capital for those in relatively peripheral positions who try to play by the dominant rules of the game – as opposed to those who are distanced by choice or by force. Finally, she hypothesizes that the constraints imposed by assumptions about model systems matter less for those with access to other forms of field-specific capital.

Christin examines an area of practice that we might expect to be fielded on a transnational level – journalism – and provides an explicit discussion of the criteria that need to be met for fieldedness more generally. Her paper draws on a comparative ethnography (we might also call it a relational ethnography) of the production and circulation of online news in the US and in France. She looks at a collaboration between two prestigious and two lowbrow partnerships across the

Atlantic and finds that online news does not circulate easily across the two contexts in either case. She argues that US and French web journalists do belong to a common, transnational journalistic field in the sense that they share terms for the contestation of legitimacy, but this is "weak" field at best. There are no reciprocal field effects and there is no mutual awareness, since US journalists are barely aware of the existence of French media, while French journalists follow US news obsessively. US and French news organizations and web journalists also do not compete for shared stakes. Christin's study thereby helps us better think about the question: when and where do social relations constitute a field? Ultimately, Christin's essay shows us how fields are limited in the sense that not everything should be theorized as a field. But in the process her analysis, along with the others in this volume, shows us the benefits of raising the question in the first place. Is all the world a field? Probably not. But it is a question worth thinking about.

Acknowledgements

The editors thank the Department of Sociology at Boston University and the College of Arts and Sciences at Boston University for funding the workshop on 'Fielding Transnationalism' during which contributions to this volume were discussed. Monika Krause would like to acknowledge support from a Future Research Leaders Grant awarded by the Economic and Social Research Council. The authors also thank the participants of the workshop and the contributors, especially Larissa Buchholz, Angèle Christin, and David Swartz, for their comments. Thanks also to two anonymous reviewers for SR for their suggestions.

Notes

1 Scholars working within the field of International Relations have been the most interested in using Bourdieu's concepts for analysing relations on scales beyond the national scale, though they have tended to focus less upon his *field* concept and more on concepts like habitus and practice, eg Adler-Nissen (2012), Berling (2012), Bigo (2007, 2011), Leander (2011), and Mérand (2010). The potential of field analysis for analysing international, transnational or global relations is indicated in the work of scholars, who have already used it to discuss a diversity of phenomena: art (Buchholz, 2013), forms of expertise associated with the European Union (Bigo, 2011; Mérand, 2010; Mudge and Vauchez, 2012; Vauchez, 2008, 2011; Georgakakis, 2011; Cohen, 2011); the field of empires (Go, 2008); colonial states (Steinmetz 2007, 2008); social science (Guilhot, 2014; Heilbron *et al.*, 2008; Heilbron, 2014), democracy promotion and humanitarian relief (Guilhot, 2001, 2005, 2007; Krause, 2014), international law and international commercial law (Dezalay and Garth, 1995, 1998, 2002a, 2002b, 2011; Hagan, 2005), among other sites (Adler-Nissen, 2012; Guilhot, 2007; Leavitt and Glick-Schiller, 2004; Marginson, 2008; Stampnitzky, 2011; see also Bohn, 2006 and Sapiro, 2013).

2 For example, this volume includes a paper by Petzke on transnational religion using a field perspective (see also McKinnon *et al.*, 2011) but, in the context of contemporary transformations of organized religion across the globe, this can only begin to highlight the potential for work that

 The Sociological Review Monographs, 64:2, pp. 6–30 (2016), DOI: 10.1111/2059-7932.12000

would ask about how different actors with which organizational features and structures position themselves vis-à-vis each other, and vis-à-vis different national settings and political fields.

3 Bourdieu stands here in the tradition of differentiation theory, following Kant and Weber (see Calhoun, 1993; Lahire, 2014; Gorski, 2013a). While it might be compatible with theories of capitalism and imperialism, field theory is a departure from all work that posits a single logic of global processes without asking also about the logic of specific practices. The picture of global order that emerges from field-oriented studies is one of differentiated space with different communities of actors and different logics of practice. Also see Buchholz (2008) on differentiation, field theory, and globalization.

References

Adler-Nissen, R. (ed.), (2012), *Bourdieu in International Relations: Rethinking IR*, London: Routledge.

Arrighi, G., (1994), *The Long Twentieth Century*, London: Verso.

Barman, E., (2013), 'Classificatory struggles in the nonprofit sector: the formation of the national taxonomy of exempt entities, 1969–1987', *Social Science History*, 37 (1): 103–141.

Beck, U., (2006), *The Cosmopolitan Vision*, Cambridge; Malden, MA: Polity.

Benson, R., (2005), 'Mapping field variation: journalism in France and the United States', in R. Benson and E. Neveu, *Bourdieu and the Journalistic Field, 85–112*, Cambridge: Polity.

Benson, R., (2013), *Shaping Immigration News: A French American Comparison*, Cambridge: Cambridge University Press.

Berling, T. V., (2012), 'Bourdieu, international relations and European security', *Theory & Society*, 41: 451–478.

Bigo, D. (ed.), (2007), *The Field of the EU Internal Security Agencies*, Paris: Centre d'études sur les conflits/l'Harmattan.

Bigo, D., (2011), 'Pierre Bourdieu and international relations: power of practices, practices of power,' *International Political Sociology*, 5 (3): 225–258.

Bockman, J. and Eyal, G., (2002), 'Eastern Europe as a laboratory for economic knowledge: the transnational roots of neoliberalism', *American Journal of Sociology*, 108 (2): 310–352.

Bohn, C., (2006), 'Une société mondiale. Les concepts de société opératories dans les théories sociales de Bourdieu et Luhmann', in H. P. Muller and Y. Sintomer (eds), *Pierre Bourdieu, théorie et pratique. Perspectives freanco-allemandess*, 101–12. Paris: La Découverte.

Boli, J. and Thomas, G. M., (1997), 'World culture in the world polity: a century of international non-governmental organization', *American Sociological Review*, 62 (2): 171–190.

Boli, J. and Thomas, G. M., (1999), *Constructing World Culture: International Nongovernmental Organizations since* 1875, Stanford, CA: Stanford University Press.

Bourdieu, P., (1959), 'Le choc des civilisations', in Secrétariat social d'Alger (ed.), *Le Sous-Développement en Algérie*, 52–64, Algiers: Secrétariat social.

Bourdieu, P., (1961 [1958]), *The Algerians*. Translated by Alan C.M. Ross with a preface by Raymond Aron, Boston: Beacon Press.

Bourdieu, P., (1971), 'Intellectual field and creative project', in M. F. D. Young (ed.), *Knowledge and Control: New Directions for the Sociology of Education*, 161–188, London: Collier-Macmillan.

Bourdieu, P., (1977), *Outline of a Theory of Practice*, Cambridge: Cambridge University Press.

Bourdieu, P., (1984a), *Homo Academicus*, Stanford, CA: Stanford University Press.

Bourdieu, P., (1984b), *Distinction: A Social Critique of the Judgement of Taste*, Cambridge, MA: Harvard University Press.

Bourdieu, P., (1986), 'The forms of capital', in J. Richardson (ed.), *Handbook of Theory and Research for the Sociology of Education*, 241–258, New York: Greenwood Press.

Bourdieu, P., (1990), *In other Words: Essays towards a Reflexive Sociology*, Stanford, CA: Stanford University Press.

Bourdieu, P., (1991a), 'Epilogue: on the possibility of a field of world sociology', in P. Bourdieu and J. Coleman (ed.), *Social Change for a Changing Society*, Boulder, CO: Westview Press.

Bourdieu, P., (1991b), 'Genesis and structure of the religious field', *Comparative Social Research*, 13: 1–44.
Bourdieu, P., (1993), *The Field of Cultural Production: Essays on Art and Literature*, New York: Columbia University Press.
Bourdieu, P., (1994), 'Rethinking the state: genesis and structure of the bureaucratic field', *Sociological Theory*, 12 (1): 1–18.
Bourdieu, P., (1996), *The Rules of Art: Genesis and Structure of the Literary Field Pierre Bourdieu*, Stanford, CA: Stanford University Press.
Bourdieu, P. (1999), *On Television*. New York: The New Press.
Bourdieu, P., (2002), 'Les conditions sociales de la circulation internationale des idées', *Actes de la Recherche en Sciences Sociales*, 145: 3–8.
Bourdieu, P., (2003), *Firing Back: Against the Tyranny of the Market* 2, London: Verso.
Bourdieu, P., (2005), 'The Political Field, the Social Science Field, and the Journalistic Field', in R. Benson and E. Neveu (eds), *Pierre Bourdieu and the Journalistic Field*, 29–47, Cambridge: Polity Press.
Bourdieu, P. *et al.*, (2000), *The Weight of the World: Social Suffering in Contemporary Society*, Palo Alto, CA: Stanford University Press.
Bourdieu, P. and Passerson, J. C., (1977), *Reproduction in Education, Society and Culture*, Beverly Hills, CA: Sage.
Bourdieu, P. and Wacquant, L., (1992), *An Invitation to Reflexive Sociology*, Chicago: University of Chicago Press.
Brand, U., Demirovic, A., Görg, C. and Hirsch, J. (eds), (2001), *Nichtregierungsorganisationen in der Transformation des Staates*, Münster: Westfälisches Dampfboot.
Breitmeier, H., Young, O. R. and Zürn, M., (2007), *Analyzing International Environmental Regimes*, Cambridge, MA: MIT Press.
Buchholz, L., (2008), 'Feldtheorie und Globalisierung' ('Field theory and globalization'), in B. von Bismarck, T. Kaufmann and U. Wuggenig (eds), *Nach Bourdieu: Visualität, Kunst, Politik*, Vienna: Turia & Kant.
Buchholz, L., (2013), 'The global rules of art', PhD Dissertation, Department of Sociology, New York: Columbia University.
Burawoy, M., (2000), 'Introduction: reaching for the global', in M. Burawoy, J. A. Blum, S. George, Z. Gille, T. Gowan, L. Haney, M. Klawitter, S. H. Lopez, S. O. Riain and M. Thayer (eds), *Global Ethnography*, 1–40, Berkeley, CA: University of California Press.
Burawoy, M., (2008), 'Rejoinder: for a subaltern global sociology?' *Current Sociology*, 56 (3): 435–444.
Calhoun, C., (1993), 'Habitus, field, and capital: the question of historical specificity', in C. Calhoun, E. Lipuma and M. Postone (eds), *Bourdieu: Critical Perspectives*, 61–88, Chicago: University of Chicago Press.
Chandler, D., (2001), 'The road to military humanitarianism: how the human rights NGOs shaped a new humanitarian agenda', *Human Rights Quarterly*, 23 (3): 678–700.
Chandler, D., (2002), *From Kosovo to Kabul: Human Rights and International Intervention*, London: Pluto Press.
Chandler, D., (2004), 'The responsibility to protect? Imposing the liberal peace', *International Peacekeeping*, 11 (1): 59–81.
Chomsky, N., (1999), *The New Military Humanism: Lessons from Kosovo*, Monroe: Common Courage Press.
Chorev, N., (2012), 'Changing global norms through reactive diffusion: the case of intellectual property protection of AIDS drugs', *American Sociological Review*, 77 (5): 831–853.
Cohen, A., (2011), 'Bourdieu hits Brussels: the genesis and structure of the European field of power', *International Political Sociology*, 5 (3): 335–339.
Desan, M., (2013), 'Bourdieu, Marx, and capital: a critique of the extension model', *Sociological Theory*, 31 (4): 318–342.

 The Sociological Review Monographs, 64:2, pp. 6–30 (2016), DOI: 10.1111/2059-7932.12000

Dezalay, Y. and Garth, B. G., (1995), 'Merchants of law as moral entrepreneurs: constructing international justice from the competition for transnational business disputes', *Law and Society Review*, 29: 27.

Dezalay, Y. and Garth, B. G., (1998), *Dealing in Virtue: International Commercial Arbitration and the Construction of a Transnational Legal Order*, Chicago: University of Chicago Press.

Dezalay, Y. and Garth, B. G., (2002a), *Global Prescriptions: The Production, Exportation, and Importation of a New Legal Orthodoxy*, Ann Arbor, MI: University of Michigan Press.

Dezalay, Y. and Garth, B. G., (2002b), *The Internationalization of Palace Wars: Lawyers, Economists, and the Contest to Transform Latin American States*, Chicago: University of Chicago Press.

Dezalay, Y. and Garth, B. G., (2011), 'Hegemonic battles, professional rivalries, and the international division of labor in the market for the import and export of state-governing expertise', *International Political Sociology*, 5 (3): 276–293.

Di Maggio, P. and Powell, W., (1991), *The New Institutionalism in Organizational Analysis*, Chicago: University of Chicago Press.

Duffield, M., (2001), *Global Governance and the New Wars: The Merging of Development and Security*, London: Zed Books.

Elias, N., (2000 [1939]), *The Civilizing Process: Sociogenetic and Psychogenetic Investigations*, Oxford: Blackwell.

Emirbayer, M. and Johnson, V., (2008), 'Bourdieu and organizational analysis', *Theory and Society*, 37 (1): 1–44.

Finnemore, M., (1996), 'Norms, culture, and world politics: insights from sociology's institutionalism', *International Organization*, 50 (2): 325–347.

Fligstein, N., (2001), 'Social skill and the theory of fields', *Sociological Theory*, 19: 105–125.

Fligstein, N. and McAdam, D., (2011), 'Toward a general theory of strategic action fields', *Sociological Theory*, 29 (1): 1–26.

Fligstein, N. and McAdam, D., (2012), *A Theory of Fields*, Oxford: Oxford University Press.

Foucault, M., Burchell, G., Gordon, C. and Miller, P., (1991), *The Foucault Effect: Studies in Governmentality (with Two Lectures by and an Interview with Michel Foucault)*. Chicago: University of Chicago Press.

Fourcade, M., (2006), 'The construction of a global profession: the transnationalization of economics', *American Journal of Sociology*, 112 (1): 145–194.

Frank, A. G., (1967), *Capitalism and Underdevelopment in Latin America*, New York: Monthly Review Press.

Furedi, F., (1994), *The New Ideology of Imperialism: Renewing the Moral Imperative*, London: Pluto Press.

Gartman, D., (2002), 'Bourdieu's theory of cultural change: explication, application, critique', *Sociological Theory*, 20 (2): 255–277.

Georgakakis, D. (2011), 'Don't throw out the "Brussels bubble" with the bathwater: from EU institutions to the field of eurocracy', *International Political Sociology*, 5 (3): 331–334.

Gingras, Y., (2002), 'Les formes spécifiques de l'internationalité du champ scientifique', *Actes de la recherche en sciences sociales*, 141–142: 31–45.

Go, J., (2008), 'Global fields and imperial forms: field theory and the British and American empires', *Sociological Theory*, 26 (3): 201–229.

Gorski, P. S., (2013a), 'Bourdieusian theory and historical analysis: maps, mechanisms, and methods', in P. S. Gorski (ed.), *Bourdieu and Historical Analysis*, 327–367, Chapel Hill, NC: Duke University Press.

Gorski, P. S. (ed.), (2013b), *Bourdieu and Historical Analysis*, Chapel Hill, NC: Duke University Press.

Guilhot, N., (2001), 'Les professionnels de la d'emocratie', *Actes de la recherche en sciences sociales* 4: 53–65.

Guilhot, N., (2005), *The Democracy Makers: Human Rights and International Order*, New York: Columbia University Press.

Guilhot, N., (2007), 'Reforming the world: George Soros, global capitalism and the philanthropic management of the social sciences', *Critical Sociology* 33 (3): 447–477.

Guilhot, N., (2014), 'The international circulation of international relations theory', in W. Keim, E. Çelik, C. Ersche and V. Wöhrer (eds), *Global Knowledge Production in the Social Sciences: Made in Circulation*, 63–87, London: Ashgate.
Hagan, J., (2005), 'Crimes of war and the force of law', *Social Forces* 83 (4): 1499–1534.
Hardt, M. and Negri, A., (2000), *Empire*, Cambridge, MA: Harvard University Press.
Hasenclever, A., Mayer, P. and Rittberger, V., (1997), *Theories of International Regimes*, New York: Cambridge University Press.
Heilbron, J., (2014), 'The social sciences as an emerging global field', *Current Sociology*, 62 (5): 685–703.
Heilbron, J., Guilhot, N. and Jeanpierre, L., (2008), 'Toward a transnational history of the social sciences', *Journal of the History of the Behavioral Sciences*, 44 (2): 146–160.
Hess, D. and Frickel, S., (2014), 'Introduction: fields of knowledge and theory traditions in the sociology of science', *Political Power and Social Theory*, 27: 1–30.
Hilbert, R. A., (1990), 'Ethnomethodology and the micro-macro order', *American Journal of Sociology*, 794–808.
Hilgers, M. and Mangez, E., (2014), 'Introduction to Pierre Bourdieu's theory of social fields', in M. Hilgers and E. Mangez (ed.), *Bourdieu's Theory of Social Fields*, 1–37. London: Routledge.
Holsti, K. J., (1985), *The Dividing Discipline: Hegemony and Diversity in International Theory*, Winchester, MA: Allen & Unwin.
Holzer, B., Kastner, F. and Werron, T. (eds.), (2014), *From Globalization to World Society: Neo-Institutional and Systems-Theoretical Perspectives*, London; New York: Routledge.
Hulme, D. and Edwards, M., (1997), *NGOs, States and Donors: Too Close for Comfort*?, New York: St Martin's Press.
Iriye, A., (1989), 'The internationalization of history', *American Historical Review*, 94 (1): 1–10.
Keck, M. E. and Sikkink, K., (1998), *Activists beyond Borders: Advocacy Networks in International Politics*, Ithaca, NY: Cornell University Press.
Keohane, R. O. and Martin, L. L., (1995), 'The promise of institutionalist theory', *International Security*, 20 (1): 39–51.
Knorr-Cetina, K., (2007), 'Microglobalization', in I. Rossi (ed.), *Frontiers of Globalization Research: Theoretical and Methodological Approaches*, 65–92, New York: Springer.
Krasner, S. D. (ed.), (1983), *International Regimes*, Ithaca, NY: Cornell University Press.
Krause, M., (2014), *The Good Project: Humanitarian NGOs and the Fragmentation of Reason*, Chicago: University of Chicago Press.
Krause, M., (n.d.), 'How fields vary', unpublished manuscript.
Lahire, B., (2014), 'The limits of the field: elements for a theory of the social differentiation of activities', in M. Hilgers and E. Mangez (eds), *Bourdieu's Theory of Social Fields*, 1–37, London: Routledge.
Larner, W. and Walters, W., (2004), *Global Governmentality: Governing International Spaces*, London: Routledge.
Latour, B., (2005), *Reassembling the Social*, Cambridge: Cambridge University Press.
Latour, B., Jensen, P., Venturini, T., Grauwin, S. and Boullier, D., (2012), 'The whole is always smaller than its parts: a digital test of Gabriel Tarde's Monads', *British Journal of Sociology*, 63 (4): 590–615.
Leander, A., (2011), 'The promises, problems, and potentials of a Bourdieu-inspired staging of international relations', *International Political Sociology*, 5 (3): 294–313.
Leavitt, P. and Glick Schiller, N., (2004), 'Conceptualizing simultaneity: a transnational social field perspective on society', *International Migration Review*, 38 (145): 595–629.
Lebaron, F., (2008), 'Central bankers in the contemporary global field of power: a "social space" approach', *Sociological Review*, 56 (1): 121–144.
Lebaron, F., (2010), 'European Central Bank leaders in the global space of central bankers: a geometric data analysis approach', *French Politics*, 8: 294–320.
Lewin, K., (1975), *Field Theory in Social Science: Selected Theoretical Papers*, Westport, CT: Greenwood Press.

The Sociological Review Monographs, 64:2, pp. 6–30 (2016), DOI: 10.1111/2059-7932.12000

Lippert, R., (1998), 'Rationalities and refugee resettlement', *Economy and Society*, 27: 380–406.

Loveman, M., (2005), 'The modern state and the primitive accumulation of symbolic power', *American Journal of Sociology*, 110 (6): 1651–1683.

Marginson, S., (2008), 'Global field and global imagining: Bourdieu and worldwide higher education', *British Journal of Sociology of Education*, 29 (3): 303–315.

Martin, J. L., (2003), 'What is field theory?', *American Journal of Sociology*, 109: 1–49.

McKinnon, A., Trzebiatowska, M. and Brittain, C. C., (2011), 'Bourdieu, capital, and conflict in a religious field: the case of the "homosexuality" conflict in the Anglican Communion', *Journal of Contemporary Religion*, 26 (3): 355–370.

Mérand, F., (2010), 'Pierre Bourdieu and the birth of European defense', *Security Studies*, 19 (2): 3342–3374.

Meyer, J., (1980), 'The world polity and the authority of the nation-state', in A. Bergesen (ed.), *Studies of the Modern World-System*, 109–137, New York: Academic Press.

Meyer, J. W., (2010), 'World society, institutional theories, and the actor', *Annual Review of Sociology*, 36: 1–20.

Meyer, J. W., Boli, J., Thomas, G. M. and Ramirez, F. O., (1997), 'World society and the nation-state', *American Journal of Sociology*, 103 (1): 144–181.

Mudge, S. L. and Vauchez, A., (2012), 'Building Europe on a weak field: law, economics and scholarly avatars in transnational politics', *American Journal of Sociology*, 118 (2): 449–492.

Neumann, I. B., (2002), 'Returning practice to the linguistic turn: the case of diplomacy', *Millennium*, 31 (3): 627–651.

O'Malley, P., Weir, L. and Shearing, C., (1997), 'Governmentality, criticism, politics', *Economy and Society*, 26: 501–17.

Rankin, K. N., (2001), 'Governing development: neoliberalism, microcredit, and rational economic woman', *Economy and Society*, 30: 18–37.

Risse, T., (2002), 'Transnational actors and world politics', in W. Carlsnaes, T. Risse and B. A. Simmons (eds), *Handbook of International Relations*, London: Sage.

Sapiro, G., (2013), 'Le Champ est-il national? La theorie de la differenciation sociale au prisme de l'histoire globale', *Actes de la Recherche en Sciences Sociales*, 200: 70–86.

Sending, O. and Neumann, I. B., (2006), 'Governance to governmentality: analyzing NGOs, states, and power', *International Studies Quarterly* 50 (3): 651–672.

Slaughter, A.-M., (2011), 'International relations, principal theories', in R. Wolfrum (ed.), *Max Planck Encyclopedia of Public International Law*, Oxford: Oxford University Press.

Stamatov, P., (2013), *The Origins of Global Humanitarianism*. Oxford: Oxford University Press.

Stampnitzky, L., (2011), 'Disciplining an unruly field: terrorism experts and theories of scientific/intellectual production', *Qualitative Sociology*, 34 (1): 1–19.

Steinmetz, G., (2007), *The Devil's Handwriting*, Chicago: Chicago University Press.

Steinmetz, G., (2008), 'The colonial state as a social field: ethnographic capital and native policy in the German overseas empire before 1914', *American Sociological Review*, 73: 589–612.

Steinmetz, G., (2011), 'Bourdieu, historicity, and historical sociology', *Cultural Sociology*, 5 (1): 45–66.

Swartz, D., (1997), *Culture and Power: The Sociology of Pierre Bourdieu*, Chicago: University of Chicago Press.

Thomas, G., (2007), 'World polity, world culture, world society', *International Political Sociology*, 3 (1): 115–119.

Thornton, P. H., Ocasio, W. and Lounsbury, M., (2012), *The Institutional Logics Perspective: A New Approach to Culture, Structure and Process*, Oxford: Oxford University Press.

Tomlinson, J., (1991), *Cultural Imperialism*, Baltimore, MD: Johns Hopkins University Press.

Vauchez, A., (2008), 'The force of a weak field: law and lawyers in the government of the European Union (for a renewed research agenda)', *International Political Sociology*, 2 (2): 128–144.

Vauchez, A., (2011), 'Interstitial power in fields of limited statehood: introducing a "weak field" approach to the study of transnational settings', *International Political Sociology*, 5 (3): 340–345.

Wallerstein, I., (1974), *The Modern World-system*, New York: Academic Press.

The Sociological Review Monographs, 64:2, pp. 6–30 (2016), DOI: 10.1111/2059-7932.12000

Wallerstein, I., (2001), *Unthinking Social Science: The Limits of Nineteenth-Century Paradigms*, Philadelphia, PA: Temple University Press.
Wallerstein, I., (2004), *World-Systems Analysis: An Introduction*, Durham, NC: Duke University Press.
Waltz, K., (1979), *A Theory of International Politics*, New York: McGraw Hill.
Wapner, P., (1996), *Environmental Activism and World Civic Politics*, Albany, NY: State University of New York Press.
Willets, P. (ed.), (1996), *The Conscience of the World*, Washington, DC: The Brookings Institution.

Please quote the article DOI when citing SR content, including monographs. Article DOIs and "How to Cite" information can be found alongside the online version of each article within Wiley Online Library. All articles published within the SR (including monograph content) are included within the ISI Journal Citation Reports® Social Science Citation Index.

The Sociological Review Monographs, 64:2, pp. 6–30 (2016), DOI: 10.1111/2059-7932.12000

What is a global field? Theorizing fields beyond the nation-state

Larissa Buchholz

Abstract: While scholarship on global and transnational fields has been emerging, hitherto contributions have rarely or not explicitly discussed how Bourdieu's field theory has to be altered when its use expands from a national to a global scale. Starting from the premise that a global field is not a national field writ large, this paper discusses strategies and elements for revising field theory for use beyond national borders. Specifically, the article first proposes analogical theorizing as a systematic approach for extending and modifying the tools of field theory at a global level. Analogical theorizing offers a method for constructing the object in a global context in a way that goes beyond rescaling and minimizes the risk of deductive reification. Against this background and drawing from research on the global visual art field, the article offers criteria for delineating a global field and distinguishes relative functional and vertical autonomy. Finally, it discusses how the concept of 'relative vertical autonomy' contributes in three ways to the development of global field analysis: for theorizing emergence; examining global-national interdependencies; and denationalizing Bourdieu's concept of 'national capital'.

Keywords: theorizing, field theory, global/transnational fields, art fields, globalization, emergence

Introduction

A key challenge in current sociological theorizing is to reassess the theoretical resources that were developed from within the frame of the Western nation-state to engage with new, and often qualitatively unique issues of transnational or global research. On one hand, we cannot simply go ahead and scale up our concepts of 'society' or 'power' from particular Western societies 'straight to the level of the global' (Connell, 2007: 373). Such a rescaling approach runs the danger of producing a reifying picture of the 'nature of global society' from the one-sided perspective of the global north (Connell, 2007: 373; cf. also Brenner, 1999: 53–60; Reed, 2013; Abbott, 2015). At the same time, we can also not afford to go to the other extreme and completely discard the tools of the

The Sociological Review Monographs, 64:2, pp. 31–60 (2016), DOI: 10.1111/2059-7932.12001

Published by John Wiley & Sons Ltd, 9600 Garsington Road, Oxford OX4 2DQ, UK and 350 Main Street, Malden, MA 02148, USA

sociological tradition. Many of today's global configurations (eg nation-state system, capitalist economy, modern science, arts, sports, etc.) indeed often reach back in their roots to European modernity (eg Giddens, 1990; Meyer *et al.*, 1997). Theories that stem from north-western contexts, despite their limitations, can still offer useful conceptual resources for transnational and global sociology.[1] Hence, beyond mere upscaling or downright dismissal, a more promising route is likely to be that of theoretical reform: to re-examine and reconceptualize the resources of the sociological tradition in the reflexive confrontation with the transnational and global problems of research.

The challenge to reassess sociological theories beyond the nation-state also pertains to burgeoning scholarship on transnational or global fields: a growing body of work builds upon and expands Bourdieu's field theory to engage with transnational or global social orders (eg Dezalay and Garth, 1996; Heilbron, 1999; Casanova, 2004; Fourcade, 2006; Steinmetz, 2008a, 2008b; Go, 2008; Buchholz, 2008, 2013; Krause, 2014). These studies demonstrate that Bourdieu's influential field theory has much to offer for transnational and global sociology when it is extended beyond national boundaries: for one, in contrast to established global paradigms, field analysis offers a mode of examination that can move beyond monolithic models of one overarching global system be it economic or cultural (eg Wallerstein, 1974, 2004; Meyer, 2000). It provides an approach that is able to map the plurality and specificity of social spheres in global context, each revolving around semi-autonomous logics and histories.[2] Indeed, by making use of field theory, scholars have engaged with such diverse cases as world literature (Casanova, 2004), the global profession of economics (Fourcade, 2006), the colonial state (Steinmetz, 2008a, 2008b), empires (Go, 2008), or humanitarian intervention (Krause, 2014). And whereas the two dominant paradigms in global sociology – world-systems and world polity analysis – are either materialist or culturalist, field theory permits to take into account both the material and cultural dimensions of global arenas (Go, 2008: 206–210).[3] Yet field theory is not just multidimensional but also multi-levelled. It equips one to examine transnational or global processes from three levels of analysis: the micro level of agents' habitus and strategies, meso-level social and cultural relations, and the macro level of larger structures or environments (Buchholz, 2008, 2013).

Nevertheless, while a multifaceted body of research on transnational and global fields has emerged and demonstrated the unique advantages of the approach, scholars have rarely or at least not explicitly discussed how field theory has to be *altered* when its use goes beyond national borders. Perhaps even more important, there has been little discussion about what kinds of analytical principles and strategies are useful to extend an entire model such as field theory from the national to the global scale in systematic and reflexive ways. The problem is not only that by not engaging in such a discussion one might end up in rescaling and thus run the danger of northern reification (Connell, 2007). It is also true that if we do not confront this problematic explicitly, we are likely to miss an important, broader question of transnational and global sociology: how are social

The Sociological Review Monographs, 64:2, pp. 31–60 (2016), DOI: 10.1111/2059-7932.12001

configurations at the transnational or global level different? What is distinctive or indeed unprecedented about them?

Given this background, the purpose of this article is twofold: first, to propose analogical theorizing as one systematic approach for extending and modifying tools of field theory at a transnational or global level in reflexive and non-reifying ways. Against this background and drawing mainly from empirical research on the global art field, the article secondly develops criteria for delineating a field in a global context. It thereby introduces the concept of vertical autonomy to account for one characteristic in which certain transnational or global fields differ significantly from the way fields were structured in Bourdieu's original theory, namely their multi-scalar architecture.

Specifically, my discussion unfolds in four parts. The first opens with an introduction to analogical theorizing, as developed by Diane Vaughan, and sketches how this method can be used to move and revise concepts and models across different scales. The second section argues that 'relative autonomy' is a defining criterion in Bourdieu's field theory and, on this basis, develops elementary criteria for identifying a social sphere as a field. The third section shows how this elementary conception of a field can be extended and revised at the global level, based on principles of analogical theorizing. Drawing from my research on the global field of the contemporary visual arts – which represents a case that has reached a particularly highly globalized state – I thereby develop a distinction between relative functional and vertical autonomy and suggest criteria for delineating a field in a global context.[4] The final part fleshes out how the new concept of relative vertical autonomy may contribute to the development of a global field analysis in three ways: for theorizing emergence; examining global-national interdependencies; and denationalizing Bourdieu's concept of national capital.

Analogical theorizing for constructing the object in a global context

Bourdieu originally developed his conception of fields in the frame of the nation-state unit, particularly France and Algeria. As I argued in previous work (Buchholz, 2006, 2008), this national origin does not mean that the idea of the field automatically falls prey to (implicit) methodological nationalism for at least two analytical reasons: First, Bourdieu's model of socially differentiated fields is, in contrast to functionalist variants of social differentiation, not tied to the idea of a functionally integrated society. In fact, Bourdieu dismissed the concept of society itself. Second and perhaps more importantly, Bourdieu advocates a pragmatic use of his theory. He considers concepts first and foremost to be 'temporary construct(s)' or 'tools kits' (Wittgenstein) (Wacquant, 1992: 31) for organizing empirical research, which can and ought to be modified in light of different cases and problems of research (Bourdieu, 1985: 11; Bourdieu and Wacquant, 1992: 95f.). This pragmatic approach also applies to field theory. Indeed, as Bourdieu emphasized:

> [T]he notion of field does not provide ready-made answers to all possible queries in the manner of the grand concepts of 'theoreticist theory' which claims to explain everything and in the right order. Rather its major virtue [...] is that it promotes a mode of construction that has to be rethought anew every time. It forces us to raise questions: about the limits of the universe under investigation, how it is 'articulated,' to what and to what degree, etc. (Bourdieu and Wacquant, 1992: 110)

Thus, Bourdieu's field theory represents not a static model with a priori determined confines. Instead, it offers a mode of analysis for constructing an 'object' of knowledge, beyond what is visible to common sense.[5] The specific boundaries and characteristics of each field have to be determined in the course of research, and they may thus transgress, principally, those of nation-states (Buchholz, 2006, 2008).[6]

In fact, Bourdieu referred to world or global fields in his later work,[7] and, as outlined in the introduction, by now a growing body of scholarship extends field theory to engage with transnational or global problems of research. The crucial question is no longer *if* his model can be expanded to transnational or global scales, but *how* this can be accomplished in systematic and reflexive ways. For this question, however, Bourdieu's writings offer us few systematic clues. For one, Bourdieu only addressed how to transpose concepts from one nation-state to the other (eg from France to the US or Japan, Bourdieu, 1984: xi, xiv, 1998: 1–3), not how to move them across different scales.[8] Furthermore, in his discussion of adjusting models to varying (national) contexts, Bourdieu refers to changes in the content of concepts, but not to modifications in the analytical architecture. For example, in the English preface of *Distinction* he suggests that his theory of inequality represents 'universal propositions' that are 'valid for every stratified society' (Bourdieu, 1984: xi). Thus, in order to transpose it to a different context, the main task would be to search for 'structural equivalents',[9] that is, substantive alternatives of principally the 'same structures' (Bourdieu, 1984: xii; cf. also Bourdieu, 1998: 1–3).

For transposing field theory to a global level, such principles of theory extension are too narrow. They imply that we would have to rescale the national field model and substantiate it with new empirical content without critically interrogating or altering its architecture. Yet if – as Bourdieu states – the 'major virtue' of the notion of field 'is that it promotes a mode of construction that has to be rethought anew every time' (Bourdieu and Wacquant, 1992: 110), then extending it to the transnational or global scale could and should be more than upscaling.

Given these limitations, I suggest that Diane Vaughan's method of analogical theorizing (AT) for cross-case comparison[10] offers a productive alternative (Vaughan, 1992, 2014). As Bourdieu remarked, 'analogical reasoning ... is a powerful instrument of construction of the object' (Bourdieu and Wacquant, 1992: 233). And Vaughan's approach to extending theory is principally akin to Bourdieu's suggestion to search for structural equivalents, since analogy is understood as a 'cognitive process' of identifying structural equivalencies 'between separate, distinctive domains and their parts' (Vaughan, 2014: 61). Yet, AT

 The Sociological Review Monographs, 64:2, pp. 31–60 (2016), DOI: 10.1111/2059-7932.12001

provides an alternative to Bourdieu in two crucial ways: first, it is explicit about – and geared toward – extending models across different levels of analysis. For example, deploying principles of AT, Vaughan moved Merton's theory of deviance from the level of individuals to organizations and, in the process, significantly innovated upon his original model (Merton, 1968 [1938]; Vaughan, 1983). Second, while Vaughan's method is based on the identification of structural similarities between cases, it does not stop at that. For AT, establishing structural similarities between cases represents only a first heuristic step. It serves to create the analytical background against which it then becomes possible to decipher differences in a systematic, controlled way. It is such differences that are critical in AT, because they are the basis for theoretical innovation (Vaughan, 2014: 66). The central principle of theory extension for AT is thus not analogical similarity (or in Bourdieu's vocabulary structural equivalents), but *analogical difference*: the use of analogy as a heuristic tool and cognitive process to *systematically identify differences against the background of equivalencies.* Hence, AT is not just relevant for adjustments in the content of concepts. Importantly, it may extend to modifications of a model's analytical architecture as well.

Deploying AT for theory extension across scales involves three main analytical moves. I only briefly summarize them here. Their application to extending field theory will be exemplified in the second and third sections of the article. The first move consists of the analytical reduction of theory. This does not just mean to formalize the model into a scheme that identifies the core concepts and their relations, which constitutes a common procedure not specific to the method of analogical theorizing. The task is, more particularly, to reconstruct the model in such a way that: (a) form is subtracted from content, and (b) properties are disentangled from scale. These two principles of analytic reduction are based on the assumption that all forms of social organization – notwithstanding variation in their size, level, complexity and function – have certain features in common: they share basic characteristics of structure (which Bourdieu would term 'structural homologies'), such as 'hierarchy, division of labor, goals or normative standards' (Vaughan, 2014: 64). In addition, they display similar processes, for example 'socialization, conflict, competition, cooperation, power, culture' (Vaughan, 2014: 64). Thus, to reconstruct a model with AT means, literally, to reduce elements of the theory to scale-invariant properties.

For example, with regard to field theory: in a scale-invariant way, one can posit in schematic terms that a field refers to a social sphere that is relatively autonomous from its environment. How to conceptualize this environment, in turn, would be scale-specific. Bourdieu's original theory tied the environment of fields like those of cultural production closely to the nation-state and the field of power more generally (eg Bourdieu, 1993a: 37–40). Yet, to move the concept beyond national borders, we need to abstract specification from this national level in a move of analytical reduction in order to construct a preliminary model. We know that fields need to be theorized in relation to their environment, yet how to conceptualize this environment, in particular, is scale-dependent and thus has to be determined in the course of research.

A second move consists of analogical extension. It means to identify to what extent and how there are structural equivalencies between the model and the characteristics of the empirical case in order to justify the transposition. The more equivalencies there are, the deeper the analogy and thus the better, principally, the fit of the theory will be for the case. At this stage it is best to work with theoretical alternatives, in order to identify comparatively the concept/model with the best fit, so that one avoids mere 'relabelling'.[11] Indeed, analogical theorizing should not be mistaken for a method that leads simply to 'the ever more extensive expansion of some theoretical system in a way that effectively closes it off from rebuttal or disconfirmation' (Healy, 2015: 3).

Finally, against this background, one arrives at the critical step of adjusting and substantiating the selected model that provided the best fit by identifying relevant empirical differences. Of course, there can be an infinite number of differences. What matters are those that are relevant for the specific research question. Thus, the identification of what needs to be adjusted or rearranged must be fundamentally problem-driven and seen against the background of the established analogies. Principally, there can be two kinds of differences: first, the specification of terms that became abstracted from the original model (eg the above example of 'environment'). Second and more profound is the identification of necessary changes in the analytical architecture of the model, for example by introducing new concepts, by reformulating or subtracting core concepts, or by changing the logic of their relationships. For example, I will discuss in the article's third section how I identified one significant difference in comparison to Bourdieu's national approach by engaging in research on the problem of the emergence of the global art field. And, thereby, how I introduced a new concept into the field model, namely 'relative vertical autonomy'. But before we get there, I would like to illustrate briefly the first two analytical moves. Thus, the next section begins by developing a basic, scale-invariant definition of a social field that is centred on the concept of 'relative autonomy'. Then, I proceed to discuss how this basic conception of a social field has been transposed to a global scale, in line with the move of analogical extension.

Relative autonomy as a defining criterion of Bourdieusian fields

The autonomy criterion

Bourdieu's field theory builds upon and expands Max Weber's notion of social differentiation (Weber, 1946 [1915]; Martin, 2003: 20).[12] Standing on Weber's shoulders, he develops a framework to account for a variety of (modern) social spheres, which each follow their own 'inherent lawfulness' (Weber, 1946 [1915]) – such as science, the arts, the bureaucratic state, or the economy (eg Bourdieu, 1996, 1999, 2004, 2005). Every social field embodies a uniquely structured, differentiated social space of specialized practice that revolves around distinctive beliefs and interests (cf. Swartz, 1997: 117–149). In Bourdieu's take on social differentiation, the concept of 'relative autonomy' is fundamental, because it

 The Sociological Review Monographs, 64:2, pp. 31–60 (2016), DOI: 10.1111/2059-7932.12001

designates how a social field is to be distinguished from others.[13] In this way, it represents the central entry point from which to delineate the analytical boundary conditions that define a social sphere as a distinctive social field. To reconstruct an elementary, that is, scale-invariant field definition, this section looks more closely at how Bourdieu introduced and used the concept – dissecting the twin components of 'autonomy' and 'relative'. This analysis will establish analytical criteria for the third part, which discusses how to extend the field model to a global level by drawing upon principles of analogical theorizing.

Bourdieu oriented his usage of 'autonomy' closely to its original meaning as a composite of the Greek words *nomos* (law) and *autós* (self). He deploys the term to account for social spheres that are governed by their own 'specific law' (Bourdieu, 2000: 15) or, as he alternatively writes, their own 'specific logic' of competition (Bourdieu, 2000: 126). But what specifically does Bourdieu mean by 'law' or 'logic'?[14] *The Rules of Art* offers specification, for here he associates the notion of a field's *nomos* with fundamental 'principles of vision and division' (Bourdieu, 1996: 223ff., 230). In this sense, the idea of a field-specific law should not be mistaken for codified legal regulations. More deeply, it refers to elementary ways in which agents perceive a particular world and through which they devise – accordingly – social categories and hierarchies that give order to that world.

At this point, we should pause and note a crucial implication of Bourdieu's use of autonomy as a differentiating concept, namely that a social field refers not just to a sphere of specialized practice – which visual art, for example, had been for centuries. Already in the Renaissance, for instance, painters underwent long and arduous periods of specialized training; and creators (and competitors) like Leonardo da Vinci and Michelangelo clearly achieved highly specific artistic mastery. Still, a social field emerges not only on the grounds of a kind of 'division of labor' or specialization. In Bourdieu's approach, this would constitute only a necessary, but not sufficient condition. What matters analytically is what I call the autonomy criterion: a stage when a social sphere of specialized practice institutionalizes categories of 'vision and division' that construe its law (or logic) of competition as relatively independent from the logics of other social spheres or the broader environment. This subtle but important distinction is crucial to keep in mind throughout the sections in which I discuss how to define and delineate a field at a transnational or global scale.

Three dimensions of autonomy

For the purposes of research, it is useful to specify the autonomy criterion along three dimensions. They can be analytically extracted from *The Rules of Art* (1996).[15] The first dimension refers to an autonomous ideology, which, at the level of agents, becomes embodied in a 'particular form of belief' (Bourdieu, 1983: 317). An autonomous ideology construes a specific sphere of practice as distinctive, independent, and 'ultimately more valuable' than other realms of practice (Gorski, 2013: 334). For example, the emergence of the modern art field hinged on the rise and legitimation of a new belief in the principle of *l'art pour l'art*. This ideology redefined art as a practice that demanded to be seen and appreciated for its own intrinsic aesthetic sake (Bourdieu, 1996: 297, 81) – independent from the worldly demands and influences of patronage, the state, or the market. In the visual arts in France, this new 'vision' was spearheaded by Édouard Manet (Bourdieu, 2013). His aesthetic strategies claimed the importance of form over content, the aesthetic 'mode of representation over the object of representation' (Bourdieu, 1996: 299). By moving the emphasis from the subject of a painting to the pure play of colours or the formal manner of brushwork, Manet sought to free visual art from its traditional duty of representing the external world, thereby bringing about what Bourdieu called a 'symbolic revolution' – the construction of an autonomous vision of artistic production (Bourdieu, 2013).

A second dimension consists of the establishment of autonomous principles of constructing hierarchy, manifested in what Bourdieu would term a distinctive type of specific symbolic capital, which, at the subjective level, becomes associated with specific interests.[16] For example, in the art field, the ideology of *l'art pour l'art* entailed new notions of artistic legitimacy. The attribution of the latter became anchored in aesthetically specific peer criteria and opposed to external evaluative principles, such as those imposed by state institutions or the commercial market. In other words, artistic legitimacy (ie symbolic capital) turned into something autonomous to the extent that it became defined in opposition to external worldly forms of economic or public artistic success, leading to a new mandate of 'interest in disinterestedness' (Bourdieu, 1996: 142; Bourdieu, 1993a: 39).[17]

A third and often underappreciated dimension of an autonomous field consists of the formation of a 'set of specific institutions' (Bourdieu, 1996: 292)[18] through which autonomous principles of vision and division become ingrained in a distinctive institutional infrastructure. In the case of the modern art field, this third dimension became manifest in what Bourdieu termed a market for 'restricted production'. It encompassed, for example, autonomously oriented 'places of exhibition (galleries, museums, etc.), institutions of consecration (academies, salons, etc.), institutions for the reproduction of producers (art schools, etc.), and specialized agents (dealers, critics, art historians, collectors, etc.)' (Bourdieu, 1996: 292).

Thus, abstracted from the substantive case of the modern art field, one can derive three principal and scale-invariant dimensions that specify when a social sphere qualifies as an autonomous field: (1) an autonomous ideology and related beliefs about a particular realm of practice (what Bourdieu also referred to as 'vision,' (2) autonomous principles of hierarchy formation as the foundation for a specific type of 'symbolic capital' and associated interests (corresponding also to his notion of 'division'); and (3) a distinctive set of 'institutions' through which autonomous principles of vision and division become objectified and perpetuated.

The Sociological Review Monographs, 64:2, pp. 31–60 (2016), DOI: 10.1111/2059-7932.12001

The historical relativity of autonomy

Bourdieu does not go as far as Max Weber (Alexander, 1995: 160) or classical field theorists in physics to assume the possibility of complete closure. As he recognizes, social fields are themselves embedded, and, as such, they are not immune to external influences. Larger societal processes, events, or crises may all impact upon field dynamics (cf. also DiMaggio, 1991; Fligstein and McAdam, 2012: 59–64). To highlight this critical point, Bourdieu adds the qualifier 'relative' to his conception of autonomy. It suggests that environments may affect fields, but in a modus that is relative to their specific 'laws' and particular historical configurations: external influences have an impact only to the extent that they become 'refracted' like a prism through the internal principles, structures and meanings of a historically given state of the field. In addition, 'relative' also means that a field's autonomy is empirically variable, and so it may range in a linear fashion from absolute autonomy to nearly complete heteronomy (Gorski, 2013: 329f): the higher the degree of autonomy, the higher in turn is the field's 'refraction effect', that is, its power to absorb and transform external influences or constraints into internal ones (Bourdieu, 1996: 220–221).

Thus, the composite of 'relative autonomy' offers a way to delineate what differentiates a field from others, while, at the same time, it also formulates a varying modus of how a field is related to other spheres or a broader environment. Taken together and concluding the move of analytical reduction that motivated this second section, a social field can be defined – in an elementary and scale-invariant sense – *as a sphere of specialized practice with a relatively autonomous logic of competition in the three dimensions of a distinctive ideology, a particular type of specific symbolic capital, and a distinctive set of organizations.*

I agree with Steinmetz that it is useful to distinguish the concept of an autonomous field clearly from a settled field (Steinmetz, 2002, cf. especially pp. 151, 193; 2008b: 595) – also in view of the notion of 'field settlement' in the theory of strategic action fields (eg Armstrong, 2005; Fligstein and McAdam, 2012). In a settled field, participants concur not only about the distinctive value of a specialized practice and the particular type of symbolic capital that is dominant. Far more, they also agree about the specific criteria of evaluation that underlie the distribution of symbolic capital (Steinmetz, 2002: 151, 2008b: 595). In this sense they have arrived at a 'field settlement', manifested in a 'stable consensus regarding rules of conduct and membership criteria' (Fligstein and McAdam, 2012: 88–90). Consequently, a settled field has reached a higher degree of consolidation, being characterized by a 'robust social order' and established 'rules of the game' (Fligstein and Adam, 2012: 92).

While one might object that the concept of a relatively autonomous field refers to a rather loose meso-level order, I suggest that this feature has unique advantages for transnational or global analysis. Insofar as transnational relations tend to be more ephemeral (Buchholz, 2013) and their meanings in flux – being marked by greater 'indeterminacy' (Madsen, 2006: 24, 33) and 'ontological openness' (Marginson, 2008: 313) – the concept of an autonomous field is principally well suited for their analysis. One can capture relatively distinct and interdependent transnational orders *as* orders *without* having to exaggerate the degree of consolidation and integration. In other words, the concept has a unique analytical purchase to enable one to grasp social spheres with 'institutionalized anomie' (Bourdieu, 1993b: 238–253), which seem to be profuse at the transnational or global level.

Extending the field concept to a global level: from functional to vertical autonomy

Analogical extension: relative autonomy and global fields

As outlined above, in an elementary sense, Bourdieu defines fields by considering relative autonomy to be a necessary condition. Fields refer not just to social spheres of specialized practice. They also designate spheres of specialized practice that have established a (relatively) autonomous logic. An intriguing body of empirical-theoretical work has transposed the concept of autonomy beyond national borders to examine fields in a global context, proceeding akin to the strategy of extension via structural equivalencies (eg Dezalay and Garth, 1996; Heilbron, 1999; Steinmetz, 2008a, 2008b; Go, 2008; Krause, 2014: 112–114).[19] These works demonstrate that at the transnational or global level, too, certain social spheres are best grasped as differentiated through relatively autonomous logics of competition.

For example, positioning himself against political economy models, Johan Heilbron shows that the global field for book translations functions in its cross-border exchanges relatively independently from the 'constraints' of the broader 'world market' (Heilbron, 1999: 432). He reveals that the share of a language group like Dutch or French in the total number of translated books worldwide is not a derivative of 'global economic structures', that is, inequalities of the world economic system. Instead, the position of a language group is influenced by the particular history and principles of hierarchy that are specific to the field of book translations, as a relatively autonomous sphere of cultural exchange (Heilbron, 1999). As another example, Monika Krause (2014) has insightfully demonstrated how a global field of humanitarian relief emerged by defining its (relative) independence from state politics, social movements and religious organizations. It is the vision of neutrality toward these institutions that provided the foundational ideology for a specific type of humanitarian symbolic capital, which, the study reveals, figures as the dominant resource and stake of competition among agents and organizations in this realm of global humanitarian practice.

By synthesizing these and other contributions, one can arrive at a preliminary, basic definition of a global field that centres, analogous to Bourdieu's national fields, on the criterion of relative autonomy. What changes in such a move of analogical extension is, first and foremost, the geographic scale, expanding from the national to the global level. Correspondingly, based on analogical equivalencies, a global field can be delineated along three basic analytical characteristics: (1) as a sphere of specialized practice; (2) with a relatively autonomous logic of competition, and (3) on a multi-continental scale of geographic expansion.[20]

Analogous difference: distinguishing functional and vertical autonomy

For my work on the contemporary visual arts, however, merely extending Bourdieu's relative-autonomy criterion proved to be insufficient. While investigating the emergence of the global art field, I had to revise Bourdieu's argument that a field emerges through increasing autonomy in relation to other fields. Extending his conception analogically – from the making of a national field to the making of a global one – it became evident that I had to supplement it with a second axis of differentiation: the global field of contemporary visual art emerged not so much by constituting its independence from other fields of practice, such as the economic, the political or even the religious field (Bourdieu, 1996). The main axis of differentiation was that it became relatively autonomous from the logics of various national art fields (Buchholz, 2008, 2013). In this case, however, the autonomy criterion assumed a new direction and meaning: rather than applying to functionally different spheres of practice, it relates to the different *levels* on which fields operate. In short, in examining the emergence of a global field in the contemporary visual arts, I was confronted with a second set of processes of differentiation across different levels of social organization – and thus, I concluded, a second kind of autonomy.

To delineate the latter for global field analysis, I suggest that it is necessary to distinguish between two types of autonomy: first, what I term functional autonomy, which designates how social spheres are differentiated by functionally different types of interests, practices and their logics, corresponding to Bourdieu's original conceptualization (cf. the 2nd section).[21] Second, vertical autonomy, which accounts for differentiation in relation to other field-levels of social organization in the same realm of specific interest and practice.

Figure 1 represents the distinction between these two kinds of autonomy in highly schematic terms with regard to the case of the global art field and respective forms of capitals (+ signifying positive volume): as illustrated, functional autonomy captures how the (global) art field is (relatively) distinct in its logics from the economic field (or political or religious etc.), while vertical autonomy refers to how the global art field is (relatively) differentiated in its logic from national fields of art (eg French, US, Japanese). Thus, it depicts differentiation between field *levels* of social organization, rather than the *type* of specialized practice. Instead of functional differentiation (broadly understood, cf. Gorski, 2013: 329), it accounts for a dynamic of vertical differentiation.

Correspondingly, by integrating 'vertical autonomy' as a feature of analogous difference – in the case of a field with different scales of social organization – the preliminary definition of a global field from the previous section has to be specified by four rather than three analytical characteristics: (1) as a sphere of specialized practice; (2) on a transcontinental scale; (3) functional autonomy in

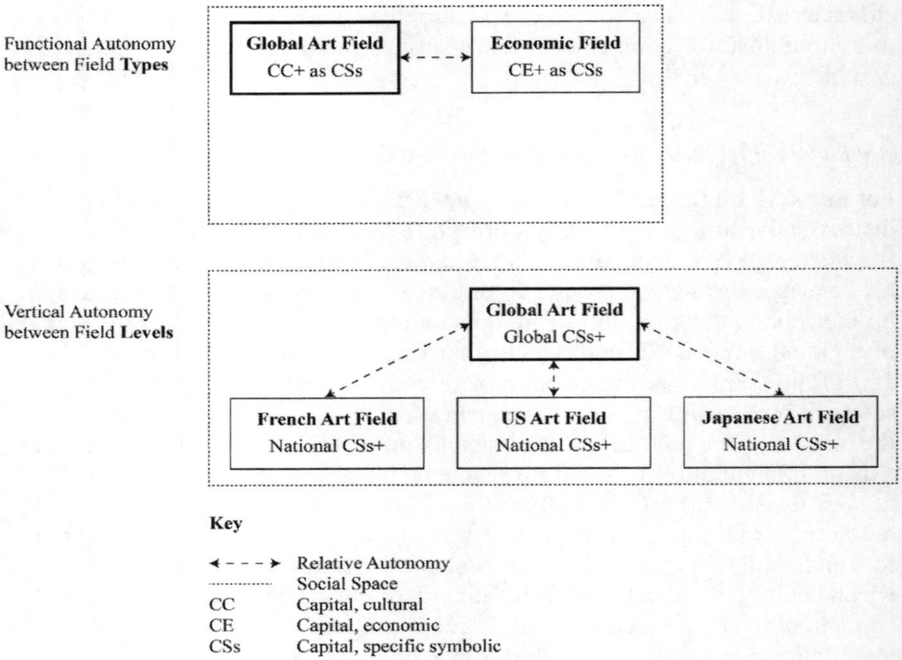

Figure 1 *Relative functional and vertical autonomy*

relation to other fields of practice; and (4) vertical autonomy from 'lower' field levels of organization within the relevant practice sphere. In short, *a multi-scalar global field can be defined as a globally extended sphere of specialized practice that displays a relatively autonomous logic of competition vis-à-vis other types of fields as well as other field levels within the same realm of practice*.

I will detail in the following paragraphs how the idea of vertical autonomy can contribute to advancement of a global field analysis more generally. But, before doing so, I would like to add three important qualifications of my conceptual distinction: first, the term vertical is not meant to designate a certain kind of hierarchical relationship between fields. In my usage, it denotes an analytically different meaning and direction of autonomy, in contrast to functional autonomy (cf. Figure 1). In this context, my conception of 'vertical' also has to be sharply distinguished from its meanings in the literature on multi-level governance in the political sciences, in which vertical governance levels refer to inequalities in political authority (eg Bache and Flinders, 2004). Second, while I develop the concept of vertical autonomy in this article with primary reference to the relations of global to national fields, it is, in principle, not limited to these field levels. It could be also used, for example, to conceptualize global fields in relation to regional fields (Heilbron, 2013), or to global fields vis-à-vis urban fields – depending on the particular research problem. Thus, the concept

 The Sociological Review Monographs, 64:2, pp. 31–60 (2016), DOI: 10.1111/2059-7932.12001

is not attached to inherent methodological nationalism. Third, this analytical flexibility also pertains to the directionality of the relationship among field levels. For example, while I focus my discussion in the following section on the emergence of a global art field as a process that involves vertical autonomy from national art fields, one could also invert the vector of analysis. In regard to a different field and historical period, one could study, for instance, how the emergence of national fields of state governance also involved the vertical differentiation from pre-existing global fields of empire (Wimmer and Feinstein, 2010) or the modern capitalist economy. In short, vertical autonomy should not be associated with a predefined directionality.

Contributions of relative vertical autonomy to the development of global field analysis

If one reads carefully, one could argue that the idea of vertical autonomy has been implicit in important contributions that define global cultural fields (eg Casanova, 2004: xii, 11f.; Kuipers, 2011: 541, 554). However, as it has not been explicitly distinguished as a *different kind* of autonomy, the vertically autonomous dimension has remained under-theorized in the actual empirical study of global fields. Pushing our analytical attention more into the direction of vertical autonomy offers, I argue, at least three contributions to the study of fields in a global context: first, it brings into sharp focus how the emergence of certain global fields involves a dynamic of vertical differentiation across field levels. As such, it provides an entry from which to theorize mechanisms of the emergence of higher-order fields out of lower-order fields – something that Bourdieu himself was not clear about. Second, it offers a lens through which we can examine how global fields remain (at least partially) articulated and interdependent with national fields (or urban or regional fields, etc.). Third, as I will detail, it also advances the conceptualization and measurement of the macro-structure of a global field.

Theorizing the emergence of multi-scalar global fields

As indicated, relative vertical autonomy was originated and developed during research on the emergence of the global art field. Taking the visual arts as an example, I would like to suggest that the concept may offer analytical purchase for examining the emergence of global fields that are multi-scalar[22] more generally, and that it thereby extends the existing literature in important ways.

For example, one of the most elaborated and convincing studies on global field emergence so far is Pascale Casanova's pioneering work on avant-garde world literature (Casanova, 2004).[23] Her approach is breathtaking in historical scope, yet it relies mainly on the vantage-point of functional autonomy. In *The World Republic of Letters,* she showed how one fundamental precondition that enabled a world literary field to arise after the nineteenth century was that literary production gained increasing independence from the nation-state and national politics within different national fields, first in Europe, then spreading around the world, also to various post-colonial states. With looser ties to national agendas and the production of propaganda, writers became able to envision an alternative, non-national conception of literature – and thus to develop a more international vision of their work (cf. also Moretti, 2000; Santana-Acuña, 2014). Yet, while Casanova's historical argument is insightful, it is incomplete. Insufficiently addressed is how, out of various national, yet autonomous literary fields, a genuinely global literary field can emerge that is not just a sum of these independent entities.

This is exactly where the concept of vertical autonomy can be productive: it offers a lens through which to theorize more explicitly a second axis of differentiation that is crucial for multi-scalar fields – to bring into clear relief how a global arena becomes relatively different in its logic and structures from national fields.[24] Vertical autonomy thereby also implies that the making of a global field is not necessarily just a question of the spatial extension of boundaries – for example, when specialized agents and institutions from different autonomous fields expand their competitive exchanges across national borders (Buchholz, 2006, 2008; Kuipers, 2011: 542f.). It also comprises another set of processes, which can be grasped, I argue, as vertical social differentiation.

To explain the vertical differentiation of a global field, the historical processes are seen to be multifaceted and complex, resonant with Bourdieu's intricate approach to historical sociology (Calhoun, 1993; Steinmetz, 2011; Gorski, 2013). By transposing Bourdieu's three-dimensional model of differentiation from functional to vertical autonomy and using it as a heuristic frame,[25] my research identified three mechanisms that have come into play in the vertical differentiation of the global art field since the 1980s. These mechanisms might be transposable for examining the historical emergence of other (multi-scalar) global fields. They encompass (a) the formation of global institutions for cross-border exchange; (b) the rise and institutionalization of a field-specific global discourse; (c) the rise of genuinely global evaluation mechanisms, which I conceptualize as institutional forms of transnational or global capital. As schematically summarized in Figure 2, it is through the interaction of these three mechanisms that the vertical differentiation of the global art field could be situated and historically explained – that is, as an interdependent global space for cultural cross-border flows and competition in which the ultimate stakes and values of contemporary art have become redefined in global terms. In the following paragraphs, I describe each mechanism separately with illustrations from my research. By considering findings of empirical studies on other cases, I seek to indicate how these mechanisms might be relevant for theorizing global field emergence beyond the visual arts.

The first mechanism consists of what I term *global institutions for cross-border exchange*, referring to the establishment of an institutional infrastructure for the worldwide circulation of ideas, persons, and goods across borders (Buchholz, 2008, 2013). In the visual arts, the two most influential global institutions for the emergence of a global field were the global art biennial circuit at the cultural pole,[26] and the global auction market at the economic pole.[27] While both institutions (ie art biennials and auction houses) had been international for a longer

The Sociological Review Monographs, 64:2, pp. 31–60 (2016), DOI: 10.1111/2059-7932.12001

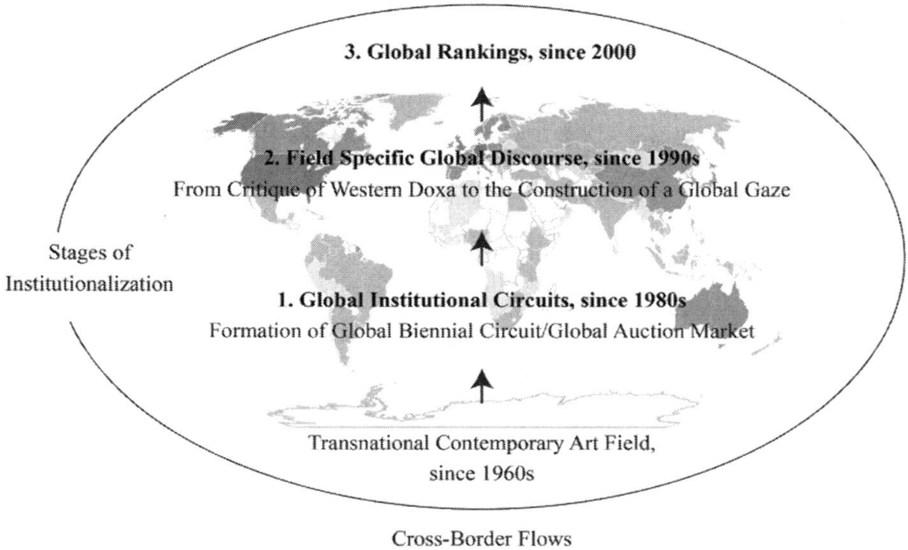

Figure 2 *The emergence of the global art field: three mechanisms*

period, over the past three decades they increasingly diffused across several continents. More importantly, they began to form interconnected circuits for the worldwide flow and valorization of contemporary art. For example, Sotheby's and Christie's underwent tremendous (and competitive) expansion since the 1980s, which entailed the formation of a partially integrated global auction market (Moulin, 2003; Horowitz, 2011; Buchholz, 2013). By the first decade of the new millennium, both houses had established sales locations in nine cities (including New York, London, Toronto, Zurich, Milan, Amsterdam, Hong Kong, Paris, Doha or Dubai). In addition, while Sotheby's could further rely on offices in 23 countries on five continents,[28] Christie's sales offices spread across 29 countries, plus Africa.

The formation of such global institutions for cross-border exchange constituted an important mechanism for the vertical emergence of a global art field because they helped to connect individual and organizational players from various national art fields around the world on a more frequent and, above all, sustained basis. Thus, they created an institutional infrastructure that made regular cultural exchange and competition with a worldwide scope possible in the first place. Beyond the visual arts, the relevance of transnational or global institutions for cross-border exchange in the formation of a global field is indicated, for example, in the literary realm, where international book fairs figure as significant institutions for enabling the cross-border circulation of cultural goods and connecting brokers from different national fields on a more frequent basis (Boschetti, 2004; Sapiro, 2010: 243). Also, in global TV, the proliferation of trade conventions or fairs has come to play a similarly connecting and integrative role (Bielby and Harrington, 2008: especially 2–8).[29] And recent work on the social sciences highlights the early relevance of international social scientific associations for an emerging global field in this realm (Heilbron, 2013: 689f.).

However, we should not assume that a global field arises quasi-mechanically out of the formation of a global institutional infrastructure. In the case of the contemporary visual arts, its emergence also hinged upon the rise of new meanings that rendered such institutional transformations intelligible and gradually redefined the 'vision' and cultural boundaries of contemporary art in global terms (Buchholz, 2013). In this regard, a second mechanism that I identified in my research is *field-specific global discourse*. In view of the art field, field-specific global discourse refers to the body of writings that engage with global issues and globalization in *specific* view of contemporary art, that is, its institutions, its artistic practices, its meanings, and its history. As Ferguson (1998) has insightfully shown at the national level, discourse is a fundamental mechanism for field autonomization. It provides tangible schemes of reference that may cohere and harden into cultural logics and beliefs that are constitutive for a particular social field (cf. also Gorski, 2013: 334f.). Regarding a global perspective, Bourdieu himself ironically stressed the performative, constructionist nature of discourse in a vehemently critical discussion of the concept of globalization, which he denounced (with a focus on its neoliberal sources) as a 'power discourse' in the 'strongest sense of the word' (Bourdieu, 2003: 84). However, in the context of global field analysis, so far, few works have fully attended to the systematic study of discourse in order to account for the constitutive role of meanings and beliefs in cross-border transformations (for an exception, cf. Steinmetz, 2008a).

In my work, I traced the dynamics of global art discourse by examining internationally influential art journals over a period of three decades. This tracking showed how field-specific global discourse rose since the 1980s, and how it entailed, over time, the emergence of new global imaginations and meanings, which, eventually, led to the gradual construction and legitimation of a 'global gaze'. This dynamic was far from straightforward. The construction of a global gaze unfolded in three stages that were each associated with different connotations of global categories and themes: first, toward the end of the 1980s, debates on multiculturalism and post-colonialism introduced global concepts and topics into the contemporary art field primarily as a normative *topos* from which to criticize (at times vehemently) Eurocentric perspectives in Western contemporary art and its institutions. Then, in the late 1990s, the global partly shed its normative connotations when it became more strongly associated with discourses on 'globalization'. In this period, the global discourse began to both express and contribute to growing awareness of actually existing global transformations in the art field, as manifested, for example, in the emergence of a global art biennial circuit[30] – which, it was lauded, enabled new kinds of cross-border exchanges and hybridizations beyond the dominant Western centers. Finally, at the beginning of the new millennium, the global assumed greater taken-for-granted status. More and more agents began to believe in the global as an actually existing (immanent) condition

 The Sociological Review Monographs, 64:2, pp. 31–60 (2016), DOI: 10.1111/2059-7932.12001

for contemporary art and its institutional landscape. At the same time, global art discourse became entrenched in novel modes of institutional and artistic classification, manifested, for example, in the proliferation of new, unifying categories, such as 'global art world', 'global art', 'global styles' or 'global artist'. Taken together, these transformations in fundamental classifications and beliefs about the scope of contemporary art and its institutions reveal how field-specific global discourse can figure both as a crucial indicator and cultural mechanism for the vertical differentiation of a global field.

A third mechanism for the vertical differentiation of the global art field rested in the rise of new institutional practices of classifying and assessing artistic recognition and value in global terms, notably in the advent of worldwide artists' rankings in the new millennium (Buchholz, 2013). Newly created rankings of the most successful artists in the global exhibition space and global auction market figured as important mechanisms, because they contributed to the construction of new principles of hierarchy and, thus, new types of 'global capital' – as both stakes and objects-of-competition among cultural agents from virtually all corners of the world.[31] For one, they globalized the parameters within which the highest stakes of artistic recognition could be represented, thought of, and referenced. In addition, such rankings had important effects on the cultural construction of a common global space of competition. Their logic of evaluation suggests that artistic production around the world – which is nested in very different local histories, contexts, and biographies – can be attributed with enough sameness so as to be comparable in the first place. Through constructing unifying representations, global rankings both presuppose and indirectly assert the very notion that there is a common global competitive game.

The relevance of institutions for global evaluation or rankings as mechanisms for the institutionalization of vertically autonomous principles of hierarchy can be generalized. Existing studies indicate their importance for the international field of literature, for example regarding the Nobel Prize (Casanova, 2004 [1999]: 126–163), or for the global field of higher education (Marginson, 2007). Extending Bourdieu's terminology, I suggest the conceptualization of such mechanisms as *institutional forms of transnational or global capital*. Because they operate as quasi formal institutions of evaluation, they solidify stakes and types of transnational or global capital in principally more-ephemeral, vertically differentiated value struggles – thus creating tangible objects of competition in an emerging global game.

In sum, it was the historical convergence and, in part, the interaction of these three mechanisms at the beginning of the new millennium – the establishment of a global art infrastructure, the cultural construction of a global gaze, and the institutionalization of new global institutional practices of evaluation such as in the form of rankings – that laid the institutional foundation for the vertical emergence of a global field in the contemporary visual arts as an interdependent and minimally integrated cultural space of exchange and competition that reaches across six continents. This nascent global art field, which is still in the process of consolidation, does not obliterate the relevance of national or regional art fields, nor does it vanquish their diversity. Thinking in terms of vertical autonomy allows one to appreciate it as an additional, relatively differentiated dimension that runs through the smaller fields and connects them with a historically unmatched worldwide scope. As I have sought to indicate throughout this section, the three identified mechanisms of vertical differentiation might be fruitful for examining the emergence of other global fields. Yet, in line with a pragmatic and analogical approach to theory, they should not be considered as exhaustive.

National-global interdependencies: degrees and modalities

Moreover, the idea of relative vertical autonomy offers a conceptual basis from which it is possible to theorize relations between global and national levels in ways that avoid simple dualisms, an issue that has been long and rightly problematized in the globalization literature (eg Brenner, 1999; Sassen, 2007; Major, 2013). As the 'relativity' of field autonomy suggests that national and global field levels are only *partially* independent, we must approach them, by the same token, as still *relatively interdependent.* Thus, the concept permits us to grasp global and national field levels as simultaneously distinct and entangled, as independent and interdependent – beyond any dualistic or even zero-sum terms.

To be sure, there are already important terms in global and transnational sociology that account for how the global and the national (or local) relate, such as 'glocalization' (Robertson, 1995), 'hybridization' (Pieterse, 2015), 'localization' (Acharya, 2004), or 'bricolage' (Fourcade and Savelsberg, 2006). Yet, for social realms that are fielded, I claim, relative vertical autonomy offers a particularly precise entry point from which to theorize global-national relations – both in regard to the *degree* as well as the *modalities* of their relative interdependence or interaction.

On one hand, the qualifier *relative* implies that vertical autonomy between national and global field levels is variable. Accordingly, the concept enables one to take into account and assess differences in *degrees* of independence/interdependence. Empirically the degree of interdependence between the global and the national could be measured, for example, by considering the extent to which hierarchies at the global level correspond to hierarchies at the national field level. Regarding my research on contemporary visual art, for instance, I found that several artists from the U.S. that were leading in global rankings were also at the top of their national field, which correctly indicated that the U.S. art field has had a high degree of interdependence with the global art field (Buchholz, 2013). The situation changes dramatically if one looks to China. Chinese contemporary artists that were recognized at the global level and those that were renowned in their own country strikingly diverged during the 1990s. This finding rightly made evident that the mainland Chinese and global field levels were separated by higher vertical autonomy in this period—and thus, in turn, they were characterized by lower interdependence. Generalizing these findings from the visual arts, I propose the following testable hypothesis: the less that hierarchies are similar between national field and global field levels, the higher is vertical autonomy, and thus the less national and global field levels are interdependent—and vice versa.

On the other hand, relative vertical autonomy offers a particular lens through which we can examine *how* the global influences the national or the national the global, that is, the *modalities* of relative interdependence. Central in this regard is the notion that relatively autonomous fields are affected by other fields or the broader environment only indirectly, namely through refraction.[32] Extended analogically to the global–national axis, relative vertical autonomy helps us to keep in mind that the global is filtered through the national; it affects the national only to the extent that it becomes refracted, like a prism, through the latter's specific characteristics. Accordingly, the concept of vertical autonomy gives us an analytical stance from which to characterize the nature of causal relations that obtain throughout different field levels and in their interaction, something that Bourdieu did not adequately address.

To illustrate this point with an empirical example from research on the valuation of contemporary art in the auction market: relative vertical autonomy was a fertile starting point from which to develop an explanation of how and why the global auction success of certain contemporary Chinese artists influenced their standing in the national auction market. Throughout the 1990s, contemporary Chinese art had been strongly marginalized in local auctions. These were frequented by wealthy mainland Chinese buyers, who had a strong preference for traditional realist painting and classical ink. This marginal local position changed after Chinese contemporary art achieved record prizes at sales in global market centres (New York and London) in the new millennium. However, as my research revealed, feedback effects from the global to the national were far from direct and did not move in lockstep. Their impact must be explained by considering the specific constellations and junctures in the national auction sub-field, as well: around 2005, classical Chinese painting and ink faced mounting problems with forgeries and sky-rocketing prices, so that investment-oriented Chinese art buyers became predisposed to look for alternatives. Although these buyers had long exhibited a cultural disdain for the Chinese contemporary art genre, under such circumstances, it became desirable for them to go beyond cultural prejudices in order to embrace contemporary art as an alternative mode of investment. In short, the rise of Chinese contemporary artists in the global auction market improved their national standing, but, as I showed, rather indirectly: by refraction through the particular (dis)tastes, investment cultures and market junctures in the Chinese auction sub-field.

Lastly and importantly, the ideas of vertical autonomy and refraction can be illuminating when one inverts the analytical perspective, as well: to examine how the national becomes refracted in the global. For instance, in my work on global art, I found that since the 1990s, certain artistic styles emerged in art exhibitions and criticism that were interpreted as 'global styles', such as global conceptualism or global pop art (Buchholz, 2013). Yet, upon closer inspection, it became clear that these global art styles were far from anything unitary or homogeneous. Rather, they represented a kind of artistic idiom through which various nationally rooted forms of aesthetic expression were brought into dialogue. Global pop art, for example, is a style that encompasses artistic variations from the US and Great Britain, as well as Japan, Italy or Germany. A similar dynamic can be observed in the case of the 'rock aesthetic' as a global idiom in popular music (Regev, 2003: 224). Rather than being homogeneous, this global musical style is constituted through numerous refracted national variations around the world, such as Russian, Chinese, Beninese or Argentine rock, representing 'diversity within sameness' (Regev, 2003: 223).

More generally, thinking about such cases with the concept of vertical autonomy provides a way to understand and explain why global culture in its expressive forms does not need to be reduced to something homogeneous; and why, and in which modalities, it is not necessarily devoid of national influences. This stands in contrast to strands of global sociology which assume that the global as a particular socio-spatial configuration makes it unnecessary to think in national terms.[33] As the cases of contemporary art or rock music reveal, to grasp certain global cultural manifestations adequately, it is indispensable to keep an eye on persistent and complex entanglements of the global with the national. And this is why, I posit, the concept of vertical autonomy provides a fertile vantage point: we can examine and theorize global culture as an (unequal) mélange of refractions of various national and local modes of cultural production; a mélange that emerged, nevertheless, through trans-border exchanges and competition. Consequently, the symbolic space of a global field can be conceived as constituted through diversity within commonality – emerging out of multiple, vertically drawn-upon cultural traditions, sources, and entanglements; that is, global refractions of national cultural varieties (or local or urban or regional ones, etc.).

Macro-structure: identifying and denationalizing Bourdieu's national capital

Finally, I argue that relative vertical autonomy offers a useful refinement of our understanding and measurement of a global field's macro-structure. As Bourdieu (2003) points out, a macro-structure is important to incorporate into the analysis of certain global fields in order to illuminate in what ways the dimensions and results of power contests in fields go beyond the meso-level properties and relations of individual or organizational participants. They are also influenced by macro-level asymmetries, that is, inequalities between, for example, national fields. For instance, in view of global economic competition, Bourdieu argued that a firm's position in the imbalanced macro-structure between national fields has a 'positive or negative multiplier' effect on its chances of success (Bourdieu, 2003: 91). Although he did not make it explicit, an agent's position in a macro-structure is thus thought to have contextual effects that function *independently* from how her agent-level forms of capital are wielded. To extend the above example, two corporate entities with comparable resources will, nonetheless, have quite different odds of succeeding in global competition depending on their relative location, if one is situated in an economically advantaged area and the other

The Sociological Review Monographs, 64:2, pp. 31–60 (2016), DOI: 10.1111/2059-7932.12001

in a disadvantaged one. So, a global macro-structure can hone our comprehension of power dynamics in transnational or global fields, as it affects them at the meso-level but cannot be reduced to that point. And this, I emphasize, is the key implication.

Both Bourdieu (2003: 91) and Casanova (2004: 94) have made pioneering suggestions for conceptualizing the macro-structure of global fields, which, however, suffer partly from methodological nationalism. They posited that a global field's macro-structure is to be conceptualized by the distribution of stocks of various forms of 'national capital', that is, economic, political, cultural or linguistic resources associated with particular national fields as a whole. Yet, in general terms, I believe that it is neither necessary nor advisable to posit 'national capital' a priori as the main structuring category. The weight of 'national' – in contrast to, for example, urban or regional macro inequalities – may be subject to change; when considering cultural spaces, their relative significance may also differ between different cultural media.[34] Also, if we look beyond cultural arenas to global finance, for instance, Saskia Sassen has insightfully demonstrated that global cities rather than nation-states define the macro power structure of this economic realm most accurately (Sassen, 1991). Thus, in order not to be blinded by presuppositions of methodological nationalism, I argue that one should treat the relevance of 'national' capital not as an axiomatic assumption but as a factor, whose empirical and analytical weight has to be determined and justified in the course of research (Buchholz, 2006, 2008).

Yet, apart from the general importance of maintaining the flexibility of forms of what I have termed 'macro capital' (Buchholz, 2013), I argue that the concept of relative vertical autonomy can advance our approach to a global field's macro-structure in two ways. For one, it allows us to distinguish in which cases such a macro-structure is relevant for global fields at all, namely, only when they are differentiated along the vertical axis and thus partly remain interdependent with lower field levels and, therefore, the latter's forms of capitals (eg national, regional or urban fields in the same practice realm, etc.). This contrasts with global fields that constitute themselves independently from any entanglements with the national level, as Krause (2014) has shown, for example, for the global field of humanitarian intervention.

Second, even if countries (rather than cities or regions) are often the most relevant sub-units in many cases, vertical autonomy suggests that what matters in a global field are only those macro-level characteristics of national fields that constitute structural asymmetries at a *global* level of rivalry and competition, that is, at a vertically relatively autonomous field level. This apparently fine distinction has important implications for how one measures the macro-inequalities of a global field. For example, for reconstructing asymmetries in the distribution of institutional resources across 149 countries in the contemporary art field, it led me to consider only those art institutions within a national field that were also oriented toward a transnational or global level in their operations, instead of a national or regional level (eg among biennials, museums, or auction houses). In other words, I made sure that my sampling was precise by including only entities of the institutional structure of a national field that entailed inequalities at the level of *transnational* culture exchange and valuations. Consequently, taking into account the idea of relative vertical autonomy, I argue, alerts us to the need to distinguish clearly between nationally and transnationally relevant 'national stocks of capital'. By implication, the concept contributes to denationalize Bourdieu's and Casanova's original formulation of 'national capital'. Macro-level global hierarchies are not a simple reflection of national hierarchies.

Conclusion

We finally return to the question that opened this paper: what is a global field? By now, it should be clear that this question is ill-posed. Instead of seeking a quasi-universal theoretical definition, it seems more fruitful to ask which are the most fertile analytical principles to examine and use in theorizing the distinctive characteristics of global fields during the course of research. In other words, what are useful methods and 'thinking tools' for advancing an empirically grounded global field analysis, and which also avoid the traps of deductive reductionism or northern-western theory reification?

I have offered some suggestions for this complex problem. First, I argue that Vaughan's analogical theorizing opens one possible path for further developing Bourdieu's nation-state-centred field analysis toward a transnational or global level. Analogical theorizing provides both the means to generate an empirically differentiated as well as theoretically cumulative global field analysis. Second, drawing upon analogical theorizing and taking the visual arts as an empirical example, I argue that one characteristic in which certain transnational or global fields differ from the way fields were conceived in Bourdieu's original theory is their multi-scalar architecture. To account for this distinctive feature, I propose the concept of relative vertical autonomy and outline how it contributes to the analysis of fields in a global context in three ways: (1) for theorizing their emergence, (2) examining their relations or interdependencies on global and national levels, and (3) their macro-structure. This concept was elaborated in research on the global visual art field. It should not be interpreted as a world-spanning generalization (Connell, 2007). Instead, and in line with principles of analogical theorizing, it should be treated as a preliminary construct that might be revised or confirmed – in the perpetual confrontation with different objects of research.

Finally, I believe that there are three further directions in which the idea of vertical autonomy may inform research on global fields and be elaborated further: the first involves the theorizing of the strategies of agents, which, in vertically differentiated fields, are more complex to grasp. They can be simultaneously oriented at a national as well as a transnational or global field level, in relation to which they can have quite different meanings (cf. also Madsen, 2006: 28, 30; Regev, 2007: 127f.). In other words, players may pursue double or multiple games in their various national or transnational positions (cf. Dezalay, 2006). Thus, it

 The Sociological Review Monographs, 64:2, pp. 31–60 (2016), DOI: 10.1111/2059-7932.12001

is important to account for and further theorize the multi-positionality of agents in a vertically nested structure. Multiple-correspondence analysis, for example, is not suitable for use in analyzing such a multi-scalar situation. Second, it would be fruitful to develop further Bourdieu's notion of social capital to detail in more conceptually refined ways how cross-border networks affect the dynamics of a global field across vertically autonomous levels. Third, as indicated in the fourth section, vertical autonomy requires one to revise one's understanding of a field's symbolic space in a global context, so that it avoids overly cohesive or structuralist presuppositions as in Bourdieu's original formulation. For, if we can grasp a global symbolic space as an assembly of vertically refracted national or local cultural forms, we need to account for local diversity within global similarity (or global similarity within local diversity), neither of which are easily mapped onto a dualist, structuralist grid (cf. Bourdieu, 1993a). In other words, the idea of vertical autonomy demands further understanding of a seemingly paradoxical cultural constellation: how multiple, vertically drawn-upon sources, refractions, and entanglements make up the *common diversity* in the culture of global fields.

Acknowledgements

I would like to thank Gil Eyal, Diane Vaughan, George Steinmetz, Phil Gorski, Michèle Lamont, Mark Gould, Ulf Wuggenig, Chris Muller, Monika Krause, Maggie Frye, Ya-wen Lei, Nick Wilson, John Lie, Dillip Goankar, Vincent Gengnagel, Carol Lindquist, Sarah Sandelbaum, and the four anonymous reviewers for their helpful feedback and suggestions. I would also like to thank Julian Go for engaging and insightful conversations on the topic. Special thanks are due to Steffen Rudolph for his assistance in the production of the graphs.

Notes

1 As one of the reviewers rightly underscored.

2 As I have argued elsewhere (Buchholz, 2006, 2008), global field analysis thus offers one theoretical way to resurrect a 'functional or institutional differentiation perspective' (Gorski, 2013: 329) for the field of global studies, which has so far remained underdeveloped – apart from other frameworks, such as the model of transnational scapes by the anthropologist Arjun Appadurai (1990) or Luhmann's world society theory (eg Luhmann, 1997).

3 This is not to say that world-systems analysis and world polity theory can't be thought of as complementary. Indeed, the latter also evolved as a response to world-systems analysis, seeking to counter-balance its materialist emphasis (conversation with George Steinmetz). Yet, as Go rightly pointed out, field theory offers a way to synthesize their insights, and thus to arrive at a multidimensional approach (Go, 2008).

4 For reasons of exposition, I will henceforth not explicitly distinguish between *transnational* or *global* fields, which define a more-extended, that is, global geographic scope. Global refers to a scale that is multi-continental; it covers several continents. For this territorial qualification of the concept 'global', see Held *et al.* (2003).

5 The contours of Bourdieu's distinctively pragmatic theoretical stance can be delineated by considering two alternative positions against which it is directed, namely so-called 'theoreticist theory'

and positivism. Regarding the former, Bourdieu sharply objected to the idea that theoretical concepts can be developed for their own sake independent of engagement with empirical research, by the mere 'dissection or by amalgamation of other theories' (Bourdieu and Wacquant, 1992: 161). At the same time, Bourdieu's stance rejects positivistic approaches. Informed by French historical epistemology (particularly the work of Bachelard and Canguilhem, cf. Wacquant, 1992: 5, 61), he opposes positivism in maintaining that theory should be accorded epistemological primacy in constructing a research problem (eg Wacquant, 1992: 35).

6 Bourdieu's approach has been criticized for being confined to the national space of France. I will bypass the complex debate about determining boundaries of fields, as it has been discussed in Swartz (1997) and Eyal (2013), but I want to point out that one should generally distinguish between two different questions: on one hand, whether Bourdieu's models of the social space or field are also applicable to other countries or scales. Here, one has to see that Bourdieu conceives of theories as models for the construction of sociological objects, which can be modified according to the specific area or object of research. In this specific regard, it would not be a decisive objection whether 'high culture' is an equally important criterion for distinction in the US as it is in France, cf. Michèle Lamont (1992). It would be more important to ask whether Bourdieu's epistemological and theoretical principles allow us to validly construct and explain the heterogeneity of practices, for example. A sounder problem, however, consists in Bourdieu's strong empirical orientation toward a nation-state or sub-national frame of analysis, beginning with his studies of Algeria. He thereby privileges an endogenous perspective. With respect to the field concept, such criticism, however, can be put into perspective, as is demonstrated by Bourdieu himself, when he began to deploy his tools to reflect about the 'Possibilities of a Field of World Sociology', for example, Bourdieu (1991), cf. also the following note.

7 Bourdieu did not elaborate a global field analysis in the context of systematic empirical research, but he referred to international or global fields in his later writings, eg in a discussion of the 'field of world sociology' (Bourdieu, 1991), the 'international legal field' as a foreword to Dezalay's and Garth's (1996) pioneering field analysis of international commercial arbitrage; the 'world media field' (Bourdieu, 1999), or the 'global economic field' (Bourdieu, 2003).

8 As noted, Bourdieu *did* write conceptually about transnational and global fields. Yet he did not discuss how to extend his concepts in systematic ways in the course of research across scales, which stands in contrast to his otherwise strong emphasis on epistemological-methodological reflexivity (eg Bourdieu and Wacquant, 1992).

9 His usage of the concept of structural equivalence should be distinguished from the meaning of the term in the context of network theory, cf. Lorrain and White (1971), whose definition is mathematical, suggesting that two actors have structural equivalence if they have identical ties to and from all the g-2 other actors in a diagram or non-directed graph.

10 Cross-case comparison is to be distinguished from same-case comparison. The former engages with cases that may vary in their size, function, or complexity (Vaughan, 2014: 63). A classic example is Goffman's concept of the 'total institution'. It originated from field work at a mental hospital (Goffman, 1961). Then, he elaborated it further through cross-case comparison with such diverse cases as prisons, army training camps, naval vessels, boarding schools, and monasteries (Goffman, 1961: 62). Same-case comparison, by contrast, refers to similar cases, such as social revolutions in different nation-states. Stinchcombe, for example, envisioned historical case comparison essentially as a search for relations of structural equivalence (Stinchcombe, 2013 [1978], cf. in Vaughan, 2014: 62).

11 Abbott rightly problematizes the tendency of theorizing without engaging with real alternatives as 'relabeling', (Abbott, 2004: 218). As he put it, 'A researcher is not in the business of simply putting someone's labels on some new situation' (Abbott, 2014: 66).

12 Among other influences, cf. Bourdieu and Wacquant (1992).

13 It should be noted that the concept of relative autonomy was originally introduced by Louis Althusser (2009 [1971]). Standing in the Marxian tradition, he sought to formulate a relationship between the base and the superstructure that is less deterministic, and acknowledges the

possibility of reciprocal effects. Bourdieu develops this idea in the context of field theory further, as a central angle of his version of social differentiated theory.

14 We might want to keep in mind that the latter notion, a specific 'logic', has been deemed as 'broad and too amorphous' to have analytical leverage in field theory (Fligstein and McAdam, 2012: 10).

15 Which Philip Gorski considers as Bourdieu's 'most sophisticated piece of historical analysis and arguably his most methodologically sophisticated work *tout court*' (Gorski, 2013: 328).

16 Bourdieu distinguishes between four main sorts of capital: apart from 'economic capital', which denotes material wealth in the form of money, stocks and shares, etc., he introduces 'cultural capital', 'social capital' and 'symbolic capital'. 'Cultural capital' refers to the possession of cultural goods (eg books, paintings), institutional academic titles or formal credentials, and the degree to which one has incorporated cultural competencies or maintains familiarity with certain cultural practices. His rather vague notion of social capital signifies the kind and amount of social relationships that can be mobilized for certain strategies in specific fields (for the idea of negative social capital, cf. Wacquant, 1998: 27f.). The concept of symbolic capital indicates a degree of social recognition or prestige as an effect of possessing some of the aforementioned sorts of capital, such as cultural capital in cultural fields, etc. (eg Bourdieu, 2001). Regarding the latter, Bourdieu frequently speaks of *specific* symbolic capital, because it refers to a form of recognition that functions only with particular forms of capital whose value depends on the field itself; symbolic capital in 'rigorous terms' thus designates 'symbolic effects of capital' (Bourdieu, 2000: 242). Wacquant remarks that the notion of symbolic capital is one of the most complex in Bourdieu's approach (Bourdieu and Wacquant, 1992: 119.)

17 Bourdieu summarized this argument in the *Field of Cultural Production* succinctly, as follows: 'Thus, at least in the most perfectly autonomous sector of the field of cultural production, where the only audience aimed at is other producers (as with Symbolist poetry), the economy of practices is based, as in a generalized game of "loser wins," on a systematic inversion of the fundamental principles of all ordinary economies: that of business (it excludes the pursuit of profit and does not guarantee any sort of correspondence between investments and monetary gains), that of power (it condemns honours and temporal greatness), and even that of institutionalized cultural authority (the absence of any academic training or consecration may be considered a virtu' (Bourdieu, 1993a: 39).

18 Which, properly translated, refers to a set of specific organizations.

19 It should be mentioned that in doing so, these studies did not refer to principles of analogical theorizing.

20 For this territorial qualification of the concept 'global', see Held *et al.* (2003).

21 In this context, I presume a clear distinction between functional and functionalist, the latter referring to an older variant of systemic social differentiation theory, as formulated, for example, by Parsons. For an insightful critique of functionalist reasoning in historical sociology, cf. Roy (1990).

22 That is, those that are already institutionalized at 'lower,' eg national levels, etc.

23 Global in the generic sense introduced in note 4.

24 Which also needs to be conceptualized as more than the 'opening up of national fields' since we are dealing with a process of veritable emergence (cf. Kuipers, 2011).

25 As the first section outlined, in a scale-invariant sense, field autonomy encompasses, at minimum, three dimensions: (1) specific ideologies/beliefs; (2) a specific type of symbolic capital/interests; and (3) a specific set of organizations.

26 Art biennials in this context can be defined as periodic group exhibitions that aspire to represent the state of international contemporary art (Boecker, 2002: 422). As several scholars have noted, since the 1980s, contemporary art biennials have proliferated all over the world, with new biennials in places in Asia, Latin America or Africa (eg Quemin, 2002; Stallabrass, 2004). Yet beyond diffusion, they have also come to form a partially integrated global institutional circuit that heightens transcontinental flows of intermediaries, artists and artefacts (Bydler, 2004: 85–169; Buchholz, 2013). Other examples of border-crossing integrated circuits, which do not necessarily reach a global scope, however, are the more ephemeral travelling exhibitions among art museums

(Crane, 2002); and certainly the Guggenheim's spectacular expansions, which have partly faltered and partly been revived, with a new, major Abu Dhabi satellite in the making.

27 My institutional analysis of globalization in the contemporary visual arts focused only on institutions that are particularly important for the global valuation of art. Other institutional phenomena that also matter for increasing artistic flows and exchange across borders are artist-in-residence programmes (Bydler, 2004; Glauser, 2009), or art fairs, which, however, with few exceptions, tend to operate more regionally (Quemin, 2012: 53–82; Baia Curioni, 2012: 115–151).

28 This analysis did not take into account consultancies, which represent a far less institutionalized, volatile form of the foreign representation of auction houses.

29 It should be added that the authors did not refer to Bourdieu's field approach.

30 It was in this period, thus, when I observed an interaction effect between mechanisms one and two, which in tandem contributed to the emergence of a global field.

31 The two most relevant rankings that played into the vertical differentiation of the global art field were, on one hand, the *Artfacts* ranking, which assesses the global symbolic recognition of artists by drawing upon information from exhibitions at contemporary art institutions worldwide, including the global art biennial circuit. On the other hand, there was the *Artprice* ranking, which determines the leading contemporary visual artists in the global auction market by assessing their total annual volume of sales. Although contentious, these institutional evaluation mechanisms are not only global in terms of the information they draw upon, but also in their reception. The *Artfacts* ranking, for example, has occupied a paradoxical position in the art field: while open criticism has never fully vanished, it has come to be regularly received and used by a silent, largely professional majority, reaching a truly global audience. Aided by tireless promotion at numerous art fairs worldwide, by 2012, *Artfacts* could count art institutions from 62 countries on six continents as its clients, while its private clients – of whom the majority are reportedly artists – came from 75 countries, overall.

32 Cf. The second section, on the historical relativity of autonomy.

33 As one of the reviewers rightly noted.

34 Casanova (2004: 35f.), for example, pointed out that literature has tended to be strongly tied to the construction of national spaces, being bound up with corresponding languages. Regarding the artistic media and visual 'languages' of the fine arts, this is not necessarily the case to the same extent (Buchholz, 2006). Also, for certain research questions, it might be more appropriate to take, for example, cities or regions and not countries as the main macro-level entities. Hence, I argue for a more flexible approach to reconstructing the macro-structure of a global field.

References

Abbott, A., (2004), *Methods of Discovery: Heuristics for the Social Sciences* (Contemporary Societies), New York: W. W. Norton.

Abbott, A., (2014), *Digital Paper. A Manual for Research and Writing with Library and Internet Materials*, Chicago: Chicago University Press.

Abbott, A., (2015), 'Reflections on the future of the social sciences', 37th Marc Bloch lecture at the École des Hautes Études En Sciences Sociales, Paris.

Acharya, A., (2004), 'How ideas spread: whose norms matter? Norm localization and institutional change in Asian regionalism', *International Organization*, 58 (2): 239–275.

Alexander, J., (1995), 'The reality of reduction: the failed synthesis of Pierre Bourdieu', in J. Alexander, *Fin de Siècle Social Theory. Relativism, Reduction, and the Problem of Reason*, 128–218, London; New York: Verso.

Althusser, L., (2009 [1971]), 'Ideology and ideological state apparatuses', in A Sharma and A. Gupta (eds), *The Anthropology of the State: A Reader*, 86–111, Chichester: John Wiley & Sons.

Appadurai, A., (1990), 'Disjuncture and difference in the global cultural economy', *Public Culture*, 2 (2): 1–24.

Armstrong, E. A., (2005), 'From struggle to settlement: the crystallization of a field of lesbian/gay organizations in San Francisco, 1969–1973', in G. Davis, D. McAdam, W. R. Scott, and M. Zald

The Sociological Review Monographs, 64:2, pp. 31–60 (2016), DOI: 10.1111/2059-7932.12001

(eds), *Social Movements and Organization Theory*, 161–187, Cambridge: Cambridge University Press.
Bache, I. and Flinders, M., (2004), *Multi-level Governance*, Oxford: Oxford University Press.
Baia Curioni, S., (2012), 'A fairy tale: the art system, globalization, and the fair movement', in M. Lind and O. Velthuis (eds), *Contemporary Art and its Commercial Markets: A Report on Current Conditions and Future Scenarios*, 115–151, Berlin: Sternberg Press.
Bielby, D. D. and Harrington, C. L., (2008), *Global TV: Exporting Television and Culture in the World Market*, New York: NYU Press.
Boecker, S., (2002), 'Austausch oder globaler Inzest? 2. Konferenz Biennalen im Dialog in Frankfurt', *Kunstforum International*, 29 (161): 422–426.
Boschetti, A., (2004), ,Vom Engagement zum Experimentalismus. Anmerkungen zum italienischen literarischen Feld seit 1945 und seinem Verhältnis zum transnationalen Raum', *Berliner Journal für Soziologie*, 2: 189–205.
Bourdieu, P., (1983), 'The field of cultural production, or: the economic world reversed', *Poetics*, 12 (4): 311–356.
Bourdieu, P., (1984), *Distinction: A Social Critique of the Judgement of Taste*, Cambridge, MA: Harvard University Press.
Bourdieu, P., (1985), 'The genesis of the concepts of habitus and field', *Sociocriticism*, 2 (2): 11–24.
Bourdieu, P., (1991), 'Epilogue: on the possibility of a field of world sociology', in P. Bourdieu and J. Coleman (eds), *Social Theory for a Changing Society*, 373–387, Boulder, CO: Westview Press.
Bourdieu, P., (1993a), *The Field of Cultural Production*, New York: Columbia University Press.
Bourdieu, P., (1993b), 'Manet and the institutionalization of anomie', in P. Bourdieu (ed.), *The Field of Cultural Production*, 238–253, Oxford: Polity Press.
Bourdieu, P., (1996), *The Rules of Art: Genesis and Structure of the Literary Field*, Cambridge: Polity Press.
Bourdieu, P., (1998), *Practical Reason: On the Theory of Action*, Stanford, CA: Stanford University Press.
Bourdieu, P., (1999), 'Rethinking the state: genesis and structure of the bureaucratic field', in G. Steinmetz (ed.), *State/culture: State-formation after the Cultural Turn*, 53–75, Ithaca, NY: Cornell University Press.
Bourdieu, P., (2000), *Pascalian Meditations*. Stanford, CA: Stanford University Press.
Bourdieu, P., (2001), 'The forms of capital', in M. Granovetter and R. Swedberg (eds), *The Sociology of Economic Life*, 96–111, Boulder, CO: Westview Press.
Bourdieu, P., (2003), 'Unite and rule', in P. Bourdieu (ed.), *Firing Back. Against the Tyranny of the Market*, 82–96, New York: The New Press.
Bourdieu, P., (2004), *Science of Science and Reflexivity*, London: Polity.
Bourdieu, P., (2005), *The Social Structures of the Economy*, London: Polity.
Bourdieu, P., (2013), *Manet: une révolution symbolique: cours au Collège de France, 1998–2000, suivis d'un manuscrit inachevé*, Paris: Seuil.
Bourdieu, P. and Wacquant, L., (1992), 'The purpose of reflexive sociology', in P. Bourdieu and L. Wacquant (eds), *Reflexive Sociology*, 61–216, Chicago: Chicago University Press.
Brenner, N., (1999), 'Beyond state-centrism? Space, territoriality, and geographical scale in globalization studies', Theory and Society, 28 (1): 39–78.
Buchholz, L., (2006), 'Field theory and the globalization of art: rethinking "interdependency"', *Practicing Bourdieu, In the Field & Across the Disciplines. An International and Interdisciplinary Conference*. University of Michigan, Ann Arbor.
Buchholz, L., (2008), 'Feldtheorie und Globalisierung', in B. Von Bismarck, T. Kaufmann and U. Wuggenig (eds), *Nach Bourdieu: Kunst, Visualität und Politik*, 211–238, Vienna: Turia + Kant.
Buchholz, L., (2013), 'The global rules of art', PhD dissertation, Columbia University, New York.
Bydler, C., (2004), *The Global Art World, Inc. On the Globalization of Contemporary Art*, Uppsala: Uppsala University Press.
Calhoun, C., (1993), 'Habitus, field and capital: the question of historical specificity', in C. Calhoun, E. Lipuma and M. Postone (eds), *Bourdieu: Critical Perspectives*, 61–88, Cambridge: Polity Press.

Casanova, P., (2004), *The World Republic of Letters*, Cambridge, MA: Harvard University Press.
Connell, R., (2007), 'The northern theory of globalization', *Sociological Theory*, 25 (4): 368–385.
Crane, D., (2002), 'Culture and globalization: theoretical models and emerging trends', in D. Crane, N. Kawashima and K. Kawasaki (eds), *Global Culture. Media, Arts, Policy and Globalization*, 1–25, London; New York: Routledge.
Dezalay, Y., (2006), 'State expertise on the international market: professional rivalries between lawyers and economists', *Practicing Bourdieu, In the Field and Across the Disciplines. An International and Interdisciplinary Conference*, University of Michigan, Ann Arbor.
Dezalay, Y., and Garth, B., (1996), *Dealing in Virtue: International Commercial Arbitration and the Construction of a Transnational Legal Order*, Chicago: University of Chicago Press.
DiMaggio, P. J., (1991), 'Constructing an organizational field as a professional project: US art museums, 1920–1940', in W. W. Powell and P. J. DiMaggio (eds), *The New Institutionalism in Organizational Analysis*, 267–292, Chicago: University of Chicago Press.
Eyal, G., (2013), 'Spaces between fields', in P. Gorski (ed.), *Pierre Bourdieu and Historical Analysis*, 159–182, Durham, NC: Duke University Press.
Ferguson, P., (1998), 'A cultural field in the making: gastronomy in 19th century France', *American Journal of Sociology*, 104 (3): 597–641.
Fligstein, N. and McAdam, D., (2012), *A Theory of Fields*, Oxford: Oxford University Press.
Fourcade, M., (2006), 'The construction of a global profession: the transnationalization of economics', *American Journal of Sociology*, 112 (1): 145–194.
Fourcade, M., and Savelsberg, J. J., (2006), 'Introduction: global processes, national institutions, local bricolage: shaping law in an era of globalization', *Law & Social Inquiry*, 31 (3): 513–519.
Giddens, A., (1990), *The Consequences of Modernity: The Raymond Fred West Memorial Lectures.*
Glauser, A., (2009), *Verordnete Entgrenzung. Kulturpolitik, Artist-in-Residence Programme und die Praxis der Kunst*, Bielefeld: Transcript.
Go, J., (2008), 'Global fields and imperial forms: field theory and the British and American empires', *Sociological Theory*, 26 (3): 201–229.
Goffman, E., (1961), *Asylums: Essays on the Social Situation of Mental Patients and Other Inmates*, Chicago: Aldine Transaction.
Gorski, P. (ed.), (2013), *Bourdieu and Historical Analysis*, New York: Duke University Press.
Healy, K., (2015), 'Fuck nuance', paper presented at the Theory Section Paper Session on the Promise and Pitfalls of Nuance in Sociological Theory, American Sociological Association Meetings.
Held, D., McGrew, A., Goldblatt, D. and Perraton, J., (2003), 'Rethinking globalization', in D. Held and A. McGrew (eds), *The Global Transformation Reader*, 67–86, Cambridge: Polity Press.
Heilbron, J., (1999), 'Toward a sociology of translation: book translations as a cultural world-system', *European Journal of Social Theory*, 2 (4): 429–444.
Heilbron, J., (2013), 'The social sciences as an emerging global field', *Current Sociology*, 62 (5): 685–703.
Horowitz, N., (2011), *Art of the Deal: Contemporary Art in a Global Financial Market*, Princeton, NJ: Princeton University Press.
Krause, M., (2014), *The Good Project. Humanitarian Relief NGOs and the Fragmentation of Reason*, Chicago: University of Chicago Press.
Kuipers, G., (2011), 'Cultural globalization as the emergence of a transnational cultural field: transnational television and national media landscapes in four European countries', *American Behavioral Scientist*, 55 (5): 541–557.
Lamont, M., (1992), *Money, Morals, and Manners: The Culture of the French and the American Upper-Middle Class*, Chicago: University of Chicago Press.
Lorrain, F., and White, H. C., (1971), Structural equivalence of individuals in social networks', *Journal of Mathematical Sociology*, 1 (1): 49–80.
Luhmann, N., (1997), 'Globalization or world society: how to conceive of modern society?', *International Review of Sociology*, 7 (1): 67–79.
Madsen, M., (2006), 'Transnational fields: elements of a reflexive sociology of the internationalisation of law', *Retfærd. Nordisk Juridisk Tidsskrift*, 114 (3): 34–41.

Major, A., (2013), 'Transnational state formation and the global politics of austerity', *Sociological Theory*, 31 (1): 24–48.
Marginson, S., (2007), 'Global university rankings', in S. Marginson (ed.), *Prospects of Higher Education: Globalisation, Market Competition, Public Goods and the Future of the University*, 79–100. Rotterdam: Sense Publishers.
Marginson, S., (2008), 'Global field and global imagining: Bourdieu and worldwide higher education', *British Journal of Sociology of Education*, 29 (3): 303–315.
Martin, J. L., (2003), 'What is field theory?' *American Journal of Sociology*, 109 (1): 1–49.
Martin, J. L. and Forest, G., (2014), 'Was Bourdieu a field theorist?', in M. Hilgers and E. Mangez (eds), *Bourdieu's Theory of Social Fields. Concepts and Applications*, London: Routledge.
Merton, R. K., (1968) [1938], *Social Theory and Social Structure*, New York: Simon and Schuster.
Meyer, J. W., (2000), 'Globalization sources and effects on national states and societies, *International Sociology*, 15 (2): 233–248.
Meyer, J. W., Boli, J., Thomas, G. M. and Ramirez, F. O., (1997), 'World society and the nation-state', *American Journal of Sociology*, 103 (1): 144–181.
Moretti, F., (2000), 'Conjectures on world literature', *New Left Review*, 54–68.
Moulin, R., (2003), *Le Marché de l'Art. Mondialisation et Nouvelles Technologies*, Paris: Flammarion.
Pieterse, J. N., (2015), *Globalization and Culture: Global Mélange*, New York: Rowman and Littlefield.
Quemin, A., (2002), *L'Art Contemporain International. Entre les Institutions et le Marché*, Nimes: Jacqueline Chambon / Artprice.
Quemin, A., (2012), 'The internationalization of the contemporary art world and market: the role of nationality and territory in a supposedly "globalized" sector', in M. Lind and O. Velthuis (eds), *Contemporary Art and its Commercial Markets: A Report on Current Conditinos and Future Scenarios*, 53–83, Berlin: Sternberg Press.
Reed, I. A., (2013), 'Theoretical labors necessary for global sociology: critique of Raewyn Connell's southern theory', *Political Power and Social Theory*, 25: 157–171.
Regev, M., (2003), '"Rockization": diversity within similarity in world popular music', in U. Beck, N. Sznaider and R. Winter (eds), *Global America? The Cultural Consequences of Globalization*, 222–234, Liverpool: Liverpool University Press.
Regev, M., (2007), 'Cultural uniqueness and aesthetic cosmopolitanism', *European Journal of Social Theory*, 10 (1): 123–138.
Robertson, R., (1995), 'Glocalization: time-space and homogenity-heterogenity', in M. Featherstone, S. Lash and R. Robertson (eds), *Global Modernities*, 15–30, London: Sage.
Roy, W. G., (1990), 'Functional and historical logics in explaining the rise of the American industrial corporation', *Comparative Social Research*, 12 (20): 19–44.
Santana-Acuña, A., (2014), 'How a literary work becomes a classic: the case of one hundred years of solitude', *American Journal of Cultural Sociology*, 2 (1): 97–149.
Sapiro, G., (2010), 'Globalization and cultural diversity in the book market: the case of translations in the US and in France', *Poetics* 38 (4): 419–439.
Sassen, S., (1991), *The Global City: London, New York, Tokyo*, Princeton: Princeton University Press.
Sassen, S., (2007), *A Sociology of Globalization*, New York: W.W. Norton & Company.
Stallabrass, J., (2004), *Art Incorporated: The Story of Contemporary Art*. Oxford: Oxford University Press.
Steinmetz, G., (2002), 'Precoloniality and colonial subjectivity: ethnographic discourse and native policy in German overseas imperialism, 1780s–1914', *Political Power and Social Theory*, 15: 135–228.
Steinmetz, G., (2008a), *The Devil's Handwriting: Precoloniality and the German Colonial State in Qingdao, Samoa, and Southwest Africa*, Chicago: University of Chicago Press.
Steinmetz, G., (2008b), 'The colonial state as a social field: ethnographic capital and native policy in the German overseas empire before 1914', *American Sociological Review*, 73 (4): 589–612.
Steinmetz, G., (2011), 'Bourdieu, historicity, and historical sociology', *Cultural Sociology*, 5 (1): 45–66.

Stinchcombe, A. L., (2013) [1978], *Theoretical Methods in Social History*, Amsterdam: Elsevier.
Swartz, D., (1997), 'Fields of struggle for power', in D. Swartz (ed.), *Culture & Power: The Sociology of Pierre Bourdieu*, 117–142, Chicago: University of Chicago Press.
Van den Bosch, A., (2005), *The Australian Art World. Aesthetics in a Global Market*, Sydney: Allen & Unwin.
Vaughan, D., (1983), *Controlling Unlawful Organizational Behavior: Social Structure and Corporate Misconduct*, Chicago: University of Chicago Press.
Vaughan, D., (1992), 'Theory elaboration: the heuristics of case analysis', in C. Ragin and H. Becker (eds), *What Is a Case? Exploring the Foundations of Social Inquiry*, 173–202, Cambridge: Cambridge University Press.
Vaughan, D., (2014), 'Analogy, cases and comparative social organization', in R. Swedberg (ed.), *Theorizing in Social Science: The Context of Discovery*, 61–84, Stanford, CA: Stanford University Press.
Wacquant, L., (1992), 'Towards a social praxeology: the structure and logic of Bourdieu's sociology', in P. Bourdieu and L. Wacquant (eds), *Reflexive Sociology*, 1–60, Chicago: Chicago University Press.
Wacquant, L., (1998), 'Negative social capital: state breakdown and social destitution in America's urban core', *Netherlands Journal of Housing and the Built Environment*, 13 (1): 25–40.
Wallerstein, I., (1974), *The Modern World-System*, New York: Academic Press.
Wallerstein, I., (2004), *World-Systems Analysis: An Introduction*, Durham, NC: Duke University Press.
Weber, M., (1946) [1915], 'Religious rejections of the world and their directions', in H. H. Gerth and C. W. Mills (eds), *From Max Weber: Essays in Sociology*, London and New York: Routledge.
Wimmer, A. and Feinstein, Y., (2010), 'The rise of the nation-state across the world, 1816 to 2001', *American Sociological Review*, 75 (5): 764–790.

Please quote the article DOI when citing SR content, including monographs. Article DOIs and "How to Cite" information can be found alongside the online version of each article within Wiley Online Library. All articles published within the SR (including monograph content) are included within the ISI Journal Citation Reports® Social Science Citation Index.

Moral accounting as field foundation in an early modern empire: the English East India Company in the late eighteenth century

Nicholas Hoover Wilson

Abstract: Field analysis and the relational approach to historical social-scientific explanation of which it is an instance – helps illuminate the administrative dynamics of empires. While most studies of imperial dynamics emphasize the 'high imperialism' of the nineteenth and twentieth centuries, this article extends field analysis to a crucial case from the second half of the eighteenth century: the English East India Company's transition from a (largely) merchant trading company to a territorial power. In this disordered space of administration, officials struggling with one another for metropolitan recognition provided moral accounts of themselves which, on the one hand, explained their behaviour in terms drawn from abstract, purportedly universal social spaces, and, on the other hand, claimed credibility through a personal 'interest in disinterest'. I argue that these moral accounts helped delimit the boundaries of and shape the dynamics within a distinctively imperial administrative field. To analyse this transformation, I suggest a synthesis of three varieties of relational analysis: Bourdieu's field theory, Fligstein and McAdam's analysis of strategic action fields, and Padgett and Powell's work on network folding and robust action.

Keywords: field theory, empire, organizations, morality, culture

Introduction

Thanks largely to the work of Pierre Bourdieu and buttressed by developments in areas as diverse as organizational analysis to international relations, the concept of a field has provided crucial intellectual purchase on the behaviour of global processes. Indeed, this article aims to extend and complement the robust body of work (in this volume, see esp. Buchholz, Dromi) – where, how, and why fields emerge in the first place. But while many applications exploring how global fields emerge operate by employing Bourdieu's whole tightly interwoven conceptual apparatus, this article instead suggests a synthesis among (and probes the

The Sociological Review Monographs, 64:2, pp. 61–78 (2016), DOI: 10.1111/2059-7932.12002

Published by John Wiley & Sons Ltd, 9600 Garsington Road, Oxford OX4 2DQ, UK and 350 Main Street, Malden, MA 02148, USA

boundaries of) three popular field-theoretic and relational approaches to field emergence: Bourdieu's approach and work inspired by it; Fligstein and McAdam's concept of 'strategic action fields'; and Padgett and Powell's perspective on network folding and robust action.

A limited synthesis among these three approaches is important because it serves a substantive aim: to contribute to burgeoning work on relational and field analysis of imperial administrations (see also Steinmetz, this volume). This work has advanced our understanding of what empires are and how they work, but they also tend to lay aside a key historical transition: the movement from early-modern patrimonial administrations, in which the line between metropolitan and imperial administrative politics was significantly blurred, to a more recognizably 'modern' bifurcation in the official imagination between colony and metropole. This article seeks to hold just such a transition at the centre of its empirical frame, focusing on aspects of a key early-modern case: the English East India Company (hereafter 'EIC' or 'Company') in the late eighteenth century.

The case of the EIC, as I will suggest below, reveals key layers of imperial field-foundation. The argument is relational at each of these layers, meaning that the 'essence' of Company agents – and indeed, the identity of the Company as a whole – is determined by how they are embedded in relationships with other actors, corporate or individual (Abbott, 1995; Emirbayer, 1997; Fuchs, 2005). At the layer of the EIC's structural relationship with the English (after the 1707 Act of Union, 'British') state, the Company entered a profound period of crisis (driven by the fiscal and military complications of acquiring territory in India after 1765) which eroded the insulation of its administrative affairs in India from metropolitan politics. In another layer, the decay of this insulation opened new avenues for officials in India bitterly struggling with one another to appeal home for help. And, in a final layer, these altered paths of appeal meant that the substance of the officials' claims about their actions shifted as well: from 'insider' accounts emphasizing the particularity of Indian administration to more abstract moral narratives stressing the derivation of official behaviour from universal justifications. Using the example of a struggle from the early 1770s between two EIC officials, which was one of the first to play out before a broad metropolitan audience, I seek to show that this transformed process of moral accounting was an indirect struggle over the limits and scope of imperial administrative politics. In other words, it represented unintended efforts to organize the boundaries and logic of a field.

I unfold this argument in three main parts. First, I discuss several field-analytic approaches to imperial administration, and suggest that they are challenged by the ambiguities of early-modern empires. Second, I suggest a synthesis among the three varieties of field analysis and relationalism mentioned above. In particular, I examine Bourdieu's account of the 'interest in disinterest' and its conditions, Fligstein and McAdam's useful attention to the external mobilization of resources (and state recognition) into a field, and Padgett and Powell's focus on the structural positioning of actors in networks of exchange and their ability to leverage 'robust action'. I then suggest all three can be placed in useful dialogue to account for the EIC's transition. Third, I apply this suggested synthesis to the exchange between Harry Verelst and William Bolts – two important EIC officials in the early 1770s – showing how Bolts offered a view of universal economic exchange as the key dynamic of imperial administration while Verelst emphasized the power of the state (based on a strict partition of Indian and British administrative orders) as the key anchor of his moral accounting.

Contemporary sociology and relational analysis of empire

Recent years have seen a proliferation of field-theoretic, and more broadly relational, studies of empires and their dynamics. These include works focusing on German colonialism (Steinmetz, 2007, 2008, this volume), the United States (Go, 2008a) – including a comparison of it with the British empire (Go, 2008b, 2011) – China's grasp of inner Mongolia (Wang, 2015), the Ottoman empire (Barkey, 1994, 2008), the making of colonial and postcolonial states in French North Africa (Wyrtzen, 2015, 2011), and the relationship between British commercial practices and market formation and integration (Erikson, 2014). Taken together, these studies emphasize that the details of imperial administration, and especially the way that metropolitan control is linked with the projection of control into colonies, are crucially important to understand outcomes as various as the nature of postcolonial identity (Kumar, 2010), modern social sciences (Steinmetz, 2013), the contemporary structure of postcolonial politics (eg, Goswami, 2004; Wyrtzen, 2015), as well as a variety of other contemporary political and economic outcomes (Acemoglu *et al.*, 2001; Banerjee and Iyer, 2005).

While these studies have provided excellent insight into the dynamics of empires and, indeed, have stretched the conceptual apparatus of social-scientific analysis by emphasizing the empirical persistence of imperial behaviour into the present day (eg, Calhoun *et al.*, 2006; Mann, 2005; Wyrtzen, 2011), their striking tendency is also to concentrate on the moments of 'high imperialism' in the nineteenth and twentieth centuries. Consider two important recent examples. Go's recent comparative analysis (2011) of American exceptionalism and the British empire centres on the comparison of equivalent hegemonic phases in relation to the global system as a whole, which for Britain stretches back to the Glorious Revolution in 1688. Yet the logic of comparing equivalent phases (rather than at the same time in history) entails, as Go recognizes, deemphasizing 'world developments across ... time periods' (2011: 23) and invites viewing both empires as occupying a similar, homogeneous analytic space. Meanwhile, Steinmetz's otherwise excellent edited volume exploring the 'Imperial Entanglements' between sociological thought and empire (2013) contains few studies addressing periods prior to 1800 in its section of substantive historical studies of empire.

Although these foci are sensible given the authors' substantive aims, attention to the dynamics of early-modern empires is warranted. One important reason is simple: modern empires arose against the backdrop, and in interaction with, their early-modern ancestors. Indeed, as Steinmetz demonstrated in *The Devil's Handwriting* (2007), modern native policies pursued in German colonies cannot be understood without appreciating the centuries-long ethnographic contact between Europeans and Asians, Pacific Islanders, and Africans. Moreover, the emergence of Britain's nineteenth-century 'second' empire in Asia and Africa emerged out of a troubled dialogue with its 'first' settler empire in the Americas (Chatterjee, 2012; Harlow, 1952; Marshall, 2005).

Yet in spite of these continuities, early-modern and modern empires still operated in very different ways. Early-modern empires were often settler societies founded on more-or-less direct rule which tended to annihilate the societies they encountered. Modern empires, meanwhile, often pursued 'indirect' rule through indigenous elites and preserved (albeit in distorted form based on colonial prejudices) a simulacrum of indigenous society. This problem of governing different, established societies from a social and physical distance, moreover, introduced a second distinction: whereas early-modern empires tended to emphasize administrative flexibility and ecumenical accommodation of difference within a patrimonial matrix emphasizing concrete connections among officials to the metropole (as, for example, Barkey (2008) traces in the case of the Ottoman empire), modern empires tended to operate according to the 'rule of colonial difference' (Chatterjee, 1993), logically separating colonizer in colonized in pseudo-essential ways that reproduced themselves over time and legitimated colonial rule (see also Steinmetz, 2014).

When considering this transition between early-modern and modern empires as an analytic puzzle, it is crucial not to overdraw the distinction between them. After all, the orientalist tropes founding the rule of colonial difference have deep historical roots (Chatterjee, 2012). Even Europeans emigrating to settler colonies occasionally found themselves described using 'the language of alterity or otherness' by those remaining at home (Greene, 2013: 50). Beyond this, the British state at the heart of what would become a world-historical empire in the eighteenth century was fundamentally 'enigmatic' (Adams, 2007), on the one hand showing precious aspects of modern bureaucratic and fiscal organization (Brewer, 1990) and 'cultural infrastructure' (Norton, 2014), while on the other hand remaining organizationally fragmented and administratively patrimonial (eg, Black, 1990; Harling, 1996).

Given all of this ambiguity, the strategy of this article is to use field analysis to help account for the transition between early-modern and modern forms of empire. It does so by examining a quintessentially enigmatic and important case: Britain's crossing of its 'imperial meridian' (Bayly, 1989) as the EIC became a territorial power in India after 1765. Field analysis is well suited to this task, because from its vantage point modern empires are characterized by a specific kind of administrative field: one guided by the rule of colonial difference. More specifically, field analysis guides us to ask more pointed questions about officials within the EIC during the period of transition: how were they positioned in relation to their metropolitan authorities and colonial elites; how did these positions change during periods of perceived crisis; and how did these changes alter the kinds of claims officials made about themselves and their actions?

The Sociological Review Monographs, 64:2, pp. 61–78 (2016), DOI: 10.1111/2059-7932.12002

The goal of this article is to show how answers to these interrelated questions shaped how the EIC's administration modernized, and how the rule of colonial difference emerged as it did. To pursue that goal, I first suggest a synthesis of several varieties of field and relational analysis.

Three varieties of relationalism

Although the terms 'field theory' and 'relational sociology' are singular, upon closer examination they represent multiple approaches. This section distinguishes three strands of relational and field analysis and suggests connections among them to help explain the transition between the early-modern and high-modern eras of EIC colonialism in India.

Arguably the best-known of the three perspectives is to be found in the work of Pierre Bourdieu. It revolves around a tight link between the concepts of habitus and field, representing people's pre-reflexive principles of judgment and the social spaces they occupy depending on their endowments of different forms of meaningful capital, respectively, as well as the subsidiary concepts of illusio and doxa, which respectively represent the kind of beliefs people hold about the nature of their behaviour and the taken-for-granted logic organizing a field. Thus people's position-takings (how they actually behave) are motivated by their illusio, drawn from their habitus, and interpreted in terms of their doxic understandings of their positions and action, which is in turn drawn from an interaction of their habitus with their position in a field.[1]

As Bourdieu repeatedly emphasized (eg Bourdieu and Wacquant, 1992: 96), each of these core concepts – including that of 'field' – is defined by its relationship to the others. Consider, for example, how a person's habitus and their position in a field together shape the 'space of possibles' for their behaviour. This space of possibles does not strictly determine action, but rather opens a range of potential lines of action. Yet it still

> impresses itself on all those who have interiorized the logic and necessity of the field as a sort of *historical transcendental*, a system of (social) categories of perception and appreciation, of social conditions of possibility and legitimacy which, like the concepts of genres, schools, manners and forms, define and delimit the universe of the thinkable and the unthinkable, that is to say, both the finite universe of potentialities capable of being thought and realized at a given moment – freedom – and the system of constraints inside which is determined what is to be done and to be thought – necessity. (Bourdieu, 1996: 326; original emphasis)

The initial clause of this passage is especially striking: 'on all those who have interiorized the logic and necessity of the field . . .'. Who takes such a step, given that doing so implies accepting limits on thinkable action within the field? For Bourdieu, the question cannot be put in this way, because

> [i]t is one and the same thing to enter into a field of cultural production, by settling an entrance fee which consists essentially of the acquisition of a *specific code* of conduct and expression, and to discover the finite universe of *freedom under constraints*

The Sociological Review Monographs, 64:2, pp. 61–78 (2016), DOI: 10.1111/2059-7932.12002

> and *objective potentialities* which it offers: problems to resolve, stylistic or theatric possibilities to exploit, contradictions to overcome, even revolutionary ruptures to effect. (Bourdieu, 1996: 235; original emphasis)

In other words, for the stakes of behaviour in a field to appear meaningful and comprehensible to someone, they must already have adopted the illusio and doxa of a particular field; to understand it they must already be in it.

Given that fields, subsuming freedom and necessity as they do, have histories, how and why do they emerge? The above passages from Bourdieu are drawn from his *The Rules of Art* (1996), which is his most systematic investigation of the emergence of a field – that of literature in nineteenth-century France. To briefly summarize his nuanced and rich analysis, a group of overeducated, underemployed, newly city-dwelling producers of cultural works were incubated in the 'bastard institutions' of the Paris salons in the early nineteenth century, allowing the field of artistic production to root itself on the one hand in a particular lifestyle (Bourdieu calls it an 'art of living') and on the other hand in a rejection of the Bourgeoisie, which had 'never before asserted so bluntly its values and its pretension to control the instruments of legitimation, both in the domain of art and in the domain of literature, and which, through the press and its hacks, now aim[ed] to impose a degraded and degrading definition of cultural production' (1996: 58). As the literary field grew increasingly autonomous in its *avant-garde* definition of 'pure' literature (and yet simultaneously dependent upon markets for its products among like-minded consumers; see Bourdieu, 1996), moreover, it increasingly fragmented among competing internal forms and genres which aligned relative to one another according to their relationship to commercial production. In other words, for Bourdieu, the field of artistic production arose because a group of cultural producers found themselves at the intersection of social forces which created a niche where they could assert their particular 'interest in disinterest', which in turn could be institutionalized into a regular system of one-upmanship as different authors attempted to produce ever-more 'artistic' literature.

This concept of an 'interest in disinterest' is crucial when thinking about the transition between early-modern and modern imperial fields. For this kind of claim – where an actor *dis*claims personal interest in the name of a higher principle, whether artistic, political, philosophical, or scientific – constitutes for Bourdieu the motor of modern 'universal' fields of practice like science and bureaucracy. Indeed, according to Bourdieu, disinterested duty to the state, for instance, emerged because

> social groups [who made up bureaucratic cadres] had an interest in the universal, and they had to invent the universal (the law, the idea of public service, the idea of general interest, etc.) and, if one may put it this way, domination in the name of the universal in order to accede to domination. (Bourdieu, 1998: 90)

Bourdieu thus emphasizes that his concepts are deeply intertwined with one another. Yet he also emphasizes the historical reality of social fields and their emergence, sometimes gradually, over time. Consequently, there seem to be

 The Sociological Review Monographs, 64:2, pp. 61–78 (2016), DOI: 10.1111/2059-7932.12002

two strategies for explaining the emergence of fields. One is to deploy the full panoply of Bourdieusian concepts and emphasize their different features over the course of a field's institutionalization. For example, Petzke's analysis (this volume) of the role of illusio in the construction of a global field of religion uses this strategy to great effect (and therefore employs the concept of illusio in a different sense than I do here). Another strategy, which I undertake here, takes a key contribution of Bourdieu's concept of a field (the legitimacy-claim of an 'interest in disinterest' as an organizing doxa of the modern imperial administrative fields) and complements it with other styles of field analysis focused on the structural conditions that can make those claims persuasive.[2]

One form of field and relational analysis which complements Bourdieu's is that of 'strategic action fields', because it contains an explicit treatment of how and where fields emerge. In their overview of the perspective, Fligstein and McAdam define strategic action fields as 'a constructed mesolevel social order in which actors ... are attuned to and interact with one another on the basis of shared ... understandings about the purposes of the field, relationships to others in the field ... and the rules governing legitimate action in the field' (2012: 24–25). The dynamics of these strategic action fields, moreover, depend on actors' 'social skill' or 'that complex mix of cognitive, affective, and linguistic facilities that render individuals more or less effective as skilled strategic actors supremely well adapted to the demands of collective action' (2012: 61) which marshals people's 'seemingly unique human capacity for collaborative symbolic activity and *need* for meaning and membership' (2012: 108; original emphasis). In other words, strategic action fields depend on two levels of organization: on the one hand, of a mid-level social space and its government by some shared logic and sense of purpose, and on the other hand, of people into groups by actors more-or-less skilled at doing so.

This emphasis on organization figures into the emergence of strategic action fields in important ways (Fligstein and McAdam, 2012). In the first place, strategic action fields come from 'emergent mobilization', in which

> collective actors fashion new lines of interaction with other actors based on altered understandings of the opportunities or threats to group interests they perceive. Typically the process is set in motion by some exogenous change that is perceived by at least two actors as posing a significant new threat to, or opportunity for, the realization of group interests. (Fligstein and McAdam 2012: 107)

In building up strategic action fields, Fligstein and McAdam emphasize how collective actors strategize with and against one another in both horizontal and vertical ways. On the one hand, people and groups in strategic action fields are locked in 'an inherently conflictual world where change is ubiquitous, incumbents worry daily about how to maintain their advantages, and challengers search for and seek to exploit any "cracks" they discern in the system' (Fligstein and McAdam, 2012: 97). Yet on the other hand, any given strategic action field is dependent for its ongoing stability on alliances with the larger strategic action fields of which it is a part (as would be a department within a corporation, for example) or the horizontal fields on which it depends for crucial resources

(2012: 3). Put differently, an entity like the early-modern British empire or the EIC itself can be viewed from one angle as a single unit, but also, as we shall see, as a set of interrelated and even competing collective actors whose mutual coordination and interest is far from a given. Thus appeals to and alliances with outsiders are a crucial way that strategic action fields are formed and maintain stability.

If Bourdieu's perspective on fields provides a useful frame for understanding the 'interest in disinterest' while Fligstein and McAdam emphasize the ongoing exchange of resources among strategic action fields which are embedded in one another, the final variety of relationalism used here articulates how and why those claims of disinterest might actually be successful in mobilizing resources. This third perspective, which is rooted in network analysis, finds systematic examination of the question of how new structural forms emerge in Padgett and Powell's *The Emergence of Organizations and Markets* (2012).

The work is organized around the concept of 'autocatalysis', a network characteristic wherein 'all nodes [in the network] are reconstructed through transformations among nodes in the set' (Padgett and Powell, 2012: loc 640). Abstracted from its origin in chemistry, the problem for Padgett and Powell is to explain how sets of relationships among people, firms, and so on can become durable over time, creating innovative social structures and even new kinds of roles and actors. In turn, the whole system of inter- and intra-network dynamism is driven by 'network folding' (2012: loc 594), one constitutive mechanism of which is 'the emergence of a new open elite of biographical flows, which broke down previous social boundaries' (2012: loc 790). This movement of people from one kind of network to another leads to a dynamic wherein 'people, practices, and relational protocols being recombined are attached to networks, with percolation consequences' (2012: locs 762–769). In other words, the durable organizations and institutionalized procedures that stabilize social life emerge because the churn of people moving among different networks puts certain actors in brokerage positions. These positions then allow people to transpose and connect procedures from one network or domain of social life into another.

Beyond their emphasis on the concrete biographical flows from one network 'domain' to another – that is, the movement from people from one concrete set of relations to another (see 2012: locs 700–745) – Padgett and Powell's emphasis on multivocality and robust action is especially useful to understand the EIC's transformation. Like Fligstein and McAdam's concept of social skill, multi-vocal 'robust action' appears as something akin to agency for Padgett and Powell. Robust action is 'the tactical capacity ... to sustain multiple attributions of identity through uttering sphinx-like statements that plausibly can be interpreted in multiple ways' (2012: loc 978) and is a strategy best pursued by people at the intersection of otherwise separated networks, such that they can utter ambiguous enough statements (or act unpredictably enough) to persuade their connected parties that support is plausible, if not forthcoming. This strategy is evident in the behaviour of leaders like the 'quiescent sphinxes' (Obert and Padgett, 2012: loc 8020) Cosimo de' Medici and Deng Xiaophong (see Padgett,

 The Sociological Review Monographs, 64:2, pp. 61–78 (2016), DOI: 10.1111/2059-7932.12002

2012; Padgett and Ansell, 1993), as well as Otto von Bismarck's notorious blustering style (Obert and Padgett, 2012: loc 8034).

To sum up Padgett and Powell's relational perspective for our purposes, a key dynamic of relational social life is the biographical movement of people among a variety of network domains and the alternative procedures and ideas they carry with them. Moreover, their capacity to effectively behave ambiguously – like 'quiescent sphinxes' – and hence to maintain a form of agency and power by strategically marshalling that very ambiguity, is driven by their ability to appear to be serving the interests of sometimes very different networks and political factions.

Standing back, it is hopefully evident that this synthesis is geared towards informing the EIC's transition from early-modern to modern imperial administration and as such is meant to be limited. Each relational and field-analytic approach still rests on very different epistemological foundations, and each is in turn embedded in very different sociological traditions of analysis. Yet there is profit in their combination. Bourdieu emphasizes the power of universal claims to operate in the 'interest of disinterest', showing how such claims (insofar as they are recognized by others) lead to the autonomization and foundation of new social fields. In turn, Fligstein and McAdam suggest how such claims to disinterest might be used to durably mobilize resources among a shifting terrain of interlocked (and sometimes overlapping) strategic action fields by people struggling to maintain their incumbency or challenging those incumbents. Finally, Padgett and Powell suggest that biographical flows along networks (and through fields) and the dynamics of multivocal action at the intersection of such structures might reveal key patterns of agency during periods of field-foundation.

The synthesis of these three approaches also specifically helps analyse modern imperial field formation. To ask how and why early-modern, patrimonial forms of imperial administration transformed into a modern rule of colonial difference means investigating the structural conditions that transformed the relationship among different parts of both the imperial and metropolitan strategic action fields. Moreover, it also requires understanding how this first transformation was shaped by and shaped the context of struggles among particular administrators (whether they would later be categorized as 'indigenous' or 'imperial') as they sought to mobilize resources to their side. Finally, it is to ask how these two changing contexts in turn affected how administrators presented themselves and one another during these struggles – that is, how they described their motivations and their social worlds.

The next section explores these themes through an analysis of the EIC's transformation in the late eighteenth century.

The case: Bolts and Verelst

This section expounds a key episode in the history of the EIC's transformation from a largely merchant organization to the major territorial power in South Asia using the analytic frame developed above. Founded in 1600 and despite its abortive military adventures at the end of the seventeenth century (see Stern,

2011), the EIC's territorial expansion only became sustained after it began military competition with French and Dutch merchant companies. The competition intensified amid the decaying central authority of the Mughal Empire, and as succession disputes among its increasingly independent satraps promised a mixture of political and commercial opportunity (Marshall, 1987). The Mughal Empire's decline is usually dated to the death of Aurangzeb in 1707, and military competition between the French and English began in South India in the 1740s (Dodwell, 1920), but a key moment of the emergence of Company territorial power was surely the Battle of Buxar in 1764, when Company forces defeated an indigenous coalition including the Mughal emperor. Shortly thereafter, the EIC signed the treaty of Allahahbad, which made it a legal vassal of the Mughal emperor and granted it revenue authority over the provinces of Bengal, Bihar and Orissa.[3]

Considered as a strategic action field during this period, the Company's behaviour in both Britain and India was a response to the very different demands being placed on it in both places. In London, the Company's stock, fiscal resources, and patronage appointments had long been an integral part of British elite politics (Bowen, 2006; Sutherland, 1952), and the EIC's Court of Directors enjoyed a usually cosy relationship with the Whig ministries, especially under its powerful mid-eighteenth century Chairman, Laurence Sulivan (McGilvary, 2006). Meanwhile, the Company's servants in India, who were increasingly made up of second and third sons of well-to-do merchant and gentry families in Britain in the second half of the eighteenth century (Cohn, 1987; Ghosh, 1970), depended on indigenous Indian rulers for permission and security to conduct the trade in goods that generated the Company's profit.

As the Company militarized and particularly as it fought proxy wars against the French during the Seven Years War (1756–1763), the relationship among the EIC's constitutive strategic action fields and to those it depended on in India and Britain transformed. The Company's military expenditures and uncertain profits and stock prices upended domestic fiscal markets (since it was the most important joint-stock firm in Britain at the time) as well as threatening the solvency of the Treasury (since it became both a creditor and debtor to the state). And in India, new military power meant increasing involvement in local affairs, as well as the frequently indulged temptation (both for the Company as a whole and for servants personally profiting through local trade) to garner tax exemptions, direct military subsidies, and other commercial concessions as part of treaties. This process certainly enriched Company servants (Marshall, 1976) and promised windfall, if risky, profits to the company as a whole (Bowen, 1991). Accordingly, Company shareholder 'general courts' and elections to the Court of Directors became increasingly tumultuous 'theatre[s] of disputes' (Leonard, 2014) among anxious government ministers intervening directly in Company affairs, old-guard Directors seeking to protect the long-term viability of the EIC, returning Company 'nabobs' (Lawson and Phillips, 1984; Nechtman, 2010) anxious to protect their personal and potentially ill-gotten fortunes, and stock speculators attempting to inflate the Company's share price and dividends at the cost of its long-term health.

This chaotic state of affairs among the Company's internal strategic action fields and those it depended on in Britain and India opened new fissures for officials struggling with one another within the EIC's organizational framework. Since territorial expansion had been coupled with difficult-to-control servants partly remunerated by the profits they could make as private traders (Furber, 1948; Hejeebu, 2005; Marshall, 1976), disputes among officials were not rare throughout the eighteenth century, and became bitter and more intense in the decades after Allahabad. What changed decisively, however, was the *audience* for these disputes. The Company's fiscal troubles and internal political chaos created an audience of previously unfamiliar readers and listeners in Britain, who were eager – beyond the often-salacious details of the disputes and potential corruption of 'asiatic despotism' – for information that could affect the Company's political and commercial fortunes. As the 1760s and 1770s wore on (that is, particularly prior to the decades-long settlement entailed by Pitt's India Act of 1784, which established ministerial oversight of many Company affairs through the Board of Control), then, there was a new kind of general political audience to struggles taking place within the Company.[4]

This changing context of disputes among Company officials altered the possibility of what could (successfully) be claimed as those disputes migrated back to Britain. For much of its history and the eighteenth century, moral regulation among Company servants was based on a model of politeness (Klein, 1994) which defined propriety as an embedded judgment of 'impartial spectators' who were 'independent' of influence yet were ambiguously also members of concrete networks of peers (Smith, 2002).[5] As struggles among administrators increasingly played out in front of audiences unfamiliar with such contextual detail, the structural position of complaining officials, between the unfamiliar world of Indian administration and metropolitan politics, offered the chance to exercise a form of robust action by translating and abstracting the administrative detail that formed the background of official struggle. However, these struggles had a more complicated structure than straightforward robust action: because they almost always involved the escalation of a multi-party dispute from colony to metropole, at least two officials disputing each other's acts of abstraction and translation of Indian affairs actually stood in the brokerage position. Because they could challenge each other's accounts (and could usually both lay claim to equal expertise and embeddedness within Company administration in India), their recourse was not to 'multivocal' ambiguity, but instead to a kind of moral earnestness that laid claim to their own 'interest in distinterest' as a basis for their appeals to outsiders in their disputes.[6]

An illustration: William Bolts, Harry Verelst, and the EIC, 1772–1775

An extended example can help clarify this process. In 1768, amid the larger conflict over the future of the Company, in India, the Governor of the Bengal 'presidency' (ie province), Harry Verelst, deported a nettlesome former official, William Bolts.[7] Verelst's reason was that Bolts misrepresented his position as

The Sociological Review Monographs, 64:2, pp. 61–78 (2016), DOI: 10.1111/2059-7932.12002

a Company official to gain trading privileges from the (now relatively subordinated) Nawab of Bengal. Upon returning to England, Bolts appealed first to the Court of Directors for reprieve, but failing there, sued (and was counter-sued by) Verelst in the Court of Chancery (Bowen, 2004; Kuiters, 2002). When these suits failed, in turn, Bolts took up the pen, and, listing himself as 'Merchant and Alderman, or Judge of the Hon. The Mayor's Court of Calcutta', published *Considerations on East India Company Affairs* (in 1772), which Verelst felt the need to answer 'The Misrepresentations of Mr. Bolts, and other writers' in his *A View of Rise, Progress, and Present State of the English Government in Bengal (also 1772)*. This published debate between Bolts and Verelst has been identified as the first serious discussion of the details of Indian administration in the eighteenth-century public sphere (Bowen, 2006).

A full analysis of these documents is outside the scope of this article, so this illustration will concentrate on two features: how each text expresses an interest in disinterest, claiming credibility through a holistic moral narrative; and how both texts root their justifications in morally disembedded spaces (namely 'the state' and 'the economy'), yet take radically different stances towards the limits of those spaces.

Consider, to start, how Bolts described his own position, at once portraying himself as 'disinterested' victim of 'oppression' at Verelst's hands in Bengal:

> The Writer of these sheets, who was many years in the service of the Company in Bengal, as is an Alderman or Judge of the Mayor's Court of Calcutta, agreeably to the charter, writes not with any view of advantage to himself. He has felt the iron rod of oppression from the Company and their servants, in many instances equally grievous with any that are herein laid before the public; but having appealed for justice to the laws of this country, (though it must be some years before he can obtain it) he forbears at present to say more of himself or his cause than, that he was marked out for vengeance in Bengal, for his professional abilities, even small as they were, and his success in such mercantile undertakings as rather entitled him to the blessings of the natives and approbation of his country, as they usefully obstructive to mischievous monopolists, and of service to the Company, though offensive to their principal servants. (Bolts 1772: x–xi)[8]

In this passage, Bolts marries a disclaimer of his own interest to a moral account by which his own 'success in such mercantile undertakings' as had gotten him ejected by Verelst to his ability to simultaneously 'usefully [obstruct]' monopoly and serve the Company though not 'their principal servants'. As his jab against monopoly suggests it might, the remainder of *Considerations* is occupied by a radical call for the installation of a universalizing free-trade relationship between India and Britain to be overseen by the direct extension of British parliamentary jurisdiction to India and the extension of quasi-citizenship rights to Indians themselves. As Bolts put it:

> It is the wisdom and power of the Legislature alone that can prevent the total improverishment or less of the Bengal provinces, either of which misfortunes might now prove fatal in its consequences to this kingdom. This can only be effected by laws for securing

 The Sociological Review Monographs, 64:2, pp. 61–78 (2016), DOI: 10.1111/2059-7932.12002

> the impartial administration of justice throughout those dominions; for preventing the commission of those oppressions and irregularities which have of late years prevailed, to the disgrace of a British government; for more easily and effectually punishing in India the authors of such enormities when committed, and for improving and rendering permanent those resources which the nation has a right to expect from the conquered countries. Such laws would equally tend to promote the laudable and desirable object of regaining and securing an interest in the hearts of the subjected natives, who wish only to receive their protection and happiness from a British Sovereign; in which state of things this nation might long possess the Bengal provinces, even against the combined efforts of Indian enemies and European rivals. (Bolts, 1772: x)

From Verelst's perspective, however, it was precisely the lack of power given to the Company state in India that was responsible for the immiseration of the Indian people (at the hands of men like Bolts). Even as he, too, coupled his moral account to a claimed interest in disinterest (or as he put it, without a 'rapacious spirit'), Verelst argued that

> ... the evils complained of in Bengal, have arisen ... [more] from the inability of the governor and council to restrain the daring and pernicious projects of private interest in others, than from a rapacious spirit in themselves. Had the higher servants of the company, as [Bolts] would wish us to believe, been alone the oppressors of Bengal, the evil could not have extended far. But when the rapacity of all who assume the English name, is let loose upon a harmless and inoffensive race of men ... every attempt of the governor and council to restrain these lawless traders, is represented as a violation of property, and [an] infringement of those laws by which only Europeans can be governed; and ... this spirit, supported by interested men, proceeds so far, that the governor, council, and commander in chief, are presented to the grand jury as conspirators against the life and fortune of an individual... (Verelst, 1772: 42)

Of course, Verelst recognized that the kind of power he asked for in the above passage, which would ratify the ability of Governors to unilaterally deport Europeans living in India and overrule their own councils, ran far beyond the imagined British citizenship protections elsewhere (as would so violently be demonstrated in the coming years in the American colonies). To justify this, however, not only did Verelst carefully attach his desire for ratified power to a disinterested moral-self presentation as a dutiful Company servant, he also carefully delimited the reach of this Company state. Bolts' argument to extend direct Parliamentary control to India would never work, Verelst argued, because after all they were radically different places, where different 'manners and habits of a people' were to be found:

> If in Great Britain, where the form of our government has grown up to maturity in the course of several ages; where the power of each magistrate has undergone frequent discussions from the united wisdom of successive generations; where all authority is committed to the hands of men formed by education for their several stations, and where the effects of its exertion may be traced in our history; if, in a country like this, we are perpetually alarmed with supposed invasions of our rights, and frightful pictures of encreasing despotism are daily held forth to terrify the people, what a portrait might the dullest imagination exhibit of Bengal? By minds open to such impressions, little

> regard will be had to the different manners and habits of a people; to the enterprising Mahomedan or Armenian opposed to the gentle native of India; to the condition of conquerors living amidst a timid and submissive race, like soldiers unrestrained by discipline; of men clamorously demanding the protections of laws ill understood and worse applied, where interest and passion unite to confound all order, and where lordly traders, impatient of controul, hope to gratify their own sordid avarice in the general wreck. (Verelst, 1772: 130)

To summarize this illustration: as intra-administrative squabbling spilled over the boundaries of the Company's organization and into the larger British public sphere, we can see strong moral claims and narratives about behaviour taking place in India. These claims not only purported to describe the rightness or wrongness of action taking place within the Company (but in a setting so distant that the claims could not be verified by anyone other than other 'interested' actors), they also appealed for intervention (being published in books meant for the general reading public in Britain) into the EIC's affairs in India. And yet to the extent that these accounts were recognized as effective and shaped subsequent such appeals, they also prospectively delimited the field of Company administration in India and transformed its nature. What had once been comprehensible as the pursuit of both 'fortune and integrity' (Nightingale, 1985) for oneself and the Company became a conflict over what Company rule in Bengal was and should represent. For Verelst, it was a carefully delimited space in which action was to be rooted in an empowered state, and which depended on a careful argument about the 'difference' of Indian people from the British. For Bolts, meanwhile, economic exchange and its stabilizing influence was the moral key to his argument (and account of himself) and that form of exchange meant that there was no meaningful, essential difference between British people and Indians. In other words, through the debate between these two officials of the Company, the terms were set for the recognizably modern character of imperial administration.

Conclusion

This struggle between Bolts and Verelst in the 1770s represents only a single case drawn from one part of what would become one modern empire, but it still suggests broader contributions to how we think about the emergence of global fields. The core of Bolts and Verelst's dispute was bitterly 'interested', in the sense that the careers and reputations of both men hinged on how their claims about the nature of EIC policy in India were received by the British public. But their argument was also much more than that: both men turned their positions into expressions of an 'interest in disinterest' and used those expressions to develop much more general moral accounts of how nascent Company rule in India should be organized, and particularly what the social and geographical limits of that organization ought to be. In other words, their argument seems to represent a key pivot from the logic of early-modern to modern forms of imperial administration.

To see how Bolts and Verelest could argue in the style they did, I have also suggested a synthesis of Bourdieu's account of the emergence of fields with an organizational and resource-mobilization perspective, provided by Fligstein and McAdam, and a network-analytic perspective developed by Padgett and Powell. Roughly put, in this synthesis Bourdieu provides the substantive moral anchor for the nascent imperial administrative field with his notion of an 'interest in disinterest' as a key claim of imperial officials. Fligtstein and McAdam, meanwhile, supply a useful vocabulary to understand the densely interwoven organizational space that Bolts and Verelst occupied, and how 'exogenous shocks' in distant parts of the world could be communicated into local political struggles among Company officials as events of deadly seriousness. Padgett and Powell, finally, help clarify how actors like Bolts and Verelst circulated through both metropolitan and colonial spaces, and how, in turn, their legitimacy and credibility depended on their ability to credibly portray themselves to a metropolitan audience as reliable narrators of events in India and their own motivations.

This analysis can be carried forward in three main ways. First, since it is built on an illustrative case, albeit one that seems historically important, a comparative analysis of cases in which colonial affairs were subjected to public metropolitan scrutiny could be used to establish the generality of the phenomenon of moral accounting I have described. Second, while this analysis has suggested how the 'interest in disinterest' became a stake in colonial administrative politics – because it supplied a ready means of appealing to observers who did not possess knowledge of the detail of administration – it did not trace out the consequence of this form of politics for the subsequent history of the colonial administrative field. Further work might, for example, examine how this emergent form of recognition affected the shape of indigenous politics, or perhaps distorted or foreclosed lines of appeal that had previously been open during administrative struggles. Finally, I have said relatively little about how and why the specific *content* of the claims made by Verelst and Bolts were seen as persuasive (or not) by metropolitan audiences. After all, an 'interest in disinterest' can be put in the service of both the modern rule of colonial difference and abstract commercial exchange. Further work on this front might therefore employ Bourdieu's concept of homology between field positions, for example, to gauge whether specific kinds of moral anchors were more or less likely to be convincing when made by officials from geographically and socially distant imperial fields.

Acknowledgements

This article has benefited greatly from constructive comments by a variety of people, including: Larissa Buchholtz, Siri Colom, Julian Go, Monika Krause, Laura Mangels, Damon Mayrl, Sarah Quinn, David Swartz, Jonathan Wyrtzen, and two anonymous reviewers. I presented an earlier version of this work and received valuable feedback at a conference on 'Global Fields' organized by Julian Go and Monika Krause in 2014 at Boston University. Errors remain my own.

Notes

1 The clearest introduction to all of these terms is in Bourdieu and Wacquant (1992), especially their discussion of fields (pp. 94–115).
2 Careful readers of Bourdieu may note that he also warned against attempts to trace field emergence back to the emergence of particular socio-historical figures, since it is possible to find, in the case of the literary field in France, for example, 'the personage of the writer', albeit one still '[dependent] on the state for the recognition and official status that it accords them' well before 'the system of characteristics constitutive of an autonomous field is found assembled together' (Bourdieu, 1996: 367, n. 1). Yet my aim here is less to trace the emergence of a habitus or illusio characteristic of an imperial interest in disinterest, and more to understand how claims to such disinterest could become stakes in the EIC's intra-administrative conflict in the second half of the eighteenth century.
3 Bowen (1991, 2006) and Marshall (1987, 2005) provide more detail on this transition.
4 For a more detailed discussion of the points in the last two paragraphs, see Wilson (2015).
5 For more detail on this point, see Wilson (2012: esp. Chs 1 and 2).
6 This line of argument is in dialog with McLean (2007) and follows Greenblatt (1980).
7 Bolts has been the subject of two biographies (Hallward, 1920; Kuiters, 2002) and an entry in the *Dictionary of National Biography* (Bowen, 2004) and other scholarly interest, while interest in Verlest has been comparative scanty (Kuiters, 2004).
8 In each of the quotes from Bolts and Verelst below, I have preserved the sometimes eccentric spelling and capitalization conventions of eighteenth-century texts.

References

Abbott, A., (1995), 'Things of boundaries', *Social Research*, 62: 857–882.

Acemoglu, D., Johnson, S. and Robinson, J. A., (2001), 'The colonial origins of comparative development: an empirical investigation', *The American Economic Review*, 91 (5): 1369–1401.

Adams, J., (2007), *The Familial State*, Ithaca, NY: Cornell University Press.

Banerjee, A. and Iyer, L., (2005), 'History, institutions, and economic performance: the legacy of colonial land tenure systems in India', *The American Economic Review*, 95 (4): 1190–1213.

Barkey, K., (1994), *Bandits and Bureaucrats: The Ottoman Route to State Centralization*, Ithaca, NY: Cornell University Press.

Barkey, K., (2008), *Empire of Difference*, Cambridge: Cambridge University Press.

Bayly, C. A., (1989), *Imperial Meridian: The British Empire and the World*, 1780–1830, London: Longman.

Black, J., (1990), *Robert Walpole and the Nature of Politics in Early Eighteenth-Century Britain*, Basingstoke: Macmillan Education.

Bolts, W., (1772), *Considerations on India Affairs*, London: Printed for J. Almon.

Bourdieu, P., (1996), *The Rules of Art: Genesis and Structure of the Literary Field*, Cambridge: Polity Press.

Bourdieu, P., (1998), 'Is a disinterested act possible?', in *Practical Reason*, 75–91. Stanford, CA: Stanford University Press.

Bourdieu, P. and Wacquant, L. J. D., (1992), *An Invitation to Reflexive Sociology*, Chicago: University of Chicago Press.

Bowen, H. V., (1991), *Revenue and Reform: The Indian Problem in British Politics*, 1757–1773, Cambridge: Cambridge University Press.

Bowen, H. V., (2004), 'Bolts, William (1739–1808)', *Oxford Dictionary of National Biography*, online edn, Oxford: Oxford University Press.

Bowen, H. V., (2006), *The Business of Empire: The East India Company and Imperial Britain*, 1756–1833, Cambridge: Cambridge University Press.

Brewer, J., (1990), *The Sinews of Power*, Cambridge, MA: Harvard University Press.

 The Sociological Review Monographs, 64:2, pp. 61–78 (2016), DOI: 10.1111/2059-7932.12002

Calhoun, C. J., Cooper, F. and Moore, K. W., (2006), *Lessons of Empire: Imperial Histories and American Power*, New York: New Press.
Chatterjee, P., (1993), *The Nation and its Fragments*, Princeton, NJ: Princeton University Press.
Chatterjee, P., (2012), *The Black Hole of Empire: History of a Global Practice of Power*, Princeton, NJ: Princeton University Press.
Cohn, B. S., (1987), 'The recruitment and training of British Civil servants in India, 1600–1860', in *An Anthropologist among the Historians and Other Essays*, 500–553. New York: Oxford University Press.
Dodwell, H., (1920), *Dupleix and Clive: The Beginning of Empire*, London: Methuen.
Emirbayer, M., (1997), 'Manifesto for a relational sociology', *American Journal of Sociology*, 103 (2): 281–317.
Erikson, E., (2014), *Between Monopoly and Free Trade: The English East India Company*, 1600–1757, Princeton, NJ: Princeton University Press.
Fligstein, N. and McAdam, D., (2012), *A Theory of Fields*, Oxford: Oxford University Press.
Fuchs, S., (2005), *Against Essentialism: A Theory of Culture and Society*, London: Harvard University Press.
Furber, H., (1948), *John Company at Work: A Study of European Expansion in India in the Late Eighteenth Century*, Cambridge, MA: Harvard University Press.
Ghosh, S. C., (1970), *The Social Condition of the British Community in Bengal: 1757–1800*, Leiden: Brill.
Go, J., (2008a), *American Empire and the Politics of Meaning*, Durham, NC: Duke University Press.
Go, J., (2008b), 'Global fields and imperial forms: field theory and the British and American empires', *Sociological Theory*, 26 (3), 201–229.
Go, J., (2011), *Patterns of Empire: The British and American Empires, 1688 to the Present*, New York: Cambridge University Press.
Goswami, M., (2004), *Producing India*, Chicago: University of Chicago Press.
Greenblatt, S., (1980), *Renaissance Self-Fashioning: From Moore to Shakespeare*, Chicago: University of Chicago Press.
Greene, J. P., (2013), *Evaluating Empire and Confronting Colonialism in Eighteenth-Century Britain*, New York: Cambridge University Press.
Hallward, N. L., (1920), *William Bolts: A Dutch Adventurer under John Company*, Cambridge: Cambridge University Press.
Harling, P., (1996), *The Waning of 'Old Corruption'*, Oxford: Oxford University Press.
Harlow, V. T., (1952), *The Founding of the Second British Empire* 1763–1793, London: Longmans, Green and Company.
Hejeebu, S., (2005), 'Contract enforcement in the English East India Company', *The Journal of Economic History*, 65 (2): 496–523.
Klein, L. E., (1994), *Shaftesbury and the Culture of Politeness*, Cambridge: Cambridge University Press.
Kuiters, W. G. J., (2002), *The British in Bengal*, 1756–1773, Paris: Indes savantes.
Kuiters, W. G. J., (2004), 'Verelst, Harry (1734–1785)', *Oxford Dictionary of National Biography*, online edn, Oxford: Oxford University Press.
Kumar, K., (2010), 'Nation-states as empires, empires as nation-states: two principles, one practice?', *Theory and Society*, 39 (2): 119–143.
Lawson, P. and Phillips, J., (1984), '"Our execrable banditti": perceptions of nabobs in mid-eighteenth century Britain', *Albion: A Quarterly Journal Concerned with British Studies*, 16(3): 225–241.
Leonard, S., (2014), '"A theatre of disputes": the East India Company election of 1764 as the founding of British India', *Journal of Imperial and Commonwealth History*, 42(4): 593–624.
Mann, M., (2005), *Incoherent Empire*, London: Verso.
Marshall, P. J., (1987), *Bengal: The British Bridgehead*, Cambridge: Cambridge University Press.
Marshall, P. J., (1976), *East Indian Fortunes*, Oxford: Clarendon Press.
Marshall, P. J., (2005), *The Making and Unmaking of Empires*, Oxford: Oxford University Press.

McGilvary, G. K., (2006), *Guardian of the East India Company: The Life of Laurence Sulivan*, London: I.B. Tauris.
McLean, P. D., (2007), *The Art of the Network: Strategic Interaction and Patronage in Renaissance Florence*, Durham, NC: Duke University Press.
Nechtman, T., (2010), *Nabobs: Empire and Identity in Eighteenth-century Britain*, New York: Cambridge University Press.
Nightingale, P., (1985), *Fortune and Integrity*, Oxford: Oxford University Press.
Norton, M., (2014), 'Classification and coercion: the destruction of piracy in the English maritime system', *American Journal of Sociology*, 119(6): 1537–1575.
Obert, J. and Padgett, J. F., (2012), 'Conflict displacement and dual inclusion in the construction of Germany', in *The Emergence of Organizations and Markets*, Princeton, NJ: Princeton University Press.
Padgett, J. F., (2012), 'The politics of communist economic reform: Soviet Union and China', in *The Emergence of Organizations and Markets*, Princeton, NJ: Princeton University Press.
Padgett, J. F. and Ansell, C. K., (1993), 'Robust action and the rise of the Medici, 1400–1434', *American Journal of Sociology*, 98: 1259–1319.
Padgett, J. F. and Powell, W. W., (2012), *The Emergence of Organizations and Markets*, Princeton, NJ: Princeton University Press.
Smith, A., (2002), *The Theory of Moral Sentiments*, Cambridge: Cambridge University Press.
Steinmetz, G., (2007), *The Devil's Handwriting*, Chicago: University of Chicago Press.
Steinmetz, G., (2008), 'The colonial state as social field: ethnographic capital and native policy in the German overseas empire before 1914', *American Sociological Review*, 73: 589–612.
Steinmetz, G., (2013), *Sociology and Empire: The Imperial Entanglements of a Discipline*, Durham, NC: Duke University Press.
Steinmetz, G., (2014), 'The sociology of empires, colonies, and postcolonialism', *Annual Review of Sociology*, 40 (1): 77–103.
Stern, P. J., (2011), *The Company-State: Corporate Sovereignty and the Early Modern Foundations of the British Empire in India*, Oxford: Oxford University Press.
Sutherland, L. S., (1952), *The East India Company in Eighteenth-Century Politics*, London: Hyperion Press.
Verelst, H., (1772), *A View of the Rise, Progress, and Present State of the English Government in Bengal: Including a Reply to the Misrepresentations of Mr. Bolts, and other Writers*, London: J. Nourse.
Wang, L., (2015), 'From masterly brokers to compliant protégées: the frontier governance system and the rise of ethnic confrontation in China-Inner Mongolia, 1900–1930', *American Journal of Sociology*, 120 (6): 1641–1689.
Wilson, N. H., (2012), *Economies, Moralities, and State Formations in British Colonial India*, Berkeley, CA: University of California.
Wilson, N. H., (2015), "'A state in disguise of a merchant'? The English East India Company as a strategic action field, ca. 1763–1834", *Political Power and Social Theory*, 29: 257–285.
Wyrtzen, J., (2011), 'Colonial state-building and the negotiation of Arab and Berber identity in protectorate Morocco', *International Journal of Middle East Studies* 43 (Special Issue 2): 227–249.
Wyrtzen, J., (2015), *Making Morocco: Colonial Intervention and the Politics of Identity*, Ithaca, NY: Cornell University Press.

Please quote the article DOI when citing SR content, including monographs. Article DOIs and "How to Cite" information can be found alongside the online version of each article within Wiley Online Library. All articles published within the SR (including monograph content) are included within the ISI Journal Citation Reports® Social Science Citation Index.

For good and country: nationalism and the diffusion of humanitarianism in the late nineteenth century

Shai M. Dromi

Abstract: Despite the growing interest in transnational fields and their influence on national-level dynamics, existing literature has not yet addressed the processes involved in creating such fields in the first place. This article provides insight into the complexities involved in national–transnational interactions amidst national and transnational field formation. It examines the nascent transnational humanitarian field of the late nineteenth century through the work of the emerging Red Cross Movement in the 1860s–1890s, drawing primarily on the archive of the International Committee of the Red Cross. The findings show that National Red Cross (NRC) societies employed a discourse drawn from a transnational cultural arena in order to gain central positioning in their national fields and to convince other parties of their necessity. Conversely, NRCs used nationalism as a form of symbolic capital in establishing themselves in their national fields, seemingly at odds with their cosmopolitan aspirations. Thus, by contrast to the ideal-typical representation of global humanitarianism as non-national, these findings suggest that nationalism and impartial humanitarianism are historically intertwined. More broadly, the article argues that national-level field dynamics as well as nationalism play important roles in the creation of transnational fields, even when field actors present themselves as acting for universal causes.

Keywords: humanitarianism, transnational advocacy, Red Cross, field theory, nationalism

Introduction

Scholars often cite humanitarian international non-governmental organizations (INGOs) as central actors in the effort to counteract the destructive effects of rampant nationalism (Kurasawa, 2012; Brysk, 2013; Balibar, 2013; Jean, 1993). Indeed, since organizations such as Oxfam and Doctors Without Borders have historically provided relief to victims of conflict and disaster regardless of ethnicity, nationality and religion, they have associated themselves with a cosmopolitan ethic that transcends state sovereignty (Davey, 2011). These

The Sociological Review Monographs, 64:2, pp. 79–97 (2016), DOI: 10.1111/2059-7932.12003

Published by John Wiley & Sons Ltd, 9600 Garsington Road, Oxford OX4 2DQ, UK and 350 Main Street, Malden, MA 02148, USA

characteristics have led scholars to identify the world of humanitarian INGOs as a *transnational field*, in which actors supersede their national positioning and work in relation to other global actors (Krause, 2014). And yet, other studies of humanitarian work have shown that activists regularly link the form of universal aid they provide with their national values and character, thereby suggesting that national-level dynamics may impact the subtleties and divisions of the transnational humanitarian field (Stroup, 2012; Redfield, 2013; Siméant, 2005).

However, there is little research about the interaction of national-level dynamics with transnational social processes in the emergence of transnational fields. While there is growing scholarship on transnational fields as a phenomenon (Dezalay and Garth, 2010; Mudge and Vauchez, 2012), there is little concrete research of the relations between transnational fields-in-formation and corresponding national fields. Instead, transnational field research has often analyzed such fields separately from nation-level specificities (Hagan and Levi, 2005; Dixon and Tenove, 2013). Furthermore, recent scalar expansions of field analysis, including contributions in this volume, have looked at the formation of supranational fields as a process of disengagement from national confines (Buchholz, this volume) or as a process of imperial expansion (Steinmetz, this volume; Wilson, this volume), but have not considered the role of nations and nationalism in transnational field formation processes. The current article presents initial insights into these issues by examining the nascent transnational humanitarian field of the late nineteenth century. It focuses on the international spread of the Red Cross movement and on its interweaving of national and global social spaces.

The article turns to the late nineteenth century because that period was pivotal for the emergence of a relatively autonomous field of humanitarian activism, and saw the emergence of the stakes and logics that ultimately came to underpin the transnational humanitarian field. The International Committee of the Red Cross (ICRC, established 1863) was central to this process as it advocated for the creation of a network of impartial aid societies, each of which would be based in each sovereign nation and would care for the battlefield wounded regardless of nationality.[1] By the turn of the century the movement expanded into most European states, as well as numerous American and Asian ones, by establishing a National Red Cross Society (NRC) in each. While the late nineteenth century humanitarian community was irreducible to the Red Cross alone, this movement was crucial in laying down the infrastructure for what would become a transnational humanitarian field: it provided a level of international cooperation that allowed actors in different locations to become cognizant of each other as participating in the same global endeavour (Moorehead, 1999); it laid down the legal and political groundwork to facilitate this type of relief work (Veuthey, 1983); and it propagated a new *ethos* sanctifying impartial and universal humanitarian care for the wounded regardless of nationality, providing humanitarian actors with markers of honour and worth over which to compete (Hutchinson, 1996). By serving as a model for other activist groups, the Red

Cross was key in disseminating an organizational template for other relief societies (Forsythe, 2005).

The article shows that the nascent transnational humanitarian field of the nineteenth century emerged through processes embedded in national-level dynamics, inextricably linked with currents of nationalism. The ICRC endorsed and enhanced pre-existing national sentiments in eliciting support for the globally relevant mission of helping all those in need. Such affirmation of nationalism, as well as the considerable autonomy afforded to the national Red Cross societies by the ICRC, allowed for the creation of nationally bounded fields devoted to long-distance humanitarianism in multiple states. In those national-level fields, local Red Cross actors drew both on symbolic resources provided by the ICRC and on local notions of nationalism in establishing themselves and promoting their work. On the one hand, they employed the internationally shared cultural resources and standards of conduct espoused by the ICRC in order to convince others in their polity of their superior adherence to universal values. On the other hand, local Red Cross activists developed ideas and beliefs about the relationship between humanitarianism and their own national identity, embedding nationalist value and imagery in the logics of their evolving humanitarian work. This hybridity allowed local actors to represent and conceive of providing aid to foreign nationals as an expression of their own patriotic spirit, and to generate a sense of pride and worth from their subscription to a global project. Thus, while the article does not deny that the nationalistic underpinnings of nineteenth-century humanitarianism occasionally inhibited cross-national humanitarian action,[2] it demonstrates that nationalism has also had a generative effect on humane conduct. The research is based on documents from the archive of the International Committee of the Red Cross (ICRC) and the Library of Geneva, as well as self-reports sent to the ICRC by national Red Cross societies and related actors in the years 1860–1900.

Theoretically, the article shows that the genesis and growth of transnational fields involves processes of translation and adaption into local contexts, which are performed by national-level actors and are embedded in national-level social dynamics. The article draws on Bourdieu's work on the international circulation of ideas to unpack the roles such processes play in the emergence of transnational fields. After outlining the theoretical approach, the article will turn to the empirical case. It will first show that, despite being presented as a transnational project by its founders, the Red Cross was deeply tied to *intra*-national processes and actors. In this, the Red Cross helped consolidate pre-existing local humanitarian communities into national humanitarian fields, and at the same time oriented those fields toward transnational stakes. The article will then show that national-level actors presented humanitarianism in their countries as aligning with their national values and character, and that this was a central aspect of the emergence and maintenance of the transnational humanitarian field. The discussion will highlight the implications for the study of transnational fields.

Transnational fields: between global and national dynamics

The notion of a 'transnational' field makes several modifications to the traditional, state-bounded concept of a social field.[3] At its most general, a field is a 'domain of relative autonomy marked off from others by its distinctive hierarchy, values, struggles, styles of improvising action, and forms of capital' (Calhoun, 2013: 37).[4] It is populated by actors who believe they are engaged in the same type of social action and therefore work in relation to each other. Those actors collectively identify a limited set of hierarchical positions and largely agree on who occupies which one. In this, they implicitly agree on a certain set of logics that dictate the norms by which action within the field ought to be conducted, and they share a belief in specific stakes that orient their work.[5] Field analysis has tended to remain confined to nationally bounded fields (Bourdieu, 1993, 1996a, 1996b), as the theory assumes elite actors in different fields within a particular state struggle for influence over its institutions and resources.

What, then, defines a 'transnational' humanitarian field? Krause's recent work (2014) demonstrates that such a field is very much in existence today and has several defining characteristics. Firstly, it involves humanitarian organizations (or, in some cases, individual actors) competing for funding, recognition, and influence on global scales, in relation to other global actors. The ICRC, Doctors without Borders, Oxfam, World Vision International, and other such associations ultimately compete over a limited pool of resources, as well as over dominance in defining what 'true' humanitarianism ought to be.[6] Secondly, it features a relatively consensual understanding of hierarchy and positioning between global humanitarian actors. While humanitarian INGOs are often critical of one another, few of them would disagree that the ICRC possesses unique prestige and influence over international and intergovernmental organizations, and that numerous 'camps' of relief organizations exist and work in relation to each other (Best, 1980; Fassin, 2011). Thirdly, their mutual critique notwithstanding, humanitarian organizations implicitly agree about a set of norms that bind their interaction regardless of their national origin (eg how funding can be secured; what types of justifications can be provided; etc.). Fourth, humanitarian INGOs subscribe to an overarching ethos, according to which social suffering must be alleviated impartially and universally, regardless of national boundaries (even though the practical interpretations of this injunction vary dramatically between organizations; see Plattner, 1996). Indeed, humanitarian INGOs have historically struggled over who best emulates this ethos (eg Fassin, 2011; Cullity, 2010).

Existing treatments of transnational field formation have tended to view national-level dynamics and culture as the context from which a transnational field gains autonomy (Buchholz, this volume) or a context into which transnational fields interject (Petzke, this volume). However, there is reason to believe that national-level factors play a more direct and positive role in transnational field formation. Despite the cosmopolitan attitudes espoused by many actors in the transnational humanitarian field, humanitarian INGOs continue to be influenced by national dynamics in their states of origin as well as by beliefs

The Sociological Review Monographs, 64:2, pp. 79–97 (2016), DOI: 10.1111/2059-7932.12003

about the relationship between their nationality and their global work. Sarah Stroup (2012) has recently shown the profound influence national organizational culture exerts on humanitarian organizations, even as they engage with global actors and action. Recent research has shown similar patterns in the environmental field, where actors in different locations engage with the global task of counteracting climate change by construing links between that ideal and their national character and values, drawing motivation from a sense of unique responsibility and dedication that makes them feel best suited for such a global task (Shani, 2011; Arnold, 2012). Since contemporary transnational domains continue to be influenced by national differences (as evidenced by these studies), nationality may play a role in the emergence of the transnational humanitarian field. Indeed, even a cursory glance at the transnational humanitarian field-information of the mid to late nineteenth century shows that much of the action in it had to do with nationally bounded dynamics within local humanitarian communities, even as those communities were adopting transnational types of discourse about impartial humanitarianism.

The international spread of field logics

Bourdieu's (1999) short essay about the complexities involved in the transnational travel of ideas is instructive for examining how the shared beliefs that are constitutive of a transnational field are circulated. While he has often been criticized for his nationally confined research (Chernilo, 2006; Beck and Sznaider, 2006), Bourdieu provided good reasons to be cautious in expanding research beyond national boundaries, especially when it comes to the diffusion of ideas such as impartial humanitarianism. According to Bourdieu, ideas circulate from their fields of production without their context or their original meaning structure, and are received in a field of reception with a set of different assumptions that brings forth reinterpretation.[7] Moreover, which texts travel and how they do so varies according to the peculiarities of the field of reception: who 'discovers' and selects the text or the idea? Who translates it to the receiving language? Finally, the way ideas are received is intertwined with the new meanings they are assigned by their importers (one might conjure up Parsons's translation of *The Protestant Ethic*[8]). Polysemic texts are in particular important here, as they can be adapted to different contexts easily (Bourdieu, 1999). Crucially, the shifts of meaning in international circulation of ideas is often independent of any conscious intention of any party to manipulate information.

Even though Bourdieu saw the international circulation of ideas, with the attendant misunderstanding and distortion, as having both good and bad consequences (Bourdieu, 1999), he ultimately saw these processes as a barrier for the creation of transnational fields. With relation to the possibility of a world field of sociology, he asked if it is 'possible to circumvent the barrier of the nationalisms that hinder the free circulation of ideas' thereby allowing 'the formation of a worldwide space of social scientific discussion and critique' (Bourdieu, 1991: 374). However, the same processes that complicate the travel of ideas between national contexts are also those that render them intelligible across boundaries, thereby facilitating the emergence of global engagement. They travel without the context in which they were produced, but their local reception may reinterpret them in a way that resonates with local meaning structures; they are selected and translated by specific agents, but those agents may thus encourage other actors to engage with global stakes and actors; and they are assigned new meanings by their importers, but those new meanings may be crucial to permeate those ideas in the first place.

The task ahead, then, is to explicate how impartial humanitarianism – advocated as a *transnational* mission by the ICRC – became meaningful in multiple *national* contexts to the extent that it was seen as a patriotic endeavour, and the extent to which this contributed to the creation of a transnational field. To this end, the next section will turn to the empirical examination of the spread of impartial humanitarianism through the work of the Red Cross and the establishment of multiple local fields dedicated to providing impartial relief. Following a brief historical context, the section will show that the ICRC advocated the transnational project of impartial humanitarianism as a *national* mission that should be undertaken independently by charitable communities in different states. In this, it will demonstrate that local humanitarian actors drew upon transnational discourse in order to gain dominance and prestige in their national communities. Second, it will demonstrate that activists also interpreted the discourse of humanitarianism through the lens of nationalism, which they presented as an important motivation for humanitarian work on a global scale.

Historical context

The ICRC was founded in Geneva in 1863 as a private association tightly connected both to Genevan civil society and to Swiss diplomats and decision makers. Drawing on firm Calvinist ideas about the need to subordinate international relations to Christian ethics, the ICRC advocated the establishment of independent volunteer societies in each state, which would provide humanitarian relief to wounded soldiers regardless of nationality. According to the ICRC proposals, each society would secure the cooperation of its host government in advance in order to ensure free access to the battlefield once war broke out (CICR, 1904). The ICRC saw the ratification of the Geneva Convention of 1864 – proposed by the ICRC and endorsed by the Swiss Federal Council – as a key condition for such cooperation (CICR, 1864). The Convention, initially signed by 12 European states including most great European powers, established that both wounded soldiers and medical workers (ranging from military medical staff to local volunteers offering help) in the battlefield are inviolable, designating the Red Cross emblem as conferring neutrality upon its bearers, and obliging armies to allow the wounded to be treated (ICRC, 1864).[9]

As a result of these efforts, National Red Cross societies (NRCs) began appearing in both core and periphery states, some of which were organized by volunteers and others by state officials. Each of these societies emerged independently

 The Sociological Review Monographs, 64:2, pp. 79–97 (2016), DOI: 10.1111/2059-7932.12003

from the ICRC, but shared with Geneva and with other NRCs knowledge, procedures, principles and symbols. In most states, the national society was joined by provincial volunteer societies, which were centralized (to varying extents) by the NRCs, and additional unaffiliated societies often worked closely with the NRC (or competed against it for funding and prestige). The ICRC coordinated NRCs in all areas concerning protection of victims of armed conflicts, as it was (and still is) the sole NGO recognized by International Humanitarian Law (Veuthey, 1983). By the end of the century 33 national Red Cross societies existed, each with its own constellation of local donors, activists, administrators, supporters, and detractors.[10] Some NRCs consisted of small groups of philanthropists whereas others employed thousands of medically trained workers. NRCs worked primarily within national boundaries – establishing hospitals, training, and accumulating funds and resources – but during wartime they also provided aid to foreign nationals. In 1919 the International Federation of the Red Cross was also established to coordinate the peace-time relief work of the NRCs.

International recognition and its uses in national-level humanitarian fields

Some scholars (Finnemore, 1996) have described the early diffusion of the Red Cross as a top-down process, with Swiss philanthropists advocating the idea of impartial aid societies to state leaders and local notables who, in turn, worked to establish NRCs. However, the road from the abstract proposals proffered by the ICRC in Geneva to the development of robust NRCs that are positioned in nationally bounded humanitarian fields involved more intricate processes of translation and adoption. A key function the ICRC played in support of the NRCs and of their dominance in their local fields was in maintaining global recognition of the Red Cross as an elite movement. NRCs drew upon the growing international prestige of the ICRC in order to gain symbolic distinction in their home countries, while at the same time being influenced by local dynamics and competition.

The ICRC, from its early years, invested considerable effort in creating a shared identity among its national chapters and to draw outside attention to its work. Red Cross activists published reports about their endeavours and achievements in newspapers, memoires and treatises (eg Pearson and MacLaughlin, 1871), and organized expositions dedicated to the movement (Barton, 1898). The ICRC established an international periodical to help coordinate activities between the various national societies and to help them publish stories of their successes and challenges. The periodical (as well as nationally based versions of it) attracted activists, decision makers, and philanthropists alike (Moynier, 1882). The Red Cross also organized international meetings for the NRCs for similar purposes (CICR, 1890, 1904). At the same time, the ICRC also worked to standardize the various organs of the movement, thereby emphasizing the relationship between the NRCs and the international movement. Key here was the proposal to adopt the name and emblem of the Red Cross in 1872 and to encourage NRCs to use them (Moynier, 1905). Since the establishment of the movement each society had been free to choose its own name, and – as the ICRC emphasized – remained free to do so. However, in order to achieve coherence in the eyes of diplomatic powers, the ICRC 'strongly urged the national societies to adopt the name Red Cross Society or, better still, Austrian, Russian, English, etc...'. (Moynier, 1905). These various efforts drew attention to the transnational features of the movement and connect NRCs symbolically to the ICRC.

Alongside these efforts to create a shared, transnational identity, the ICRC was concerned about unwittingly undermining trust between local governments and their respective NRCs. If an NRC appeared to bear allegiance to an international cause over a national one, it could appear as a threat in the eyes of its governments. In France, for example, the identification of the Paris-based NRC with international agents caused the Paris Commune to accuse it of spying in 1871 and to confiscate its supplies (Cte. de Beaufort, 1871). Thus, the ICRC exercised its influence cautiously so as not to exacerbate such suspicions, and placed much of the responsibility for the creation of local organizational structures on local volunteers.[11] The reasoning was that local notables (state officials, philanthropists, physicians) would be more likely to move state governments to establish aid societies than a foreign committee that may be unaware of local specificities or be perceived as interfering in domestic affairs (CICR, 1863). Since there has never been a formal hierarchy between the ICRC and the NRCs, the ICRC even resisted the label of the leader of the movement and its identification as a 'central' committee (Moynier, 1905; CICR, 1904). This was easier said than done, as the ICRC gained public visibility that attracted unwelcome attention by enthusiastic actors believing it to possess powers it did not have. A report of ICRC activities during the Franco-Prussian War complained:

> There have been some grave misconceptions about our responsibilities. We have seen, for example, people of all countries pouring into our offices, coming to join the *International*, as they say, thinking that there was only one society operating on both sides, and that we have the capacity to enlist them or to direct sanitary societies, and the ability to confer upon them absolute inviolability by giving them an international armband. The need to disabuse these applicants and to refer them to the proper authorities has been, for some weeks, fairly demanding work (CICR, 1870a: 8).

However, since the ICRC adopted a policy to communicate with only one central NRC per state (Moynier, 1905), it kept control of an important resource: recognition of the official NRC in each state.[12] Recognition by the ICRC as a national Red Cross society had clear advantages. First, it provided societies with access to an alternate source of funding that, once emergency struck, could circumvent the state's financial influence on the organization. Second, it gave societies access to a channel of information and a network by which to exercise moral agency (either by sending donations or by travelling to disaster-ridden areas). Third, it conferred distinction and prestige upon the recognized society, marking it as part of an internationally acclaimed group of elite institutions and – no less important – marked it as being an exemplary carrier of impartial humanitarianism.[13] Fourth, these benefits – taken together – provided NRCs

 The Sociological Review Monographs, 64:2, pp. 79–97 (2016), DOI: 10.1111/2059-7932.12003

with considerable leverage in their home countries and attracted the attention of royal houses and volunteers alike (with Japan, Prussia and Saxony being prime examples).

These rewards have led to various local squabbles between societies presenting themselves as belonging to the movement, as being impartial, and as representing the international Red Cross in their country (Gautier, 1890). In Belgium, the NRC warned about a competing society, going by the name of 'Société nationale belge de la Croix-Rouge', which 'did not possess as recommendable a character as its name suggests' (Moynier, 1905: 29). In France and Britain, 'copycat' Red Cross societies appeared – often taking similar organizational forms as the official NRC – and vied for funds and prestige. An English letter to the Genevan society warned that a competing society was a 'political and combatant aid society',[14] and another confessed that 'the National Red Cross Society has many enemies in England and among the worst are those who try to take its place in order to obtain the credit for its work'.[15]

Whether in competition or cooperation, the emergence of new NRCs had the effect of orienting existing charitable societies, which had already been a staple of mid-century aristocratic social life, toward the template of the Red Cross (eg the 'Samaritan Society', which was educating volunteers in first aid and formed strong ties to the Red Cross in numerous locales[16]). NRCs often formed close relations with pre-existing charitable religious societies of similar aims (CICR, 1870c).

The nature and extent of the competition in each national-level humanitarian field greatly depended on the level of state contribution and support. In some states, enthusiastic state involvement produced highly hierarchical and structured NRCs that were quasi-state organizations and produced little competition between actors over symbolic capital. In other cases (eg the Ottoman Empire), Red Cross societies remained weak and, with little interest from the state level, gave rise to weak field dynamics. But in most cases, NRC work interacted with varying levels of state involvement to consolidate nationally bounded fields of humanitarianism, in which providing impartial help (and, no less importantly, being recognized for this) was an object for some competition. In Prussia (and later Germany), the NRC enjoyed the strong support and, to a large extent, the cooperation of hundreds of local volunteer societies (von Itzenplitz, 1870).

The emergence of the transnational humanitarian field, then, involved the adoption (and competition over) a set of discursive and symbolic resources proffered by the ICRC and their deployment in national settings as a way to attain funding and prestige. Thus, a project that has prided itself as promoting impartial aid to victims regardless of their nationality did not emerge only as a cosmopolitan, boundary-defying construct but also as a set of nationally bounded fields, operating around stakes that were drawn from a transnational discourse arena. But how were these adopted codes culturally adapted in each setting for the promotion of the global Red Cross aims? The next section will take a closer look at the symbolic roles and discourses adopted by the ICRC and the NRCs in order to answer this question.

Humanitarianism between patriotism and transnationalism

From its original conception the movement did not position itself as defying national sovereignty or denying nations of any right, thereby allowing nationally situated actors to 'translate' the ICRC framework to local codes that resonate with local notions of patriotism. In this, the movement greatly differed from many of its peers that called for disarmament and saw their mission as restricting belligerents (CICR, 1863). ICRC leaders – alongside their critique of the brutalities of war – espoused a positive view of the potential of patriotism to motivate humane conduct (Hutchinson, 1996). Indeed, Red Cross advocates described nationalism and humane conduct as fully compatible with each other, often citing the United States as the model of such patriotic humanitarianism:

> America ... with the energy, spontaneity, and unwavering commitment that distinguish its children, and also – we should add – with a deep sense of patriotism and a tender and compassionate love which is one of the most previous fruits of Christianity, responded without hesitation [to the Civil War] (Maunoir, 1864: 179–180).

In keeping with this worldview, ICRC leaders spoke of NRCs as 'primarily *national*, and not *international*, as they are often believed to be', for each one of them was 'born under the joint inspiration of charity and patriotism' (Moynier, 1874: 4):

> What is essentially *international* in the Red Cross Societies is the spirit that animates them, that spirit of charity that moves them to wherever blood flows on the battlefield, experiencing as much solicitude for foreigners as for their compatriots when they are injured ... [but] most of the work of each society will concern the army of its country; they are thus eminently *national* institutions ... they cannot repudiate this character. By proclaiming it, they affirm their autonomy which is a condition for their vitality .... this is a guaranty for their success both with relation to their nation and with relation to their government (CICR, 1870b).

The ICRC aimed, then, at drawing upon the perceived positive effects of national commitment in order to promote an overarching transnational humanitarian project that would alleviate suffering in battlefields worldwide.

Such endorsements of patriotism made it easier for NRCs to present the Red Cross project to local contributors and statesmen as directly aligning with their national interest and well-being. For example, the statute declaration of the Magdeburg provincial society explained:

> The international character the [Red Cross] project takes does not only respond to the voice of philanthropy, but also satisfies national patriotism. We find in it a guaranty that the wounded and the sick of the Prussian army will be treated fraternally, even if they are in an enemy country, and our own assistance could not reach them (CICR, 1864: 208).

Indeed, in various parts of Europe and in the United States, the equivalence of nationalism and charity latched on to already-existing types of charitable volunteer work that had become popular among aristocratic women (Quataert, 2001;

The Sociological Review Monographs, 64:2, pp. 79–97 (2016), DOI: 10.1111/2059-7932.12003

Lawson, 2002). With the mass conscription of men and with the multiple wars that erupted in the second half of the nineteenth century, this equivalent system of quasi-national service provided women and non-combatant men with prestige and recognition that greatly resembled military honours. In Prussia and post-unification Germany, Empress Augusta provided humanitarian volunteers (both in the service of the Red Cross and in other societies) medals of honour, and the Japanese empress followed suit in the 1890s (Richardson, 1905). By creating NRCs (or relabelling an existing society as such) and providing it with national recognition, state leaders singled out the Red Cross as occupying an elite position which, as we have seen, often created competition among different humanitarian actors.

The growing legitimacy of Red Cross societies helped state leaders present themselves as morally superior to their neighbours once their NRC was well established. They did so, however, in different tenors. The Franco-Prussian War saw both belligerents exchanging accusations of mistreatment of enemy wounded soldiers, with Prussia in particular brandishing its compliance with the Geneva Convention, its superior Red Cross society, and the generosity and compassion of its broader humanitarian community in the face of its enemy (CICR, 1871).[17] This type of legalistic claims for national superiority were a common way in which nations competed in the late nineteenth century (Mazower, 2012). Other types of claims for superiority were also made by NRCs. The Dutch NRC, for example, erroneously congratulated its nation for being the 'only country in which an aid society was established by the initiative of the King himself ... for the good of the nation and of humanity' (CICR, 1869). The Austrian society prided itself with caring even for the 'infidels', the Ottoman soldiers in a Dalmatian conflict in 1870, when no equivalent care was offered by their enemies (d'Arneth, 1870).

The additional meanings given to the idea of Red Cross humanitarian relief in different countries through the particular aspects of national identity can be illustrated by comparing the early Japanese and United States societies. Figure 1 presents a Japanese woodblock print depicting the Red Cross volunteers at work in the Russo-Japanese War. The well-organized and compassionate Japanese aid workers are seen recovering the wounded Russian soldiers and meticulously caring for them in a field hospital, under a proud Japanese flag. A smaller frame at the top of the print depicts Russian soldiers kicking Japanese women and children. Indeed, European visitors to Japanese Red Cross hospitals reported an unusually large, orderly, and hierarchical society, with staff members professing their devotion to their work as an expression of their devotion to the Empress (who headed the society) and to Japan itself (eg Richardson, 1905), in particular during war. The society worked closely with the military and thus often presented itself as an auxiliary to the armed forces. In short, the Japanese Red Cross presented itself (and was presented by others) as an extension of Japanese moral superiority in relation to its enemies.

By contrast, the aid society founded in New York by Henry Whitney Bellows in 1866 failed to gain much government or public support and disbanded in the mid-1870s (Ador and Moynier, 1876). While appreciative of the initiative, the

Figure 1 *"Russo-Japanese War: Great Japan Red Cross Battlefield Hospital Treating Injured" (Utagawa Kokunimasa (Ryûa), 1904)*
Source: *Jean S. and Frederic A. Sharf Collection, The Museum of Fine Arts in Boston.*

US Government (like many potential donors) was confident of existing medical facilities and, with the Civil War concluded, had little interest in making new arrangements for wartime relief. The relief society itself remained small and failed to represent itself as bearing a national mission. When Clara Barton reconstituted the American National Red Cross in 1881, she drew attention to the society through natural disaster relief work (given the relative peacefulness of the 1880s, battlefield relief would have been untimely). Thus, the society grew to fame by helping (both domestically and internationally) victims of floods, famines and fires, with wartime relief being only one of its many functions. Being less affected by the government than its Japanese counterpart, and having little contact with the armed forces in its first decades, the ANRC grew decentralized with many of its interventions obtaining a distinct grassroots character (Barton, 1898; Jones, 2013). By the end of the century, the ANRC presented itself as being an international carrier of American charity and voluntarism, supplying gifts provided 'by the people of America for the innocent, unfortunate sufferers' in other countries (Barton, 1904: 347), as opposed to the more militarized Japanese Red Cross.

The NRC official names and imagery are also indicative as to the patriotic terms in which they conceived of their missions and the nature of the fields in which they stood (the Austrian society, for example, was officially named the Patriotic Aid Society for Wounded Soldiers). Early Red Cross societies saw no contradiction between the Red Cross flag and their own national flag, which were raised side by side in the field and in promotional material. NRCs also recruited local mythical figures and imagery to promote the Red Cross: in the United States

 The Sociological Review Monographs, 64:2, pp. 79–97 (2016), DOI: 10.1111/2059-7932.12003

it was Columbia, the feminine personification of the nation; in France it was Joan of Arc, the patron saint of the French Red Cross; and in Germany it was a medieval armour-clad Red Cross nurse slaying tuberculosis, in the form of a dragon. Presentation as an active expression of nationalism in an era of rising nationalist sentiments in Europe and the United States (Brubaker, 1992) was crucial for the widening influence of the Red Cross.

The Red Cross also helped model ideas of what the nation ought to look like for emerging nation-states. The newly unified German Red Cross cited proudly a letter sent by Emperor Wilhelm I to Empress Augusta in 1871, discussing the co-operation of the pre-unification German NRCs during the Franco-Prussian War: '...my heart was profoundly and joyfully moved by the loving care devoted to the army by the entire German homeland under your direction ... German unity has already been achieved in the field of humanitarianism by the Central Committee of the German Aid Societies for Wounded Soldiers' (Comité central allemand, 1871: 202–203). For the new nation-states that fought for independence in the 1870s and 1880s, establishing a Red Cross Society was a declaration of self-determination and of belonging to the family of nations. Montenegro, Serbia and Romania featured national Red Cross societies months and even years before they were recognized as independent states by the international community. The national revival of Hungary under the Habsburg Empire saw the establishment of a Hungarian society in 1881, which mobilized its own imagery, language and bureaucracy to distinguish itself from the Vienna-based society, which until then had represented all of Austro-Hungary.

In the non-European world, some states supported a strong humanitarian field led by a national Red Cross society for similar reasons. The Ottoman Empire, Siam and Japan established their own Red Cross societies (with Constantinople eventually replacing the cross with a crescent), as part of a general wave of reforms aimed at presenting themselves as equals to Western nations. These states faced considerable threats of coercion and domination by the West, and thus struggled to assert their independence and equal worthiness in the 'civilized' family of nations (Horowitz, 2004). ICRC members were initially incredulous, but were surprised to find that the Japanese emissaries to Geneva 'could not be more charitable, even at the era of enlightened men, who observed the committee's efforts sympathetically' (CICR, 1873: 13). Indeed, reports of the devoted care extended to wounded enemy soldiers, including approximately 70,000 Russian prisoners of war in the 1905 Russo-Japanese War, contradicted the initial scepticism toward the Japanese Red Cross (Checkland, 1994). Siam modelled its own NRC after the Japanese chapter, as officials were taken by what they saw in a visit to Japan (Siamese Red Cross Society, 1934).

To summarize, then, NRCs saw themselves and represented themselves as nationalistic, and intertwined specific representations of nationalism with the transnational discourse they adopted from the ICRC. This way, the notion of transnational humanitarianism compelled actors in different nations as – through 'translation' into locally recognizable codes – it became intertwined in a national ethos, but also oriented toward a transnational humanitarian mission.

Conclusion

The findings have shown that the late nineteenth century proliferation of transnational humanitarianism in different states was associated with the adaptability of the Red Cross to the wave of nationalist sentiments of the same era. National Red Cross societies drew upon a transnational source of prestige and worth – the ICRC – but at the same time adapted their discourse and self-presentation to their local contexts. Theoretically, the paper has argued for increased attention to the roles national-level dynamics and nationalism play in the foundation and expansion of transnational fields. Heeding Bourdieu's cautions about the assumption that ideas traverse boundaries unchanged is thus fruitful for examining the emergence of transnational fields and the effects of national dynamics on the process.

While the twentieth century has seen the increasing association of nationalism with violence and of humanitarianism with non-nationalism, national dynamics continue to matter in the transnational humanitarian field. These national considerations occasionally constrain its work. For example, during the 1998–99 Kosovo War, the humanitarian organization MSF was split when its Greek section, motivated by an expressed pro-Serbian sentiment that was pervasive in Greece, dispatched into Kosovo and Belgrade to provide humanitarian assistance against the position of the worldwide MSF. As MSF-Greece acted under the auspices of the Greek government, thus breaching the non-national principles of the movement, it was ostracized and expelled from the movement for several years (Fox, 2014). Since other instances of national boundary making within the humanitarian community have occurred (Stroup, 2012), it is important to acknowledge that the humanitarian field is rooted in national culture and institutions, and that these may pose challenges to actors who promote a truly cosmopolitan field.

At the same time, this study also questions the assumption of scholars that patriotism necessarily obstructs humanitarianism and is inherently tied to aggression (Kaldor, 2012; Held, 2010). While national attachment often presents obstacles to the provision of impartial relief, at other times it also facilitates and intensifies that same goal, as actors identify helping others with their national values and interests. Thus, to the extent that nationalism involves 'an idealization of the nation' and the 'conviction of one's own national superiority' (Blank, 2003: 262), the category of the nation may also serve as 'a helpful mediation between the local and the global' (Calhoun, 2007: 100). Indeed, existing research has raised the possibility of 'cosmopolitan nationalism' (West, 2008), as actors sympathize with others and wish to act on their behalf while drawing on a nationally defined sense of purpose and meaning.

Admittedly, focusing on the Red Cross as the harbinger of the transnational humanitarian field presents us with an extreme example of the effects of nationalism on the creation of new field forms. The ICRC explicitly identified its mission as building a set of national humanitarian fields that would work together to provide universal relief, thereby forming a transnational field. Other

 The Sociological Review Monographs, 64:2, pp. 79–97 (2016), DOI: 10.1111/2059-7932.12003

transnational fields, for example that of environmental activism, are likely to be less coordinated and less explicit about such aims. Furthermore, due to a growing tendency to view nationalism negatively since the late twentieth century (Alexander, 2003), contemporary transnational movements are unlikely to invoke it in support of their transnational growth. However, the model proposed in this article can help identify the multiple layers that comprise interscalar fields, and can help pinpoint the independent role of cultural adaption and translation in making broad, abstract transnational projects achievable in local field contexts.

Acknowledgements

The author is indebted to Jeffrey C. Alexander, Julian Go, Philip S. Gorski, Monika Krause and Philip Smith for their valuable suggestions. The author also thanks Matthew A. Andersson, Noli B. Brazil, and Samuel D. Stabler, for their close reading and comments on previous versions of this article. This research was supported by the Lake Institute on Faith and Giving at the Indiana University Lilly Family School of Philanthropy.

Notes

1 While the movement officially adopted the Red Cross as its name in the mid-1870s, this article refers to these organizations as the ICRC and the NRCs from their inception for clarity.
2 Hutchinson (1996) and Moorehead (1999) provide numerous example of local activists identifying with their national armies rather than the transnational aid movement.
3 This article departs from the concept of transnational social field as used in the context of migration; see Levitt and Glick Schiller (2004).
4 For further elaboration see Gorski (2013).
5 For elaborate discussion see Bourdieu (1993).
6 For further discussion of domination of the 'principles of vision and di-vision' see Bourdieu (1991).
7 In this, Bourdieu's views align with the claims of the transnational constructivist school in international relations. See Risse-Kappen (1994) and Checkel (1998) for examples. Neoinstitutional studies similarly demonstrate the ways global models undergo local adaptations (Boyle, 2005).
8 See Gorski (2003).
9 For full historical context see Boissier (1985).
10 See Online Appendix 1 for specific details at http://onlinelibrary.wiley.com/doi/10.1111/2059-7932.12003/suppinfo.
11 This was often complicated when Red Cross advocates requested that the ICRC or the Swiss Federal Council intervene on their behalf and convince their local government (eg, letter from Dr W. Schlesinger to Gustave Moynier, November 14, 1869, Vienna. ICRC Archive, AF 1,3/30(T)).
12 However, aid societies that were not officially related to the Red Cross remained active and, oftentimes, quite powerful (the Order of St John of Jerusalem in Germany and the Knights of Malta in numerous Catholic states, for example).
13 Today, inclusion as part of the movement requires the approval of both the ICRC and the IFRC, and remains contentious grounds, with NGOs such as the North Cyprus Red Crescent Society and the Taipei-based Red Cross Society of the Republic of China achieving only limited recognition.

14 Letter from Thomas Longmore to Gustave Moynier, 14 April 1872, Wortley. ICRC Archive, AF 8,2 (116).
15 Letter from C. Burgess to Gustave Ador, 17 January 1877, London. ICRC Archive, AF 8,2 (190).
16 Letter from Emilio R. Coni to the ICRC, 25 February 1885, Buenos Aires. Archive de la CICR, ARG AF 1,2 (2). See also Glasgow and West of Scotland Medical Association (1888: 151).
17 In particular, a report published by the Berlin NRC titled *Les violations de la Convention de Genève par les Français en 1870–71* accused France of complete disregard for the convention.

Supporting Information

Additional Supporting Information may be found in the online version of this article:

Doc S1. Chronological list of signatories to the 1864 Geneva Convention and National Red Cross Societies established, 1863–1899.

References

Ador, G. and Moynier, G., (1876), 'Fondation d'une société en Roumanie et dissolution de celle des Etats-Unis'. *Bulletin international des sociétés de secours aux militaires bléssés*, 7 (28): 159–161.

Alexander, J. C., (2003), 'Modern, anti, post, and neo: how intellectuals explain "our time"', in J. C. Alexander, *The Meanings of Social Life: A Cultural Sociology*, 193–228, Oxford and New York: Oxford University Press.

Arnold, A., (2012), 'Towards a transcultural community of climate change: adapting Max Weber's distinction of vergemeinschaftung and vergesellschaftung', in M. Arnold and P. Łukasik (eds), *Europe and America in the Mirror: Culture, Economy, and History*, 107–123, Kraków: NOMOS.

Balibar, É., (2013), 'On the politics of human rights', *Constellations*, 20 (1): 18–26.

Barton, C., (1898), *The Red Cross: A History of this Remarkable International Movement in the Interest of Humanity*, Washington, DC: The American National Red Cross.

Barton, C., (1904), *The Red Cross in Peace and War*, Washington, DC: American Historical Press.

Beck, U. and Sznaider, N., (2006), 'Unpacking cosmopolitanism for the social sciences: a research agenda', *British Journal of Sociology*, 57 (1): 1–23.

Best, G. F., (1980), *Humanity in Warfare*, New York: Columbia University Press.

Blank, T., (2003), 'Determinants of national identity in East and West Germany: an empirical comparison of theories on the significance of authoritarianism, anomie, and general self-esteem', *Political Psychology*, 24 (2): 259–288.

Boissier, P., (1985), *From Solferino to Tsushima: History of the International Committee of the Red Cross*, Geneva: Henry Dunant Institute.

Bourdieu, P., (1991), *Language and Symbolic Power*, (ed. J. Thompson; trans. G. Raymond and M. Adamson), Cambridge, MA: Harvard University Press.

Bourdieu, P., (1993), *The Field of Cultural Production: Essays on Art and Literature*, Cambridge: Polity Press.

Bourdieu, P., (1996a), *The Rules of Art: Genesis and Structure of the Literary Field*, Cambridge: Polity Press.

Bourdieu, P., (1996b), *The State Nobility: Elite Schools in the Field of Power*, (trans. L. C. Clough), Oxford: Polity Press.

Bourdieu, P., (1999), 'The social conditions of the international circulation of ideas', in R. Shusterman (ed.), *Bourdieu: A Critical Reader*, 220–228, Oxford and Malden, MA: Blackwell.

Boyle, E. H., (2005), *Female Genital Cutting: Cultural Conflict in the Global Community*, Baltimore, MD: Johns Hopkins University Press.

Brubaker, R., (1992), *Citizenship and Nationhood in France and Germany*, Cambridge, MA: Harvard University Press.

Brysk, A., (2013), *Speaking Rights to Power: Constructing Political Will*, New York: Oxford University Press.
Calhoun, C., (2007), 'Nationalism and civil society: democracy, diversity, and self-determination', in C. Calhoun, *Nations Matter: Culture, History, and the Cosmopolitan Dream*, 77–101, London and New York: Routledge.
Calhoun, C., (2013), 'For the social history of the present: Bourdieu as historical sociologist', in P. S. Gorski (ed.), *Bourdieu and Historical Analysis*, 36–66, Durham, NC: Duke University Press.
Checkel, J. T., (1998), 'The constructive turn in international relations theory', *World Politics*, 50 (2): 324–348.
Checkland, O., (1994), *Humanitarianism and the Emperor's Japan*, 1877–1977, Basingstoke and New York: Macmillan and St Martin's Press.
Chernilo, D., (2006), 'Social theory's methodological nationalism: myth and reality', *European Journal of Social Theory*, 9 (1): 5–22.
CICR, (1863), *Compte-rendu de la Conférence internationale réunie a Genève les 26, 27, 28, 29 Oct. 1863 pour étudier les moyens de pourvoir a l'insuffisance du Service sanitaire dans les Armées en campagne*, Genève: Imprimerie de Jules-Guillaume Fick.
CICR, (1864), *Secours aux blessés: Communication du Comité international faisant suite au compte rendu de la conférence internationale de Genève*. Genève: Imprimerie de Jules-Guillaume Fick.
CICR, (1869), 'Assemblée générale de la société néerlandaise', *Bulletin international des sociétés de secours*, 1 (1): 31–35.
CICR, (1870a), 'Comité international', *Bulletin international des sociétés de secours aux militaires blessés*, 2 (5): 3–13.
CICR, (1870b), 'Du double caractère, national et international, des sociétés de secours', *Bulletin internationale des sociétés de secours aux militaires bléssés*, 1 (4): 11–14.
CICR, (1870c), 'Progrès de l'oeuvre de la Croix Rouge', *Bulletin international des sociétés de secours aux militaires blessés*, 1 (4): 173–174.
CICR, (1871), 'Travaux du Comité international pendant le dernier trimestre de l'année 1870', *Bulletin internationl des sociétés de secours aux militaires blessés*, 2 (6): 77–91.
CICR, (1873), 'L'ambassade japonaise', *Bulletin international des sociétés de secours aux militaires blessés*, 5 (17): 11–16.
CICR, (1890), *Résumé des travaux du Comité International de la Croix-Rouge de 1884–1890, lu à la séance du 14 Novembre 1890 par son président*, Geneva: O. and Aut. de B. Soullier.
CICR, (1904), *La Conférence Internationale réunie à Genève les 26, 27, 28, et 29 Octobre 1863 pour étudier les moyens de pourvoir a l'insuffisance du service sanitaire dans les armées en campagne, deuxième édition*, Genève: Publication du Comité International de la Croix-Rouge.
Comité central allemand, (1871), 'Le Comité central allemand', *Bulletin international des sociétés de secours aux militaires bléssés*, 2 (7–8): 202–206.
Cte. de Beaufort, (1871), 'Déclaration du conseil de la Société française de secours aux blessés des armées de terre et de mer', *Bulletin international des sociétés de secours aux militaires bléssés*, 2 (7–8): 208–212.
Cullity, G., (2010), 'Compromised humanitarianism', in K. Horton and C. Roche (eds), *Ethical Questions and International NGOs: An Exchange between Philosophers and NGOs*, 157–173, Dordrecht: Springer.
d'Arneth, D. F.-H., (1870), 'Evénements de Dalmatie', *Bulletin international des Sociétés de Secours aux Militaires Bléssés*, 1 (3): 123–124.
Davey, E., (2011), 'Famine, aid, and ideology: the political activism of Médecins sans Frontières in the 1980s', *French Historical Studies*, 34 (3): 529–558.
Dezalay, Y. and Garth, B. G., (2010), *The Internationalization of Palace Wars: Lawyers, Economists, and the Contest to Transform Latin American States*, Chicago: University of Chicago Press.
Dixon, P. and Tenove, C., (2013), 'International criminal justice as a transnational field: rules, authority and victims', *The International Journal of Transitional Justice*, 7 (3): 393–412.
Fassin, D., (2011), *Humanitarian Reason: A Moral History of the Present*, Berkeley, CA: University of California Press.

Finnemore, M., (1996), *National Interests in International Society*, Ithaca, NY and London: Cornell University Press.
Forsythe, D. P., (2005), *The Humanitarians: The International Committee of the Red Cross*, Cambridge: Cambridge University Press.
Fox, R., (2014), *Doctors without Borders: Humanitarian Quests, Impossible Dreams of Médecins sans frontières*, Baltimore, MD: Johns Hopkins University Press.
Gautier, A., (1890), *Résultat du Concours relatif à l'emploi abusif du signe et du nom de la Croix-Rouge*, Genève: Imprimerie B. and I. Soullier.
Glasgow and West of Scotland Medical Association, (1888), *Glasgow Medical Journal* (Vol. XIX (January to June 1888)), Glasgow: Glasgow and West of Scotland Medical Association.
Gorski, P. S., (2003), 'Review: The Protestant Ethic and the Spirit of Capitalism by Max Weber; Stephen Kalberg; The Protestant Ethic and the Spirit of Capitalism and Other Writings by Max Weber; Peter Baehr; Gordon C. Wells', *Social Forces*, 82 (2): 833–839.
Gorski, P. S., (2013), 'Bourdieusian theory and historical anaylsis: maps, mechanisms, and methods', in P. S. Gorski (ed.), *Bourdieu and Historical Analysis*, 327–367, Durham, NC: Duke University Press.
Hagan, J. and Levi, R., (2005), 'Crimes of war and the force of law', *Social Forces*, 83 (4): 1499–1534.
Held, D., (2010), *Cosmopolitanism: Ideals and Realities*, Cambridge and Malden, MA: Polity Press.
Horowitz, R. S., (2004), 'International law and state transformation in China, Siam, and the Ottoman Empire during the nineteenth century', *Journal of World History*, 15 (4): 445–486.
Hutchinson, J. F., (1996), *Champions of Charity: War and the Rise of the Red Cross*, Boulder, CO: Westview Press.
ICRC, (1864), *Convention for the Amelioration of the Condition of the Wounded in Armies in the Field*, Geneva.
Jean, F. (ed.), (1993), *Life, Death, and Aid: The Médecins sans Frontières Report on World Crisis Intervention*, London and New York: Routledge.
Jones, M. M., (2013), *The American Red Cross from Clara Barton to the New Deal*, Baltimore, MD: Johns Hopkins University Press.
Kaldor, M., (2012), *New and Old Wars*, Cambridge and Malden, MA: Polity Press.
Krause, M., (2014), *The Good Project: Humanitarian Relief NGOs and the Fragmentation of Reason*, Chicago: The University of Chicago Press.
Kurasawa, F., (2012), 'L'humanitaire, manifestation du cosmopolitisme?', *Sociologie et sociétés*, 44 (1): 217–237.
Lawson, M., (2002), *Patriot Fires: Forging a New American Nationalism in the Civil War North*, Lawrence, KS: University Press of Kansas.
Levitt, P. and Glick Schiller, N., (2004), 'Conceptualizing simultaneity: a transnational social field perspective on society', *International Migration Review*, 38 (3): 1002–1039.
Maunoir, T., (1864), 'Note sur l'oeuvre des comités de secours aux Etats-Unis D'Amérique', in Comité international (ed.), *Secours aux blessés: Communication du Comité international faisant suite au compte rendu de la conférence internationale de Genève*, 179–187. Genève: Imprimerie de Jules-Guillaume Fick.
Mazower, M., (2012), *Governing the World: The History of an Idea, 1815 to the Present*, New York: Penguin Books.
Moorehead, C., (1999), *Dunant's Dream: War, Switzerland, and the History of the Red Cross*, New York: Carrol and Graf Publishers.
Moynier, G., (1874), *Ce que c'est que la Croix-Rouge*, Genève: Imprimerie B. Soullier.
Moynier, G., (1882), *La Croix-Rouge: son passé et son avenir*, Paris: Sandoz and Thuillier.
Moynier, G., (1905), *Rappel succinct de l'activité déployée par le comité international de la Croix-Rouge à Genève pendant les quarante premières années de son existence (1863 à 1904)*, Genève: Comité international de la Croix-Rouge.
Mudge, S. L. and Vauchez, A., (2012), 'Building Europe on a weak field: law, economics, and scholarly avatars in transnational politics', *American Journal of Sociology*, 118 (2): 449–492.

 The Sociological Review Monographs, 64:2, pp. 79–97 (2016), DOI: 10.1111/2059-7932.12003

Pearson, E. M. and MacLaughlin, L., (1871), *Our Adventures during the War of 1870*, London: R. Bentley and Son.
Plattner, D., (1996), 'ICRC neutrality and neutrality in humanitarian assistance', *International Review of the Red Cross*, 36 (311): 161–180.
Quataert, J. H., (2001), *Staging Philanthropy: Patriotic Women and the National Imagination in Dynastic Germany*, 1813–1916, Ann Arbor, MI: University of Michigan Press.
Redfield, P., (2013), *Life in Crisis: The Ethical Journey of Doctors without Borders*, Berkeley, CA: University of California Press.
Richardson, T. E.-S., (1905), *In Japanese Hospitals during War-Time: Fifteen Months with the Red Cross Society of Japan*, Edinburgh: W. Blackwood and Sons.
Risse-Kappen, T., (1994), 'Ideas do not float freely: transnational coalitions, domestic structures, and the end of the cold war', *International Organization*, 48 (2): 185–214.
Shani, L., (2011), 'Nationalism between land and environment: the conflict between "oranges" and "greens" over settling in the East Lakhish area', *The University of Maryland Institute for Israel Studies Research Papers Series*.
Siamese Red Cross Society, (1934), *The Siamese Red Cross Society: Its Origin and Activities*, Bangkok: Siamese Red Cross Society.
Siméant, J., (2005), 'What is going global? The internationalization of French NGOs "without borders"', *Review of International Political Economy*, 12 (5): 851–883.
Stroup, S. S., (2012), *Borders Among Activists: International NGOs in the United States, Britain, and France*, Ithaca, NY: Cornell University Press.
Veuthey, M., (1983), 'Implementation and enforcement of humanitarian law and human rights law in non-international armed conflicts: the role of the International Committee of the Red Cross', *American University Law Review*, 33: 83–98.
von Itzenplitz, C., (1870), 'Association patriotique de dames à Berlin', *Bulletin international des sociétés de secours aux militaires blessés*, 1 (2): 68–69.
West, B., (2008), 'Collective memory and crisis: the 2002 Bali bombing, national heroic archetypes, and the counter-narrative of cosmopolitan nationalism', *Journal of Sociology*, 44 (4): 337–353.

Social fields, subfields and social spaces at the scale of empires: explaining the colonial state and colonial sociology

George Steinmetz

Abstract: This article develops a series of arguments about social fields, subfields, and social spaces that can help us understand empires and colonies. First, we have to assume that the scale of fields is not always coextensive with the boundaries of the national state but is often much larger, or smaller. Imperial fields are among the most spatially extensive ones, though they may not be as territorially extensive as truly global fields. Second, we need to make a distinction between *imperial fields* and *imperial social spaces* (based on Bourdieu's distinction between social fields and social spaces). The third argument is that colonies in modern empires were characterized by two different kinds of fields: fields that were simply extended into the overseas territories, versus completely separate fields unique to one or more of the colonies. The colonial state is an example of a field that is specific to the colony. By contrast, scientific fields were often simply extended from the metropole into the colonies, encompassing both. The fourth argument concerns subfields. Transported into imperial realms, this distinction suggests that some colonial offshoots of fielded metropolitan practices do not constitute separate fields but are nonetheless differentiated from their main overarching field. These four points are illustrated with examples from British, French and German imperial policy, colonial statecraft and colonial sociology.

Keywords: Bourdieu, field theory, empires, colonies, British sociology, French sociology

> In the long term, globalization does not mean that we will all eat hamburgers; globalization means that a true *global field* will emerge. (Žižek, 2013: 37)

This paper discloses a neo-Bourdieusian theory of fields, subfields, and spaces at the scale of colonial and non-colonial empires. Bourdieu is not generally seen as a theorist of empire, even though his research career originated in late colonial French Algeria (Yacine *et al.*, 2013; Yacine, 2013; Pérez, 2015). Some of the difficulties in making Bourdieu's work useful for imperial historians stem from the fact that he never tried to integrate his early work on colonial Algeria with

The Sociological Review Monographs, 64:2, pp. 98–123 (2016), DOI: 10.1111/2059-7932.12004

Published by John Wiley & Sons Ltd, 9600 Garsington Road, Oxford OX4 2DQ, UK and 350 Main Street, Malden, MA 02148, USA

his later thinking on field theory. Nor did Bourdieu think systematically about the distinctive features of colonial states as compared to non-colonial ones. His writings on Algeria between 1958 and 1964 do not thematize the country's place in the wider French empire, even though his secret reports for the French army's Information Service dealt with these sorts of questions (Pérez, 2015). Bourdieu analysed 'the structure of European society' in Algeria in the second edition of *Sociologie de l'Algérie* (Bourdieu, 1958: 117, n. 1; 1961: 107–118; Steinmetz, 2009), but he largely ignored the relations between colonizer and colonized or among different groups of colonizers inside the colonial state or the colonial field of power. Bourdieu never systematically asked whether his field theory applied to 'indigenous' Algerian society before 1962, although he endorsed a field-theoretic analysis of the historical Chinese empire (Will, 2000; Bourdieu *et al.*, 2000). We cannot criticize Bourdieu for failing to accomplish these tasks, of course, since he allowed us to ask these questions and contributed in so many other ways to the reconstitution of sociology and sociological theory.

It is well known that Bourdieu's concept of habitus emerged in a preliminary, rough-cast form during his Algerian work (Sapiro, 2004). The same can be said of some of the building blocks of his concept of field – especially the idea of relative autonomy as applied to social science.[1] But he did not use the word 'field' in a conceptual rather than a descriptive way until 1965, when he had finished publishing his Algerian fieldwork and was turning his attention to metropolitan cultural practices.[2] There is a disjuncture between the period of Bourdieu's research in Algeria (1956–early 1960s) and his explicit deployment of the field concept starting in 1965.[3]

Bourdieu's mature theoretical approach nonetheless provides an extremely fruitful starting point for solving some of the main analytic puzzles raised by colonialism and empires. His theory of fields suggests a framework for analysing metropolitan states and their colonial offices, colonial states, and overseas settler societies (Bourdieu, 1999, 2014; Steinmetz, 2002, 2003, 2014a). Bourdieu's concepts help to explain shifts and variations in colonial 'native policies' and transformations in the habitus of colonial officials, settlers and civil servants (Steinmetz, 2007, 2008). Bourdieu provides a corrective to prevailing fashions in the historiography of colonialism and empire. Many historians consider a focus on colonial officials and colonizing elites as old-fashioned and prefer to focus exclusively on the colonized, anticolonial resistance, or imperial culture. A relational field-theoretic approach refuses to separate colonizer and colonized, metropole and colony, culture and economics, but sees these as inextricably linked elements of an extremely complex figurational and relational whole.

In the first section of this paper I will provide a brief survey of Bourdieusian field theory or BFT. In the second section I will suggest two main extensions of BFT. The first involves extending the concepts of social field and social space to the scale of empires. I draw a distinction between imperial *social spaces* and imperial *fields*, arguing that both were present in empires as in the metropoles. The example of the research on the colonial state and colonial civil society (Goh, 2007; Steinmetz, 2002, 2003) illustrates the explanatory payoff

The Sociological Review Monographs, 64:2, pp. 98–123 (2016), DOI: 10.1111/2059-7932.12004

of these theoretical moves: without specifying the boundaries of the colonial administrative field we cannot properly situate the efficacy and weakness of resistance by the colonized; without specifying the definition of the specific form of symbolic capital governing conflicts within the colonial state bureaucracy and without analysing those struggles internal to the colonial state field we cannot understand the course of individual colonies' policies (Steinmetz, 2007, 2008).

The second revision foregrounds the analytical difference between *fields* and *subfields*. Once we have determined that some metropolitan field is present in a colony we still need to determine whether the relevant activities are simply extensions of metropolitan ones, or whether they instead reveal the reversals and inversions typical of subfields or the revisions that are characteristic of all extensions of national-level practices beyond their original locales. Here I focus on the example of colonial studies within French sociology between the 1940s and the 1960s, arguing that colonial sociology emerged as a semi-coherent subfield of the overarching sociology field but that it was neither simply an extension of metropolitan ways of doing sociology nor an entirely new field. After providing some evidence that colonial sociology was indeed a subfield I ask how the subfield related to the rest of the field. Here we can begin to see the explanatory payoff of field theory's relational approach, by showing that the relative coherence and expansion of colonial sociology after 1945 was due to a contingent alliance of interests with the field's 'intellectual' pole against the dominant metro-empiricist pole (see below).

Field theory and its basic extensions

To set the stage we need to establish the basic parameters of BFT. Bourdieu discussed the field concept in 1965 in a publication that appeared the following year in a special issue on 'problems of structuralism' in Sartre's journal *Les temps modernes* (Bourdieu, 1966). This structuralist context provides an important clue to BFT's lasting commitment to a fully relational analytic approach. Bourdieu taught seminars on field theory between 1972 and 1975 (Bourdieu, 2013) and lectured on different fields (the state, art, science) at the Collège de France between 1982 and 2001.[4]

Bourdieusian field theory allows the analyst to hold two seemingly opposing socioanalytic viewpoints simultaneously while keeping them in a dialectical tension with one another: (1) an image of society as a congeries of diverse realms of social practice, each characterized by distinct logics that are irreducible to external causalities; and (2) an image of society as a historical totality in which disparate realms of social and symbolic practice are interconnected through homologies, refracted logics, and indirect transfers of value, and through a distinctive architecture of relations among different fields and social spaces.

This architecture is specific and closely elaborated in BFT (*pace* Fligstein and McAdam, 2012). The most encompassing space, according to Bourdieu, is the *social space*, a concept referring to the overall distribution of the generic resources

 The Sociological Review Monographs, 64:2, pp. 98–123 (2016), DOI: 10.1111/2059-7932.12004

valued within a particular 'society'. A social space is an arrangement of social relations among actors competing for the same resources (economic and cultural capital) and occupying different social positions but which does not have a constitutive social outside against which it defines itself and is not governed by a specific form of symbolic capital.

Bourdieu argues explicitly that not all specialized practices arrange themselves into fields. *Fieldness* is a continuous variable, not a binary, either-or condition. The thrust of Bourdieu's own work is not to apply the field concept to almost everything, as is clear in his diagrams (for example in *Distinction* or *The Rules of Art*), which show fields nesting within the 'field of power' (see below), and the latter located in the upper reaches of the encompassing social space. Certain practices do not have enough separateness from the outside or enough inter-actor coordination to be seen as fields.

It follows that some human practices exist entirely outside of both social fields and social spaces. For a practice to be outside of social space, as that term is defined by Bourdieu, means to lack control over any and all power or resources. Complete powerlessness or lack of resources is an extreme boundary condition of the sort discussed by Agamben (1998) as 'bare life', and characterized by Lawson (2013) as the limit of the social, since social practice for Lawson is predicated on possession on some sort of power. This is compatible with neo-Aristotelian theories of human virtues insofar as the latter are rooted in essential powers that may be universally possessed by all humans but sometimes not expressed at all due to evil social conditions (Smith, 2010; Groff, 2013).

It is as crucial for sociology to establish the limits of sociology as it is to determine the boundaries between social space and social field, between the field of power and specific fields, and so on. The question of practices existing outside of social space is perhaps particularly crucial in colonial situations, where pre-existing social relations and institutions are often shattered without anything new taking their place. The radical juxtaposition of fragments of destroyed older social practices with the practices of the foreign conquerors sometimes leads to a complete lack of commensurability between the culture of the colonizer and the colonized, and colonial native policy can be interpreted as an effort to provide enough common cultural ground to allow the colonizers to attain their political, economic and cultural goals (Steinmetz, 2002, 2003, 2007; Liu, 2004). But these policies are not always sufficient to stitch together a common social fabric. Practices that have lost their grounding in the old but not found a place in the new may continue to wander through a-social space like ghostly revenants or Agamben's figures at the boundary zone of indistinction between the human and the inhuman. Societalization, or the constitution of social space, is a variable condition, a political accomplishment, not a universal feature of human life. Bourdieu does not explicitly discuss the notion of social practices existing outside social space, to my knowledge, but there is nothing that makes this argument incompatible with BFT. This argument does not transcend BFT but *extends* it by specifying its limits. I will not have more to say about this empirically in this paper but would suggest that those working on colonial history pay as much attention to it as those investigating slavery, concentration camps and other extreme antisocial situations.

Although I do not want to return to the basic defining features of BFT, which have been amply discussed by Bourdieu himself, I want to make one additional clarification or extension of the basic approach before turning to the question of empires. This is the distinction between field autonomy and field *settlement* (Steinmetz, 2002, 2005a). We are justified in describing a particular resource as a field specific form of symbolic capital when it is recognized as legitimate by all of the field's agents – that is, when all participants in a given game, a given realm of activity, agree on what it is they are doing and what they are striving for. For example, the autonomy of an artistic field requires that artists (and critics) agree that judgments should take an aesthetic (or 'artistic') form, rather than being based on external criteria such as economic profitability or political efficacy. Both the dominant and dominated agree that the determinant criterion should take a field-specific form. A field whose participants no longer agree about the definition of the stakes is likely to suffer a catastrophic collapse of its autonomy. By contrast, it is quite possible and even normal for the participants in a given field to disagree about the criteria used to rank different artists, artworks, or aesthetic judgments. This sort of disagreement is what Bourdieu refers to as conflict over the 'dominant form of domination'. Such a field is an unsettled rather than a settled one, but it is still a coherent field.

A *settled* field, by contrast, is one in which all participants agree not only about what it is they are fighting for but also about how that capital should be measured, that is, about the principles of its distribution (Bourdieu, 2000). Such agreement is enforced informally in many fields, since they typically have 'a weak degree of codification' (Bourdieu, 1996: 226). In other fields, agreement on the criteria of evaluation is enforced by some institution that monopolizes the definition of distinction. In the French educational field this institution is the state, which codifies valuation explicitly through 'the possession of scholarly titles, success in competition, etc., or by measures of exclusion and discrimination, such as laws intended to assure a *numerus clausus*' (Bourdieu, 1996: 226). Fligstein and McAdam (2012) label such institutions 'internal governance units', but it is important to note that they do not have to be formal organizations. Unanimity among all participants in a field is often enough.[5]

What about the assertion (by Fligstein and McAdam, 2012: 24) that 'Bourdieu does not have much to say about the relationships between fields'? Here it is important to recognize that Bourdieu's field theory does not emerge from some sort of generic 'classical social theory' (2012: 24), but from a much more specific set of sources. These sources do include Durkheim, Weber, and a little bit of Marx, of course, but they also include the specific philosophy of science associated with Bachelard, Koyré, Canguilhem, and Cassirer; phenomenology, and perhaps most importantly, linguistic and Levi-Straussian structuralism. Of course, Bourdieu broke early on with what he later called 'blissful' structuralism (Bourdieu, 1990b: 9) – blissful, because structuralism makes explanation of individual practices so straightforward. Bourdieu moved quickly beyond

The Sociological Review Monographs, 64:2, pp. 98–123 (2016), DOI: 10.1111/2059-7932.12004

structuralism to a practice-based, dynamic, constructionist social ontology mixed with structuralism (Burke, 1990: 80; Steinmetz, 2011; Mead, 2013). As Bourdieu explained in his lectures on the state, his entire project was to integrate structuralism with 'the fact that the human agent is creative, generative, producing mythical representations by applying mental functions, symbolic forms' (Bourdieu, 2012: 170). This evolution in Bourdieu's work is best captured by his concept of habitus (Bourdieu, 2002). Over time he came to argue that habitus does not result automatically from the subject's passive imitation of his social environment but is generated through the selective identification by the subject with parts of that environment (or 'surroundings'). This active engagement with the world confers on agents a social knowledge that is practical and partly unconscious, and that allows them to position themselves in social space and to respond to novel situations rather than simply applying a template of rules in a mechanical way (Mead, 2013). Habitus *does* innovate Bourdieu's formula of 'regulated improvisation' captures this combination of constructive freedom and structured constraint. This is Bourdieu's take on Kant's combination of causation and moral freedom.

Like habitus, Bourdieu's concept and theory of fields retain key ideas from structuralism. Most significant is the basic idea that fields, practices and positions within fields are defined relationally, with and against other fields, practices and positions. The idea of the relational definition of practices is captured by the idea of *homologies*. This fundamental structuralist idea is defined as 'a resemblance with a difference' (Bourdieu and Wacquant, 1992: 106). It designates a 'morphological resemblance between the structures of different fields' resulting from a common 'underlying logic of social classification' (Wang, forthcoming). A homological relationship is regulated by the habitus, which can 'function as a translating machine' (Bourdieu, 1993: 72) between different fields or realms of activity. Homologies do not produce the same structures over and over, but produce structures that are related to one other analogically. Homology is in this respect the structuralist term for analogical thinking.

Homology differs from *isomorphism*, a term widely used in organizational sociology, which points to a simpler *diffusion* of institutional patterns (Wang, forthcoming). When I discuss fields that are simply extended into new territories, this is not necessarily the same thing as isomorphism. Field extension in the spatial, geographic sense may simply involve inviting new members who are located somewhere else into an existing field. The idea of 'foreign corresponding members' of learned societies corresponds to this approach. There are also cases in which field extension involves setting up a new organization outside the field's original territory, as when the United States exports prefabricated American military bases overseas. Cases in which overseas fields simply serially replicate a metropolitan practice may be the limited exceptions in which social isomorphism as envisioned by John Meyer's world polity model actually exists. In other realms more is involved than a simple extension of metropolitan practices into new territories. In each case it remains to be seen whether an exported social structure remains unchanged by its new social surroundings. This seems unlikely, especially to a colonial historian.[6]

Other principles relevant to the relations among fields include the distinction within the field of power between cultural and economic capital, and the axis of autonomy versus heteronomy. Bourdieu's familiar diagrams divide the field of power into sectors high in cultural capital and low in economic capital, and vice versa. We can locate entire fields along the autonomy-heteronomy axis. Sociology, pulled inexorably toward the political field, is a more heteronomous field, overall, than physics (Bourdieu, 1991). The field of think tanks, constitutionally committed to generating useful knowledge for external actors, is located near the heteronomous extreme. Indeed, Medvetz (2012) calls think tanks *hybrid* organizations because of this interstitial location and suggests they may be better conceived of as 'subspaces' rather than subfields. This points to the distinction between space and field, discussed below.

A field-theoretic account of society-wide crisis and change necessarily involves analyzing multiple fields in relation to one another (Bourdieu, 1988). In non-crisis situations, fields maintain their relative autonomy and are governed mainly by internal temporalities and rhythms. Changes at the societal level may involve events that erode the autonomy of several fields simultaneously or that bring fields into a condition of temporary harmony with one another. We should also entertain the possibility of *accidental* resonances among autonomous fields that produce unpredictable changes.

Thus while Bourdieu's fundamental (neo)historicism[7] militates against his proposing any general laws of fields' relations to one another (Bourdieu and Wacquant, 1992: 100; Steinmetz, 2011), his central concepts suggest a number of causal mechanisms or powers that may combine to produce a temporarily stabilized arrangement of fields. However, these mechanisms should also be expected to recombine periodically in unpredictable ways, disrupting any temporarily stabilized regularities (Lawson, 1998, 2013), giving rise to new fields and eliminating others, and restructuring the relations among fields. The absence of an overall blueprint of the array of fields does not represent a shortcoming in BFT but is consistent with its anti-positivist epistemology, that is, its rejection of Humean general covering laws (Bhaskar, 1979; Steinmetz, 1998; Gorski, 2013; Porpora, 2015). Asking for a permanent architecture of fields requires acceptance at the metaphilosophical level of the idea of a general theory of society acceptance, that is, of a philosophically positivist premise.

In sum, we need to distinguish between social fields, social spaces and social practices existing outside shared systems of social meaning and therefore outside of social space. We can distinguish between settled and unsettled fields and between fields and their subfields. We can specify in advance two of the central axes defining the internal architecture of any field (although other axes may reveal themselves empirically): the axis of autonomy versus heteronomy, which points to the very definition of the field as a semi-autonomous realm of activity, and the axis of unequally distributed power resources, which defines fields as systems of domination. We can posit that while the state and the field of power tend to

 The Sociological Review Monographs, 64:2, pp. 98–123 (2016), DOI: 10.1111/2059-7932.12004

assume dominant positions in social space vis-à-vis all other fields, relations among the other fields obey no transhistorical logic.

Field theory and its imperial and colonial extensions

Bourdieu's field theory requires further extensions in order to make it suited for the historical study of empires. By way of introduction it is crucial that empires need to be distinguished from colonies, since not all empires are colonial and since colonies are the building blocs of colonial empires. Empires and colonies need to be distinguished from nation-states and from social spaces existing at the scale of national states (Steinmetz, 2014b). Moreover, no empire has ever covered the entire Earth, which means that 'imperial' cannot be equated with 'global.' Empires have usually coexisted with other empires, giving rise of inter-imperial dynamics, spaces, and fields. Finally, there are trans-imperial or meta-imperial practices. The precursors of transimperial practices included the Belgian Congo before 1908, which was regulated in principle by the Great Powers that met at the Berlin West Africa conference and remained open in principle to exploitation by all nations. A second precursor was the League of Nations Mandates system within which the former German colonies and Ottoman provinces were governed after World War I by a consortium of Great Powers. The twentieth century also saw the rise of trans-imperial scientific organizations such as the International African Institute (founded in 1926) and the Scientific Council for Africa South of the Sahara (created in 1950), organizations that were not controlled by any one imperial centre and that promoted scientific activity in European colonies carried out by scientists from all of the imperial nation-states.

What other extensions are required to make BFT suited for the historical study of empires? The first involves a further specification of the distinction between social fields and social spaces. This difference takes on a new importance once it is projected up to the geopolitical scale of empires. Social practices only rarely attain the distinctive characteristics that qualify them to be referred to fields even within a limited national social space. There are specific barriers to the extension of fields across the vast and hybrid social spaces of empires. Of course this does not mean that basic resources such as economic capital or military power cannot be extended into imperial territories. Once these sorts of resources begin to structure ongoing activity in overseas imperial zones and colonies we can speak of imperial and colonial social spaces.

What about imperial and colonial fields? What processes generate such fields, and what are their basic types, or social kinds? First, some fields are simply *extended* from metropoles into colonies with little alteration in form. Settler institutions such as the University of Algiers in the first half of the twentieth century or the colleges in the 13 American colonies illustrate a logic of extending fields. Some scientific practices were directly exported to the colonies with no alteration. One example of this was psychological testing for intelligence, aptitudes and work motivations, which was widely used in the selection of labourers and managers in colonial industry with little adjustment for context (see Études Sociales Nord Africaines, 1952; Trystram, 1953; Xydias, 1955, 1959; Juan, 1958–60). Metropolitan scholars posted to the colonial universities in British Bombay, French Algiers, or Belgian Léopoldville, to the *lycées* of the French settler colonies, or to the Nazi *Reichsuniversitäten* in occupied Eastern Europe often taught the same curriculum as in their respective metropoles.

Of course we cannot decide whether we are in the presence of simple extension or something else simply on the basis of appearances. Twentieth-century British colonial universities, for example, were directly modelled on metropolitan ones. The University College of the Gold Coast was modelled on Cambridge, complete with Halls of Residence and 'gowns, high tables, [and] Latin grace read by a scholar' (Ashby, 1961: 234). But that does not mean that these were mere extensions of the metropolitan university field. Among other things, several of the colonial university colleges in British Africa had sociology departments that directly thematized the specificity of colonial society (see Busia, 1946, 1953).

Second, some activities are constituted as differentiated *subfields* of overarching metropole-based fields. This idea is illustrated by some of the colonial sciences. Rather than simply exporting extant sciences to the colonies, Europeans developed new scientific subfields and applications tailored to the peculiarities of overseas colonial conditions. In tropical medicine, for example, there was a shift from the study of 'diseases in the tropics' to the study of 'tropical diseases' (Worboys, 1996). This process of specification also took place in the social sciences, where, as Singaravélou (2009: 98) argues, colonial experts were able to 'emancipate themselves from disciplinary traditions and elaborate new methods and categories of analysis'. I will illustrate this latter point below, using the example of the French sociology field and its colonial subfield after World War II. In most respects, however, colonial offshoots of science continued to participate in the metropolitan science fields; colonial scientists were trained in the same schools, received the same degrees, and competed for the same honours and positions as their metro-centric colleagues, while pursuing specifically colonial specialities.

Imperial scientific fields with their subfields did not necessarily correspond exactly to the exact contours of the empires in which they were located. They were structured around cores and peripheries, contained blank spots and points of concentrated activity, well-worn paths as well as paths that were rarely used. The French field of colonial sociology was concentrated in West and Equatorial Africa and the Maghreb, for example, while the British field was concentrated in Southern, Central, and West Africa (Steinmetz, 2015). As an example of the wide reach of these fields showing that they were nonetheless restricted to specific parts of geopolitical territory, consider the peripatetic career of ethno-sociologist David Bettison (Figure 1). A British-born disciple of Max Gluckman, Bettison earned his BA, MA and PhD at Rhodes University in South Africa, worked at the Rhodes-Livingstone-Institute in Lusaka between 1956 and the early 1960s, and taught sociology at the University of Rhodesia, Simon Fraser and Alberta in Canada, Australian National University, and University of Waikato in New

The Sociological Review Monographs, 64:2, pp. 98–123 (2016), DOI: 10.1111/2059-7932.12004

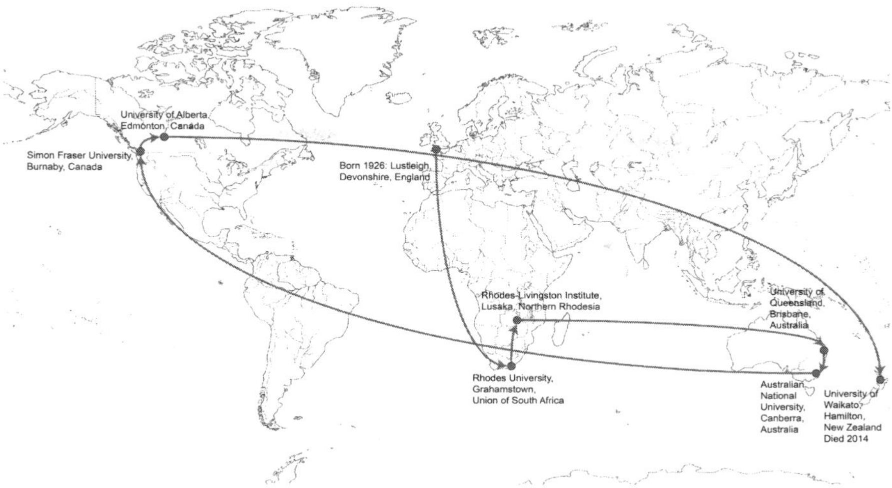

Figure 1 *Career trajectory of David Bettison*

Zealand. His career was this concentrated in the African and Commonwealth areas of the British Empire and 'British world' and did not include the Francophone parts of Africa or India, with its distinct history of distinguishing between sociology and anthropology (Uberoi *et al.*, 2007), so different from Africa where the boundaries between the two disciplines were more fluid and evolving (Steinmetz, 2013a, 2013b).

A third possibility is that certain realms of colonial activity are constituted as entirely separate fields in their own right. The colonial state exemplifies this possibility: colonial states were different in important respects from metropolitan states, and in most cases they were autonomous enough from the latter to be considered separate fields rather than subfields (Steinmetz, 2008). Limits on the circulation of officials and civil servants between colonial and metropolitan states, discussed below, underscore this point.

Imperial fields and imperial social spaces

Bourdieusian field theory rejects the assumption that all social practices take a fielded form.[8] This is an especially important precaution in studies of imperial, global, and transnational practices. Metropolitan practices are often fundamentally transformed by colonial and imperial contexts. Geopolitical boundaries and cultural barriers interrupt the flow of signifiers and resources across the colony-metropole boundary. It may be especially difficult for emigrated practices to maintain their fieldness.

Even where imperial practices are not configured as fields, however, they may still constitute colonial or imperial social spaces, defined as arenas in which commensurable practices and exchangeable capitals are circulating. Indeed, without some commensurability of this sort it is impossible to imagine how economic imperialism could work at all – how there could be extraction of resources and exploitation of labour and the export of metropolitan commodities. The settlers and officials of the British, French, Belgian, Portuguese, Dutch, and American empires participated in a common space defined by empire-wide cultural, social, and economic currencies.

Modern empires represented congeries of social fields and non-fielded social spaces. As a social space, any European empire was integrated around shared forms of generic cultural, social, and economic capital – forms that were found in the metropole and in all of its colonial outposts. Within these social spaces were specific fields. The clearest example of a colonial field involves colonial administration itself. The colonial state was separate from the metropolitan state in the ways that are relevant for determining whether it was an extended field, an extended subfield, or an entirely distinct field. The argument that the colonial state was a different field is based on several arguments. First, metropolitan colonial offices and overseas colonial states were organized around different forms of symbolic capital. For example, the German colonial state field before 1914 was governed by competition for a kind of ethnographic capital (Steinmetz, 2007, 2008), unlike the German metropolitan state and colonial office, where displays of ethnographic sagacity would be irrelevant at best, and could even be awkward or damaging. The British colonial state fields in twentieth-century Africa were organized around different forms of symbolic capital than the Colonial Office (see below). Second, if the colonial state were a mere subfield of the metropolitan state this would mean that all members of the former also qualified as members of the latter. But that was not the case. It was possible to become a 'member' (that is, an official or a civil servant) of a colonial administration without being accepted as a member of the metropolitan state. 'Vertical' mobility between metropolitan colonial offices and the overseas colonial service was limited and often impossible. The French colonies in the twentieth century had two levels of colonial civil servants, one set appointed by the metropolitan Colonial Ministry (called the Colonial Corps), the other recruited locally, consisting of contractual personnel (Cohen, 1971; Jumper, 1955). In the mid-twentieth century British empire, the Colonial Office and Administrative Service was responsible for the African colonies; India was the exclusive responsibility of the India Office and Indian Civil Service; Sudan was dealt with by the Sudan Political Service; and the Dominions Office dealt with Canada, Australia, New Zealand, South Africa, and independent post-colonies. Each of these offices guarded its prerogative to select its own personnel. Particular colonial states sometimes walled themselves off in ways that prevented penetration by officials from other colonies in the same empire.[9]

Nor was there a unified field consisting of all of the colonial states of a particular European empire, which would have allowed unfettered horizontal or 'lateral' movement. Officials could move back and forth among colonies in some cases but not others. Although many officials and experts moved readily among the three French North African colonies (Algeria, Morocco and Tunisia), there

 The Sociological Review Monographs, 64:2, pp. 98–123 (2016), DOI: 10.1111/2059-7932.12004

was much less movement between those colonies and the rest of the empire, and vice versa. The colonial administrations of the British Empire were even more fragmented. Entry into the British colonial service in India was controlled by competitive examination. Selection into the African service was governed by less formal qualifications (Austen, 1967; Furse, 1962). While there was some career mobility at the highest levels between the Indian administration and African governorships, the difference in training and recruitment practices limited movement at the lower levels of the colonial civil service. Given the limits on a civil servant's career mobility between, say, Kenya and India, and the separate legislation and informal official culture pertaining to each sub-empire and colony, the various colonies of the British Empire cannot be characterized as belonging to a single administrative field.

Imperial fields and subfields

A subfield is a differentiation internal to a field (Steinmetz, 2005a, 2010). A subfield shares certain features with its environing field while differing in other ways. But all of a subfield's members also participate in the environing field. They have to pass through the same gate-keeping mechanisms as all other participants in the larger field. Some discussions of this topic misleadingly fall back on the image of 'Russian dolls' to describe these kinds of relations, but this suggests that subfields simply mimic the larger model. This would be an image of isomorphism rather than homology. Instead, a subfield can differ formally, substantively and functionally from the surrounding field. A subfield may be governed by competition for subfield-specific stakes in addition to the stakes of the surrounding field. A subfield sometimes revises or inverts the values associated with particular practices in the broader field. In this respect much of the activity within a subfield is defined by its relations to the environing field even when the relationship is an entirely negative one. The case of political theory within US political science, for example, illustrates a systematic reversal of the discipline's dominant values: a preference for non-empirical rather than empirical and explicitly normative rather than value-neutral work, etc. (see Mihic *et al.*, 2005). At the same time, most political theorists have political science PhDs, are located in the same departments as those in the broader field, and attend the same national political science meetings.

Like fields, subfields are usually defined by at least two main axes: a 'vertical' one concerned with the volume of subfield-specific symbolic capital and a 'horizontal' one measuring autonomy from external forces. Within a subfield, however – and in contrast to dynamics within the generic, enveloping field – the external forces that are relevant include the surrounding field itself. One's own field represents a kind of outside to those in the subfield. Scholars located at the autonomous pole of a scientific subfield often seek allies and orientations beyond the field, while those at the subfield's heteronomous pole tend to mimic the values of the environing field.[10] Subfields can shield unorthodox and innovative work in a settled field, but they can also function as traps for peripheral or dominated members of fields.

Subfields sometimes play a key role in imperial fields. Medicine, architecture, urban planning, literature, and the military developed tropical specializations. Colonial specializations also developed within most of the natural and social sciences. In these colonial offshoots of metropolitan fields, the immediate context was explicitly taken into account, underwriting a series of distinctions between subfield and field.

Colonial sociology as the imperial subfield of metropolitan sociology

The example of a nascent colonial subfield that I want to discuss in some detail is colonial sociology in the British and French empires between the 1940s and 1950s (Steinmetz, 2013a, 2013b, 2015). These sociologists were also members of their overarching national sociological fields, which means that they formed a subfield and did not constitute an entirely separate field. They attended the same institutions of higher learning as their metropolitan-oriented colleagues; they obtained the same academic degrees;[11] they oriented themselves toward the same scholarly journals and canonical works.[12] They competed for the same posts in universities and research institutes and operated under the assumption that overseas postings were not permanent – although some opted to remain abroad after independence.

At the same time, members of the colonial subfield tended to define themselves against various mainstays of the dominant metropolitan discipline. The first and most obvious difference was their empirical focus on processes that encompassed metropoles and peripheries or linked multiple peripheries. Some of them explicitly thematized the differences that resulted from what Balandier (1951) defined as the 'colonial situation'. Others insisted that African or Asian realities could not be analysed using the categories deployed in metropolitan sociology (Mercier, 1954, 1965) – an argument akin to those being made here about field theory not simply being re-scalable up to the level of empire or the globe but requiring specific revisions. Some colonial sociologists opposed linear models of development. They called attention to the ways in which empire exploded the bounds of what is nowadays called 'methodological nationalism' by studying cycles of migration between colony and metropole (Banton, 1955; Montagne, 1957). Colonial sociologists were often more attentive to racial domination than their metrocentric colleagues; indeed one can say that the European sociology of race and ethnic studies grew directly out of the colonial engagement.[13] Finally, colonial sociologists after 1945 specifically valorized *fieldwork* over the compilation of existing ethnographies, although they also combined fieldwork with surveys, statistics, experimental methods, and archival research (eg Dampierre, 1967). Ethnographic fieldwork or community studies also arose in the French or British metropoles, but it tended to be conducted by sociologists or anthropologists who had experience in the colonies.[14] These colonial specialists tended to approach the familiar metropole as a foreign country.[15]

 The Sociological Review Monographs, 64:2, pp. 98–123 (2016), DOI: 10.1111/2059-7932.12004

The colonial subfield was defined relationally vis-à-vis other sectors of the French sociology field, other national sociologies and other disciplines. Colonial sociologists struggled to wrest sovereignty over the colonial object away from anthropologists during the 1940s and 1950s (Steinmetz, 2013a, 2013b, 2015). At the same time, sociologists in the colonial subfield were much more involved with anthropologists than the rest of the sociological discipline. Many British colonial sociologists had Anthropology PhDs, while many French colonial sociologists studied alongside ethnology students at the Paris *Institut d'ethnologie* and the *Centre de formation aux recherches ethnologiques*.[16] Quarrels between the two disciplines were partially attenuated by their shared educational and fieldwork experiences and their common commitment to ethnographic methods. Sociologists and anthropologists met at conferences and worked together on projects sponsored by agencies like UNESCO, whose postwar project on race and racism brought together sociologists, ethnologists, physical anthropologists, and social psychologists. The UNESCO-sponsored study of Stanleyville in the Belgian Congo was headed by an anthropologist (Forde) working with a psychologist and a sociologist, Valdo Pons (see Pons, 1956). The international 'Conference of Social Scientists on the Social Impact of Industrialization and Urban Conditions in Africa,' sponsored by UNESCO and held in Abidjan in 1954, was dominated by sociologists, despite the traditional influence of ethnologists over the study of Africa. Sociology and anthropology were on relatively equal footing at many international conferences in African during the 1950s (Figure 2). The colonial sociologists' partial affinity for anthropology was not shared by most of their metrocentric sociological colleagues.

The photograph in Figure 2[17] underscores another relational peculiarity of sociology's colonial subfields. The privileged international interlocutors of most metro-centred European sociologists after WWII were Americans,[18] although European sociologists located at the 'intellectual' pole (see below) gravitated toward other European social scientists and philosophers. Colonial sociologists' main interlocutors outside their own empires were other colonial sociologists and ethnologists. This photograph also points to a further peculiarity, since there are no Africans present. Nonetheless, colonial specialists like Balandier were the first European sociologists to work closely with African researchers, and Bourdieu was the first to coauthor an important study of a colonial situation with a sociologist who was born as a colonized subject, Abdelmalek Sayad.[19]

In order to better understand the web of relations that defined colonial subfields we need to reconstruct in the structure of the overall sociology fields in broad strokes. Consider the postwar French sociology field. As Heilbron (1991, 2015) has shown, the largest group within postwar French sociology was one that declared its independence from the Durkheimian traditions and tried to reorient the discipline toward empirical, presentist, and policy-oriented research. For this group American sociology seemed like 'Eldorado' and a study grant in the United States was like 'a voyage to Mecca' (Mendras, 1995: 43–44). Sociologists located at this pole were drawn toward psychology, economics and statistics. These disciplinary 'modernizers' were concentrated in the Sociology Section of the *Centre national de la recherche scientifique* (CNRS, the main national organization funding scientific research) and the CNRS-subsidized *Centre d'études sociologiques*, where the number of research posts grew steadily from the 1940s onward. This group was weakened, however, by the fact that most of its members did not have teaching positions in French universities and had not earned the higher prestige *agrégation* degree from the *École normale supérieure* (ENS) (Heilbron, 1991).

The other main pole in postwar French sociology was an 'intellectual' one associated with 'the theoretical and political concerns that dominated the intellectual field as a whole, especially by 'philosophers around Jean-Paul Sartre and his journal *Les Temps Modernes*' (Heilbron, 2015: 167–168). Georges Gurvitch and Raymond Aron were located at the centre of this grouping. The residual Durkheimian cluster, associated with the revived *Année sociologique*, was also linked to the intellectual pole.[20]

The powerful relational dynamics within the French sociology field are revealed by the fact that the colonial specialists were drawn into an alliance with the intellectual pole. The exemplary pairings in this respect were Georges Gurvitch with Georges Balandier and Raymond Aron with Pierre Bourdieu. Gurvitch was a grand theorist who resembled the Durkheimians in his orientation toward European social theory and philosophy but who developed

Figure 2 *Participants in the International African Institute seminar at Makerere University College, Kampala, Uganda, January 1959 (photo by Michael Banton, courtesy of Michael Banton)*

The Sociological Review Monographs, 64:2, pp. 98–123 (2016), DOI: 10.1111/2059-7932.12004

his own idiosyncratic approach. His work had no obvious connections with Balandier's colonial ethnography, but Balandier nonetheless became Gurvitch's protégé. Gurvitch invited Balandier to take over as editor of the journal *Cahiers internationaux de sociologie*, the first new sociology journal created after 1945 in France. Gurvitch co-founded the *Association internationale des sociologues de langue française*, whose first conference in 1958 was organized around the theme 'La sociologie des pays d'Outremer' (*outremer* was the official euphemism for the colonies at the time). Gurvitch was the only non-colonial specialist who participated in the sixth meeting of the *Association internationale des sociologues de langue française* in 1965. Thirteen of the chapters in Gurvitch's influential *Traité de sociologie* (1958) were written by colonial specialists such as Bastide, Balandier, Cazeneuve, Granaï, Mercier and Memmi.

What about Aron? He had published on the French empire starting in 1945 but in a more theoretical and journalistic manner (Aron, 1945, 1951, 1957). Aron was attracted to Bourdieu, whom he met in Algeria in 1959, because Bourdieu was an *agrégé* in philosophy and also perhaps because of Bourdieu's 'centre right' political stance at the time (Pérez, 2015: 92). Aron had already recruited another assistant, Eric de Dampierre, an ethnographer working in French Equatorial Africa. One might explain this affiliation through resonances of social class habitus – Dampierre was from the French aristocracy, Aron from the Parisian upper bourgeoisie. Also important was the style of Dampierre's work, which was distinctly non-scientistic.[21] Another sociologist whom Aron recruited to join the Center of European Sociology at the end of the 1950s was Jean Cuisenier, who had been associated with the Tunisian Institut des Hautes Études since 1954 and had published on Tunisian rural underdevelopment (Cuisenier, 1958). Like Bourdieu (and unlike Dampierre), Cuisenier had a philosophy *agrégation*.

Colonial sociology also received strong support from the remaining members of the old Durkheimian milieu after 1945. The revived Durkheimian journal *Année sociologique* devoted a great deal of space to colonial problems. Georges Davy, the last survivor of the original Dukheimian cluster, was involved in teaching sociology to students earning a *Licence* (master's) degree in Colonial Studies (*license d'études coloniales*) at the Sorbonne starting in 1945. Davy supported colonial social science as head of the 'Sociological Committee' of the national Superior Council of Overseas Sociological Research (*Conseil supérieur des recherches sociologiques outre-mer*) during the 1950s. Indeed, there was a smooth transition from the older style of Durkheimian sociology based on secondary sources to the newer style of colonial fieldwork carried out by professional sociologists. The easy coexistence between the two styles is revealed by their collaboration on the postwar *Année sociologique* and by various careers that straddled two formations.

The career of sociologist Jean Cazeneuve illustrates this transition from library research to fieldwork. Cazeneuve was born in 1915, a decade or two earlier than most of the colonial sociologists of the 1950s. He obtained the agrégation in philosophy with a diploma in ethnology before the war and then began work on his doctoral thesis, but was captured by the Wehrmacht in 1940 and spent the war as a POW in Germany. After spending two years teaching at the University of Alexandria, Cazeneuve returned to France and resumed work on his doctorate. His thesis supervisors were the Durkheimians Davy and H. Levy-Bruhl and his topic was Ur-Durkheimian: rites and symbols within 'primitive mentality'. In 1951 Cazeneuve described his research methodology in a report to the CNRS, and this consisted of reading books in the library. Three years later, a Rockefeller grant allowed Cazeneuve to carry out fieldwork among the New Mexican Zuñi. Cazeneuve had made the transition from philosopher to sociologist, from prewar Durkheimian to postwar fieldworker.[22] Bourdieu's own transition from philosopher to sociologist was more rapid but can be tracked in his shift from his library-based first book on Algeria (1958) to the subsequent fieldwork based work (eg Bourdieu, 1963).

In short, the colonial studies subfield was not a passive component of the enveloping field but evolved in dynamic relation to the environing sociology discipline. Colonial researchers entered into a somewhat contingent alliance with French sociology's intellectual pole and into a less surprising alliance with the remaining Durkheimian cluster.

The distribution of generic and field-specific symbolic capital within the French sociology field and its colonial subfield, 1940s–1960s

There is a widespread misunderstanding of fields as being defined solely by dynamics of contestation. Fields are relational spaces, but not all relations are conflictual. Fields are also spaces of reciprocal recognition and joint activity. It would be difficult to speak of a field at all in the absence of a fundamental, shared agreement among all field participants on a number things: the definition of their ongoing activity, the stakes of competition, the location of boundaries against the outside world, and the history of their particular practices. Processes of field formation are as important as internal conflicts within a field. To understand the colonial subfield of sociology in the 1940s–1950s, for example, we first need to explore sociologists' joint battle to extend their sovereignty over the colonial object, a battle that mainly involved seizing ontological territory from anthropologists (Steinmetz, 2013b, 2015).

That said, fields are also arenas of division, domination and struggle. They are characterized by unequal distributions of generic resources and field-specific types of capital. In light of the case study discussed above, what can we say about the relative positioning of colonial specialists in these sociological fields?

First, colonial sociologists did not have less sociological symbolic capital, on average, than non-colonial sociologists. They were not a uniformly dominated sector of the sociology field. Colonial specialists occupied many of the key positions in the French (and British) sociological fields. There were only a few sociologists at the Sorbonne and Collège de France, but many of these were oriented toward colonial or imperial questions (Aron, Bastide, Berque, Maunier, and Montagne); others promoted colonial research with their institutional resources (Cazeneuve, Davy). Three other institutions had larger concentrations

The Sociological Review Monographs, 64:2, pp. 98–123 (2016), DOI: 10.1111/2059-7932.12004

of professional sociologists: the Sixth Section of the *École pratique des hautes études* (EPHE; which became the *École des hautes études en sciences sociales* or EHESS in 1975), the Centre d'études sociologiques or CES (the main CNRS-financed Sociological Research Center), and the CNRS, which had a separate Sociology section starting in 1945 (Lautman, 2013). The sociology teaching staff at the Sixth Section during the second half of the 1950s included Bastide, Balandier and Berque. By 1961–62 there were 36 professors (*Directeurs d'études*) and one associate professor teaching in the 'Sociology and Ethnology' division of the Sixth Section. Of these, 18 were associated with research on colonized populations or empires.[23] An analysis of students' thesis committees (*juries de thèse*) at the Sixth Section of the EPHE finds that Balandier, Bastide and Mercier, together with Africanist ethnologist Denise Paulme, constituted the core cluster of supervisors in the entire school between 1960 and 1964, suggesting the centrality of colonial and postcolonial questions (Godechot, 2011). A detailed examination of the PhD dissertations directed by Balandier in the 1950s and 1960s demonstrates that they were indeed framed in terms of sociology (sometimes combined with ethnology) and that colonial practices of domination played a central role in their explanatory accounts and were not bracketed, as in most prewar ethnology. Balandier's foundational essay on the 'colonial situation' (1951) played a talismanic role in this Africanist sociology, as can be seen in a series of doctoral dissertations written at the EPHE's Sixth Section in the late 1950s and early 1960s in the area of 'regional sociology'.[24]

Another way to detect power asymmetries within a discipline is to reconstruct participants' inherited and accumulated resources. Although a full analysis of this sort is beyond the scope of this paper, we can say a few general things about the colonial grouping in French sociology. Here we need first to recall that there were two main educational trajectories into sociological careers in France. One route was based on the *agrégation* in philosophy. Karady notes that all of the 'major newcomers in the central teaching positions devoted to the social sciences' after 1945 'had in common a high level of formal training in philosophy' (1981: 42), and that this was true not just of 'Europeanists' like Aron and Bourdieu but also of the leading 'modernizers' in quantitative methods and industrial and social psychology such as Jean Stoetzel and Georges Friedmann. A second trajectory path was quite common among social scientists carrying out fieldwork in the colonies and holding research posts with ORSTOM, IFAN, and the like. This trajectory started with coursework at the Paris Ethnological Institute (the *Institut d'ethnologie*, created in 1925), followed by an internship at the Centre for Education in Ethnographic Research (*Centre de formation aux recherches ethnologiques,* created in 1946). The majority of these researchers eventually earned a doctoral dissertation at the EPHE or the Sorbonne, many were employed at one of the overseas branches of the Office of Colonial Research (ORSC, later ORSTOM) or the French Institute of Black Africa (IFAN), and some obtained professorships in the colonial and postcolonial universities or the French metropole. A typical example of this second trajectory is Georges Balandier, whose lack of a philosophy background was compensated to some extent by his literary affiliations (with Leiris, Sartre, and the journal *Présence africaine*), political connections (Balandier worked for the French Colonial/Overseas Ministry for a year), and his doctoral thesis in 1955, not to mention a huge array of additional teaching appointments and doctoral students.

The most important point in the present context is that there were leading figures in both the colonial and non-colonial groupings. The colonial subfield grouping had a slightly stronger representation at the *Collège de France* and the Sorbonne than the non-colonial grouping. Although the modernizing pole and the metrocentric French sociologists were predominant quantitatively in the field, with 60–75 per cent of the members, this does not necessarily entail qualitative dominance.

Conclusion

Fields, as Bourdieu argued, are entirely relational structures, defined by positions rather than substances, by homological relations, structural reversals and inversions, etc. The present article suggested that the surprisingly strong position of colonial sociology within French sociology after 1945 resulted partly from a rather contingent alliance with the other dominated grouping in the field – the 'intellectual' pole, with its residual Durkheimians and its European-oriented theorists. This alliance occurred despite strong political differences within the 'colonial camp' and despite the apparent polarization between the philosophical sociologists' disdain for fieldwork and the strongly empirical orientation of the colonial specialists.

This paper also proposed a theory of social fields at the scale of empires. I argued that the fields cannot be assumed to be coextensive with the nation-state but often extend beyond those boundaries. I then argued that metropolitan expansion may create imperial social spaces, introducing economic, cultural, military and scientific resources into new geographic spaces, but that this does not yet tell us whether social fields have been extended or created in the conquered territories. An *imperial social space* was defined as a realm of empire-spanning practice whose organization lacks a specific form of symbolic capital, stakes, habitus and illusio, and lacks border-policing mechanisms and 'internal governance units'.

On the other hand, modern colonial empires were characterized by different kinds of fields: fields that were simply extended into the overseas territories, fields that generated colonial subfields, and completely new, separate fields located only within overseas territories. The colonial state field is an example of a type of field that is unique, new and specific to the colony. By contrast, scientific fields provide examples of fields that are sometimes simply extended from the metropole into the colonies and in other cases lead to colonial subfields. The extension of certain fields brought with it the elaboration of new forms of practice that were organized around coloniality itself. While remaining part of the metropolitan field, these

 The Sociological Review Monographs, 64:2, pp. 98–123 (2016), DOI: 10.1111/2059-7932.12004

practices had *differentia specifica* linked to their colonial orientation. In sociology the relevant subfield was characterized by an emphasis on the colonial territory as research site and colonialism as object of analysis. Colonial sociology was an example of this subfield logic.

Acknowledgments

The author would like to acknowledge the helpful comments of the SR reviewers. Special thanks to Larissa Buchholz for reading and commenting on several versions of the essay, to Yingyao Wang for sharing her forthcoming article with me and to Amin Perez for copies of Pierre Bourdieu's unpublished correspondence.

Notes

1 Bourdieu's (1963) vehement rejection of Michel Leiris' criticism of colonial ethnography can be understood in light of Bourdieu's contributions to the French propaganda campaign in Algeria as a 'rédacteur-concepteur' for the French Military Cabinet's Information Service (Pérez, 2015) and his subsequent efforts to carry out scientifically autonomous research on such controversial policies as the army's resettlement camps (Jammet, 2013).

2 None of the major projects (on photography, museums, universities, peasant marriage patterns, and 'the bank and its clientele') that Bourdieu carried out between the end of his Algerian fieldwork in 1960 and the 1965 article on the field deployed the field concept, although the word field ('champ') is used several times in *Les Héritiers* (1965). Nonetheless, Bourdieu already noted in a letter to his Algerian collaborator Abdelmalak Sayad in 1959 that he was rethinking his analysis of honor in Kabyle culture through "a Lewinian perspective". It is widely recognized that Bourdieu's field concept originally drew on Kurt Lewin's field theory, but his interest in Lewin is usually dated to the mid-1960s when his first articles using the field concept appeared in print. Letter from Bourdieu to Sayad, in Fonds d'Archives Abdelmalek Sayad (FAAS), Musée de l'Histoire de l'Immigration (MHI), Paris, France.

3 Bourdieu returned briefly to the colonial context in Bourdieu (1976) and in his self-analysis (Bourdieu, 2000). He mentioned the colonial context only fleetingly in his Collège de France lectures on the state in 1989–92 (Bourdieu, 2013: 233, 354).

4 Some commentators trace Bourdieu's field theory to his reading of Weber's sociology of religion. It is clear, however, that many of the core concepts, including symbolic capital, recognition, *nomos* and *nomothète*, relative autonomy, and the ideas of a space of positions, position taking, and homologies, have very different sources. Bourdieu's first article on field theory (1965) refers more frequently to Althusser and Panofsky than to Weber.

5 At the opposite extreme from realms in which there is not even agreement about the basic stakes of competition are realms in which there is lockstep agreement not just about the stakes of competition and their principle of distribution but also about the relative ranking of every single position and actor in the field. Cases like this, however improbable, are too rigid to be called fields. Bourdieu discusses the possibility of a field becoming an *apparatus,* when 'all movements go exclusively from the top down … such that the struggle and the dialectic that are constitutive of the field cease' (Bourdieu and Wacquant, 1992: 102). The idea of apparatus corresponds to a rigid structuralist logic, the conversion of every action into 'the simple *execution* of a rule' (Bourdieu, 1990a: 88).

6 Thanks to Larissa Buchholz for discussing these ideas with me.

7 Bourdieu's historicism is not the same as nineteenth-century historicism, which refused all explanation and comparison, but is closer to the neo-historicist philosophy of Heinrich Rickert and

Max Weber. This twentieth-century *neo*-historicism preserves the uniqueness of the event while arguing that it is possible to explain the singular event in terms of a conjuncture of separate, contingently intersecting causal chains.

8 See for example Mathieu (2007), who argues that social movements are best construed as a social space rather than a field, even if specific movements may have fieldlike characteristics.

9 The German colony of Kiaochow, for example, was overseen by the Navy rather than the Colonial Office; this meant that the colony's governors had to be navy captains and that none of them could transfer out to governorships of other German colonies. Officers who received training for service in the *Affaires Indigènes* office of the French Algerian administration were not qualified for service in other colonies, and vice versa.

10 This argument is based on studies of several different field-subfield relations. The American sociological subfield of historical sociology, for example, is divided between an autonomous pole that interacts mainly with historians and a heteronomous pole that configures its work along the lines of what it understands as mainstream sociology; see Calhoun (1996); Steinmetz (2005b).

11 Members of the colonial sociological subfield sometimes earned specialized degrees such as the French colonial 'Licence' degree, but they always also obtained a generic academic degree such as the philosophy *agrégation* or the *doctorat-ès-lettres*.

12 John Barnes had his African students in Lusaka read Parsons in the late 1940s; Clyde Mitchell referred to the American sociologists Shils and Homans as the 'heavenly twins'. Mitchell papers, Rhodes House, Barnes to Mitchell, 21 February 1949. MSS.Afr.s.1998, Box 4, file 1, p. 26; Mitchell to Merran, 1 April 1953, MSS.Afr.s.1998, Box 2, File 1, p. 43.

13 The leading social scientific journal of race relations studies in Britain, *Race* (later *Race and Class*), was oriented in its first few years mainly toward colonial problems.

14 One of the two creators of the British Mass Observation project before WWII was Tom Harrisson, who had worked as a government anthropologist in Sarawak. British community studies were carried out by colonial ethnographers in Liverpool, Edinburgh, London and Wales. French community studies were sponsored by UNESCO during the 1940s and 1950s in Asnières-sur-Oise (Dampierre, 1956), Vienne sur le Rhône (Clément and Xydias, 1955), and 'Nouville' (Bernot, 1953) in Normandy. At the time of publication Dampierre had already started his fieldwork in Ubangi; Clément had published on African culture; and Bernot was working toward a *Licence* degree in sociology, ethnology, Chinese civilization and colonial history.

15 British ethnosociologist Ronnie Frankenberg, a student of Max Gluckman, was prevented from carrying out his doctoral research in the British West Indies due to his Communist politics and instead wrote an ethnographic study of a Welsh village as a sort of internal colony (Frankenberg, 1957). René Gouellain, urban sociologist in French Cameroon, worked on a doctoral thesis on 'activités lointaines' and 'espaces non-continentaux' in which he developed a 'colonial' critique of 'notre sociologie "continentale"' and criticized a sociological language that was 'instinctivement terrien'. Gouellain, 'Sur l'état de ma thèse en vue du Doctorat d'État' (report to CNRS, September 1971: 1, 9–10), in CNRS Dépôt des archives, Gif-sur-Yvette, France. My thanks to archivist Isabelle Dujonc for help with Gouellain's file,

16 See Conklin (2013) and Gutwirth (2001) on these institutions.

17 Seven of the people shown in the photo were anthropologists; six were more closely associated with sociology. Another participant in the volume that came out of this conference was René Gouellain, who held the post of sociologist at the IFAN Center in Yaoundé, Cameroon at the time (see n. 15).

18 See Kropp (2015), for a telling but less familiar case, Danish sociology.

19 See Pérez (2015) on the decades-long intellectual and political relationship between the two sociologists.

20 The editors of the first postwar volume of *Année sociologique* included Georges Davy, Sorbonne sociology professor and a contemporary of Durkheim, and Maurice Leenhardt, who had been a student of Mauss.

 The Sociological Review Monographs, 64:2, pp. 98–123 (2016), DOI: 10.1111/2059-7932.12004

21 Dampierre published translations of Leo Strauss and E. Franklin Frazier's *Black Bourgeoisie*, and he asked Aron to write an introduction to his translation of Weber's *Wissenschaft als Beruf*. Aron involved Dampierre in the creation of the *Centre de sociologie européenne*, even before involving Bourdieu, and he worked closely with Dampierre in launching the new sociology journal, *Archives européennes de sociologie*. Both the *Centre* and the *Archives* represented a strong pushback against the Americanizing tendencies within French Sociology at the time. On Dampierre see Buckner (2010); also Dampierre papers, Nanterre; Author's interview with Ms. Catherine Perlès at MAE, Nanterre, February 2014.

22 See Rapport to CNRS, 20 Feb. 1951, CNRS archives, Cazeneuve dossier; also Cazeneuve (1957, 1989).

23 EPHE, Section des sciences économiques et sociales, *Annuaire* (1956/57–1965/66).

24 See for example the doctoral theses of Agblémagnon (1964); Clignet (1963); Gosselin (1964); and Gouellain (1969).

References

Agamben, G., (1998), *Homo Sacer: Sovereign Power and Bare Life*, Stanford, CA: Stanford University Press.

Agblémagnon, F. N'S., (1964), 'Rôle sociologique du matériel oral dans une société africaine: les Eue du Sud-Togo', Thèse 3ème cycle, Sociologie régionale, Paris, E.P.H.E., VI^0 sec.

Aron, R., (1945), *L'Âge des empires et l'Avenir de la France*, Paris: Défense de la France.

Aron, R., (1951), *Les Guerres en chaîne*, Paris: Gallimard.

Aron, R., (1957), *La Tragédie algérienne*, Paris: Plon.

Ashby, E., (1961), *Patterns of Universities in Non-European Societies*, London: School of Oriental and African Studies.

Austen, R., (1967), 'The official mind of indirect rule: British policy in Tanganyika, 1916–1939', in P. Gifford and W. R. Louis (eds.), *Britain and Germany in Africa: Imperial Rivalry and Colonial Rule*, New Haven: Yale University Press.

Balandier, G., (1951), 'La situation coloniale: approche théorique', *Cahiers internationaux de sociologie*, 11: 44–79.

Banton, M., (1955), *The Coloured Quarter: Negro Immigrants in an English City*, London: Cape.

Bernot, L., (1953), *Nouville, un village français*, Paris: Institut d'ethnologie.

Bhaskar, R., (1979), *The Possibility of Naturalism*, New York: Humanities.

Bourdieu, P., (1958), *Sociologie de l'Algérie*, 1st edn, Paris: Presses Universitaires de France.

Bourdieu, P., (1961), *Sociologie de l'Algérie*, 2nd edn, Paris: Presses Universitaires de France.

Bourdieu, P., (1963), 'Étude sociologique', in P. Bourdieu, A. Darbel, J.-P. Rivet and C. Seibel, *Travail et travailleurs en Algérie*, 253–562, Paris: Mouton.

Bourdieu, P., (1965), 'Projet créateur et champ intellectuel', Paris: Centre de Sociologie Européenne (unpublished document).

Bourdieu, P., (1966), 'Champ intellectuel et projet créateur', *Les temps modernes*, 22 (246): 865–890.

Bourdieu, P., (1976), 'Les conditions sociales de la production sociologique. Sociologie coloniale et décolonisation de la sociologie', in H. Moniot (ed.), *Le mal de voir*, 416–427, Paris: Union Générale d'Éditions.

Bourdieu, P., (1988), *Homo academicus*, Cambridge: Polity Press.

Bourdieu, P., (1990a), 'Droit et passe-droit', *Actes de la recherche en sciences sociales*, 81–82, 86–96.

Bourdieu, P., (1990b), *The Logic of Practice*, Cambridge: Polity Press.

Bourdieu, P., (1991), 'On the possibility of a field of world sociology', in P. Bourdieu and J. S. Coleman (eds.), *Social Theory for a Changing Society*, 373–387, Boulder, CO: Westview Press.

Bourdieu, P., (1993), 'Some properties of fields', in Bourdieu, *Sociology in Question*, 72–77, London: Sage.

Bourdieu, P., (1996), *The Rules of Art*, Cambridge: Polity Press.

Bourdieu, P., (2000), *Propos sur le champ politique*, Lyon: Presses universitaires de Lyon.

Bourdieu, P., (2002), 'Habitus', in J. Hillier and E. Rooksby (eds), *Habitus: A Sense of Place*, 27–34, Aldershot: Ashgate.
Bourdieu, P., (2012). *Sur l'état*, Paris: Seuil.
Bourdieu, P., (2013), 'Séminaires sur le concept de champ, 1972–1975', *Actes de la recherche en sciences sociales*, 200 (Dec.): 4–37.
Bourdieu, P., Christin, O. and Will, P.-E., (2000), 'Sur la science de l'État', *Actes de la recherche en sciences sociales*, 133: 3–11.
Bourdieu, P. and Wacquant, L., (1992), *An Invitation to Reflexive Sociology*, Chicago: University of Chicago Press.
Buckner, M., (2010), 'Eric de Dampierre and the art of fieldwork', in R. Parkin and A. de Sales (eds), *Out of the Study and into the Field: Ethnographic Theory and Practice in French Anthropology*, 103–124, New York: Berghahn.
Burke, P., (1990), *The French Historical Revolution: The Annales School*, 1929–1989, Stanford, CA: Stanford University Press.
Busia, K. A., (1946), 'Educational policy in West Africa: a rejoinder', *Oversea Education*, 17 (4): 343–345.
Busia, K. A., (1953), 'Recent developments in sociological research in West Africa', International Sociological Association, *Communications, Papers*, vol. 1.
Calhoun, C., (1996), 'The rise and domestication of historical sociology', in T. J. McDonald (ed.), *The Historic Turn in the Human Sciences*, 305–338, Ann Arbor, MI: University of Michigan Press.
Cazeneuve, J., (1957), *Les dieux dansent à Cibola le Shalako des indiens Zuñis*, Paris: Gallimard.
Cazeneuve, J., (1989), *Les hasards d'une vie*, Paris: Buchet.
Clément, P. and Xydias, N., (1955), *Vienne-sur-le-Rhône. La ville et les habitants, situations et attitudes. Sociologie d'une cité française*, Paris: Unesco.
Clignet, R. (1963), 'Tradition et Evolution de la vie familiale en Côte d'Ivoire', Thèse 3ème cycle, Sociologie régionale, Paris, E.P.H.E., VI^0 sec.
Cohen, W. B. (1971), *Rulers of Empire: The French Colonial Service in Africa*, Stanford, CA: Hoover Institution Press.
Conklin, A. L., (2013), *In the Museum of Man: Race, Anthropology, and Empire in France*, 1850–1950, Ithaca, NY: Cornell University Press.
Cuisenier, J., (1958), 'Le sous-developpment economique dans une groupement rural en Tunisie: le Djebel Lansarine', *Cahiers de Tunisie* 6 (23–24): 219–266.
Dampierre, E. de, (1956), 'Malvire-sur-Desle. Une commune aux franges de la region parisienne', *L'information géographique*, 20: 68–73.
Dampierre, E. de, (1967), *Un ancien royaume Bandia du Haut-Oubangui*, Paris: Plon.
Études Sociales Nord Africaines, (1952), 'La psychotechnique au service des Nord-Africains', *Cahiers nord-africains no*. 20.
Fligstein, N. and McAdam, D., (2012), *A Theory of Fields*, Oxford: Oxford University Press.
Frankenberg, R., (1957), *Village on the Border; a Social Study of Religion, Politics and Football in a North Wales Community*, London: Cohen & West.
Furse, Sir R., (1962), *Aucuparius. Recollections of a Recruiting Officer*, London: Oxford University Press.
Godechot, O., (2011), 'La formation des relations académiques au sein de l'EHESS', *Histoire et mesure*, 26: 223–260.
Goh, D. P. S., (2007), 'States of ethnography: colonialism, resistance and cultural transcription in Malaya and the Philippines, 1890s–1930s', *Comparative Studies in Society and History*, 49 (1): 109–142.
Gorski, P. S., (2013), 'What is critical realism? And why should you care?', *Contemporary Sociology: A Journal of Reviews*, 42: 658–670.
Gosselin, G., (1964), 'Sociologie du travail en pays Gbeya: R.C.A.', Thèse 3ème cycle, Sociologie régionale, Paris, E.P.H.E., VI^0 sec.
Gouellain, R., (1969), 'Douala, Sociologie d'une ville colonial', Thèse 3ème cycle, Sociologie régionale, Paris, E.P.H.E., VI^0 sec.

 The Sociological Review Monographs, 64:2, pp. 98–123 (2016), DOI: 10.1111/2059-7932.12004

Groff, R. (ed.), (2013), *Powers and Capacities in Philosophy: The New Aristotelianism*, New York: Routledge.
Gurvitch, G. (ed.), (1958), *Traité de sociologie*, Paris: Presses universitaires de France.
Gutwirth, J., (2001), 'La professionnalisation d'une discipline: Le centre de formation aux recherches ethnologiques', *Gradhiva*, 29: 25–41.
Heilbron, J., (1991), 'Pionniers par défaut? Les débuts de la recherche au Centre d'études sociologiques (1946–1960)', *Revue française de sociologie*, 32: 365–379.
Heilbron, J., (2015), *French Sociology*, Ithaca, NY: Cornell University Press.
Jammet, Y., (2013), 'Abdelmalek Sayad, les années d'apprentissage', in T. Yacine, Y. Jammet and C. de Montlibert (eds), *Abdelemalek Sayad. La découverte de la sociologie en tamps de guerre*, 17–127, Nantes: Éditions Nouvelles Cécile Defaut.
Juan, M., (1958–1960), *Recherche de certaines bases psychotechniques pour le mieux être des travailleurs maliens. Études réalisées avec le concours de l'Office du Niger (en 1958 et 1960), sous la patronage technique de PROHUZA*, Paris, n.p.
Jumper, R., (1955), 'The recruitment and training of civil administrators for overseas France: a case study of French bureaucracy', PhD dissertation, Duke University.
Karady, V., (1981), 'Prehistory of present day French sociology (1917–1957)', in C. Lemert (ed.), *French Sociology Today*, 33–47, New York: Columbia University Press.
Kropp, K., (2015), *A Historical Account of Danish Sociology – A Troubled Sociology*, Basingstoke: Palgrave Macmillan.
Lautman, J., (2013), 'Le CNRS et la sociologie', *Histoire de la recherche contemporaine* 2 (2).
Lawson, T., (1998), 'Economic science without experimentation/abstraction', in R. Bhaskar, A. Collier, T. Lawson, M. Archer and A. Norrie, *Critical Realism, Essential Readings*, 144–185, London: Routledge.
Lawson, T., (2013), 'Emergence and causation', in R. Groff (ed.), *Powers and Capacities in Philosophy: The New Aristotelianism*, 285–307, New York: Routledge.
Liu, L. H., (2004), *The Clash of Empires: The Invention of China in Modern World Making*, Cambridge, MA: Harvard University Press.
Mathieu, L., (2007), 'L'espace des mouvements sociaux', *Politix*, 77: 131–151.
Mead, G., (2013), 'Sense of structure and structure of sense: Pierre Bourdieu's habitus as a generative principle', PhD thesis, School of Social and Political Sciences, University of Melbourne.
Medvetz, T., (2012), *Think Tanks in America*, Chicago: University of Chicago Press.
Mendras, H., (1995), *Comment devenir sociologue ou les mémoires d'un vieux mandarin*, Arles: Actes Sud.
Mercier, P., (1965), 'Les classes sociales et les changements politiques récentes en Afrique noire.' *Cahiers internationaux de sociologie*, 38 (N.S. 12): 143–154.
Mercier, P., (1954), 'Aspects des problèmes de stratification sociale dans l'Ouest Africain', *Cahiers internationaux de sociologie*, 17: 47–65.
Mihic, S., Engelmann, S. G. and Wingrove, E. R., (2005), 'Facts, values, and "real" numbers', in G. Steinmetz (ed.), *The Politics of Method in the Human Sciences: Positivism and its Epistemological Others*, 470–495, Durham, NC: Duke University Press.
Montagne, R., (1957), *Étude sociologique de la migration des travailleurs musulmans d'Algérie en métropole*, 8 vols., Paris.
Pérez, A., (2015), 'Rendre le social plus politique. Guerre coloniale, immigration et pratiques sociologiques d'Abdelmalek Sayad et de Pierre Bourdieu', Thèse pour le doctorat de sociologie, EHESS, Paris.
Pons, P., (1956), 'The growth of Stanleyville and the composition of its African population', in D. Forde (ed.), *Social Implications of Industrialization and Urbanization in Africa South of the Sahara*, 229–274, Paris: UNESCO.
Porpora, D., (2015), *Reconstructing Sociology: The Critical Realist Approach*, Cambridge: Cambridge University Press.
Sapiro, G., (2004), 'La formation de la théorie de l'*habitus*', in L. Pinto, G. Sapiro and P. Champagne (eds), *Pierre Bourdieu, sociologue*, 49–92, Paris: Fayard.

Singaravélou, P., (2009), 'Le moment "impérial" de l'histoire des sciences sociales (1880–1910)', *Mil neuf cent. Revue d'histoire intellectuelle*, 27: 87–102.
Smith, C., (2010), *What Is a Person? Rethinking Humanity, Social Life, and the Moral Good from the Person Up*, Chicago: University of Chicago Press.
Steinmetz, G., (1998), 'Critical realism and historical sociology', *Comparative Studies in Society and History*, 40 (1): 170–186.
Steinmetz, G., (2002), 'Precoloniality and colonial subjectivity: ethnographic discourse and native policy in German overseas imperialism, 1780s–1914', *Political Power and Social Theory*, 15: 135–228.
Steinmetz, G., (2003), 'The devil's handwriting: precolonial discourse, ethnographic acuity and cross-identification in German colonialism', *Comparative Studies in Society and History*, 45 (1): 41–95.
Steinmetz, G., (2005a), 'Scientific authority and the transition to post-Fordism: the plausibility of positivism in American sociology since 1945', in G. Steinmetz (ed.), *The Politics of Method in the Human Sciences: Positivism and its Epistemological Others*, 275–323, Durham, NC, Duke University Press.
Steinmetz, G., (2005b), 'American sociology's epistemological unconscious and the transition to post-Fordism: the case of historical sociology', in J. Adams, E. Clemens and A. Orloff (eds), *Remaking Modernity: Politics, Processes and History in Sociology*, 109–157, Durham, NC: Duke University Press.
Steinmetz, G., (2007), *The Devil's Handwriting: Precoloniality and the German Colonial State in Qingdao, Samoa, and Southwest Africa*, Chicago: University of Chicago Press.
Steinmetz, G., (2008), 'The colonial state as a social field', *American Sociological Review*, 73: 589–612.
Steinmetz, G., (2009), 'The imperial entanglements of sociology in the United States, Britain, and France since the 19th century', *Ab Imperio*, 4: 1–56.
Steinmetz, G., (2010), 'Ideas in exile: refugees from Nazi Germany and the failure to transplant historical sociology into the United States', *International Journal of Politics, Culture, and Society*, 23 (1): 1–27.
Steinmetz, G., (2011), 'Bourdieu, historicity, and historical sociology', *Cultural Sociology*, 5 (1): 45–66.
Steinmetz, G., (2013a), 'A child of the Empire: British sociology and colonialism, 1940s–1960s', *Journal of the History of the Behavioral Sciences*, 49 (4): 353–378.
Steinmetz, G., (2013b), 'British sociology in the metropole and the colonies, 1940s–1960s', in J. Scott and J. Holmwood (eds), *The Palgrave Handbook of Sociology in Britain*, 302–337, Basingstoke: Palgrave Macmillan.
Steinmetz, G., (2014a), 'État-mort, État-fort, État-empire', *Actes de la recherche en sciences sociales*, 201: 112–119.
Steinmetz, G., (2014b), 'The sociology of empires, colonialism, and postcolonialism', *Annual Review of Sociology*, 40: 77–103.
Steinmetz, G., (2015), 'Sociology and colonialism in the British and French Empires (1940s–1960s): the forgotten origins of a discipline', *Journal of Modern History*.
Trystram, J. P., (1953), 'Recherches psychotechniques au Maroc : principes et applications', *Bulletin économique et Social du Maroc*, 57: 219–225.
Uberoi, P., Sundar, N. and Deshpane S. (eds), (2007), *Anthropology in the East: Founders of Indian Sociology and Anthropology*, New Delhi: Permanent Black.
Wang, Y., (forthcoming), 'Homology and isomorphism: Bourdieu in conversation with New institutionalism', *British Journal of Sociology*.
Will, P.-E., (2000), 'Science et sublimation de l'État', *Actes de la recherche en sciences sociales*, 133: 13–25.
Worboys, M., (1996), 'Germs, malaria and the invention of Mansonian tropical medicine: from "diseases in the tropics" to "tropical diseases"', *Clio medica*, 35: 181–207.
Xydias, N., (1955), 'Un test de situations appliqué au Congo belge', *Le Travail Humain*, 18 (1): 109–123.

The Sociological Review Monographs, 64:2, pp. 98–123 (2016), DOI: 10.1111/2059-7932.12004

Xydias, N., (1959), 'Sélection psychotechnique et main-d'œuvre au Sahara', in Comité de coordination scientifique de Sahara (ed.), *Journées d'information Médico-sociales sahariennes*, 223–228, Paris: Arts et métiers graphiques.
Yacine, T., (2013), 'At the origins of a singular ethnosociology', in P. Bourdieu, *Algerian Sketches*, 13–34, Cambridge: Polity Press.
Yacine, T., Jammet, Y. and Montlibert, C. de, (2013), *Abdelemalek Sayad. La découverte de la sociologie en tamps de guerre*, Nantes.
Žižek, J., (2013), *Demanding the Impossible*, Cambridge: Polity Press.

Please quote the article DOI when citing SR content, including monographs. Article DOIs and "How to Cite" information can be found alongside the online version of each article within Wiley Online Library. All articles published within the SR (including monograph content) are included within the ISI Journal Citation Reports® Social Science Citation Index.

Taken in by the numbers game: the globalization of a religious 'illusio' and 'doxa' in nineteenth-century evangelical missions to India

Martin Petzke

Abstract: While the Bourdieusian concepts of capital and relational configurations of positions and position-takings have recently been fruitfully employed to theorize global fields, this paper argues that the concepts of *illusio* and *doxa* are especially conducive to analyzing the *globalization* of a field as an expansion into and transformation of formerly independent national arenas. In deploying the concept of *illusio* as a (quasi-libidinous) investment in the game, globalization is here first and foremost framed as a process in which more and more actors in various contexts 'succumb' to specific field logics that orient them to transnational structures. By emphasizing the concept of *doxa* as the taken-for-granted fundamentals of a field, the paper furthermore calls attention to the mechanisms that help forge and globalize the tacit presuppositions and shared ontologies on which such logics build. Focusing on a field of global Christian missions that emerged during the nineteenth century, the paper illustrates how its competitive logic of proselytization was introduced into the religious arena of India. It highlights how Western notions of religion gained ground among local traditions and pulled them into a game in which numerical relations of adherents mattered.

Keywords: religion, globalization, Pierre Bourdieu, 19th century, India, quantification

Introduction

Recent endeavours to theorize global fields from a perspective of Bourdieusian field theory have broadened our understanding of transnational institutional orders in highlighting how action in these domains is structured by competitive struggles for legitimacy and relational configurations of positions and position-takings (eg Casanova, 2004; Dezalay and Garth, 1996; Go, 2008; Krause, 2014; for a theoretical comparison of global perspectives in the works of Luhmann and Bourdieu see Bohn, 2006). However, while this literature has also described the emergence of such field logics, the submission to which marks the entry into

The Sociological Review Monograph, 64:2, pp. 124–145 (2016), DOI: 10.1111/2059-7932.12005

Published by John Wiley & Sons Ltd, 9600 Garsington Road, Oxford OX4 2DQ, UK and 350 Main Street, Malden, MA 02148, USA

a potentially global competition, less attention has been devoted to the actual process of transnationalization or globalization of a field, that is, to the mechanisms and dynamics that cause actors from different geographical locations and cultural contexts to commit to such a game in the first place.

The contribution of this paper lies precisely in offering such an account of a *transnational expansion* of an institutional sphere that merits the description of a Bourdieusian field. It aims to show how the field of global Christian missions that emerged in the nineteenth century affected other religious traditions in such a way that they themselves were to some extent drawn into the logic of competitive proselytization. Focusing on India and using secondary sources on Indian religion, nineteenth-century Christian missions and the British Empire as data, the paper analyses how local religious dynamics were penetrated and supplanted by 'Western' logics of religious competition that centre on religious affiliation and individual conversion. It thus traces the process of formerly separate and locally distinct 'rules of the game' aligning themselves with a transnational structure as it shows how 'Hinduism', 'Sikhism' and 'corporate' Islam surfaced as religious actors in India and assumed positions in a potentially global struggle for religious adherents.

With the different theoretical focus of this paper comes an emphasis on a particular set of field-theoretical concepts. Indeed, the conceptual apparatus of Bourdieusian field theory is as well-equipped to capture transformative and expansionary processes as it is for the analysis of the more persisting features of distinct social dynamics.[1] It is in this context that I suggest that the concepts of 'illusio' and 'doxa' offer substantial analytical utility (see Bourdieu and Wacquant, 1992). Defined as the (quasi-libidinous) investment in the game and the unquestioned belief in its stakes, *illusio* can serve as a conceptual tool to assess the extent to which formerly independent (and thus 'indifferent') religious entities succumb to the 'gravitational pull' of a field and its specific logics – in other words, the extent to which they 'buy into' the game and become subject to 'field effects' (see the articles by Mudge and Vauchez, Stampnitzky, and Christin in this volume for a similar analytical focus on 'field effects') . By emphasizing the notion of *illusio*, one can thus conceive of the globalization of a field as a gradual process in which more and more actors within an analytically defined institutional sector (eg religion, politics, the economy) pay tribute to specific norms and the dominant worldview in a field regardless of their geographical location. Such an analysis necessarily needs to be complemented by investigating the proliferation of a specific 'doxa' (Bourdieu, 1990: 66) – the tacit agreement on the fundamental ontological structures of a field on which particular field dynamics build.

With these concepts, I focus on three major traditions in India as I discuss how, in the context of nineteenth-century missions in British India, 'Hinduism', 'Sikhism' and Islam were '*taken in*' by an outlook on religion that competitively compares numerical distributions of religious adherents. The argument will pay somewhat greater attention to 'Hinduism', not just for reasons of demographic proportion: for one, as a religious tradition that is culturally very distant from

Christianity, it serves particularly well to highlight the *doxic* presuppositions that underlie the diffusion of a historically contingent *illusio*. Second, to some extent the rise of 'Hinduism' as a religious contender can be seen to have served as an 'accelerant' in the transformation and competitive commitment of the other religious traditions in India.

The paper sets out with a discussion of Bourdieu's own field-theoretical writings on religion; this section serves to highlight some of the fundamental presuppositions of Bourdieusian field theory as well as to clarify how and why I will deviate from some of its central intuitions. I then briefly discuss the unprecedented surge of global missions in the nineteenth century and outline how quantitative surveys and religious comparisons fabricated the notion of an interreligious competition for adherents. The main focus of the paper, however, lies on the globalization of this competitive dynamic through missionary activities in India, originating predominantly from the US and Great Britain. In order to throw the transformative effect of Christian missions on Indian religion into sharp relief, I first delineate the religious situation on the subcontinent as it presented itself in the centuries prior to British rule: here, a plurality of religious actors with comparatively diffuse religious identities competed for public space in locally confined arenas to display their religious symbols and practise their religious rituals. I then highlight how Orientalist constructions of Indian religions, Christian polemics, and, not least, the religious census by the British administration cultivated Western notions of religion among Indian natives and made them susceptible to competitive dynamics that centre on numerical distributions of adherents. The paper thus shows how the dominant law of the field, or its '*nomos*' (Bourdieu, 1996: 223), shifted from local struggles for the symbolic occupation of public space to a translocal 'communal' logic of exclusive religious affiliation and demographic preponderance – a *nomos* that became largely taken for granted as Hindus, Sikhs and Muslims gave in to the *illusio* of numerical comparisons which rested on *doxic* understandings of what constitutes a religion.[2]

Bourdieu's writings on the religious field

Bourdieu deals with religion in his earliest field-theoretical exercises.[3] His 'relational' concept of a field was first derived from a reinterpretation of Max Weber's sociology of religion in *Economy and Society,* where an invariant dynamic among the ideal-types of the priest, the prophet, the sorcerer, and the laity is delineated (Bourdieu, 1987 [1971]). In a likewise seminal and more extensive article published the same year, Bourdieu (1991 [1971]) elaborated on the 'Genesis and Structure of the Religious Field', again drawing heavily on the writings of Weber.

These two essays already introduce most of the fundamental notions of Bourdieu's field theory. They depict the religious field as an arena of struggle for the legitimacy of different forms of religious *capital*: that is, the institutionalized religious authority of priests, guaranteed by a church, versus the personalized charisma of prophets and sorcerers. They exemplify the binary opposition between an *autonomous* and a *heteronomous pole* by pitting the spiritual

 The Sociological Review Monograph, 64:2, pp. 124–145 (2016), DOI: 10.1111/2059-7932.12005

orientations of priests and prophets against the this-worldly services and 'profanities' of the sorcerer. First and foremost, however, they emphasize the *relative autonomy* of the field, which is neither determined by nor entirely independent from class relations but rather translates broader social oppositions into field-specific antagonisms. The essays thus already advance the notion of a *structural homology* between class hierarchies, field-specific hierarchies and hierarchies among the symbolic products of the field: differences in cultural capital, for instance, are transfigured into differences of religious qualification and resonate with the opposition of religion and magic and, on a symbolic level, of gods and demons. Accordingly, religious manoeuvres of actors struggling for religious legitimacy are necessarily *over-determined* by class struggles without being recognized as such. Such homologies furthermore organize the '*pre-established harmony*' of a diversified supply of religious products and the varying demands of religious consumers in various social positions; with this perspective on 'elective affinities', Bourdieu again employs a structuralist reading of the more materialistic points in Weber's sociology of religion. Finally, in producing and inculcating a symbolic universe that echoes and transposes the fundamental hierarchies of a class structure, religion as a field inevitably *legitimizes and naturalizes* the established social order; here as in other fields, the homologous logic in the realm of cultural production exerts a symbolic violence that serves to reinforce the prevailing divisions of society.

For Bourdieu, then, the logic of a field is not adequately understood unless the field itself is mapped onto the larger field of class relations (see Bourdieu, 1998; Bourdieu and Wacquant, 1992).[4] It thus may seem to go against the grain of his theory to dissociate field analysis from class analysis. And yet, I will largely do so in my examination of religious fields that follows, which will mostly stay silent on how such fields are situated in and influenced by broader class relations. I will proceed in this fashion for primarily two reasons. For one, as I aim to focus on the transnationalization of a field, matters of class would significantly complicate the argument. Addressing comparability of status orders across national societies or even hypothesizing a global order of class relations in which a potentially global field might be embedded is beyond the scope of this paper. Second, I argue that with his more recent field-theoretical notions of *nomos* as the fundamental law of the field, *enjeux* as the stakes of the game, and, first and foremost, *illusio* as cathectic investment in the game and *doxa* as the shared stock of taken-for-granted presuppositions, Bourdieu provides a set of concepts that allows focusing primarily on the specific logics of a particular field and grants some licence to 'bracket' the larger implications of class. Indeed, the nascent approach to global fields has largely refrained from the more 'class-laden' concepts of habitus and homologies, and has instead focused on specific forms of capital and the general relational thrust of field theory, all notions that are more easily dissoluble from considerations of social stratification (eg Go, 2008; Krause, 2014). The aforementioned formula of concepts may prove likewise fruitful in capturing not only the emergence but also the transnational expansion of field structures.

In concentrating on these aspects of fields, I furthermore deviate from the conventional heuristic of identifying an opposition of heteronomous and autonomous positions, which, while not posited as an elementary property of fields as such, is introduced by Bourdieu (1996) as a general characteristic of *cultural* fields. Rather, my emphasis in theorizing Bourdieusian fields lies more generally on the shared understandings that underlie a particular form of competition. In the case at hand, my focus is on the implicit prerequisites of buying into a competitive game of proselytization as it was transnationalized by evangelical missions. It is to this emergence of a global missionary endeavour in the nineteenth century that I now turn.

The emergence of a global field of competitive religion

The nineteenth century saw the emergence of a Christian missionary enterprise theretofore unparalleled in magnitude, global scope and organizational rationality (Latourette, 1937–45; Neill, 1987; Porter, 2004; Stanley, 1990). It was triggered by several factors. First, Calvinist doctrines of predestination within Protestantism were gradually supplanted by the notion that the conversion and salvation of mankind could be effectuated by human means. Second, as evangelical revivalism was sweeping the US and parts of Europe, especially Great Britain, at the close of the eighteenth century, it was also stirring ambitions for foreign missions. As it itself was taken as a sign of end times, revivalism was heavily imbued with a millenarian outlook: pre-millennialists thought the Second Coming of Christ imminent and consequently urged for the immediate conversion of as many souls as possible in order to save them from eternal damnation; post-millennialists saw the conversion of the world and the establishment of God's Kingdom on Earth within reach, upon which Christ's return was assumed to follow. Both strands of chiliastic expectation thus converged in their conviction that global evangelization was urgent and critical. Third, technological innovations in communication and transport as well as geographical discoveries and the colonial expansion of European empires opened up unprecedented opportunities for missions abroad, which were again construed as Divine Providence and as indicative of an imminent end of the world.

Moreover, the missionary enterprise was fuelled by novel undertakings in *quantifying religions* worldwide. The treatise generally seen as the founding document of nineteenth-century evangelical missions, *An Enquiry into the Obligation of Christians to Use Means for the Conversion of the Heathens* by British Baptist William Carey (1792), provided one of the first estimates of a *global distribution* of religious adherence. This is, to the best of my knowledge, the first instance of a survey segmenting the *world's population* into aggregates of *religious followers*, thus, in effect, comparing 'religious populations' on a global scale and across national boundaries. It inaugurated a continual quantitative self-monitoring of a global missionary enterprise and its progress in converting the world to Christianity: general interest missionary journals regularly pooled statistical information on conversions and religious adherence retrieved from censuses and

The Sociological Review Monograph, 64:2, pp. 124–145 (2016), DOI: 10.1111/2059-7932.12005

reports of the various missionary societies. By drawing attention to the 'vast multitudes' of non-Christians and pleading for foreign missions, such publications effectively projected a field of interreligious competition onto a global level – a field in which *numbers of religious followers* were at stake.

The Protestant view of other religions was thus informed by a competitive logic. Anti-Catholic sentiments, for instance, were a powerful driving force in evangelical missions; indeed, a rivalry in global missions soon unfolded between Catholicism and Protestantism as Catholic missionary orders rose to the challenge of the unprecedented surge in Protestant missions (Stanley, 2006). Muslims were seen in terms no less combative: evangelical appeals to direct missions into the Muslim territories of the Levant often spoke of 'spiritual conquests' and 'invasions' into an 'empire of sin' (Khalaf, 2012). Islam was furthermore considered a major contender in winning the souls of Africans (Porter, 2008). 'Mohammedanism' and Catholicism were even equated as two 'Antichrist forces' of which Protestant missions were to rid the world (Dwight, 1812, cited in Khalaf, 2012: 71). Moreover, as the Christian view on 'heathendom' became increasingly differentiated and scholars of 'comparative religion' began to distinguish between 'Hinduism', 'Buddhism', etc. (see Masuzawa, 2005), such 'religions' also came to figure as 'competitors' in Western missionary discourse. Using the template of Catholicism once again, Protestant missionaries construed 'the Hindoo system' as a religious adversary as their views of Brahmans began to resonate with notions of Catholic 'priestcraft' deceiving the masses into idolatry and subordination (Oddie, 2006). Furthermore, as various practices came to be synthesized into 'Buddhism' by Western observers, the projected number of 'Buddhists' worldwide, seemingly outnumbering Christians, gave rise to widespread concern if not alarm (Almond, 1988; Masuzawa, 2005).

Thus, quantitative surveys projecting global figures of religious adherence and pointing to geographical locations of unevangelized 'heathens', as well as qualitative comparisons of religions delineating the competing dogmas of the religious 'other' fuelled a missionary enterprise couched in terms of an interreligious struggle and spiritual warfare. Even *within* Protestantism, missionary societies often saw themselves in competition with those from other denominations and countries, interdenominational cooperation and coordination notwithstanding (Tyrell, 2004). What we find here, then, is a field in which competition was in some regards very real (as among Protestant missionary societies and Catholic missionary orders) and in some regards more of an unreciprocated ascription and imposed construction (as, initially, in missionary views of Eastern religions).

On the basis of such constructions, however, Christian missionaries generally acted upon the notion that they were in fact dealing with religious competitors in their encounters with local traditions as they polemically attacked the veracity of their 'creeds' and derided the supposed barbarism of their practices. As shall be seen in the following sections, such challenges did not leave the indigenous populations unfazed. In a sense, Christian missionaries unwittingly helped create the interreligious competition they were counterfactually projecting from the outset. Before turning to such transformative effects of Christian missions on

Indian religion, I will briefly outline the religious situation of pre-colonial India in the following section.

The religious scene in eighteenth-century India

In order to fully appreciate the fundamental changes introduced by the advent of Christian missionaries, it is important to glean an understanding of what the religious landscape in India looked like in the eighteenth century.

First and foremost, the religious scene during this period was thoroughly *syncretistic* in nature (C. Bayly, 1985, 1988; S. Bayly, 1989; Copland *et al.*, 2012): in the post-Mughal successor states and petty kingdoms, Hindu, Sikh or Muslim kings and chieftains sponsored shrines and festivals of multifarious local cults, saints and deities and were eager to associate themselves or at least maintain some connection with venerable figures from religious traditions other than their own. Such patronage was a politically expedient means to establish legitimacy, especially as these rulers rose to independence and power with the decentralization and dissolution of the Mughal Empire. Furthermore, as the Empire was losing its grip, an increase in interregional warfare contributed to an 'eclectic warrior culture' (C. Bayly, 1985: 184) as socially diverse warbands accommodated and amalgamated a broad range of religious practices and idols.

Second, religious life in eighteenth-century India had a very *local* outlook. Localities often constituted self-sufficient symbolic orders with their own sacred cosmos of deities and sanctuaries as well as separate ritual orders regulating interaction among the different groups and castes (S. Bayly, 1989). Indeed, even local instantiations of expansive cults such as the devotional Bhakti cult often operated without an awareness of earlier or contemporary followers in other localities (Thapar, 1989). Most importantly, Hindu, Sikh and Muslim identities did not distinguish themselves along the translocal communal lines that would later come to dominate domestic politics and religious relations in India. Though the extent to which such identities may be postulated at all for pre-colonial India is still contentiously debated, there is wide agreement that they were hardly anchored in distinct and exclusive solidarities extending the immediate context (eg Freitag, 1980; Pandey, 1990). In contrast to other religions where different sects usually cast themselves as unique interpretations of an original teaching, religious observances that would later be subsumed under 'Hinduism' often had entirely independent origins and histories (Thapar, 1989). Accordingly, the Vedas, far from being an equivalent to the Bible or the Qur'an, had little relevance to the realities of Hindu religious life; indeed, they contain hardly any ethical elements and know nothing of karma and transmigration, the reverence of cows, or other dogmatic elements that have to some extent come to be identified as 'Hindu' fundamentals (Weber, 1958). But even for the Muslims of the pre-British period, communal consciousness was largely deterred by sectarian divisions, dietary habits, language, social rank, and even the partaking in the devotional cults at local shrines – much opposed to the picture later painted by the British, who imagined Muslims as a homogenous, egalitarian and monotheistic class of rulers

 The Sociological Review Monograph, 64:2, pp. 124–145 (2016), DOI: 10.1111/2059-7932.12005

during the Mughal Empire (Hardy, 1972; Metcalf, 1995). Locally circumscribed identities of (sub-)caste, sect and language thus allowed for little more than very proximate and elusive religious solidarities.

However, despite these syncretistic and ill-defined features, the religious situation in eighteenth-century India did in fact exhibit a particular logic amenable to a field-theoretical account. It was not uncommon for villages or urban localities in pre-colonial India to be the site of competitive tensions surrounding matters of *religious symbolism* (C. Bayly, 1985; Prior, 1993). As public space was necessarily limited, religious festivals and other expressions of piety were bound to conflict at one point or another. Consequently, a more or less distinct understanding of religious dominance and ceremonial right-of-way was usually inscribed into the local culture. As Katherine Prior (1993) notes, the relative prominence of particular shrines and festivals generally reflected economic and political relations among the towns' inhabitants; likewise, in the provincial centres the religious atmosphere was to a large extent defined by the ruler's primary donorship and patronage of particular sanctuaries. Accordingly, a shift in such relations or a change of power would open up opportunities to also challenge and renegotiate the symbolic order of the local setting and would occasionally give rise to more overt religious altercations.

In a sense, then, each of these local religious scenes constituted a religious field unto itself, though not a very autonomous one. Broader power relations were here quite directly translated into hierarchical relations of religious signifiers. What was at stake – that is, the principal *enjeu* of the field – was the legitimate occupation of *public space* with specific religious symbols. For instance, where Muslims predominantly shaped the locality's cultural order, solemn restraint was also expected of Hindu ceremonies whenever they fell into the period of mourning during the sacred month of Muharram (Prior, 1993). Likewise, Muslim activities were expected to yield to Hindu observances where Hindus were politically or economically dominant. First and foremost, as cows were considered sacred entities among Hindus and Sikhs, the established policy on cow slaughter was a telling indicator of a town's current religious as well as political state of affairs (C. Bayly, 1985; Prior, 1993). Where power relations were evenly distributed, the compromise usually lay in Muslims butchering cattle discreetly and unobtrusively so as not to offend Hindu and Sikh inhabitants. Where demographic change or upward social mobility tilted relations in favour of Muslims, however, such respectful considerations were often abandoned and cow slaughter moved out into the open; conversely, if the shift was to their disadvantage, protest against such practices would become more adamant and often result in banning them altogether.

Even though such religious contentions seem marked by symbolic boundaries between Hindus, Sikhs and Muslims, such competition does not presuppose 'communal' identities as they would come to be understood in colonial and post-colonial India. Rather, such strife most likely transpired without significant reference to abstract religious identities and was deeply immersed into the concreteness and immediacy of the local scene. After all, many of the potentially contentious village festivals were generally of only local or regional importance, and even local ceremonies that were more common in India still constituted a very particular selection from a wide range of possible festivities (Freitag, 1989). Moreover, many religious symbols and practices were caste-specific; abstract religious identities among communal lines were thus undermined by local caste and lineage groups who all had a separate stake in the symbolic order (Freitag, 1989). Hence, a certain religious self-awareness may be postulated but should be seen as largely escaping the antithesis of communal identity and diffuse religious symbiosis, which has dominated the scholarly debate (C. Bayly, 1985). In a sense, religious symbols stood for themselves in this competition for local supremacy without galvanizing distinct religious communities with enduringly salient religious identities.

In no small part due to the intervention of Christian missionaries, however, the religious landscape on the subcontinent took on a different and thoroughly communal logic of religious competition in the nineteenth century. This transformation, as I will argue, constituted a shift in the scope of the field, from local to supralocal, as well as in the fundamental law and stakes of the field, from the supremacy of religious symbolism to the preponderance of specific religious affiliations in India.

'Re-fielding' India

In order to demonstrate how 'Hinduism', 'Sikhism' and 'Islam' in India emerged as religious entities and aligned themselves with a field of religious competition as it was globally projected by the nineteenth-century missionary enterprise, or how they 'bought into' a particular field logic, I focus on two fundamental aspects: I highlight how Hindus, Sikhs and Muslims came to adopt a specific religious *doxa*, that is, unquestioned and implicitly shared assumptions on what constitutes a religion, as the taken-for-granted foundation of the competitive game. Second, I address the aspect of *illusio* in showing how the *quantitative* magnitude of 'Hinduism', 'Sikhism' and 'Islam' as well as shifts in numerical proportions among the religions in India increasingly gained significance for Hindu, Sikh and Muslim observers and became the focal point of strategic intervention. In both regards, I argue that a combination of direct challenges by Christian missionaries and the continual quantification of religious change by the religious census produced the cognitive presuppositions necessary for a competitive engagement of the religions of India. I conclude this section by recapitulating how the religious field was transformed as a result of these developments.

Establishing a religious doxa

As already indicated in the last section, scholars of religion have highlighted the essentialism behind communal concepts of Indian religion. 'Hinduism' was in many ways a fabrication of Western Orientalists, synthesizing very disparate traditions under a common signifier, with the suffix '–ism' counterfactually

 The Sociological Review Monograph, 64:2, pp. 124–145 (2016), DOI: 10.1111/2059-7932.12005

suggesting a coherent body of religious thought that allows it to be compared with other 'faiths' and defined as a specific instantiation of a generic concept of religion.[5] Much the same can be said for 'Sikhism' (Ballantyne, 2006). Similarly, the socially diverse Muslims scattered across the subcontinent and subsumed under 'Islam' hardly felt as having much of a common identity (Hardy, 1972; Sikand, 2002).

However, these religious labels soon gained currency and salience for the first time among the indigenes of the Indian subcontinent as well, with the polemics of Christian missionaries significantly contributing to their diffusion. For one, missionaries raised a sense of unity by indiscriminately attacking and disparaging local traditions, the followers of which were consequently inclined to unite in common opposition to a religious antagonist and thus found utility in such umbrella terms themselves. Second, through their – albeit unfavourable – comparisons with Christianity, Christian invectives inadvertently solidified the notion that these labels stood for religious entities paralleling Western religions (Oddie, 1982, 2003).

Moreover, the institutional environment of the British colonial regime itself helped consolidate the notion of Indian religions as monolithic blocs. Since the mid-nineteenth century, the colonial government had been regularly undertaking a religious census on the Indian subcontinent. Such quantifications had far-reaching effects on the religious situation in India (Jones, 1981): not only did the census contribute to the genesis of a Hindu, Sikh and Muslim consciousness through classifications that officially established 'Hinduism', 'Sikhism' and 'Islam' as distinct and universal religious categories; by counting individual adherents, it also promoted a 'corporate' concept of religion as an aggregate of followers while unequivocally suggesting that it applied to Indian religions no less than to Christianity.[6] The mere format of the census, allowing for only one religious identification and neatly dissolving the Indian population into disjunct religious segments, thus ingrained a typically 'Western' definition of religion into the minds of the colonial subjects: here, religions figure as associations with *mutually exclusive* memberships. Whereas religious identity in pre-colonial India was diffuse and deeply situated in local contexts, religion now increasingly came to be understood as a supralocal, pan-Indian 'community' with distinct boundaries separating Hindus from an equally distinct body of Muslims on the subcontinent (Pandey, 1990). Hindu–Sikh relations proved more complicated but eventually also culminated in a religious separatism of Sikhism (Jones, 1976).

As such a notion of religion gained plausibility among the indigenous people of India, Hindu, Sikh and Muslim associations sprung up that modelled themselves rather closely after Christian organizations and saw their own traditions through an essentially 'Protestant' lens (Jones, 1989).

Of these, perhaps the most fundamental contribution to the 're-fielding' of India came from the Arya Samaj, a Hindu reform movement founded by Swami Dayanand Saraswati, the son of a Brahmin, in 1875 (Jones, 1976). The Arya Samaj propagated a highly 'rationalized', egalitarian and 'scriptural' version of 'Hinduism', purged from idolatry, polytheism and excessive ritualism while relying on the 'word' of the Vedas. Not surprisingly, Dayanand's vision of 'Hinduism' had a high appeal among the 'literate, semi-Westernized segment of the Hindu community' (Jones, 1968), that is, the educated elite that had already been thoroughly exposed to the plausibility structures of an 'occidental rationalism'.[7] As opposed to the far less successful Brahmo Samaj, whose own version of an enlightened 'Hinduism' exhibited a somewhat blatant admiration for its Christian role model, the combatively anti-Christian Arya Samaj was able to cater to the ambivalent stance of a population who had come to internalize Western ideas and standards against which it was simultaneously struggling to assert a sense of self-worth and dignity. Indeed, as Barbara Metcalf (1982: 257) points out, around 'three-fourths of the early members of the Samaj were government servants who welcomed an ideology of such clear psychological and social benefit'.

In redefining 'Hinduism' for themselves and in opposition to Christianity, Aryas became more and more susceptible to a competitive perspective that pays special heed to numerical relations among religions. Their activities were not only to have a significant impact on 'Hinduism' as a whole and its outlook on the religious scene in India and beyond; they also played a decisive role in the mobilization and competitive engagement of Islam as well as in the religious 'secessionism' of the Sikhs. Thus, the Arya Samaj can be seen as an important 'catalyst' in the institutionalization of a novel religious *illusio* on the subcontinent. It is to this aspect that I now turn.

Giving in to a specific illusio

While the internal structure and implicit logic of the census was reinforcing a concept of religion as mutually exclusive associations of individuals, it was its temporal dimension that was quickly raising a sense for the competitive game among Indians. For each religion on the subcontinent, census officials closely recorded and examined numerical size as well as relative and absolute growth (Jones, 1981). This left quite an impression on Hindus, especially, as such statistics were regularly displaying the devastating effects of Christian proselytization on 'Hinduism' in terms of lost 'adherents'. Census publications soon caught the attention of educated natives, who voiced their concern in the indigenous press. In 1883, an article in *The Regenerator of Arya Varta*, an organ of the Arya Samaj, pointed to the dramatic increase of Christians to 417,372 from 19,092 in just a few decades (Jones, 1981). Before long, Hindu intellectuals resorted to census data to make predictions as to when Hindus would entirely vanish from the subcontinent if their numerical decline continued at the current pace. Such considerations brought a relative disadvantage of 'Hinduism' into blatant view; on 14 September 1886, the *Arya Patrika*, another publication of the Arya Samaj, noted:

> The absence of proselytism in Hindu society is certainly a very important drawback in the way of its reform. No *increase* can now take place in the *number of the Hindus* and even persons gone out of their society can not [sic] enter it without undergoing a set

 The Sociological Review Monograph, 64:2, pp. 124–145 (2016), DOI: 10.1111/2059-7932.12005

> of ceremonies to submit to which would reflect volumes of discredit upon an educated person. (Cited in Jones, 1976: 130; emphasis mine)

As this editorial shows, the fundamental relevance of quantitative proportion already went without saying. The considerable extent to which the 'numbers game' had taken a hold on Hindus is markedly displayed by the fact that, soon, the Aryas invented their own means of bringing converts back into the Hindu fold. In applying 'shuddhi', a former purification ritual, the Samaj now reconverted Hindus that had switched to Islam or Christianity (Jaffrelot, 1996). While in theory reconversion was limited to former Hindus, this restriction was interpreted quite liberally in practice. Since descendants of converts were also regarded as Hindus in fact, only *immigrants* of other faiths were not subject to a 'shuddhi' reconversion – according to an estimate by the Aryas, however, Muslim immigrants, for instance, amounted to merely 5–10 per cent of all Muslims in India (Jones, 1976). Indeed, the 'theme of forced conversion and its corollary that the Muslims of today were the Hindus of the past' (Jones, 1976: 151) increasingly informed the Aryas' view on the history of Hindu–Muslim relations in India.

Still, the potential base for applying 'shuddhi' was to be extended even further. As made evident by the census, Christian mission was having the greatest effect among outcasts and lower-caste Hindus. Indeed, while conversions among the highly educated upper castes were usually isolated instances, recruitment among the lower, less well-off castes were occurring on a scale of 'mass conversions', often by converting entire communities en bloc. For them, turning Christian not only meant a change of faith, it also came with an improvement in social standing: a conversion opened the door to privileges generally withheld from 'untouchables' but not from Christians (see Fischer, 1991). Often, economic aid was already incentive enough for lower-caste Hindus to convert. Hence, dramatic surges in conversions were usually recorded during periods of great famine (Forrester, 1991). In the decade of 1881–91, the Christian community in the Sialkot District of the Punjab province saw an increase from 253 to 9,711 Christian converts (Jones, 1976). Again, numerical accounts of such 'defections' from the lower echelons aroused great concern among Hindu intellectuals (Jones, 1976, 1981; Jordens, 1991). For instance, an article in the *Tribune* from 19 October 1891, read:

> Few people have any idea about the rapidity with which the number of the Indian Christian community is being swollen by the conversion of the people of the lowest castes. In fact if conversions go on at this rate there will no longer remain any 'low castes' at a not very distant date and the 'higher castes' will have to exert all their energies in protecting themselves from being pushed to the wall by aggressive *mehters* and *chamars* elevated from their degraded position to the religious level of their rulers. (Cited in Jones, 1976: 144; emphasis in original)

Consequently, in a remarkable 'pre-emptive' move, rituals of 'shuddhi' were soon performed on lower-caste Hindus in order to elevate them to a higher position within the caste structure and thus render them more 'immune' to advances of Christian missionaries (Jones, 1981). Moreover, the Arya Samaj increasingly resorted to mass conversions themselves as they rose to the challenge of the Christian missionary endeavour in dedicating entire 'reconversion campaigns' to returning Indians to the Hindu fold or bolstering their adherence. With the foundation of the *All India Shuddhi Sabha*, the movement spread well into the Kashmir region and the United Provinces. In the Punjab province alone, close to 70,000 'shuddhis' were performed before 1910. In the United Provinces the number of Aryas had climbed to 205,000 by the year 1921 (Jordens, 1991).

Aside from these strategic interventions, pragmatically directed at the problem of numerical decline, the reactions of the Hindu orthodoxy also highlight the grave import that quantitative considerations had gained within 'Hinduism'. After all, the Arya Samaj organization and its measures of reform were by no means uncontroversial among Hindus.[8] Ironically, just as caste was becoming more standardized and the boundaries between the pure and the polluted were growing more salient in Indian life (S. Bayly, 1999), due not least to the same ethnographic surveys that were solidifying communal conceptions of 'Hinduism', the Aryas felt compelled to undermine caste hierarchies in order to hold conversions to other religions at bay. The egalitarian element of 'shuddhi' posed a fundamental challenge to Hindu traditionalists, who were appalled at formerly 'untouchables' gaining access to Vedic rituals and privileges. And yet, even though these 'reconversions' profaned the sacred norms of caste, orthodox leaders soon acknowledged 'shuddhi' as a necessary evil in light of the quantitative depletion of 'Hinduism' manifested by the British-Indian census. The converts were thus accepted as touchable and non-polluting even though social contact was still largely avoided (Jordens, 1991).

The Arya Samaj was thus no longer a heterodox outlier with an idiosyncratic perspective on Indian religion; rather, its conversionist stance now represented the majority of the Hindu population (Sikand, 2002). Commenting on this growing approval by the orthodoxy, Ganga Prasad, a leading figure of the Samaj, would observe in 1939: 'Forty years ago the Arya Samaj was looked upon as a great defiler of the Hindu religion by bringing in an alloy from outside. Today the Arya Samajist is counted as a great defender of the faith' (cited in Jones, 1968: 53).

Such momentous concessions indicate the tacit recognition of a game in which numerical proportions of religious adherents are at stake. They attest to the transnationalization of a specific religious *doxa* and *illusio*. Contrary to merely establishing an 'imagined community' in the sense of Anderson (1991), the religious census and the religious change it quantified and depicted fostered a *specific interest* and an *investment* in 'numbers' that drew Hindus into a particular struggle for religious 'followers'. Consequently, Hindu 'reconversions' generally paralleled the cycle of the census, with each new publication of data rekindling and propelling 'shuddhi' campaigns on the subcontinent (Jones, 1981).

Muslims were no less 'taken in' by this novel quantitative outlook on religion. Indeed, the Arya Samaj served as a crucial 'relay' in the transformation of the field: many influential Muslim associations of the region took shape in reaction not just to Christian missionaries and the colonial environment but in great part

 The Sociological Review Monograph, 64:2, pp. 124–145 (2016), DOI: 10.1111/2059-7932.12005

to the newly emerging assertiveness of 'Hinduism'. The Ahmadiyahs, originating in the Punjab province during the final decades of the nineteenth century, are an early example of a movement considerably moulded through its antagonism and polemic disputes with the Arya Samaj (Lavan, 1989). More strikingly, however, the Muslim missionary awakening of the early twentieth century, which united several Muslim reform organizations in British India, was a direct result of the 'shuddhi' activities of the Hindu community (Sikand, 2002). The incursion of reconversion campaigns into the nominally Muslim segments of Indian society galvanized the Muslim elite, who had hitherto shown very little interest in a thoroughgoing Islamization of, or even association with, those who had turned Muslim through a process of gradual cultural transformation during the Mughal regime. After all, as reconversion campaigns reached a new height following reports of forced conversions to Islam during the Moplah uprising in 1921, Muslims, too, now saw themselves facing 'virtual extinction' (Sikand, 2002: 46) on the subcontinent – a threat once again made apparent by the decennial census as well as by the numerical triumphalism of the Hindu press (Jones, 1981; Minault, 1982). As a result, Muslims now re-evaluated their own missionary arsenal and re-animated the tradition of 'tabligh', the proclamation of Islam, as a means to win back converts and bolster the adherence of those most vulnerable to reconversion, most prominently the tribal Muslims who were being reconverted to 'Hinduism' by the thousands. In this sense, 'tabligh' can be seen as a direct response to 'shuddhi', and was indeed understood as such by many Muslim activists (Minault, 1982; Sikand, 2002).

In a similar fashion, the Arya Samaj was also a decisive factor in the growing self-awareness and sense of 'religious sovereignty' of the Sikhs, who initially cooperated in the 'shuddhi'-movement (Jones, 1968). As the Aryas amplified their polemics against Sikhism and began to purify Sikhs by shaving their heads and beards, the latter felt increasingly antagonized, and more and more frequently refused to register with the Hindu community in the census. Again, communal distinctions hardened as many Sikhs now found themselves beleaguered not only by Christian and Muslim proselytization but by Arya reconversion as well.

Such clear-cut boundaries between the various religious segments of India were even further reinforced and the quantitative stakes heightened as constitutional reforms increasingly introduced communal representation into the political domain during the first decades of the twentieth century (Jones, 1981). Religious adherents had now become political capital as well, adding to the consequentiality of conversions and the weight of census statistics.

Thus, much in line with what Wendy Espeland and her collaborators argue, the competitive dynamic of India rested on a 'commensuration' of religions through quantitative measures as well as on the 'reactivity' of such measures, eliciting reactions from those who were subjected to them (Espeland and Sauder, 2007; Espeland and Stevens, 1998). Quantification in the context of the census was the fundamental instrument that reorganized a local religious arena and attuned it to the logic of an interreligious competition for adherents.[9]

A field transformed

The fundamental law of the religious field in India, that is, its *nomos*, had thus changed in the course of the nineteenth century. The primary stake of the game, and with it the dominant principle of religious legitimacy, now lay in the numerical preponderance of a religious community.

This did not mean that struggles for the supremacy of specific religious symbols had ceased in India. However, by the end of the nineteenth century such conflicts had become over-determined by a competitive assertion of *religious affiliation* and imbued with translocal references to an all-Indian religious community (Freitag, 1989). Symbolic struggles thus acquired a subordinate or supplemental function in the rivalry of religious associations. This is perhaps best evidenced by a subtle yet fundamental shift in the meaning of initiatives to ban cow slaughter. As we have seen, the 'cow' had already been a continual bone of contention in the circumscribed public arenas of pre-colonial India, its fortune signifying the relative supremacy of particular religious observances in the locality. In contrast, the North-Indian Cow Protection movement of the late nineteenth century had farther-reaching implications (Freitag, 1980; Pandey, 1990; Yang, 1980). Initiated in the early 1880s, the movement gained momentum in 1888 when a court decision effectively permitted the slaughter of cows. As it availed itself of the new communication technologies of a modernizing infrastructure, the movement soon spread from the urban centres to the countryside, rallying broad and often violent support. In a sense, it was able to utilize the 'cow' as the lowest common denominator of an ample spectrum of religious practices as well as of people of very different social standing. The movement thereby managed to forge a link between urban and rural regions, orthodox and reformist Hindus, higher castes and lower castes; it thus played into a newly shared sense of a *Hindu community* that was asserting itself vis-à-vis its religious 'others', first and foremost Muslims and Christians. And among Muslims, too, the cow-slaughter controversy served to bridge the social divide, foregrounding religious commonalities against class differences and the distinction of *ashraf* and *ailaf* that used to separate the Muslim elite from Muslim descendants of lower caste indigenes (Hardy, 1972; Sikand, 2002). Unlike before, the 'cow' was no longer a stake in itself but now served as a prop in a broader struggle for communal predominance. The late-nineteenth-century Cow Protection initiative thus dovetailed with the emerging logic of competitive numerical comparisons among religious associations; in itself a levelling 'metric', the 'cow' became an empty signifier structurally equivalent to census figures that were likewise fabricating corporatist notions of 'Hinduism' and Islam.

Not only did the local religious arena in India acquire a new communal logic of quantitative comparisons – a logic that would spill over into communalist politics and culminate in the partition of India and Pakistan as Hindu and Muslim communities vied for political representation. In addition, through these transformations, the religious field of India essentially assumed the position it was assigned within the globally projected meaning structure of *interreligious*

 The Sociological Review Monograph, 64:2, pp. 124–145 (2016), DOI: 10.1111/2059-7932.12005

competition. As a 'harvest field' of souls, the Indian subcontinent with its vast populations of 'Hindu idolaters' figured prominently in the appeals of evangelicals to increase missionary efforts abroad, and continues to do so today. Missions to India still form part of an ongoing enterprise of *world evangelization* and *global* Christian conversion as evangelical missions continue to proselytize in India. More importantly, however, Hindu fundamentalists, still active in reconversions, now *also* infuse the local religious dynamics with *global references*. They are not just alert to missionary activities in India, but also keep a vigilant eye on Christian proselytization efforts in *other* regions and directed towards *other* religions. In the past, Hindu intellectuals have pointed to the publicly available progress reports on global evangelization to call attention to, and make inferences about, the Christian missionary threat in the local context of India.[10] Moreover, Muslim organizations such as the Tablighi-Jama'at, spawned by the competitive dynamics of colonial India, have since established themselves as global players in their effort to preach Islam and integrate Muslims into a worldwide community (Sikand, 2002).

In independent India, then, Christian missionaries and Hindu fundamentalists, especially, share a common *doxa* and *illusio* that orient them to *global relations of religions*, even though evangelicals have an ambition to produce conversions while the others are primarily looking to avert or reverse them. Indeed, to some extent it is precisely the *nationalist* agenda of Hindu fundamentalism, that is, the ideology of 'Hindutva' (see Frykenberg, 2004), that has Hindus defensively engaged in a *transnational* competition: for fundamentalist Hindus, India can be said to figure as a Hindu bastion in a global arena of religions.[11] What unites Christians and fundamentalist Hindus in this conflict – that is, what has them committed to the same field logic – is the implicit understanding of religions as mutually exclusive collectives and the undisputed belief that their relative numerical magnitude is at stake. Through the events of the nineteenth century, then, the religious field of India in many regards aligned itself with a transnational field of religious competition, projected by evangelical missionaries, and its logic of conversion.

Conclusion

The paper has tried to highlight the utility of the concepts of *doxa* and *illusio* in analysing the transnationalization of particular field logics or 'rules of the game'. Indeed, these concepts may be especially conducive to a *historically* oriented sociological analysis. First and foremost, they are able to capture the transnational expansion of a specific field as a *process*: as more and more actors within an analytically defined institutional sector commit to a specific worldview and interest, both of which bring them into a relation of mutual orientation to one another, this can be understood as globalization in progress. Second, data pointing to an implicit recognition of the stakes in a field can readily be ascertained from historical documents such as editorials, memos, letters and other primary sources.[12] An investment in a game can be inferred not only from what is said in these documents but perhaps even more so from what goes without saying. Finally, strategic action taken and not taken at important historical junctures are likely to expose a commitment to specific relevance structures of a field as exemplified above by such measures as the introduction of 'shuddhi' or 'tabligh' and the pre-emptive promotion of lower-caste Hindus or the thorough Islamization of tribal Muslims. In utilizing *doxa* and *illusio* as analytical tools, research can take a 'microscopic' approach to investigating how specific macrostructures or logics of a field take root in different historical and cultural settings.

Aside from these historical perspectives, concepts such as *doxa* and *illusio* generally point to the cultural preconditions and implicit presuppositions that are often overlooked in the analysis of specific institutional orders. In the case of religion, for instance, the rational-choice approach of Stark and Finke (2000) and others has primarily focused on more overt developments such as the disestablishment of a state church in order to predict or explain competitive dynamics among religious suppliers. It has thus neglected the *doxic* assumptions that underlie such dynamics and has shown itself hardly attentive to a specifically religious *illusio* irreducible to materialistic interests of a disestablished clergy (see, eg, most notably Iannaccone, 1991). Above all, the approach has unduly universalized a typically Western, if not American, notion of religion and is thus conceptually ill-equipped to account for cultural particularities that may inhibit or facilitate the emergence of religious competition in different contexts.

Furthermore, the paper has pointed to a decisive role of quantification in the transnational expansion of a field. As demonstrated in this case, quantification and quantitative comparisons can be forceful factors in translating particular competitive logics across cultural and linguistic boundaries. The reductionist features of numbers serve well to succinctly boil down the stakes of the game to a few elementary indicators while their ordinal logic in itself bears competitive implications. Quantitative comparisons furthermore highlight the scope of the field in comparing a particular range of actors and can thereby even exhibit appellative, 'subjectivating' effects relevant to the expansion of a field.

Finally, Bourdieu's field theory sees fields primarily as sites of a competition for legitimacy and a struggle over the relative value of specific forms of capital (see Go and Krause, this volume). While the concept of capital has not figured prominently in the analysis above, numerical proportion can in a sense be conceived of as a specific form of capital nonetheless. However, while Hindus certainly seem to have come to recognize the relevance of quantitative relations, this recognition only goes so far – after all, there is little evidence for any ambition on the Hindu part to convert anyone outside of India or even 'genuine' Christians or Muslims within India to 'Hinduism'. Indeed, as a more thorough investigation into the religious dynamics in colonial India can show, Hindus have tried to distinguish themselves from Christians, especially, in accentuating – and 'capitalizing' on – other religious characteristics of 'Hinduism'. For instance, in a tacit embracement of Western enlightenment, Hindus presented themselves as the more *rational* religion, with scriptures and doctrines more in tune with the tenets of the natural sciences than those of Christianity (Prakash, 1999). More

The Sociological Review Monograph, 64:2, pp. 124–145 (2016), DOI: 10.1111/2059-7932.12005

importantly, they advertised religious tolerance or, more specifically, respect for the 'dharma' of other religions within an encompassing soteriology as a fundamental asset of 'Hinduism', thus introducing a true alternative to the exclusivist stance of Christianity and its logic of conversion – an alternative, which ironically, in turn again served as grounds for claims to religious superiority (Kim, 2003; van der Veer, 1994). Hence, as in any other field, a rivalry of principles of legitimacy can be observed. And yet, just as dominated artists on the economically oriented heteronomous pole in the field of art must in one way or the other pay tribute to the dominant law of 'l'art pour l'art' so as not to discredit themselves as artists entirely (see Bourdieu, 1996), so do we find a fundamental recognition of the importance of quantitative relations on the part of the Hindus even as they aim to promote alternative forms of legitimation. It is precisely this recognition as *illusio* that points to their engagement in a competitive religious field.

Acknowledgements

I thank the editors, the series editor, the participants at the workshops 'Global Fields and Historical Sociology' at the University of Lucerne and 'Fielding Transnationalism' at Boston University as well as three anonymous reviewers for helpful comments and suggestions on earlier versions of this article.

Notes

1 See Steinmetz (2011) for a general discussion on the inherently historical perspectives of Bourdieu's central concepts; see also Gorski (2013a) on perspectives of social change in the work of Bourdieu as well as Gorski (2013b) for innovative suggestions on how to apply field theory in historical analysis.

2 Beyer (2006) also points to the globalization of shared models of religion in his systems-theoretical account of global religion. For him, local traditions (re-)construct themselves as religions in global society by providing distinct variants of a religious 'code', 'program', and 'power medium'; in articulating the universal and the particular, such constructions continually reconfigure and contest the global model of religion. Beyer's subscription to systems-theoretical perspectives notwithstanding, his idea that the legitimate model of religion is constantly at stake in a global system of mutually identifying religions bears some Bourdieusian implications as well, though not expressly so. For a critical discussion of Beyer's theory see Petzke (2014).

3 On Bourdieu's sociology of religion see Rey (2007); Swartz (1996).

4 Indeed, this is further manifested by his later empirical study on the French episcopate (Bourdieu and de Saint Martine, 1982). Here, Bourdieu argues that the episcopate constitutes a microcosm of the more deep-seated differences within French Catholicism while it simultaneously strives to conciliate these differences. For Bourdieu, it is the class position of bishops that predisposes them to such an orchestration and reconciliation of competing views: members of the episcopate are disproportionally often recruited from positions in the broader field of class relations that exhibit similar structural tensions and ambiguities as those they then later come to inhabit in the religious field.

5 See Frykenberg (1997); King (1999); Marshall (1970); Stietencron (1997). See Bloch *et al.* (2010) for a recent overview over the still lively debate.

6 For a similar argument regarding the relationship of census classifications, quantification and (post-)colonial identity see Anderson (1991), Appadurai (1996) and Cohn (1987); with these authors, the emphasis lies more on ethnicity and caste and less on religion.
7 I have elaborated on how the colonial environment fostered ideas of religious individualism, organizational rationality and secular neutrality on the subcontinent from a perspective of neo-institutionalism in Petzke (2014).
8 Indeed, the construction of 'Hinduism' itself gave rise to disputes regarding the legitimate definition of the same. This holds true for 'Sikhism' and 'Islam' as well. While these struggles would also lend themselves to a field-theoretical analysis, this is beyond the scope of this paper.
9 On the relationship of quantitative comparisons and globalization see Heintz (2010); Heintz and Werron (2011). As the article of Buchholz (this volume) suggests, global rankings of artists seem to play a similar role in the globalization of a field of the visual arts and its fundamental stakes as religious statistics do in the field of interreligious competition discussed here.
10 See Kim (2003). Examples are Swarup (1985, 1988); Shourie (1994, 2000).
11 For a different take on the interplay between the global and the local, focusing less on local orientations to global meaning structures than on their national *translation* and *articulation*, see Dromi (this volume).
12 For an instructive example using policy articles and memos in analyzing the recognition of 'anti-colonial nationalism' as symbolic capital in the global political field see Go (2008).

References

Almond, P. C., (1988), *The British Discovery of Buddhism*, Cambridge: Cambridge University Press.

Anderson, B., (1991), *Imagined Communities*, rev. edn, London/New York: Verso.

Appadurai, A., (1996), *Modernity at Large: Cultural Dimensions of Globalization*, Minneapolis: University of Minnesota Press.

Ballantyne, T., (2006), *Between Colonialism and Diaspora: Sikh Cultural Formations in an Imperial World*, Durham, NC: Duke University Press.

Bayly, C. A., (1985), 'The pre-history of "communalism"? Religious conflict in India, 1700–1860', *Modern Asian Studies*, 19: 177–203.

Bayly, C. A., (1988), *Indian Society and the Making of the British Empire*, Cambridge: Cambridge University Press.

Bayly, S., (1989), *Saints, Goddessses and Kings: Mulsims and Christians in South Indian Society, 1700–1900*, Cambridge: Cambridge University Press.

Bayly, S., (1999), *Caste, Society and Politics in India from the Eighteenth Century to the Modern Age*, Cambridge: Cambridge University Press.

Beyer, P., (2006), *Religions in Global Society*, London: Routledge.

Bloch, E., Keppens, M. and Hegde, R. (eds), (2010), *Rethinking Religion in India: The Colonial Construction of Hinduism*, London/New York: Routledge.

Bohn, C., (2006), 'Une société mondiale. Les concepts sociaux de Bourdieu et Luhmann' in H.-P. Müller and Y. Sintomer (eds), *Pierre Bourdieu, théorie et pratique. Perspectives franço-allemandes*, 101–127, Paris: La Découvert.

Bourdieu, P., (1987 [1971]), 'Legitimation and structured interests in Weber's Sociology of Religion', in S. Lash and S. Whimster (eds), *Max Weber, Rationality, and Modernity*, 119–136, London: Allen and Unwin.

Bourdieu, P., (1990), *The Logic of Practice*, Stanford, CA: Stanford University Press.

Bourdieu, P., (1991 [1971]), 'Genesis and structure of the religious field', *Comparative Social Research*, 13: 1–44.

Bourdieu, P., (1996), *The Rules of Art: Genesis and Structure of the Literary Field*, Stanford, CA: Stanford University Press.

Bourdieu, P., (1998), *Practical Reason: On the Theory of Action*, Stanford, CA: Stanford University Press.

 The Sociological Review Monograph, 64:2, pp. 124–145 (2016), DOI: 10.1111/2059-7932.12005

Bourdieu, P. and de Saint Martin, M., (1982), 'La sainte famille: L'épiscopat français dans le champ du pouvoir', *Actes de la recherche en sciences sociales*, 44–45: 2–53.
Bourdieu, P. and Wacquant, L. J. D., (1992), *An Invitation to Reflexive Sociology*, Chicago: University of Chicago Press.
Carey, W., (1792), *An Enquiry into the Obligations of Christians to Use Means for the Conversion of the Heathens*, Leicester: Ann Ireland.
Casanova, P., (2004), *The World Republic of Letters*, Cambridge, MA: Harvard University Press.
Cohn, B. S., (1987), *An Anthropologist among the Historians and Other Essays*, Delhi: Oxford University Press.
Copland, I., Mabbett, I., Roy, A., Brittlebank, K. and Bowles, A., (2012), *A History of State and Religion in India*, London/New York: Routledge.
Dezalay, Y. and Garth, B. G., (1996), *Dealing in Virtue: International Commercial Arbitration and the Construction of a Transnational Legal Order*, Chicago/London: University of Chicago Press.
Dwight, T., (1812), *Sermon Delivered before the American Board of Commissioners for Foreign Missions*, Boston, 4 September.
Espeland, W. E. and Sauder, M., (2007), 'Rankings and reactivity: how public measures recreate social worlds', *American Journal of Sociology*, 113: 1–40.
Espeland, W. E. and Stevens, M. L., (1998), 'Commensuration as a social process', *Annual Review of Sociology*, 24: 313–343.
Fischer, R. H., (1991), 'Christianisation and social mobility in nineteenth-century South Kanara and Malabar: a look at the Basel mission experience', in G. A. Oddie (ed.), *Religions in South Asia: Religious Conversion and Revival Movements in South Asia in Medieval and Modern Times*, 125–154, New Delhi: Manohar.
Forrester, D. B., (1991), 'The depressed classes and conversion to Christianity, 1860–1960', in G. A. Oddie (ed.), *Religions in South Asia: Religious Conversion and Revival Movements in South Asia in Medieval and Modern Times*, 65–93, New Delhi: Manohar.
Freitag, S. B., (1980), 'Sacred symbol as mobilizing ideology: the North Indian search for a "Hindu" community', *Comparative Studies in Society and History*, 22: 597–625.
Freitag, S. B., (1989), *Collective Action and Community: Public Arenas and the Emergence of Communalism in North India*, Berkeley, CA: University of California Press.
Frykenberg, R. E., (1997), 'The emergence of modern "Hinduism" as a concept and as an institution: a reappraisal with special reference to South India', in G.-D. Sontheimer (ed.), *Hinduism Reconsidered*, reprint, 29–49, New Delhi: Manohar.
Frykenberg, R. E., (2004), 'Gospel, globalization, and Hindutva: the politics of "conversion" in India', in D. M. Lewis (ed.), *Christianity Reborn: The Global Expansion of Evangelicalism in the Twentieth Century*, 108–133, Grand Rapids, MI: Eerdmans.
Go, J., (2008), 'Global fields and imperial forms: field theory and the British and American Empires', *Sociological Theory*, 26: 201–229.
Gorski, P. S., (2013a), 'Bourdieu as a theorist of change', in P. S. Gorski (ed.), *Bourdieu and Historical Analysis*, 1–17, Durham, NC: Duke University Press.
Gorski, P.S., (2013b), 'Bourdieusian theory and historical analysis: maps, mechanisms, and methods', in P. S. Gorski (ed.), *Bourdieu and Historical Analysis*, 327–366, Durham, NC: Duke University Press.
Hardy, P., (1972), *The Muslims of British India*, Cambridge: Cambridge University Press.
Heintz, B., (2010), 'Numerische Differenz. Überlegungen zu einer Soziologie des quantitativen Vergleichs', *Zeitschrift für Soziologie*, 39: 162–181.
Heintz, B. and Werron, T., (2011), 'Wie ist Globalisierung möglich? Zur Entstehung globaler Vergleichshorizonte am Beispiel von Wissenschaft und Sport', *Kölner Zeitschrift für Soziologie und Sozialpsychologie*, 63: 359–394.
Iannaccone, L. R., (1991), 'The consequences of religious market structure', *Rationality and Society*, 372: 156–177.
Jaffrelot, C., (1996), *The Hindu Nationalist Movement in India*, New York: Columbia University Press.
Jones, K. W., (1968), 'Communalism in the Punjab: the Arya Samaj contribution', *Journal of Asian Studies*, 28: 39–54.

Jones, K. W., (1976), *Arya Dharm: Hindu Consciousness in 19th Century Punjab*, Berkeley, CA: University of California Press.
Jones, K. W., (1981), 'Religious identity and the Indian census', in N. G. Barrier (ed.), *The Census in British India*, 73–101, New Delhi: Manohar.
Jones, K. W., (1989), *Socio-religious Reform Movements in British India*, Cambridge: Cambridge University Press.
Jordens, J. T. F., (1991), 'Reconversion to Hinduism: the Shuddhi of the Arya Samaj', in G. A. Oddie (ed.), *Religions in South Asia: Religious Conversion and Revival Movements in South Asia in Medieval and Modern Times*, 215–230, New Delhi: Manohar.
Khalaf, S., (2012), *Protestant Missionaries in the Levant: Ungodly Puritans*, 1820–60, *Abingdon*: Routledge.
Kim, S. C. H., (2003), *In Search of Identity: Debates on Religious Conversions in India*, New Delhi: Oxford University Press.
King, R., (1999), 'Orientalism and the modern myth of "Hinduism"', *Numen*, 46: 146–185.
Krause, M., (2014), *The Good Project: Humanitarian Relief NGOs and the Fragmentation of Reason*, Chicago: University of Chicago Press.
Latourette, K. S., (1937–45), *A History of the Expansion of Christianity*, 7 vols, New York: Harper.
Lavan, S., (1989), 'The Ahmadiyah Movement: Islamic religious reform in modern India', in R. D. Baird (ed.), *Religion in Modern India*, 113–138, New Delhi: Manohar.
Marshall, P. J. (ed.), (1970), *The British Discovery of Hinduism in the Eighteenth Century*, Cambridge: Cambridge University Press.
Masuzawa, T., (2005), *The Invention of World Religions*, Chicago: University of Chicago Press.
Metcalf, B., (1982), *Islamic Revival in British India: Deoband*, 1860–1900, Princeton, NJ: Princeton University Press.
Metcalf, B., (1995), 'Too little and too much: reflections on Muslims in the history of India', *Journal of Asian Studies*, 54: 951–967.
Minault, G., (1982), *The Khilafat Movement. Religious Symbolism and Political Mobilization in India*, New York: Columbia University Press.
Neill, S., (1987), *A History of Christian Missions*, Harmondsworth: Penguin Books.
Oddie, G. A., (1982), 'Anti-missionary feeling and Hindu revivalism in Madras: the Hindu preaching and tract societies, c. 1886–1891', in F. W. Clothey (ed.), *Images of Man: Religion and Historical Process in South Asia*, 217–243, Madras: New Era.
Oddie, G. A., (2003), 'Constructing Hinduism: the impact of the Protestant Missionary Movement on Hindu self-understanding', in R. E. Frykenberg (ed.), *Christians and Missionaries in India: Cross-cultural Communication since 1500, with Special Reference to Caste, Conversion, and Colonialism*, 155–182, Grand Rapids, MI: Eerdmans.
Oddie, G. A., (2006), *Imagined Hinduism: British Protestant Missionary Constructions of Hinduism*, 1793–1900, New Delhi: Sage.
Pandey, G., (1990), *The Construction of Communalism in Colonial North India*, Delhi: Oxford University Press.
Petzke, M., (2014), 'Religious differentiation and world culture: on the complementary relationship of systems theory and neo-institutionalism', in B. Holzer, F. Kastner and T. Werron (eds), *From Globalization to World Society. Neo-Institutional and Systems-Theoretical Perspectives*, 148–176, New York/London: Routledge.
Porter, A., (2004), *Religion vs. Empire: British Protestant Missionaries and Overseas Expansion*, 1700–1914, Manchester: Manchester University Press.
Porter, A., (2008), 'Evangelicalism, Islam, and millennial expectation in the nineteenth century', in D. L. Robert (ed.), *Converting Colonialism: Visions and Realities in Mission History*, 1706–1914, 60–85, Grand Rapids, MI: Eerdmans.
Prakash, G., (1999), *Another Reason: Science and the Imagination of Modern India*, Princeton, NJ: Princeton University Press.
Prior, K., (1993), 'Making history: the state's intervention in urban religious disputes in the north-western provinces in the early nineteenth century', *Modern Asian Studies*, 27: 179–203.

Rey, T., (2007), *Bourdieu on Religion: Imposing Faith and Legitimacy*, London: Equinox.
Shourie, A., (1994), *Missionaries in India: Continuities, Changes, Dilemmas*, New Delhi: ASA Publications.
Shourie, A., (2000), *Harvesting our Souls: Missionaries, their Design, their Claims*, New Delhi: Rupa.
Sikand, Y., (2002), *The Origins and Development of Tablighi Jama'at*, New Delhi: Orient Longman.
Stanley, B., (1990), *The Bible and the Flag: Protestant Missions and British Imperialism in the Nineteenth and Twentieth Centuries*, Leicester: Apollos.
Stanley, B., (2006), 'Christian missions, antislavery and the claims of humanity, c. 1813–1873', in G. Sheridan and B. Stanley (eds), *The Cambridge History of Christianity, Vol 8: World Christianities, c.* 1815–1914, 443–457, Cambridge: Cambridge University of Press.
Stark, R. and Finke, R., (2000), *Acts of Faith: Explaining the Human Side of Religion*, Berkeley, CA: University of California Press.
Steinmetz, G., (2011), 'Bourdieu, historicity, and historical sociology', *Cultural Sociology*, 5: 45–66.
Stietencron, H. v., (1997), 'Hinduism: on the proper use of a deceptive term', in G.-D. Sontheimer (ed.), *Hinduism Reconsidered*, 32–53, rev. edn, New Delhi: Manohar.
Swartz, D., (1996), 'Bridging the study of culture and religion: Pierre Bourdieu's political economy of power', *Sociology of Religion*, 57: 71–85.
Swarup, R., (1985), 'Thy kingdom is the third world', *Times of India*, 14 July.
Swarup, R., (1988), 'Christianity mainly for export'. *Times of India*, 14–15 March.
Thapar, R., (1989), 'Imagined religious communities? Ancient history and the modern search for a Hindu identity', *Modern Asian Studies*, 23: 209–231.
Tyrell, H., (2004), 'Weltgesellschaft, Weltmission und religiöse Organisationen – Einleitung', in A. Bogner, B. Holtwick and H. Tyrell (eds), *Weltmission und religiöse Organisationen. Protestantische Missionsgesellschaften im 19. und 20. Jahrhundert*, 14–134, Würzburg: Ergon.
van der Veer, P., (1994), 'Hindu nationalism and the discourse of modernity: the Vishva Hindu Parishad', in M. E. Marty and R. S. Appleby (eds), *Accounting for Fundamentalisms: The Dynamic Character of Movements*, 653–668, Chicago: University of Chicago Press.
Weber, M., (1958), *Religion in India: The Sociology of Hinduism and Buddhism*. trans. and ed. H. Gerth and D. Martindale, Glencoe, IL: Free Press.
Yang, A. A., (1980), 'Sacred symbol and sacred space in Rural India: community mobilization in the "Anti-Cow Killing" riot of 1893', *Comparative Studies in Society and History*, 22: 576–596.

Fielding supranationalism: the European Central Bank as a field effect

Stephanie L. Mudge and Antoine Vauchez

Abstract: The European Central Bank (ECB), like all European institutions, poses basic problems of definition and comparability. Mobilizing Bourdieusian field theory (BFT) to resolve them, we map out the ECB's deep investments in scientific prestige and scholarly productivity – that is, its *hyper-scientization* – and the ambiguities therein, and then set out to explain them. Mobilizing diverse sources that include official documents, on-site interviews, and comparative data, we argue that hyper-scientization is a *field effect* expressing the ECB's origins and cross-location in three worlds: financial institutions, professional economics, and European politics. We then trace out the signs and symptoms of cross-location. First, we trace the origins of the ECB's directorate for research, DGR, which differentiated the ECB from most other European central banks at the time of its founding. Thus invested, the ECB accelerated its scholarly activities in step with the internationalization and scientization of economics. But this also expressed the ECB's stake in European authority struggles: research exchanges are a means of building relationships with national central banks, which was especially crucial in the lead-up to the European Union's (EU) 2004 enlargement. We thus argue that there is more to the ECB than its independence and policy operations, and that some of its most striking features are best explained as effects of its multiple field locations.

Keywords: field theory, field effect, European Central Bank, expertise, European integration, economics

Introduction

With the arrival of the financial crisis in the Eurozone, the European Central Bank (ECB) came to occupy an increasingly central, and visible, position in European politics. Long a target of left criticism in the European Parliament (EP) for its insistent independence and tight monetary policies (Adolph, 2013; Issing, 2008), controversies over the ECB intensified in both professional economics and the public sphere since 2010. In the former, old arguments that currency union was never scientifically justified are back, with new calls for a correction of past

The Sociological Review Monographs, 64:2, pp. 146–169 (2016), DOI: 10.1111/2059-7932.12006

Published by John Wiley & Sons Ltd, 9600 Garsington Road, Oxford OX4 2DQ, UK and 350 Main Street, Malden, MA 02148, USA

errors by 'completing the euro' (Enderlein *et al.*, 2012; De Grauwe, 2013). In the latter case, the ECB – once a relatively low profile EU institution – now finds itself a target of protest. Demonstrations at the ECB's (new) doorstep are making headline news, even as we write.[1] Political discontent's arrival in Frankfurt, rather than Brussels, is a novelty. According to Eurobarometer surveys, between 1999 and 2008 only about 70 per cent of EU citizens reported awareness of the ECB's very existence, versus a fairly consistent 80–90 per cent for the European Commission and EP, respectively. But by June 2014 the ECB was as politicized, if not more, than the EP: awareness of it reached 84 per cent, but trust in it dipped to an all-time low (31 per cent).[2] Struggles in and over Europe have thus shifted in ways that now situate the ECB, not yet 20 years old, centre-stage.

The ECB's growing visibility has been matched by growth in its size and purview. Since 2010 it acquired significant powers over bailed-out member states (Greece, Portugal, Ireland) in the form of unconventional policies of quantitative easing that commit national governments to wide-ranging reforms spanning pension systems, labour markets, health care provision, and local government. With the Banking Union (2014), the ECB acquired supervisory responsibility over the 130 largest Eurozone banks, and is also responsible for coordinating the supervision of about 3,000 others. Not surprisingly, the ECB's staff – which stood at 1,638 full-time equivalent (FTE) at the end of 2013 – reportedly added about 1,000 recruits in just the last year.[3]

Through it all, the ECB's self-presentation as a bearer of stability, scientific acuity, and technocratic professionalism changed little. Even as crisis set in, its presidents (Jean-Claude Trichet, then Mario Draghi as of November 2011) celebrated the euro as an against-the-odds success and maintained the bank's claim to scientifically informed monetary management. The ECB's scientific professionalism and close identification with the European project is comparable to the comportment of the ECJ – except that the ECJ is not similarly politicized (Vauchez, 2014).[4]

Understanding the ECB in all its complexities is arguably now more important than ever, but like all European institutions it presents particular analytical difficulties. In this contribution we mobilize Bourdieusian field theory (BFT) to analyse the ECB's history, development and peculiarities, which we intend partly as a demonstration of BFT's advantages for the analysis of supranational phenomena (see also Lebaron, 2000, 2013). One is that the term 'field', in itself, has no particular territorial or scalar implications. The assumption is simply that the thing to be analysed is organized relationally – that is, it exists within sets of relations, and it is internally structured in ways that express that situation. Taking this to heart, we focus on understanding the ECB's situation in various kinds of struggles, including scientific and scholarly ones, in order to render it more intelligible.

Using historical documents, comparative data, on-site interviews and other sources, we focus especially on what we term *hyper-scientization*. The ECB is well noted for its high degree of independence and its modelling on the German *Bundesbank*, but this is a partial story. As we establish below, one of the ECB's most striking features has been its unusually intense investment in scientific prestige and scholarly research from its beginnings, which set it apart from most European central banks, including the *Bundesbank*. By *hyper-scientization* we do not mean that the ECB is the only central bank that practises scientific policymaking, or that grounds its authority in scientific claims. What we do mean is that the ECB's organizational investments in scientific prestige played an unusually central role in its making and development. Hyper-scientization offers an interesting empirical inroad into an otherwise tricky analytical object.

We argue that hyper-scientization cannot be explained by the influence of the German *Bundesbank*, the ECB's formal independence, or its policy mandates. It also cannot be chalked up in any satisfying way to the general tendencies of central banks. Rather, it is a *field effect*. By this we mean a social phenomenon that is a combined effect of the topography of social space and the ECB's positioning within it, as well as the organizational characteristics of the ECB itself – all of which are continually shaped by authority struggles that unfold in time (Bourdieu, 1993; Martin, 2003).

Our analysis thus starts not with any essential argument about the ECB, but rather with an analysis of its history, endowments and self-understandings. We treat these as indicators of the ECB's cross-location within at least three systems of relations: the world of central banks and other financial institutions, the European political order, and the internationalized economics profession. This cross-location gave rise to a bank with scientific research capacities that stand out relative to most other central banks in Europe, and that facilitate strong connections to internationalized economics. But this by itself is not a full account of hyper-scientization; underlying the ECB's scientific and scholarly investments are ambiguities that render them, alone, an inadequate explanation of why the ECB intensified its research activities at such a rapid clip. For a full account, the ECB also needs to be seen in its European context: its research activities double as a means to bureaucratic authority, which became especially important in the run-up to the 2004 enlargement.

Fielding supranationalism: the case of the ECB

The study of Europe has long presented difficulties, including how to acquire analytical leverage on a phenomenon that has no historical parallel. This problem has tended to foster debates over Europe's essence: for instance, whether it is more 'intergovernmental' or 'supranational' or a case of 'multi-level governance'. Expressing close ties between European scholars and the institutions they study – as between, for instance, constitutional scholars and constitutional conventions (Chambers, 2003; Cohen, 2010) or between economists studying international macroeconomics and the European Commission's economic directorates (Mudge and Vauchez, 2012) – the line between 'is' and 'ought' in these debates can be blurry. Another difficulty is that there is no definitive way to verify or reject essentialist claims about what Europe is, or what its institutions 'really' are: the EU exhibits many tendencies that may be more or less salient depending on

 The Sociological Review Monographs, 64:2, pp. 146–169 (2016), DOI: 10.1111/2059-7932.12006

where one chooses to look; it is not a stable entity geographically, institutionally or symbolically; it has no definite comparative yardstick.

As a result, while the ECB is increasingly worthy of attention, its supranationalism presents analytical problems. It bears similarities with many other institutions – central banks, centres of economic research, international financial institutions – but, at the same time, it is not like any of them. Its relative youth, its origins in the integration project, its 'über-independent' status (Adolph, 2013: 5; McNamara, 1998), not to mention its peculiar comportment (further documented below), render the basic question of what the ECB is, and thus how it should be analysed, difficult to answer.

Research in a field-theoretic vein gets around this problem by reconfiguring the object, taking European struggles and institutions as sets of overlapping social relations-in-formation. In a BFT perspective, European field struggles are dominated by elites bearing different forms of capital, in which the ultimate prizes are those of any modern political setting: political and bureaucratic authority. These struggles are multi-scalar: they are centred in and around Brussels, but 'European' authority by its very nature depends on an ability to exert authority well beyond. In particular, it requires efforts to extend one's reach into national settings. This is true, certainly, of the ECB, which has had to work very hard to shore up its authority by developing exchange relations with national central banks, notwithstanding its official jurisdictions. Indeed, one of the peculiar stakes of European field struggles is precisely to blur the boundary between 'European' and 'national' authority – that is, to call that boundary into question.

But there is no reason to think that struggles in and over Europe play out in complete separation from other kinds of contests. Here it is important to attend to the players themselves: the ECB has multiple investments that are not simply 'European'. Its striving for scientific distinction relative to other financial institutions is wrapped up with investments in professional economics, but the ECB also maintains a technocratic stance that, at times, trumps its scientific and scholarly pursuits. The ECB's multiple investments – in European authority, in scientific prestige, and in technocratic professionalism – are indicators of its cross-field location.

Our field-theoretic approach to the study of Europe (see also Vauchez, 2008; Mudge and Vauchez 2012) – akin to Yves Dezalay and Bryant Garth's analyses of 'palace wars', as well as the work of Didier Georgakakis, Jay Rowell and others on the 'field of Eurocracy' (Dezalay and Garth, 2002; Georgakakis and Rowell, 2013) – contrasts with approaches that treat supranational institutions as static entities, or that align too easily with Europe's own self-narrative of integration as a smooth, linear process. It also allows Europe and its institutions to be placed alongside the contested histories of others, national or otherwise, without taking 'convergence' as a key problematic or assuming any essential or eternal sameness. The ECB is one among many central banks, but this does not mean that it is the same *kind of actor* or that it *has the same investments* as other central banks; it is a European institution, but it is not the same kind of actor as, say, the European Commission or the ECJ. In each case, the matter of investment is an empirical question, which can be mapped by looking into the historical and present-day characteristics, orientations, and practices of the bank, its leadership, and its staff.

Theoretical and empirical approach

Our most general claim is that the ECB's institutional peculiarities can be explained, in a BFT perspective, as a field effect. Bourdieu did not use this term very often, but it is a useful way to capture, in shorthand, the causal logic of field-theoretic thinking.

In a BFT perspective social causality does not lie in actors, or even in the relations between them, but rather in the relations between actors' attributes, their positioning, and the topography of the field. None of these are static; they unfold in time, and condition each other. The key point is that causality is not to be found in the intrinsic or essential properties of players. In Bourdieu's words, 'we may think of a field as a space in which a *field effect* is exercised, so that what happens to any object that traverses this space cannot be explained solely by the intrinsic properties of the object in question' (Bourdieu and Wacquant, 1992: 100, emphasis added). Bourdieu later stated this a little differently, explaining 'field effect' by noting the unintelligibility of artworks without knowledge of the worlds that produce them:

> There is a *field effect* when it is no longer possible to understand a work (and the value, i.e. the belief, that it is granted) without knowing the history of the field of production of the work (Bourdieu, 1993).

John Levi Martin (2003), meanwhile, discusses 'field effect' in classical electromagnetism with emphasis on the interaction between the attributes of elements and the field: field theory 'purports to explain changes in the states of some elements' in terms of 'an interaction between the field and the existing states of the elements'; a 'field effect' occurs because 'elements have particular attributes that make them susceptible' to them (2003: 4; see also Go, 2008; Hilgers and Mangez, 2014).

With this understanding of field effect in mind, in the present analysis we mobilize an array of empirics to grasp how the worlds that produced the ECB instilled in it certain characteristic features and orientations, and how those characteristic features continue to shape its practices and significance. Our main empirics include ten on-site interviews, conducted in March 2015, with managers and staff across four ECB directorates, six of whom had been with the ECB for ten years or more – that is, for most or all of its years of existence. Most interviewees (seven) had PhDs in economics and past experience in other financial institutions (six in national central banks, one in the International Monetary Fund [IMF]). Two had been involved with the making of the ECB's research directorate, DG Research, from its beginnings. Our aim in the interviews – which were somewhat difficult to arrange, perhaps due to the ECB's reputational concerns, and were largely organized and pre-agreed by DG Research – was to get a historical

 The Sociological Review Monographs, 64:2, pp. 146–169 (2016), DOI: 10.1111/2059-7932.12006

perspective on the bank's organization and research activities, gain insights into the relationship between those activities and policymaking, and to grasp how the bank sees itself relative to other financial institutions, research centres, and academic settings, in Europe and beyond. We interpret interview data in light of a broader picture of the ECB's situation that draws from historical and comparative measures of staffing, research products (working papers); scientific prestige rankings; speeches and annual reports from the ECB, the Bank of England (BOE), and the Federal Reserve Board (FRB); and secondary sources.[5]

The ECB as a (recent) historical object

The ECB is particularly interesting because of its power and youth, not to mention its recent politicization. Relative to, in some cases, centuries-old national counterparts, the ECB has yet to celebrate its twentieth anniversary – having been founded on 1 June 1998, alongside the European System of Central Banks (ESCB, consisting in 1998 of 11 Eurozone national central banks and four others[6]). The January 1994 establishment of the ECB's precursor, the European Monetary Institute (EMI), coincided with a process meant to autonomize national central banks, to be completed by 1998; the EMI was based in increased cooperation among national central banks starting in 1990. On 1 January 1999, conversion rates were fixed and the euro was introduced.

Independence has always been one the most striking aspects of the ECB (Tangourdeau and Vincensini, 2009). Its autonomy was written directly into the 1992 Treaty on European Union (TEU), which prohibited it and the national banks of the Eurozone members from either seeking or taking 'instructions from Community institutions or bodies, from any government of a Member State or from any other body' (ECB, 1999: 130). Likewise, the Treaty prohibits EU institutions and national governments from seeking to influence the decisions of either the ECB or the Eurozone national central banks. In short, while other national central banks achieved independence via contentious, long-term historical processes, the ECB was unusually independent at birth (see Table 1).

The ECB's independence has thus been taken as its defining feature. As such, its tendencies are often chalked up to the model of independence it expressly emulated, the German *Bundesbank*. And yet it also has features that are not easily explained with reference to the *Bundesbank*, nor indeed to national central banks (NCBs) in Europe more generally.

Symptoms and origins of a hyper-scientized ECB

The behaviour of the ECB and its leadership since the 2007–2008 financial crisis offer a window into some of the institution's peculiarities. Since 2008 central banking came under greater scrutiny from many quarters, but at first the ECB appeared to float more or less above the fray. As the first wave of crisis hit in August 2007, ECB President Jean-Claude Trichet's response (to immediately inject €95 billion into the banking sector – reportedly via 'fixed and mobile phone

Table 1: *Comparative central bank independence (CBI), as of 2000*

CBI Index (authors)	Alesina	Grilli *et al.*	Eijffinger and Schaling	Cukierman
Maximum value	*4*	*16*	*5*	*1*
ECB	**4**	**14**	**5**	**0.94**
Bank of Japan	3	6	3	0.16
US Federal Reserve	3	12	3	0.51
Bank of Canada	2	11	1	0.46
Bank of England	2	6	2	0.31

Source: de Haan and Eijffinger, 2000: 396, Table 1.

and old-fashioned fax' while on vacation on France's Brittany coast) was much admired by political elites and financial reporters alike (Atkins, 2007). Not long after Trichet was named 'Person of the Year' by the *Financial Times*, and then 'European Banker of the Year 2007' by The Group of 20+1, 'Central Banker of the Year' by *The Banker*, and 'Central Bank Governor of the Year' by *Euromoney* (in 2008).[7]

Praise for Trichet surely had to do with an understanding that the financial crisis was mostly made in the United States, not to mention its delayed manifestations in the Eurozone, but it also had to do with the particular significance of monetary unification in the context of the European project. Along with emphases on foresight, competence and adaptability, both Trichet and Draghi were notable for their defence of the ECB and the euro as embodiments of the European promise even as the Eurozone crisis set in (eg Trichet, 2009c; Draghi, 2012). The responses of representatives of other central banks, albeit at times similarly defensive, were decidedly less saturated with symbolic portent.

Especially when presenting to academic audiences, central bank governors' commentary occasionally drifted from the question of crisis-time central banking to that of central banking's relationship to economics. Here ECB representatives also tended to stand out. Unlike former Fed Chairman Alan Greenspan, who made a striking declaration of the collapse of 'the whole intellectual edifice' underlying financial markets before the US Congress in 2008, Trichet admitted that economic knowledge had been incomplete prior to the crisis but offered no indication of concerns over fundamental flaws (Greenspan, 2008; Trichet, 2009). While Bernanke, like other Fed representatives before him, was careful to make a distinction between policy-making and economic science (Meyer, 1997; Bernanke, 2010), ECB governors outwardly dwelled on the question of what kind of economics to use – for instance, whether and in what way Keynes might be recovered, or whether central banking should bring network analysis to bear on the analysis of risk – in order to better manage the economy (Bini Smaghi, 2010;

Tumpell-Gugerell, 2009). Speaking in Venice in October 2009, Trichet affirmed the bank's dependence on scientific and academic economics – and, in turn, economics' dependence on the ECB:

> As a central bank, we are prime consumers of economic research. For this reason, we maintain very close interactions with the academic world. We import tools and ideas and are eager to employ excellent economists from centres of advanced economic studies ... At the same time, the ECB is an active source of cutting edge economic thinking. (Trichet, 2009d)

This differs, especially, from the crisis-time rhetoric of the Bank of England (BOE). In 2008, for instance, Mervyn King opened the BOE's Annual Report by noting his foresight of the crisis (that is, his anticipation of a 'much bumpier' economic future for some time) and convictions that the BOE had responded swiftly, pragmatically, and appropriately – but in no clear sense scientifically (King, in BOE, 2008: 4). Unlike the ECB's annual reports, the BOE's 2008 and 2009 reports make not a single reference to the discipline of economics or its centrality to the operations of the bank (BOE, 2008, 2009).

As the ECB became newly responsible for financial stability, if anything the Eurozone crisis strengthened the Bank's resolve to anchor policy-making in science. In February 2010, for instance, the ECB requested a second external evaluation of DGR,[8] inviting four economists – two of them with high-profile backgrounds in central banks, as well – to carry out the task. In the report that resulted (Freedman *et al.*, 2011), its authors noted with disapproval 'that DG Research has only seen a small increase in resources devoted to research on financial stability, and almost none in the international and fiscal policy areas', and called for the expansion of the DGR's Financial Research Division (2011: 5–6, 13). This division, the report argues, needed 'to be closely involved in new financial stability developments but ... shielded to the extent possible from day to day pressures, since research in this area will have to be leading-edge it if it is to contribute significantly to the financial stability responsibilities of the ECB' (Freedman *et al.*, 2011). After the report was issued, the ECB was quick to affirm its agreement.

Behind the ECB's technical and scientific rhetoric are heavy investments in theory-building and statistical production (Tognato, 2012; Fontan, 2013, 2015). This 'scientization' is to some degree symptomatic of a more general phenomenon that stretches across central banks (Marcussen, 2009), but it also reflects an organizational feature that, when it was established, set it apart from many of its European counterparts: a standalone research division, DG Research (DGR). The ECB, like other central banks, also has an array of other research-intensive directorates – DG Economics (DGE) and, to a lesser extent, DG International (DGI) (Freedman *et al.*, 2011) – but the presence of a separate, dedicated research directorate was, by European standards, unusual. What explains this unusual feature of the ECB? In the following, we suggest that it had to do with the making of monetary union in the context not only of European politics, but also the making of 'European' economics amidst an internationalized profession in which American institutions were, and remain, an important centre of gravity.

Making the bumblebee fly

The ECB consistently defends its independence not only on a legal basis, but also by invoking the orthodox truth claims of economic science. Its first *Annual Report* emphasizes the strong scientific basis of 'the view that central bank independence leads to an improved design and implementation of monetary policy and, therefore, to more stable prices' (ECB, 1999: 129; see also Trichet, 2009). More than mere imitation of the *Bundesbank*, the coherence and strength of this consensus was rooted in a long historical coalescence of a US-dominated, nationally centred, increasingly formalized economics profession (Fourcade, 2006) – that is, a profession that simply did not exist before the advent of Keynesianism.[9] As Milton Friedman himself argued, it was not until Keynes' development of an economics grounded in statistical reasoning that monetary policy came to be truly scientific.[10]

And yet, partly because of the profession's US-centrism, the ECB's relationship with the economics profession has certain historical tensions. While the scientific consensus around central bank independence backed the view that the ECB, once created, should be free of political influences, it did not justify the project of monetary union in the first place. Developments in economic theory that spoke to the question were born mainly of economists situated in international centres of research – in particular, the International Monetary Fund's (IMF) research department – and are closely associated with Robert Mundell. On the one hand, Mundell's theory of an optimum currency area (OCA) laid important groundwork for the making of new field, 'international macroeconomics,' in which Europe was the focal case (Mundell, 1961; Tangourdeau and Vincensini, 2009; Mudge and Vauchez, 2012). But, on the other hand, an OCA did not justify monetary union in any clear way. American economists, who played 'a dominant role in both international research and policy debate around the euro', were highly critical of the economic rationale behind it (Jonung and Drea, 1999: 2). From the Delors Report of April 1989, which recommended the creation of the Economic and Monetary Union (EMU) in three stages, to the actual introduction of the euro in January 2002, they 'displayed considerable scepticism towards the single currency' (Jonung and Drea, 1999).

But by this time the profession, albeit internationalized, also had regional fractures that could be exploited. The European project had been fuelling the making of a specifically 'European' economics for several decades, which grew up within but also *against* an otherwise US-dominated profession (Mudge and Vauchez, 2012; Mudge, 2015). Faced with scepticism in the US-dominated mainstream, the Commission thus mobilized economists closer to home. In the words of then-President Jacques Delors, the Commission asked 'its own staff in the Directorate-General for Economic and Financial Affairs [DG EcFin] to build a bridge between the political negotiators on the one hand and the community of academic economists on the other, and to stimulate a two-way process of motivation of economic research and supply of economic advice' (Delors and Christopherson, 1990). The effort, headed by Michael Emerson[11] from DG EcFin, was asked to

The Sociological Review Monographs, 64:2, pp. 146–169 (2016), DOI: 10.1111/2059-7932.12006

report on the question of monetary union, with contributions from high civil servants and economic advisors of the Commmission's Directorate-General (Daniel Gros and Jean Pisani-Ferry) (Emerson *et al.,* 1992).[12]

The originality of the report had to do with its underlining of the outdatedness of OCA theory and the articulation of a patchwork alternative: based on a pragmatic assessment of the added value of the EMU in terms of micro and macroeconomic 'costs and benefits', the report asserted unambiguously that the balance was strongly positive (Emerson *et al.*, 1992). The approach was less academically grounded than OCA, but it had the advantage of being in line with the Commission's and EU policy-makers objectives. Followed by a report of the Delors committee composed of national central bankers (cf. James, 2012; Dyson and Featherstone, 2000), it contributed to an argumentative weaponry that, bridging bits of economic rationales, theoretical schools, and policy objectives into a 'bricolage' (Levi-Strauss, 1960: 27) attesting to the feasibility and desirability of a unified European monetary system. For all its scientific claims, the ECB's establishment was thus made possible by a whole collective labour of European economists linked to the Commission who, particularly on the question of the single currency, were reacting partly *against* the scepticism of US-based economists.

This history remains an important part of the ECB's consciousness. Memory of the ECB's birth in the face of scepticism featured, for instance, in a 2012 speech by Mario Draghi. Famous in part for the assertion that the ECB would save the euro 'whatever it takes', the speech opened with an account of the euro as a mystery analogous to that of the bumblebee:

> The euro is like a bumblebee. This is a mystery of nature because it shouldn't fly but instead it does. … I think people ask 'how come?' – probably there was something in the atmosphere, in the air, that made the bumblebee fly. (Draghi, 2012)

When Draghi points to this mystery, he is referring partly to the ECB's historical backdrop of professional scepticism, especially from across the Atlantic. And an important force that made the bumblebee fly was the capacity of the European Commission to mobilize European economics, and European economists, in defence of monetary union.

The ECB's cross-field investments

Our brief account of the complex historical relationship between the making of the ECB and contests in professional economics makes it clear that the ECB was not strictly a European effect (see also Lebaron, 2013); it was also born of professional struggles in which the axis between European and American economics loomed large. At the same time, of course, it was an initiative in the internationalized world of finance, grounded in a 'vision of a greater, more powerful Europe' (Marshall, 1999: 224) – and here, too, the US figured prominently. In the words of Francesco Papadia, chief of ECB operations, '[t]he Federal Reserve [the Fed] is our standard of comparison' (Papadia, quoted in Marshall, 1999: 225).[13] In short, the ECB was born of at least three different worlds: of finance, economics and European politics.

Investments in 'scientized' central banking

The struggle for scientific legitimation that was background to the making of the ECB, the way in which that struggle was linked with the making of European economics, and the US-centred orientations of ECB-makers concerned with questions of financial power, all help to explain why the ECB was, from the start, designed not only to carry out monetary policy, but also to become an anchor and engine of economic research. When it came to the question of organizational research capacity, and in particular a separate DG for Research (DGR), the model was the Fed – not the *Bundesbank*. The ECB's first president, Wim Duisenberg, himself a former IMF economist and a Dutch professor of economics, set up the ECB's organigramme with the separate research function of not only the Dutch central bank, but especially the Fed, squarely in view. According to an ECB manager with a long experience with DGR, and with the EMI before it:

> DG Research was an empty department and the plan was to do as well as the Fed; that's the plan; we were led by the US example and the Anglo-Saxon tradition that has a strong scientific tradition; that's our paradigm.[14]

This aim, once realized in the form of the DGR, would also look to the US for recruiting purposes. Despite the inclusion of 'EU-mindedness' among the bank's six corporate values, the interviewee notes that 'we [the DGR] recruit primarily through the US-job market – less and less through seconding from NCBs'.[15]

The designers of DGR were well aware that the DGR differentiated the ECB from most other European central banks – indeed, they assessed this explicitly, using their own measure of 'journal publication per employee' in the 1990s. By this measure they established that only the central banks of the Netherlands (with a strong tradition in econometric modelling), Austria, Portugal and Finland could be singled out as research powerhouses. Although systematic data were not available for France and Germany, they knew there was no research unit at the *Banque de France*, whose employees were high civil servants with minimal research credentials; nor was there one at the *Bundesbank*, which had no specialized research unit until the year 2000 (Deutsche Bundesbank, 2001; Eijffinger, 2002; de Haan, 2001).

The result was a new central bank that stood out not only for its independence, but also for an atypically strong research capacity that mirrored the structure of the Fed, and also drew primarily from the American economics job market. Aware that 'national central banks are … moving to that scientific understanding', the ECB looks 'to be a research-oriented central bank, "first in class," at the frontier of research'.[16] And indeed, the ECB was ahead of its European peers, having established a very strong scholarly profile, as measured in terms of the production of working and discussion papers, in a very short time (see Figure 1).

 The Sociological Review Monographs, 64:2, pp. 146–169 (2016), DOI: 10.1111/2059-7932.12006

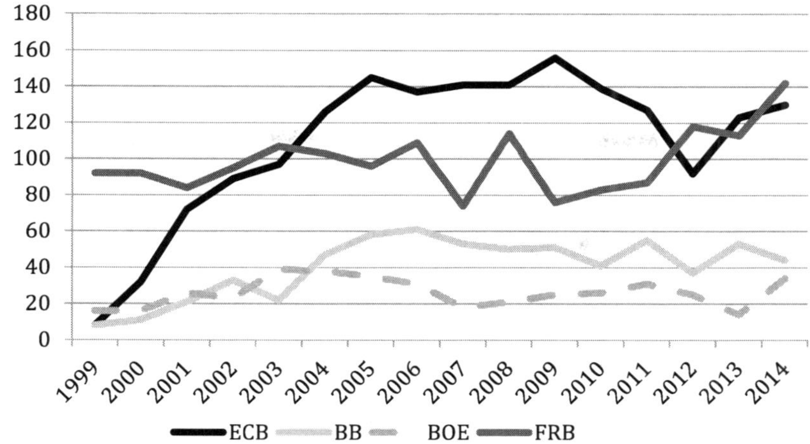

Figure 1 *Central bank working papers (counts), 1999–2014*
Sources: *Central bank website searches, by publication year, of BB discussion papers; FRB FEDS + IFDP paper series; ECB working papers. Accessed March and September 2015. Author calculations.*

As Figure 1 shows, the ECB's working paper productivity always surpassed the *Bundesbank* (labelled 'BB') and the Bank of England (labelled 'BOE'), but it also, for a time, outpaced the famously research-centric Federal Reserve Board (FRB) (Woolley, 2009).

Investments in an internationalized economics profession

The ECB's birth and early development overlapped with broader processes in disciplinary economics that had little to do with central banking per se: the internationalization of the profession on the one hand, and the crystallization of a specifically European economics on the other. The ECB's important place as a node and anchor of European economics of a particularly scientific sort is reflected not only in its profile relative to other European banks, but also its relationship to, and perceptions of, the Commission's research-heavy economic directorates (especially DG EcFin). For our interviewees, even the Commission's most economist-heavy DGs (Market and EcFin) were not peer organizations: DG EcFin has 'far less expertise' says one interviewee.[17] Another, asked about research at DG EcFin, remarks:

> DG EcFin? I have not seen anything interesting coming from the Commission; it's terribly political and legalistic. As we say in Italy, I am Catholic although I know the Church. The same here: I am European although I know the Commission. [It is] completely self-referential, they never quote any academic work.[18]

Some researchers within the ECB thus perceive the Commission as a world apart, lacking scientific rigour or political objectivity. The Commission, meanwhile,

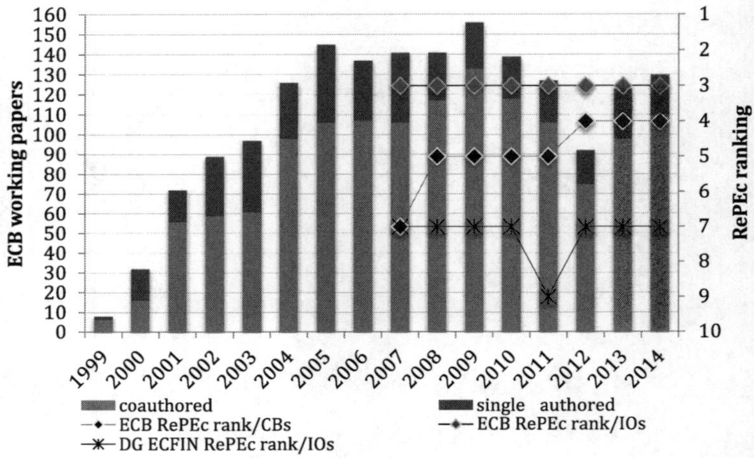

Figure 2 *ECB working papers and RePEc rankings, 1999–2014*

through DG EcFin and Eurogroup committees, increasingly relies on the ECB as a producer of scientific economic knowledge and an authority on Eurozone economics (Fontan, 2013).

The ECB's investments in professional economics, not to mention that of its research staff, can also be read in how it, and its economists, have internationalized and scientized in-step with the economics profession. Economics' internationalization has been facilitated by the development of a powerful tool of cross-national professional evaluation – born initially of computer science and physics – in the form of RePEc, a volunteer-driven, international repository of information on current research in economics, journals, research-producing institutions, and economists. RePEc emerged in 1997.[19] Within two years it became a major reference point in economics, gaining 'wide acceptance within the discipline' and establishing itself as 'the premier source of information' on developments in economic research (Karlsson and Krichel, 1999). By March 1999 it grew 'into an interconnected network of over 60 archives holding over 13,000 downloadable papers and over 50,000 descriptions of offline papers from close to 1,000 series, as well as data about over 4,000 academic Economics department and research institutes' (Karlsson and Krichel, 1999).

The ECB's first RePEc-listed publication appeared in 2003 (Castelnuovo, 2003); historical and comparative rankings are available from 2007. As Figure 2 shows, by RePEc measures – which, one should note, are built based on the voluntary participation of institutions and economists – the ECB quickly distinguished itself relative to other central banks (CBs), international organizations (IOs), and the Commission (DG EcFin).

The ECB's rank among international organizations was always higher than DG EcFin's. But during the same period the ECB also climbed in rankings of central banks, achieving a rank that placed it among the various banks of

 The Sociological Review Monographs, 64:2, pp. 146–169 (2016), DOI: 10.1111/2059-7932.12006

Table 2: *Comparison of RePEc h-indices (if h-index≥3). As of March 2015*

	H-Index min	H-Index max	H-Index median	H-Index mean	Author count	Rank: # of authors w/h-index ≥3, all institution types
IMF	3	51	6	7.6	190	1
ECB	3	25	7	7.9	115	4
FRB	3	52	6	8.8	96	6
BOE	3	18	4	5.8	37	27
BB	3	20	5	5.8	37	27

the Federal Reserve System, and even approaching the (consistently first-place) IMF.[20]

Aside from offering useful comparative metrics for present purposes, the RePEc has allowed the ECB to prove its scientificity in a whole new way. In 2004, the authors of the ECB's first research evaluation report developed their own *ad hoc* impact factors and other metrics of influence (Goodfriend *et al.,* 2004). By the time of the second evaluation in 2011, via RePEc it was possible to evaluate the ECB's standing relative to other central banks, IFIs, think tanks, academic departments, and an array of other research-producing organizations. In short time the RePec also made possible the evaluation of individual researchers (via the h-index) against a very large cross-national population of professional economists.[21] And, as shown in Table 2, at present ECB economists rank very favourably against bank and non-bank economists alike.

The RePEc standing of ECB economists is in most ways more comparable to the FRB and IMF than to the BOE or the *Bundesbank*. One might reasonably suppose that this reflects differing orientations across institutions toward the importance of RePEc listings and rankings, since authors have to sign up themselves. In any case, it leaves little doubt that ECB economists are strongly invested in the game of professional prestige.

Investments in European authority struggles

What explains the ECB's unusually rapid expansion as a research institution, and its striking investments in building scientific prestige? We have already provided evidence that it cannot be explained by the influence of other European central banks, including the *Bundesbank*. Rather, it has to do in part with the investments of the ECB's economist-designers in distinction, especially with respect to the Fed. This then provided a specific organizational research capacity, in the form of DGR, through which the ECB and its economists have rapidly expanded their scientific activities alongside the scientization and internationalization of the economics profession.

There are, of course, other ways of accounting for hyper-scientization. For instance, perhaps it is true that, as ECB representatives are prone to declaring, science and policymaking are indeed deeply interdependent. The trouble with this explanation, however, is that inside the ECB such interdependence is by no means taken for granted. Rather, interviewees conveyed a definite sense that a deep research-policy relationship is questioned by some ECB staff: 'The Buba has no tradition of research. I was once told: "the proof that you don't need a research function to succeed in monetary policy is the *Buba*; while to the contrary the *Banca d'Italia* has had a strong research tradition but poor results in terms of monetary policy!"'[22] While one DGR interviewee echoes the ECB's official position that it aims 'at policies that are scientifically founded',[23] another noted that research and policy functions have different timescales and end-goals: 'direct policy' involves the rapid production of guidelines, notes for speeches, and the like, but research works on longer time horizons and targets external, academic outlets.[24] A practical disjuncture exists between the ECB's academic and policy work:

> I have seen how the different services bombard the Executive Board members with briefs that end up in the bin because they don't read them; the biggest challenge is to catch the attention of the Board members. ... My experience is that the only way to have access to the Board is the monthly presentation to the Board, otherwise they're lost.[25]

And then there is the problem of limited access time, plus inter-departmental competition:

> The monthly presentation lasts for 70–80 minutes, each DG has a slot of ten minutes. We are asking for more, but the ECB is full of turf issues. If we want to talk about exchange rates at the monthly meeting, we have to agree with [another DG] because they do that as well ...[26]

In fact, at least two interviewees suggested that the very existence of a separate research directorate had a polarizing effect inside the bank, creating an axis of competition between two kinds of research activities that are actually, in some respects, at odds with each other. In one interviewee's comment:

> Here at the ECB, there is bit of polarization due to the existence of a specific DG Research. On the one hand, there is research detached from policy making, far away from the interest of the ECB, completely targeted to the academic market. But what is sexy for journals is certainly not sexy for Draghi ... And on the other hand, there is policy making without any reference to research, people don't have knowledge about what has been produced on the argument elsewhere, they make no reference to any paper.[27]

Another expresses a similar sentiment:

> Today, I cannot draw from DG Research because they choose individually their research subjects. For example, I'll be interested to know about [an issue concerning credit supply], this is important for us but I know I can't ask the DG Research ...[28]

It appears, then, that the ECB's in-house, academically oriented research is at most loosely coupled with the bank's policy operations, and in some respects at odds with it.

Why, then, does the ECB invest so heavily in its scholarly and scientific profile? Part of the reason is surely that the ECB, like other central banks, competes for PhD-level economists who want to be able to move between the bank and an academic career. But this is belied by the ECB's more technocratic treatment and presentation of its researchers – relative, for instance, to the Fed. Here we might consider the institutions' online presentation of researchers as scholarly professionals versus technocratic staff. Fed researchers are clearly the former: a visit to the Federal Reserve Board's 'Economic Research & Data' page presents the user with an invitation, at the top right of the screen, to 'Meet the Economists'. From here one can view images and titles of all FRB economists, listed by last name or sorted by field of interest (first) or organizational division (second), and then link to their individual profiles. The webpage's introduction is also telling: it presents the FRB's more than '300 Ph.D. economists, who ... conduct cutting edge research ... and are among the leading contributors at professional meetings and in major journals'.[29]

The ECB's 'Economic Research' page now also offers links to individual profiles (of 61 researchers, credentials unspecified on the main page), under the heading of 'ECB staff-authored research papers'.[30] But ECB researchers appear beneath a very different introduction, not of 'the economists' but rather 'economic research at the ECB', which is less about scholarly presence and professional influence and more about the necessities of technocratic policymaking. In particular, ECB economic research aims 'to provide a strong conceptual and empirical basis for policy-making and to better communicate policy to the markets and to the public'. Its 'most important task ... within the Eurosystem' is not to contribute to external professional fora, but rather 'to increase knowledge of the functioning of the euro area economy and, more specifically, to provide models, tools and analyses relevant to the conduct of monetary policy and the fulfillment of other tasks of the Eurosystem'.

We might also consider how the two institutions' research trajectories responded to the financial and Eurozone crises. Referring back to Figure 1, both appear to have been sensitive to the crises. And again, the ECB stands out relative to other European banks: the BOE's and BB's research remained fairly stable.[31] But the ECB's and FRB's research patterns were not the same: the ECB's output steadily declined as the Eurozone crisis set in, before bouncing back; the FRB's response was erratic, and not as pronounced. Here the ECB reacted more like an administrative-technocratic institution, whose first responsibility was policy rather than science.

There is another sign of technocratic primacy inside the ECB: deviation from official positions, even in external scholarly publications, is not the normative thing to do. One interviewee remarked on an informal expectation that academic papers should reinforce, rather than challenge, bank policies: '[W]ould we publish a paper that is contrary to the ECB policy? I don't think so ... Sometimes you read the ECB WP series and you already know the conclusion.' [32] And, here too, there are symptoms of European investment: while the ECB clearly values scientific training and skills, specifically European credentials – for instance, training at the European University Institute (EUI) or the *Collège d'Europe* in Bruges – can have a special value, as they allow the bank to validate its 'EU-mindedness'.[33]

Perhaps the clearest indication that hyper-scientization is not only about scientific and scholarly prestige, and is *also* an effect of European investments, is the way in which the timing and structure of integration shapes the ECB's research activities and – more importantly – the way in which the ECB uses research activities *as a means to bureaucratic authority*. Contrarily to the European legal system, which never set any formal coordination between the ECJ and national supreme courts, the European monetary system integrates NCBs within the ECB through its Governing Council in charge of determining the monetary policy, which is then implemented by the Executive Board. National central banks actually represent an important share of the votes (19 out of 25, with the other six coming from the Executive Board) – much more than it is the case in either the Fed or in the *Bundesbank*.

As a result, the ECB's autonomy from, and power over, NCBs was unsettled from the start. The ECB initially staffed mainly by civil servants seconded by NCBs and depended on them as a means to policy implementation. NCBs are the operational arms of the ECB, the source of data needed to provide a euro-wide picture of economic and financial markets.

In this context, research and academic credentials have been an important lever for the ECB's Executive Board to affirm its leadership in the Eurosystem and build its capacity to work autonomously, in time, from NCBs. Its elevated productivity had partly to do with the ECB's peculiar relations of dependence on, yet authority over, national central banks. In short, academic research and scientific prestige are, for the ECB, a means to bureaucratic power.

This becomes particularly clear in annual reports during the lead up to the EU's single-largest enlargement in 2004. Significant glimmers of academicization first appeared in 2002 (reporting on 2001). Initially preoccupied with the formidable task of generating European statistics and time series, between 2000 and 2004 the ECB introduced a series of programmes meant to link its research staff more closely with that of other central banks, and with university-based economics.[34] These included a Research Visitors programme (established 2001) in the DGR, focused on monetary policy. Bringing in visiting researchers for about two months, the initiative was complemented by a Graduate Research programme 'aimed at highly talented research students' in the final stages of their doctoral studies. Across all the ECB's departments, in 2001 programmes like this brought in 87 'students and graduates, mainly with an economics background' (ECB, 2002, reporting on 2001: 177).

In the lead-up to 2004 the ECB pursued deeper connections with other central banks, as well as academic departments, via personnel exchanges and visiting appointments. The number of the ECB's visiting students and researchers increased

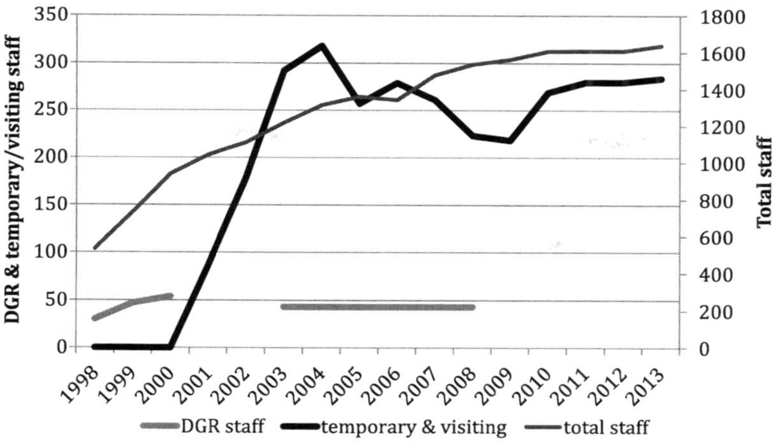

Figure 3 *ECB total and research staff (DGR + visiting/temporary), 1998–2013*
Source/notes: *Sources are ECB Annual Reports for the indicated years. For 2003 through 2008, the figures for DGR staff are rough estimates, based on language in annual reports. Figures for 'temporary and visiting' include temporary employees visiting from Eurozone member national central banks (NCBs), (estimated) participants in the ECB's 2-year postgraduate programme, interns, and fellowship programme participants. The majority are visitors from NCBs.*

to at least 179 in 2002, partly due to visits from personnel of central banks in accession countries.[35] In January 2003 the ECB institutionalized a reciprocal effort, the External Work Experience Scheme, to send its research staff to 'central banks inside and outside the ESCB or at European or international organisations' in order to foster 'ties between the ECB and its counterparts' (ECB, 2003, reporting on 2002: 191). Between 2002 and 2004 the ECB's visiting and short-term contract researchers (around 318) nearly doubled (ECB, 2005, reporting on 2004: 172). As shown in Figure 3, the ECB's visiting and temporary researchers between about 1999 and 2004 accelerated in numbers at a disproportionate pace.

In short, the immediate run-up to final accession spurred an intense effort to extend the ECB's research network into the central banks of acceding member states, as well as a new emphasis from the ECB on its research capacities and achievements.

It is thus no mistake that, by 2004 – only six years after the ECB was created – its scientization was on full display. The 2004 Annual Report, packaged in a noticeably more polished format, featured a new section on 'Economic Research' that tallied the ECB's research activities, accomplishments, and academic profile. Defining ECB economic research's aim in terms of providing 'a strong conceptual and empirical basis for policy-making and to better communicate policy to the markets and the public', the new section opened with strong claims as to the centrality of in-house research as a means to the optimal conduct of monetary policy in an enlarged EU:

> High-quality research is essential to ensure that the ECB is well equipped to cope with the unprecedented challenges associated with conducting a single monetary policy for a group of sovereign countries. The most important task of economic research within the Eurosystem is to increase knowledge of the functioning of the euro area economy and, more specifically, to provide models, tools and analyses relevant to the conduct of monetary policy and the fulfilment of other tasks of the Eurosystem. (ECB, 2004, on the year 2003: 100–102)

By this time, still well before the financial crisis, DGR's focus extended well beyond monetary policy. By 2003 its purview dealt not only with 'monetary policy strategy, rules and indicators' and 'the transmission of monetary policy', but also 'financial markets and institutions; international economics and finance; the macroeconomic modelling of the euro area; and general economic and structural issues'. At the same time the ECB was developing formal networks to bring together economists from Eurosystem NCBs via, for instance, its Macroprudential Research Network (Mars) and CompNet on competitiveness. All can be read as part of the ECB's scientific and scholarly enterprise, and yet also of a piece with the ECB's efforts to establish and sustain its institutional authority in the European political order.

Conclusion

Just like it is impossible to understand *avant-garde* art without an analysis of the field of painting, it is difficult to make sense of the ECB without placing it in the fields from which it emerged, and in which it is located still. To our knowledge, Bourdieu never elaborated on the notion of 'field effect'. It is nonetheless a useful shorthand for field-theoretic notions of causality, pointing down an analytical path in which the ECB's supranationality, per se, is not at issue: taking institutional characteristics, strategies and self-presentation as both contingent historical outcomes and indicators of its fielded location. While the ECB's hyper-scientization might appear as merely an historical accident, and perhaps even an irrationality from the perspective of its policy-making imperatives, we argue that by fielding supranationalism it becomes fully intelligible. At the same time, as the above seeks to demonstrate, a BFT facilitates a meaningful comparative and historical analysis of a world that is sometimes considered an incomparable 'N of 1'.

It also leads to other, interesting questions, about the making of specifically European forms of authority – and authority figures. For instance, if our thesis is correct, then we might expect to find that the ECB cultivates a specific kind of central banker who is encouraged to maintain three commitments at once: to scientific achievement, comparable to other economists; to the official positions and policies of the bank, comparable to other central bankers; and to a specifically European political identity, comparable to other occupants of European institutions. We found indications of this kind of juggling, reminiscent of other 'hybrid' locations (Medvetz, 2012). One interviewee noted, for instance, that despite the opposition between scholarly and policy-supporting research inside the bank, even policy-supporting work requires a degree of academic validation.[36] Another indication is that, more than a means of external validation, academic achievement is also a means to upward mobility inside the ECB; the trajectory of a former director of DGR notable for his innovations in forecasting and computational modelling, Frank Smets, into an assistant position to Mario Draghi in November 2013, attests to this.

In sum, a BFT approach offers a means not only of advancing the comparative and historical study of integration and European institutions, but also a means of understanding the making and remaking of political and bureaucratic authority in, between, and beyond national settings.

Notes

1 On 18 March 2015 the *New York Times* and other news outlets reported on a protest of about 8,000 people at the ECB's new headquarters, organized by Blockupy (an alliance of left activists and political parties) and German workers' unions (Wessel and Ewing, 2015).

2 In the same year awareness of the EP stood at 93 per cent, and trust at 37 per cent. Source: European Union 1995–2015, Eurobarometer survey, http://ec.europa.eu/publicopinion. Tables and figures are available from the authors upon request.

3 ECB Annual Report, 2014; ECB interview, March 2015. See also Black and Speciale (2014).

4 Levels of awareness of, and trust in, the ECJ as of May 2013 – the most recent round of Eurobarometer survey items on these questions – were 77 per cent and 48 per cent, respectively. Trust levels in the ECJ ranged between 48 per cent and 57 per cent in 2004 and 2005 (European Union, 1995–2014, Eurobarometer). Tables and figures are available from Stephanie Mudge on request.

5 Official documents and comparative data were collected mainly from online sources (as noted, and in the bibliography) and via two ECB site visits by Antoine Vauchez in March and June 2015. This research was funded by the France-Berkeley Fund and the University of California, Davis.

6 Initial members of the euro were Belgium, Germany, Spain, France, Ireland, Italy, Luxembourg, the Netherlands, Austria, Portugal and Finland. The other four members, of non-euro countries (at that time), were the banks of Greece, Sweden, England, and Denmark.

7 http://www.ecb.int/ecb/orga/decisions/html/cvtrichet.en.html (accessed 4 April 2010).

8 The report argues that 'those economists whose main responsibility is to work on the regular forecast will be stretched in carrying out longer-term research projects' (Freedman *et al.*, 2011: 12).

9 Central banking was occasionally defended on scientific grounds before mid-century, but 'scientific' did not necessarily imply groundedness in academic economic theory. In the 1920s, for instance, US Senator Carter Glass – the largely self-taught co-founder of the Federal Reserve System – argued before the Senate that the then-incipient FRB's operations were 'scientifically' justified, but this was not grounded in any particular economic theory (Glass, 1922).

10 Friedman famously complained that in the 1930s the Fed was guided by 'theory by aphorism' (Friedman, 1967 [1968]: 1).

11 Emerson holds a master's degree in politics, philosophy and economics (PPE). See http://www.ceps.eu/member/michael-emerson (accessed 24 March 2015).

12 This report, initially issued by DG EcFin in 1990, followed a 1987 report by Tommaso Padoa Schioppa (then a former EU top civil servant and vice-director general of the Bank of Italy) commissioned by the European Commission (Padoa Schioppa *et al.*, 1987) – on which Michael Emerson served as a rapporteur (Dyson and Featherstone, 2000; Maes, 2010).

13 Papadia became chief of operations at the ECB after more than twenty years at the *Banca d'Italia* (Marshall, 1999: 222).
14 ECB interview No. 4, manager, male, PhD, more than 10 years at ECB, March 2015.
15 ECB interview No. 4, manager, male, PhD, more than 10 years at ECB, March 2015.
16 ECB interview No. 4, manager, male, PhD, more than 10 years at ECB, March 2015.
17 ECB interview No. 1, manager, male, more than 5 years at the ECB, March 2015.
18 ECB interview No. 3, manager, male, less than 5 years at the ECB, March 2015.
19 See http://nginx.org/en/ and http://repec.org/docs/RePEcIntro.html (accessed 13 March 2015). With the establishment of RePEc, WoPEc's ceased being grant-dependent, guaranteeing that it would 'remain free for all parties.'
20 Detailed tables are available from Stephanie Mudge on request.
21 The H-Index was created by a physicist at the University of California-San Diego, Jorge Hirsch, in 2005 (Hirsch, 2005). As Freedman *et al.* (2011) explain: 'the overall RePEc ranking is driven by a scale effect, since it measures aggregate research performance and the ECB is large relative to most other institutions. One sub-measure that partially adjusts for the scale effect is the "institutional *h* index" where *h* is the number of individuals in an organization that have *h* articles cited in the RePEc database at least *h* times. The development of author-level data in RePEc started as a separate project (HoPEc), funded by the Open Society Institute (see http://acis.openlib.org/idea/, accessed 16 March 2015).
22 ECB interview No. 1, manager, male, more than 5 years at the ECB, March 2015.
23 ECB interview No. 4, manager, male, PhD, more than 10 years at ECB, March 2015.
24 ECB interview No. 1, manager, male, more than 5 years at the ECB, March 2015.
25 ECB interview No. 1, manager, male, more than 5 years at the ECB, March 2015.
26 ECB interview No. 1, manager, male, more than 5 years at the ECB, March 2015.
27 ECB interview No. 1, manager, male, more than 5 years at the ECB, March 2015.
28 ECB interview No. 3, manager, male, less than 5 years at the ECB, March 2015.
29 http://www.federalreserve.gov/econresdata/theeconomists.htm (accessed 30 September 2015).
30 See https://www.ecb.europa.eu/home/html/researcher.en.html (accessed 16 March 2015); and https://www.ecb.europa.eu/pub/economic-research/html/index.en.html (accessed 30 September 2015). On the later date we returned to the first link listed, which now arrives at a different address (the second one listed). In between times the ECB appears to have added individual, CV-like profiles.
31 Bundesbank staffing declined between 2001 and 2013, from 14,800 to 9,532 'core staff' – a decline of about 36 per cent. So this needs to be taken into consideration. The BB reports a near-doubling of academic publications between 2013 and 2014. See: http://www.bundesbank.de/Redaktion/EN/Standardartikel/Bundesbank/Tasksandorganisation/thebundesbankkeyfigures.html#doc15820bodyText1 (accessed 13 March 2015).
32 Interview No. 4, ECB Manager, Male, PhD, more than 10 years of seniority at the ECB, March 2015.
33 Interview No. 4, ECB Manager, Male, PhD, more than 10 years of seniority at the ECB, March 2015.
34 Clément Fontan relates the growth of the ECB's powers to, first, the development of its statistical capacities, then its increasingly recognized expertise over the EU financial system, and finally dominance (at the expense of DG EcFin) in the new European Systemic Risk Board.
35 Author calculations based on ECB, 2003, reporting on 2002: 191.
36 Interview No. 3, ECB Manager, Male, PhD, less than 5 years of seniority at the ECB, March 2015.

References

Adolph, C., (2013), *Bankers, Bureaucrats, and Central Bank Politics: The Myth of Neutrality*, Cambridge: Cambridge University Press.

Atkins, R., (2007), 'Cultivated polymath with a sure hand on the financial tiller of Europe', Financial Times, Asia Edition 1, FT Person of the Year – Jean-Claude Trichet, 7.

Bank of England (BOE), (1995–2010), Annual Reports.

Bernanke, B. S., (2010), 'On the implications of the financial crisis for economics', Remarks by Ben S. Bernanke, Chairman, Board of Governors of the Federal Reserve System at the conference co-sponsored by the Bendheim Center for Finance and the Center for Economic Policy Studies. Princeton, NJ, 24 September.

Bini Smaghi, L., (2010), 'Slaves of defunct economists', speech by Lorenzo Bini Smaghi, Member of the Executive Board of the ECB, at the Master Programme in International Business and Economics, Università di Pavia, 24 February.

Black, J. and Speciale, A., (2014), 'Draghi summons banking know-how for ECB posts as role shifts', *Bloomberg Business*, 10 November, available at: http://www.bloomberg.com/news/articles/2014-11-10/draghi-summons-banking-know-how-for-top-posts-as-ecb-role-shifts (accessed 25 March 2015).

Bourdieu, P., (1993), 'Some properties of fields', in *Sociology in Question*, 72–77, Basingstoke: Palgrave.

Bourdieu, P. and Wacquant, L., (1992), *Invitation to Reflexive Sociology*, Chicago: University of Chicago Press.

Castelnuovo, E., (2003), 'Describing the Fed's conduct with Taylor Rules: is interest rate smoothing important?', European Central Bank Working Paper No. 232, Frankfurt am Main.

Chambers, S., (2003), 'Deliberative democratic theory', *Annual Review of Political Science*, 6: 307–326.

Cohen, A., (2010), 'Legal professionals or political entrepreneurs. constitution-making as a process of social construction and political mobilization', *Law and Social Inquiry*, 4: 107–123.

de Grauwe, P., (2013), 'The political economy of the euro', *Annual Review of Political Science*, 16: 153–170.

de Haan, J., (2001), *The History of the Bundesbank. Lessons for the European Central Bank*, London: Routledge.

de Haan, J. and Eijffinger, S., (2000), 'The democratic accountability of the European Central Bank: a comment on two fairytales', *Journal of Common Market Studies*, 38 (3): 393–407.

Delors, J. and Christopherson, H., (1990), 'Preface', in E. Emerson, D. Gros, A. Italianer, J. Pisani-Ferry and H. Reichenbach, *One Market, One Money, An Evaluation of the Potential Costs and Benefits of Forming an Economic and Monetary Union*, Oxford: Oxford University Press.

Deutsche Bundesbank, (2001), *Annual Report 2000*, Frankfurt am Main.

Dezalay, Y. and Garth, B., (2002), *The Internationalization of Palace Wars*, Chicago: University of Chicago Press.

Draghi, M., (2012), Speech by Mario Draghi, President of the European Central Bank, Global Investment Conference, 26 July, London.

Dyson, K. and Featherstone, K., (2000), *The Road to Maastricht. Negotiating Economic and Monetary Union*, Oxford: Oxford University Press.

Eijffinger, S., (2002), 'The federal design of central bank in a monetary union: the case of the European System of Central Banks', Central Bank of Chile Working Paper No. 160.

Emerson, E., Gros, D., Italianer, A., Pisani-Ferry, J. and Reichenbach, H., (1992), *One Market, One Money, An Evaluation of the Potential Costs and Benefits of Forming an Economic and Monetary Union*, Oxford: Oxford University Press [originally produced in 1990 as a report of the staff of the Commission's DG for Economic and Financial Affairs].

Enderlein, H., Bofinger, P., Boone, L., de Grauwe, P., Piris, J-C., Pisani-Ferry, J., Rodrigues, M. J., Sapir, A. and Vitorino, A., (2012), *Completing the Euro. A Road Map towards Fiscal Union in Europe*, Report of the 'Tommaso Padoa-Schioppa Group', *Notre Europe*.

European Central Bank (ECB), (2000–2014), *Annual Reports*.

European Monetary Institute (EMI), (1995 and 1997), *Annual Reports*.

Federal Reserve Board (FRB), (1995–2010), *Annual Reports*.

Fontan, C., (2013), 'Une institution politique à l'épreuve de la crise. La Banque centrale européenne dans l'Union monétaire (2007–2012)', PhD in political science, Université de Grenoble.
Fontan, C., (2015), 'L'art du grand écart. La Banque central européenne face au dilemmes provoqués par la crise de la zone euro, *Gouvernement et action publique*, 2: 103–123.
Fourcade, M., (2006), 'The construction of a global profession: the transnationalization of economics', *American Journal of Sociology*, 112: 145–194.
Freedman, C., Lane, P. R., Repullo, R. and Schmidt-Hebbel, K., (2011), 'External evaluation of the Directorate General Research of the European Central Bank'.
Friedman, M., (1967 [1968]), 'The role of monetary policy', *The American Economic Review*, 58 (1): 1–17.
Georgakakis, M. and Rowell, J., (2013), *The Field of Eurocracy*, Basingstoke: Palgrave.
Glass, C., (1922), 'The truth about the Federal Reserve System', speech in the US Senate, 16–17 January, Washington DC.
Go, J., (2008), 'Global fields and imperial forms: field theory and the British and American Empires', *Sociological Theory*, 26 (3): 201–229.
Goodfriend, M., König, R. and Repullo, R., (2004), 'External evaluation of the economic research activities of the European Central Bank', 20 February.
Greenspan, A., (2008), 'Testimony of Dr. Alan Greenspan', *Committee of Government Oversight and Reform*, 23 October.
Hilgers, M. and Mangez, E., (2014), 'Introduction to Pierre Bourdieu's theory of social fields', in M. Hilgers and E. Mangez (eds), *Bourdieu's Theory of Social Fields: Concepts and Applications*, 1–36, London: Routledge.
Hirsch, J. E., (2005), 'An index to quantify an individual's scientific research output', *PNAS* 102 (46): 16569–16572.
Issing, O., (2008), *The Birth of the Euro*. Cambridge: Cambridge University Press.
James, H., (2012), *Making the Monetary Union*, Cambridge, MA: Harvard University Press.
Jonung, L. and Drea, E., (2009), 'The euro: It can't happen. It's a bad idea. It won't last. US economists on the EMU, 1989–2002." *Economic Papers 395* (December). Brussels: European Commission DG Economic and Financial Affairs.
Karlsson, S. and Krichel, T., (1999), 'RePEc and S-WoPEc: Internet access to electronic preprints in economics', available at: http://openlib.org/home/krichel/papers/lindi.html (accessed 10 December 2015).
Lebaron, F., (2000), 'The space of economic neutrality. trajectories and types of legitimacy of central bank managers', *International Journal of Contemporary Sociology*, 37 (2): 208–229.
Lebaron, F., (2013), 'ECB leaders: a new European monetary elite?' in D. Georgakakis and J. Rowell (eds), *The Field of Eurocracy*, 87–103, Basingstoke: Palgrave.
Levi Strauss, C., (1960), *La pensée sauvage*, Paris: Plon.
Marcussen, M., (2009), 'The scientization of central banking, the politics of apoliticization', in K. Dyson and M. Marcussen (eds), *Central Banks in the Age of the Euro: Europeanization, Convergence, and Power*, 373–390, Oxford: Oxford University Press.
Maes, I., (2010), 'Economic thought at the European Commission and the creation of EMU (1957–1991)', *Storia del Pensiero Economico*, 2: 63–80.
Marshall, M., (1999), *The Bank*, London: Random House.
Martin, J. L., (2003), 'What is field theory?' *American Journal of Sociology*, 109 (1): 1–49.
McNamara, K. R., (1998), *The Currency of Ideas: Monetary Politics in the European Union*, Ithaca, NY: Cornell University Press.
Medvetz, T., (2012), *Think Tanks in America*. Chicago: University of Chicago Press.
Meyer, L. H., (1997), 'Conduct of monetary policy', testimony of Governor Laurence H. Meyer before the Committee on Banking and Financial Services, US House of Representatives, 23 July.
Mudge, S. L., (2015), 'Explaining political tunnel vision: politics and economics in crisis-ridden Europe, then and now', *European Journal of Sociology*, 56 (1): 63–91.
Mudge, S. and Vauchez, A., (2012), 'Building Europe on a weak field. law, economics, scholarly avatars and transnational fields', *American Journal of Sociology*, 118 (2): 449–492.

Mundell, R. (1961), 'A theory of optimum currency areas', *American Economic Review*, 51: 657–667.
Padoa-Schioppa, T., King, M., Paelinck, J.-H.P., Papademos, L. D., Pastor, A. and Scharpf, F. W., (1987), *Efficiency Stability and Equity: A Strategy for the Evolution of the Economic System of the European Community*, report of a study group appointed by the Commission of the European Communities, II/49/87. Available at: http://ec.europa.eu/archives/emu_history/documentation/chapter12/19870410en149efficiencstabil_a.pdf (accessed 10 December 2015).
Taugourdeau, E. and Vincensini, C., (2009), 'La justification économique de l'Union écnomique et monétaire: ex ante, ex post ou inexistence?', *Revue française d'économie*, 24 (2): 57–83.
Tognato, C., (2012), *Central Bank Independence: Cultural Codes and Symbolic Performance*, Basingstoke: Palgrave Macmillan.
Trichet, J-C., (2009a), 'Ten years of the euro: successes and challenges', speech by Jean-Claude Trichet, President of the ECB, Osnabrück, 12 February.
Trichet, J-C., (2009b), 'Systemic risk', Clare Distinguished Lecture in Economic Policy, Clare College, University of Cambridge, Cambridge, 10 December.
Trichet, J-C., (2009c), 'Interview with Jean-Claude Trichet, President of the European Central Bank, and Le Figaro Magazine conducted by Ghislain de Montalembert', ECB.
Trichet, J-C., (2009d), 'The crisis and its lessons', Lecture by Jean-Claude Trichet, President of the ECB at the University of Venice, Venice, 9 October.
Tumpell-Gugerell, G., (2009), 'Recent advances in modeling systemic risk using network analysis', introductory remarks, ECB workshop. Frankfurt.
Vauchez, A., (2008), 'The force of a weak field: law and lawyers in the government of Europe', *International Political Sociology*, 5: 128–144.
Vauchez, A., (2014), *Democratizing Europe*, Basingstoke: Palgrave.
Wessel, R. and Ewing, J., (2015), 'Protesters and the police clash near E.C.B.'s new headquarters', International Business, *New York Times*, 18 March, available at: http://www.nytimes.com/2015/03/19/business/european-central-bank-protests-frankfurt.html?r=0.
Woolley, J., (2009), 'The US Federal Reserve and the politics of monetary and financial regulatory policies', in K. Dyson and M. Marcussen (eds), *Central Banks in the Age of the Euro: Europeanization, Convergence, and Power*, 307–336, Oxford: Oxford University Press.

The lawyers' war: states and human rights in a transnational field

Lisa Stampnitzky

Abstract: While torture and assassination have not infrequently been used by states, the post 9/11 'war on terror' waged by the US has been distinguished by the open acknowledgement of, and political and legal justifications put forward in support of, these practices. This is surprising insofar as the primary theories that have been mobilized by sociologists and political scientists to understand the relation between the spread of human rights norms and state action presume that states will increasingly adhere to such norms in their rhetoric, if not always in practice. Thus, while it is not inconceivable that the US would engage in torture and assassination, we would expect these acts would be conducted under a cloak of deniability. Yet rather than pure hypocrisy, the US war on terror has been characterized by the development of a legal infrastructure to support the use of 'forbidden' practices such as torture and assassination, along with varying degrees of open defence of such tactics. Drawing on first-order accounts presented in published memoirs, this paper argues that the Bush administration developed such openness as a purposeful strategy, in response to the rise of a legal, technological, and institutional transnational human rights infrastructure which had turned deniability into a less sustainable option. It concludes by suggesting that a more robust theory of state action, drawing on sociological field theory, can help better explain the ways that transnational norms and institutions affect states.

Keywords: human rights, torture, law, lawyers, transnational field, war on terror

> In the aftermath of 9/11, the White House went beyond the CIA's highly secretive practice of torture during the Cold War to its open, even defiant use of coercive interrogation as a formal weapon of the arsenal of American power – a historic shift with profound implications for this nation's international standing. (McCoy 2006: 211)

> Many people think the Bush administration has been indifferent to wartime legal constraints. But the opposite is true: the administration has been strangled by law, and since September 11, 2001, this war has been lawyered to death. (Goldsmith 2007: 68–69)

The Sociological Review Monographs, 64:2, pp. 170–193 (2016), DOI: 10.1111/2059-7932.12007

Published by John Wiley & Sons Ltd, 9600 Garsington Road, Oxford OX4 2DQ, UK and 350 Main Street, Malden, MA 02148, USA

Introduction

After 9/11, American officials developed an explicit legal framework to support the use of practices such as waterboarding, sleep deprivation, and physical confinement – practices that, when used by other nations, have generally been understood as torture. While the practice of torture itself is neither rare nor fully unexpected in times of 'terror' and heightened security threats, both the literature on states and human rights violations, and the recent history of state use of torture, would lead us to expect that any such use of torture, especially by states identifying as Western, advanced, and democratic, would be cloaked within an apparatus of secrecy and denial. Yet in the post-9/11 war on terror, not only did state agents engage in torture, officials developed both political and legal justifications for the practice. Furthermore, these justifications cannot be understood as merely *post hoc* attempts to save face, as they were developed both before and after the use of torture became widely known.

This paper thus asks: why construct an explicit legal architecture for practices which, until recently, if engaged in at all, would have been subject to the highest levels of secrecy, and certainly not documented by lawyers? It further asks, how can we square this development with the spread of human rights norms over the course of the twentieth century? The key puzzle is thus not merely why did the US government make use of torture in the aftermath of 9/11, but why it did so in a relatively open fashion.[1] The conduct of the American state in engaging in practices of torture and 'enhanced interrogation' was, if not necessarily predictable, certainly comprehensible in light of 9/11 and the apparatus of 'terrorism' through which Americans made sense of the attacks. Nor can the adoption of these practices after 9/11 be seen as completely surprising, given the history of their use throughout the 20th century.[2] But why not proceed in clandestine fashion? And why has the war on terror, and particularly the use of torture and assassination, been so saturated with legal expertise? In sum, why bother developing an explicit justification for practices that, in the past, would have simply been undertaken covertly?

I argue that we can best understand the open defence of torture and assassination as a response to the rise of a transnational field of legal regulation of human rights that sought to encompass both states and individual state officials.[3] In other words, the appearance of explicit legal justification of human rights violations, at the very moment when the international human rights field seems to have attained its peak, should not be seen as a paradox, but rather as two interrelated developments. I develop support for this argument by drawing on the accounts of these events presented in memoirs of direct participants, treating these as primary sources.

The 'legalization' of torture presents a circumstance not predicted or conceptualized by the primary theories mobilized in sociology and political science to understand how human rights norms affect states. These tend to suggest that we will observe an increasing adherence to such norms, at least at the level of states' rhetoric, if not always in their practices. The general expectation has been that

The Sociological Review Monographs, 64:2, pp. 170–193 (2016), DOI: 10.1111/2059-7932.12007

states will increasingly move in the direction of greater respect for human rights, and that even when states commit violations of human rights, they will still affirm the respect for human rights treaties and norms at the level of rhetoric and ideals. Within this framework, the actions of the US in the war on terror seem almost inexplicable.

One might argue that this is simply a case of American exceptionalism (eg Mertus, 2008: 17), or that the US, as the globally hegemonic power, is not subject to the rules shaping the conduct of other states. In the view of this paper, however, these explanations are inadequate, because the quasi-open breaking of the torture taboo is not a unique event, even in the contemporary era of the human rights regime. There have been similar transformations elsewhere; perhaps most notably the Israeli 'Landau Commission' of the 1980s which ruled on the legality of torture. And earlier in the century, albeit before the adoption of the UN Convention Against Torture, both France and the UK attempted to legalize the use of torture. In France, the 1955 Wuillame report 'called for the "veil of hypocrisy" to be lifted and for "safe and controlled" interrogation techniques to be authorized' (Bellamy, 2006: 128) in Algeria, while in Britain, the 1971 Compton Commission to investigate claims of state torture in Northern Ireland heard similar claims (Bellamy, 2006). Furthermore, the claim to American exceptionalism is also belied by the fact that the US did, in fact, until quite recently, hold to international human rights norms, at least rhetorically, if not always in practice.

Others have suggested that the actions of the Bush administration should be seen as a temporary aberration. But while the Obama administration has stepped back from its predecessor's justifications of torture, the larger pattern of open justification, and legalization of violations of international law has continued (Hajjar, 2010). Furthermore, although the signature practice of the war on terror under Obama has shifted from torture and indefinite detention to 'targeted killing', the US remains engaged in a practice forbidden under both domestic and international law, and yet openly defended in political rhetoric and legalized.

A third possible explanation arises from the literature theorizing the US after 9/11 as exemplifying a 'state of exception' (van Munster, 2004; Agamben, 2005; Aradau and van Munster, 2009). This approach suggests that under conditions of emergency, the state declares itself outside, or not subject to, the law (in this case, the international laws of war and human rights), thus enabling a wider range of action. This interpretation is echoed by those critics who have cast the prison at Guantanamo, and sometimes the 'war on terror' as a whole, as a 'legal black hole':[4] a space wholly *outside* the law. But while it is true that many analyses of the role of law in the post 9/11 war on terror have focused upon the ways in which the Bush administration violated, or seemed to ignore, the law, my focus here is the opposite, the central role played by lawyers in these very developments. Recent American counterterrorism policy has been thoroughly imbued with concern for the law, and lawyers and legal experts have been among the most prominent actors in the shaping of these policies (and their subsequent contestation).

Instead, this paper develops a framework for explaining the legal justification of torture as a strategic response to structural shifts in the transnational arena.

 The Sociological Review Monographs, 64:2, pp. 170–193 (2016), DOI: 10.1111/2059-7932.12007

It argues that American state actors found themselves in a new strategic position as a result of the rise of a transnational field of human rights advocacy. This new field, which developed and grew in strength over the course of the twentieth century, was composed of individuals and organizations that sought to enact new human rights norms that would constrain states. Through key practices, including the enactment of international laws to protect human rights, the collection, verification, and publication of evidence of human rights violations, and the prosecution of individual state actors for violations, these actors sought to reduce the presence of torture and other violations in the world. Yet one unintended, and likely unforeseen, consequence of these developments was to shift the strategic context within which states acted. While the rise of the human rights field may have shifted the calculus made by states as to *whether* to violate or respect human rights,[5] a surely unintended consequence was that it also shifted the context within which states that made the decision to engage in violations would act. I argue that such states now find themselves in a context in which the decision to encompass torture within an apparatus of secrecy and denial is less obvious than it was before, and in which the possible choice to openly acknowledge and legally justify such practices becomes more thinkable than before.

This argument draws upon the sociological framework of field theory (Bourdieu, 1977, 1990), which has the key advantage of enabling researchers to analyse the movements of actors and social structures together. While field theory has most often been used to analyse action at the level of the *individual,* and *within* states this paper builds on a recent move to apply field theory at the transnational level, and to state and other collective actors (eg Go, 2008; Mudge and Vauchez, 2012). This field approach allows us to conceptualize not only how transnational actors and movements might not only try to constrain states, but to reconceptualize the transnational arena as a space within which states may also 'act back' upon these constraints and aim to change the so-called 'rules of the game' in response.

Methods/data

To support the argument that the 'legalization' of torture was a purposeful strategy enacted in response to the rise of human rights norms and the overall 'legalization' of warfare, I draw on first-person accounts of those who enacted these policies, in the form of published memoirs. In studying events which are not available through the release of archival records, and whose participants are not all likely to be accessible for direct interviews, memoirs can function as a suitable proxy, providing first-hand accounts, in their own words, of those who developed these policies. While memoirs are but one possible source where one might look for first-hand accounts of those involved in the decision to 'legalize' torture, I have chosen to focus on the accounts found in memoirs rather than in alternate sources such as published interviews, or the 'torture memos' and accompanying documents themselves, first, because these are the sources where individuals put forth their accounts for posterity, and second, because they are a presently under-utilized source.[6]

Memoirs are a complex and potentially problematic source of data. Gocek's (2015) historical study of the denial of Turkish violence against the Armenians, which relies on memoirs as its primary source, contains a thoughtful discussion of the advantages and limitations of such a data source, highlighting that memoirs will limit one to the voices of the relatively elite, and the challenge posed by the difficulty in how to 'differentiate fact from fiction, knowledge based on sources from rhetoric, and historical events from their mythified recollections' (Gocek, 2015: xxi). In the case of the present study, however, the focus on elites is a purposeful feature of the study, and while the difficulty of separating 'fact from fiction' is still a concern, the fact that this study is focused on interpretations themselves makes memoirs an appropriate source. I take memoirs as a proxy form of ethnographic data, or self-reporting on the events in question. They are not to be taken as pure fact/transparent reporting of the events that occurred, but rather, taken as a source of the individuals' framings and justification of the events as they went down – which is exactly why memoirs are useful/appropriate sources for this investigation. A list of the memoirs analysed is included as an appendix to the paper.

Theorizing 'human rights' and how international 'norms' affect states

With the rise of human rights, there has been a corresponding rise of *studies* of human rights. Much of this literature has focused on analysing the effects of these norms, laws and institutions, with the question usually posed as, do these norms and laws have effects upon the actual occurrence of torture? (eg Hafner-Burton *et al.,* 2008; Cole, 2012; Hafner-Burton, 2013; Hafner-Burton and Tsutsui, 2013; Fariss, 2014).[7] However, such studies have come to no agreement on this question, with some studies even finding a *negative* correlation between the spread of treaties and states' adherence to norms of human rights! Rather than assuming that these contradictory findings are the result of errors in measurement or ambiguities in operationalization, I propose that these 'untidy' results should prompt those who wish to understand the effects of the new 'human rights regime' to look in an alternative direction.

In more general form, this is the question of how international norms and international laws affect states. The extant literature is dominated by two theoretical frameworks, international relations theory (including both realist and constructivist variants), and sociological 'world-society' theory. A key weakness of realist IR theories is their inability to grapple with the power of culture. Constructivist IR theories, on the other hand, give culture central significance, but tend to lack a developed theory of exactly how culture has influence, particularly over relatively powerful states, or under what circumstances states might be able to resist cultural norms.

World-society theory has been a key theoretical approach for much of the sociological work on states and human rights. For example, Meyer *et al.* trace 'the

 The Sociological Review Monographs, 64:2, pp. 170–193 (2016), DOI: 10.1111/2059-7932.12007

rise of human rights themes in secondary school social science textbooks around the world since 1970', finding support for 'the arguments of institutional theories that the contemporary "globalized" world is one in which the standing of the participatory and empowered individual person has very great legitimacy' (Meyer *et al.*, 2010: 111), while Levy and Sznaider examine 'how global interdependencies and the consolidation of a human rights discourse are transforming national sovereignty' given that 'adherence to global human rights norms confers legitimacy' (2006: 657). The key weaknesses of the 'world-society' approach is that it tends to assume that all states will eventually (and consensually) shift towards an agreed upon set of norms and practices, and further, it tends to assume that norms will diffuse outward from more powerful to less powerful states (Go, 2008). There is thus little room in such a theoretical framework for reactive shifts, *away* from a norm, particularly when such shifts are taken by a powerful state.[8]

The dominant conceptualizations of relations between state discourse and practices on human rights presume, first, that only certain alignments are likely: those which I have labelled in Table 1 as 1 (hypocrisy), 2A (barbarism[9]), and 3 (enlightenment), and yet misses out on others (2B: brazenness).[10] Further, this literature presumes a narrative teleology; it presumes that states will progress in only in one direction, 'forward'. The unspoken teleology of this literature is that the effect of the human rights field (norms, treaties, laws, and beliefs) upon states will be to move them from status 2A (barbarism, in which they fail to acknowledge the value of human rights either in rhetoric or in practice) towards status 3 (enlightenment) in which they affirm the value of human rights both rhetorically in practice, or at the very least, towards status 1 (hypocrisy) in which states affirm the value of human rights in discourse but not in practice. The trajectory which this paper observes in the US war on terror, from status 1 or 3 *back*, to box 2, is not conceptualized as a possibility.

Rather than presuming that the rise of the 'human rights regime' has its most significant effect upon concrete violations of human rights themselves, I argue that they may instead have their most significant effects upon what I refer to

Table 1: *States and human rights*

	States rhetorically affirm value of human rights	States fail to affirm (or actively deny) value of human rights[11]
State practices violate human rights	1. 'hypocrisy'	2A. 'barbarism' 2B. 'brazenness'
State practice respect human rights	3. 'enlightenment'	4. 'naivete'

as states' 'strategies' towards the protection and/or violation of human rights. I suggest that the Bush administration turned to the strategy of 'brazenness' not because they were oblivious to the rise of the international human rights field, but rather, as a conscious strategic response to it.[12] By using the term 'strategy' here, I intend to encompass not just states' violations (or positive protections) of human rights, but also the ways in which a state negotiates, frames and defends these actions in both its domestic and its international political contexts.[13] In other words, extant studies of human rights have been missing out on a significant effect of human rights 'culture/discourse' upon states, because they have a relatively constrained conceptualization of 'practices'. This is different from arguments suggesting that states' 'speech' about human rights, and their concrete 'practices' of respect or violation are disjointed – that is, that there is no necessary connection between the two, although it is generally assumed that, since 'talk is cheap', the usual pattern will be either for states to affirm their respect for human rights rhetorically yet violate them in practice, or to respect human rights both in speech and in practice. My argument instead is that the line of effect from norms to action is not so direct. Rather than assuming that the norm of respect for human rights is settled, second, that norms exert a fairly strong and unilateral power upon the speech of both states and publics (ie, that once the norm of respect for human rights is settled, actors will necessarily at least give lip service to it); and third, that norms also exert a fairly unilateral, yet somewhat weaker, force upon the actions of states (that is, whether or not they will actually violate or respect the human rights of those under their domain), I argue that we need to think about how practices, norms and speech interact in more complex ways, and in which both the affirmation of the norm against torture and the rejection or redefinition of such norms can be seen as strategic.

From denial to justification: American torture after 9/11

By the end of the twentieth century, not only had the right not to be tortured become a well-established norm, but open support for torture had become almost unspeakable, if not unthinkable. It seemed that respect for human rights had become something almost universally adhered to in rhetoric, if not always in practice. As philosopher Henry Shue wrote in his classic essay of 1978: 'No other practice except slavery is so universally and unanimously condemned in law and human convention' (Shue, 1978: 4, in Levinson, 2004), while more recently, Rosemary Foot declared that, 'While the practice of torture has been widespread, until recently it had come to be understood that no representatives of the state could openly admit that they would use torture for fear of being removed from office and of having their state ostracized by "civilized" nations' (Foot, 2006: 131). In America's 1999 report to the UN committee against torture, the US government stated clearly and emphatically that,

> torture is prohibited by law throughout the United States. It is categorically denounced as a matter of policy and as a tool of state authority. Every act constituting torture

The Sociological Review Monographs, 64:2, pp. 170–193 (2016), DOI: 10.1111/2059-7932.12007

> under the Convention constitutes a criminal offense under the law of the United States. No official of the government, federal, state or local, civilian or military, is authorized to commit or to instruct anyone else to commit torture. Nor may any official condone or tolerate torture in any form. No exceptional circumstances may be invoked as a justification of torture.

Katherine Sikkink quotes this passage at length, noting that, 'there was little ambiguity in US legal and ethical commitments to the prohibition on torture and cruel and unusual punishment prior to 2002' (Sikkink, 2011: 196–197).

In sum, while one may doubt the sincerity of such statements – that is, whether states were actually abiding by the moral platitudes which they officially endorsed, it appeared to be a matter of little contention that states *should* and *would* endorse human rights, and particularly, the right not to be tortured, at least in principle. By the end of the twentieth century, opposition to torture had, in the US and elsewhere, attained the status of what social scientists sometimes refer to as a norm – a settled, institutionalized, moral position. Some have even argued that the problem of torture had attained the status of a sacred boundary which might not be crossed (eg Ignatieff, 2003).

Following the attacks of September 11, 2001, however, the legal and moral permissibility of torture seemed to suddenly take on the status of an open question. Debate erupted in the public sphere, as well as within the government, over both the efficacy, and the legal and ethical permissibility, of torture. Popular magazines such as *Newsweek, The Atlantic*, and *The Economist* published cover stories arguing for and against, and a number of prominent philosophers and lawyers came out publicly in favour of the permissibility of torture, and its legalization. Newspapers reported that FBI counterterrorism agents were 'frustrated' and considering the use of 'pressure' or 'harsh interrogations'. The *New York Times* would write that it had become a topic of conversation 'in bars, on commuter trains, and at dinner tables'.[14]

Another writer notes that, '[e]arnest public discussion of the pros and cons of torture gained momentum in the United States shortly after the 9/11 attacks. . . and continued to unfold until, and beyond, the May 2004 publication of the first photographs from Abu Ghraib' (Hannah, 2006: 624). On December 26, 2002 the *Washington Post* ran a front-page story on allegations of torture and inhumane treatment. They quote officials as saying, 'If you don't violate someone's human rights some of the time, you probably aren't doing your job', and, 'We don't kick the [expletive] out of them ... We send them to other countries so they can kick the [expletive] out of them' (cited in Press, 2003).

Meanwhile, public opinion surveys began to suggest that opposition to torture was on the wane. A November 2001 survey found that 32 per cent of Americans favoured torturing terror suspects, while lawyer Alan Dershowitz, one of the key proponents of the legalization of torture, reported that '[d]uring numerous public appearances since September 11, 2001, I have asked audiences for a show of hands as to how many would support the use of nonlethal torture in a ticking bomb case. Virtually every hand is raised' (cited in Luban, 2006: 35). Now, of course, we don't know what proportion of Americans would have favoured torturing terror suspects before 9/11 – because no one was asking, which is the point: the question was virtually unspeakable. Furthermore, this shift in favour of relatively open debate over the permissibility of torture, including affirmations of its use, cannot be understood as simply a matter of post hoc justification, for it developed alongside, and in some cases prior to, the shift in concrete practices, rather than simply in response to it. Even before the revelations that the US was, in fact, torturing prisoners in the war on terror[15] the question of whether or not we *should* torture terrorist suspects came to occupy a key role in public discourse.

After 9/11, lawyers were enrolled in interpreting the law so as to give the president as much leeway as possible in working unilaterally, often explicitly against the spirit, if not the letter, of the law enshrined in international treaties such as the Geneva accords. Legal expertise was used to delineate the boundaries of exceptional treatment that could be used in a pre-emptive approach to counterterrorism. For example, Pfiffner (2010) identifies three key policy decisions on the use of torture, each of which supported by legal expertise: the first, President Bush's Military Order of 13 November 2001, 'which authorized military commissions, defined enemy combatants, and set the conditions of their imprisonment'; the second, the suspension of the Geneva Agreements, ordered by President Bush on 7 February 2002; and the third, Secretary of Defense Rumsfeld's decision of 2 December 2002 that 'allowed military interrogators to use techniques that were not allowed by the Army Field Manual on interrogation' (Pfiffner, 2010: 14). Critical geographer Derek Gregory argues that while the

> very language of extraordinary rendition, ghost prisoners, and black sites implies something out of the ordinary, spectral, a twilight zone: a serial space of exception . . . this performative spacing works through the law to annul the law: it is not a state of exception that can be counterpoised to a rule governed world of normal politics . . . it is a, at bottom, a process of juridical othering. (Gregory and Pred, 2007: 226)

Similarly, Fleur Johns has written that 'the plight of the Guantanamo detainees is less an outcome of law's suspension or evisceration than of elaborate regulatory efforts by a range of legal authority. The detention camps are above all works of legal representation and classification. They are spaces where law and liberal proceduralism speak and operate in excess' (Johns, 2005, cited in Gregory and Pred, 2007). Similar arguments regarding the very centrality of law have also been made by Khalili (2008), Dayan (2011), and Hajjar (2011).

The final extent of openness around torture is illustrated by the fact that state officials defended the use of torture even after the practice had become a public scandal. The story of torture at Abu Ghraib prison began to break in late 2003, and in April 2004 photos depicting abuse of prisoners were published in the *Washington Post* and by the television show *60 minutes*. In May of that year, a previously internal Red Cross report on conditions at the prison was leaked to the *Wall Street Journal*. While the scandal following the release of shocking explicit photographs from the now-notorious Iraqi prison, did lead to a resurgence of condemnation, more recent surveys have actually found that increasing percentages of Americans now profess support for torture under certain circumstances (Zegart, 2012; Brooks and Manza, 2013). And even more puzzlingly, while the scandal was followed at first by the expected denials, the resolution took the form of overt approvals of torture (even if not always labelled as such). While the reaction we might expect would have been, 'first, an absolutely unambiguous cessation of questionable interrogation practices by the administration; and second, a major domestic political upheaval in which broad swaths of the American public loudly insist that anything smacking of torture stop immediately and that top-level officials on whose watch earlier abuses occurred be thrown out of office', neither the 'unambiguous cessation' of torture, nor the broad 'political upheaval' occurred (Hannah, 2006: 622). Exposure did not put an end to the practice of torture, nor did it lead to a clear moral and political condemnation of those who had authorized and carried it out. Instead, '[t]he system of torture has . . . survived its disclosure' (Danner, 2005, quoted in Ip, 2009: 39).

The Bush administration at first engaged in a strategy of denial, claiming that the photos from Abu Ghraib reflected only the work of a few 'bad apples'. Yet, as time went by, the administration turned to policies that would allow the continued use of the techniques exposed, and open defence of 'harsh interrogation', their euphemism for torture. When Congress sought to reign in the use of torture, as in the McCain amendment, which would ban the use of torture on any detainees in US custody, 'Vice President Cheney and CIA director Porter Goss publicly urged Congress to exempt the CIA' (Mertus, 2008: 74–75). And when the amendment passed regardless, 'The administration did little to alleviate suspicions when President Bush attached a "signing statement" to the amendment, declaring that the president had the right at any point not to comply with the ban on cruel, inhumane, and degrading punishment' (Mertus, 2008: 75). When the Army released a new field manual in September 2006, which reaffirmed the need to adhere to the Geneva Conventions and barring torture, President Bush asserted that the new regulations would not apply to the CIA: 'In a speech that sharply contrasted with the Pentagon speech in both tone and substance, President Bush confirmed the existence of a secret CIA detention program, defended CIA officials' use of "alternative" interrogation methods, and called on Congress to pass proposed legislation on military commissions to try detainees at Guantanamo Bay' (Mertus, 2008: 75–76).

A second instance of exposure followed by overt affirmation of 'forbidden practices' can be seen in the administration's reaction to the *Hamdan v. Rumsfeld* Supreme Court decision, which ruled that the military commissions set up to try those held at the Guantanamo prison were illegal, and violated both the Uniform Code of Military Justice and the Geneva Conventions. The *Hamdan* decision was issued on June 29, 2006. Two months later, on 'September 6, 2006, in a nationally televised address, President Bush acknowledged the existence of CIA black sites and the authorization of waterboarding and other "alternative" interrogation tactics, which he characterized as "tough," "safe," "lawful" and "necessary"' (Hajjar, 2011). And the following month, the Military Commissions Act, which brought back the military commissions, and allowed the use of evidence and confessions gained via torture, was passed in Congress. The Military Commissions Act 'also amended the War Crimes Act to provide immunity for past violations of the Geneva Conventions by US officials dating back to 1997, and stripped the federal courts of jurisdiction over all prisoners detained in the context of the "war on terror"' (Hajjar, 2011).

Analysis: why legalize torture?

Why did the Bush administration choose to govern terrorism through the law? I argue that it was in response to the rise of the transnational human rights field, which, with its key practice of documentation and exposure of human rights violations, altered incentives for states, making denial, or complete cover-ups, less viable. While the intent of human rights advocates in so doing was to eliminate human rights violations, an unforeseen consequence has been the opening up of new incentive structures, making not just open adherence to human rights norms, but also their open violation, more likely. I thus argue that the 'brazenness' of the Bush administration's use of torture in the war on terror should be understood as a response to the rise of this transnational human rights field. In this section I focus on two consequences of the rise of the human rights field: two ways in which the rise of human rights has altered the 'field' of forces in which states act, and which shape their practices and strategic moves in the international arena. First, state use of violence (both within and outside of formal 'warfare') has become increasingly legalized (subject to legal regulation, justification, and contention/pushback). Second, the possibility and practicability of keeping large-scale state secrets has shifted, making denial a less feasible long-term strategy. These developments can be traced back over (at least) several decades – concurrent with the rise of the human rights field. And while neither the legalization of warfare/state violence, nor the declining feasibility of state secrecy can been attributed solely to the rise of the transnational human rights field, the rise of human rights has had a significant effect on both of these transformations.

The rise of a transnational human rights field

The latter half of the twentieth century and the early years of the 21st have seen the emergence of international law and legal expertise as spaces of contestation in which states, lawyers, human rights organizations and international institutions contest the legitimacy of states' use of violence against both citizens and foreigners (Keck and Sikkink, 1998; Dezalay and Garth, 2006). This field is transnational, but acts upon and through particular states and state and international and non-governmental institutions. And this field has a history, which entails the merging of several different fields of international law, including human rights law and the wars of law (which previously were largely separate). What is this 'transnational field of human rights', and where did it come from?

When I write here of 'fields', I draw primarily on the work of Pierre Bourdieu, who developed the field analysis as a theoretical apparatus that could include both structure and agency in the same framework. What is key about a 'field' is that it is a space of 'position-takings' of various actors *in relation to one another,* with conflict a constant feature of these relations: 'When we speak of a *field* of position-takings, we are insisting that what can be constituted as a *system* for the sake of analysis is not the product of a coherence-seeking intention or an objective consensus . . . but the product and prize of a permanent conflict' (Bourdieu, 1993: 34). More recently, Krause has described a field as 'a realm in which actors take each other into account … a space of shared taken-for granteds and interpretations, or, to use Pierre Bourdieu's term *doxa'*, and suggests that we might ask 'of any given space … is it fielded?' (Krause, 2014: 22). Julian Go suggests that a global field is 'an arena of struggle in which actors compete for a variety of valued resources, that is, different species of "capital" that are potentially convertible to each other' and that 'fields consist of two related but analytically separable dimensions: (1) the objective configuration of actor-positions and (2) the subjective meanings guiding actors in the struggle, that is the "rules of the game"' (Go, 2008: 206). I suggest that the transnational arena of human rights became 'fielded' in the period between the 1970s and 1990s, thus coming to exert more potential influence on state action (although not necessarily determining the particular actions of any one state) during that time.

Histories of human rights differ in when they argue the concept emerged. Although some suggest we can trace it all the way back to the eighteenth century (Hunt, 2007), most locate the key turning point either to the aftermath of World War II and the Universal Declaration of Human Rights (Borgwardt, 2007) or in the 1970s (Kelly, 2012; Moyn, 2012a; Keys, 2014). For the purposes of this article, I take the latter date to be the site of the key shift, with additional important developments taking place in the 1980s and 1990s: for while *ideas* about human rights may have begun to take shape earlier, it was not until the 1970s that the key elements of a *transnational field* of human rights, consisting of not just laws and treaties, but also significant numbers of governmental and non-governmental organizations (such as Amnesty International and Human Rights Watch), and institutional sites such as truth commissions and international courts, operating in relation to one another, began to take shape. For in order for us to say that there is a *field* of human rights, there must be not just ideas, but also actors (individual and collective) who are oriented towards one another in their actions, with some of the aforementioned 'ideas' taking the form of what is valued, or what underlies action, in the field.

Amnesty International, now one of the best known human rights organizations, was founded in 1961. According to one account, while

> The United Nations (UN) set down core human rights principles in 1948 in the form of the Universal Declaration of Human rights (UDHR) … the governmental representatives who made up the UN Commission on Human Rights ruled that it had no power to act . . . since 1961, the entire context for international human rights discussions has changed. In contrast to the weak human rights norms of the 1960s, it is now possible to point to the fruits of Amnesty's efforts to build norms and elicit behavior more consistent with human rights principles. (Clark, 2001: 3–4)

In sum, 'When Amnesty was founded, an international "human rights" regime, or complex of rules, as we now know it did not exist – and there was no good reason to expect one' (Clark, 2001: 4). In 1972, Amnesty launched the first worldwide 'campaign for the abolition of torture' (Sikkink, 2011: 40). Membership in national chapters grew quickly during this period, with the US chapter growing from 3,000 to 50,000 between 1974 and 1976 (Sikkink, 2011: 41), while the NGO, Helsinki Watch, would merge with a number of other regional groups to form Human Rights Watch in 1988, becoming 'one of the world's largest and most influential human rights organizations' (Keys, 2014: 265).

Calls for the criminal prosecution of individual state leaders for human rights violations took off in the 1980s and 1990s. In 1983, Argentinean activists began demanding trials of leaders who had engaged in human rights violations during the 'Dirty War', and in 1998, Pinochet was extradited from London. In 1990, Margaret Thatcher and George H. W. Bush endorsed the idea of a war crimes trial for Saddam Hussein after he invaded Kuwait, and in 1991 and 1992 there were calls for war crimes trials of leaders in the former Yugoslavia (Sikkink, 2011: 110). In 1999, Slobodan Milosevic would become 'the first sitting head of state to be indicted for war crimes', in 2003, Charles Taylor would become the second, and in 2009 Omar al Bashir the third (Sikkink, 2011: 4).

The rise of calls for individual accountability was in part a story about the bringing together of several previously separate fields of law: human rights law, humanitarian law/ the laws of war, and international criminal law (Sikkink, 2011: 100). It was this new merger, beginning in the 'discovery' and activation of the laws of war by human rights activists in the 1980s, and cemented by the establishment of the International Criminal Tribunal for the former Yugoslavia (ICTY) in 1993, and then the International Criminal Court in 1998,[16] that enabled the prosecution of individuals for human rights crimes (Sikkink, 2011: 106).

As the field developed, there came to be two core practices through which human rights advocates attempted to enforce norms. These were, first, the use of documentation and exposure of human rights violations as a key form of 'naming and shaming' human rights violators, and, second, the mobilization of law to hold states and individuals accountable. As one account puts it, '[c]urrent debates about torture are saturated with law' (Kelly, 2012: 3). Information collection and dissemination took on a central role in the practices of human rights advocates (Moon, 2012: 876), aided by new technological developments: 'It became possible to collect information about victims of repression abroad more cheaply, easily, and rapidly than before' (Keys, 2014: 10). As Moon (2012: 876) puts it, 'The single most important activity that human rights organizations (HROs) undertake to promote human rights is that of documenting human rights violations'. This practice is foregrounded on an assumption that exposure of human rights violations will lead to their elimination: that 'if only people knew they would act' (Moon, 2012: 877), with the 'human rights report . . . now firmly established as a literary genre "with its own rules of style and presentation" (Dudai, 2006, 783)' (Moon, 2012: 877).

 The Sociological Review Monographs, 64:2, pp. 170–193 (2016), DOI: 10.1111/2059-7932.12007

I argue that 'naming and shaming' – the documentation and dissemination of evidence of human rights violations – along with the rise of legal regulation and particularly prosecution, form key practices in the transnational human rights field. And while neither of these practices have been able to *compel* states to change their relations to the norms of human rights, they have, I suggest, sufficiently shifted the forces at play in the international field so as to exert leverage on states' relational approach to human rights norms. This relational approach should be conceptualized as including both concrete practices (do states violate human rights of individuals or not) as well as states' rhetoric (do states affirm rhetorically that they respect human rights). This is a somewhat different approach from those who would conceptualize 'practices' and 'discourses' as operating in distinct registers. Further, this allows us to analyse practices and discourses together. And while prior literature has largely focused on two relational modes (which I have earlier called 'enlightenment' and 'hypocrisy'), the case of the US after 9/11 presents a third mode of state relation to human rights, which is what I have called 'brazenness'.[17] My argument is that 'brazenness' (like the other relational modes) is best understood as a strategic response to the shifting forces affecting states in the transnational human rights field: in this case, the rise of 'naming and shaming' along with legal remedies, which have acted to make 'hypocrisy' a less viable option for states that wish to engage in torture.

The 'legalization' of torture as a response to the international human rights field

In this section, I draw on evidence from the published memoirs of participants in the Bush administration in support of this argument, demonstrating that these two shifts – the 'legalization' of state violence and the shifting feasibility of state secrecy – were on the minds of those who enacted the legal justification of torture, and, further, were often explicitly referenced when providing explanations for why torture was 'legalized'. First, there was a sense of the seeming inevitability of the release of secrets, sometimes framed as a relatively new problem. Second, there was an awareness of the rising importance of law and lawyers as a constraint on state action, which, on the part of some actors, was joined with an interpretation of international law, and the international criminal court in particular, but also sometimes extending to international treaties and laws more generally, as 'lawfare': a form of war by other means. These themes were not present in every memoir, but there were also no instances of contradictory claims: that is, none of the accounts claimed that law and lawyers had become less of a constraint on state action, nor did any of the accounts presume that secrets could easily and indefinitely be kept.

The first recurring theme in the memoirs is the seeming inevitability of the release of secrets. In his memoir, *Decision Points,* former President G. W. Bush wrote, on his decision to approve the use of 'controversial' interrogation techniques, that:

> I knew that an interrogation program this sensitive and controversial would one day become public . . . I would have preferred that we get the information another way.

> But the choice between security and values was real . . . I approved the use of the interrogation techniques. (Bush, 2010: 169)

While John Kiriakou, a CIA analyst now best known for being the first official in the US government to confirm the use of waterboarding, wrote that: 'Even though enhanced techniques were supposed to be used only on the highest-profile, toughest, most important al-Qaeda prisoners, word of their existence got out pretty quickly' (Kiriakou and Ruby, 2009: 140). And later, when discussing his acknowledgement that Abu Zubaydah had been waterboarded, noted that:

> President Bush had talked about the use of enhanced interrogation techniques on al-Qaeda prisoners, although he and others in the administration had never addressed the specifics. At that point, the torture memos were classified . . . Still, Human Rights Watch and other nongovernmental organizations had been saying for more than two years that waterboarding was one of the enhanced techniques; if it was a secret . . . it was the worst-kept secret in Washington by December 2007. (Kiriakou and Ruby, 2009: 187)

What all of these excerpts indicate are a shared awareness of the fleeting nature of secrets, and possible dangers of attempting to conceal information that would likely become public after a time.

Second, was an awareness of the increased importance of law/lawyers as a constraint on governments. Donald Rumsfeld, who served as Secretary of Defense under President Bush, writes in his memoir that:

> One of the notable changes I had observed from my service in the Pentagon in the 1970s was the prevalence of lawyers . . . By the time I returned as secretary in 2001, there were a breathtaking ten thousand lawyers . . . involved at nearly every level of the chain of command. (Rumsfeld, 2011: 557)

While General Richard Myers, who served as Chairman of the Joint Chiefs of Staff under President Bush from 2001 to 2005, observed at a meeting to discuss the question of interrogation practices that, 'I noted the government attorneys sitting along the walls behind each of their principals' (Myers and McConnell, 2009: 205).

A related, and perhaps even more important, theme that emerges from the memoirs is the rise of a shared perception of international law as 'lawfare': a harnessing of legal strategies to wage war by other means, which must therefore be resisted.[18] On law as 'lawfare', Donald Rumsfeld writes:

> Besides contending with enemy bullets and bombs, the men and women in our nation's military and intelligence services must also navigate legal traps set by our enemies, by some of our fellow citizens, by some foreigners, and even by some members of Congress and officials at international institutions such as the United Nations. . . This is a new kind of asymmetric war waged by our enemies – 'lawfare'. (Rumsfeld, 2011: 595)

Like several others, Rumsfeld points to the experiences of Henry Kissinger, who was facing threats of prosecution in the early 2000s, as well as the naming of General Tommy Franks in a lawsuit before a Belgian court in 2003, as a crucial turning point in his consciousness of the threat (Rumsfeld, 2011: 596).[19] Nor was the danger of 'lawfare' limited to those in high positions: the International Criminal Court was, in 2003, 'being discussed as a possible forum to try US military and civilian personnel involved in the Iraq war' (Rumsfeld, 2011: 598).

In John Yoo's account of his time in the Office of Legal Counsel from 2001 to 2003, three themes leap out: a view of law/lawyers as the enemy, and law and the courts as a battlefield; a view of the period preceding 9/11 as excessively legally regulated, so much so that it impeded national security; and a view of law itself, consequently, as a necessary defence against these constraints. Yoo repeatedly portrays the law itself as a site of conflict: for example, 'The group of us who landed that day in Cuba surely had no idea then that the front in the war on terrorism would soon move from the battlefields of Afghanistan to the cells of Gitmo and the federal courtrooms' (Yoo, 2006: 20); and lawyers as the enemy to be overtaken: for example, 'Human rights lawyers, law professors, and activists who oppose the war on terror' who 'have filed many lawsuits' (Yoo, 2006: 129). The pre-9/11 period is portrayed as a hyper-regulated era in which an abundance of caution prevented any effective action against al-Qaeda: 'Efforts to capture or kill al Qaeda leader Osama bin Laden throughout the 1990s were shelved, out of concerns that the Justice Department did not have enough evidence to satisfy the legal standard for a criminal arrest. A return to this state of affairs would be a huge mistake' (Yoo, 2006: 3). The legal restraint on counter-terrorism is presented by Yoo as a serious constraint, necessitating a legal counteroffensive to permit effective counter-terrorism action.

In the memoir of Jack Goldsmith, head of the Office of Legal Counsel from autumn 2003, until he resigned in July 2004, law is also viewed as an encumbrance upon the proper functioning of the state. Goldsmith argues, first, that the US has been subject to a rising legalization of warfare over the course of the twentieth century (encompassing both domestic and international legal regulation), and second, that these pressures particularly mounted at the end of the twentieth century and the start of the twenty-first, leading to heightened concern about prosecution among both government officials and military and intelligence operatives. The response to this was either a cowed executive (exemplified by the Clinton administration) or the attempt to provide legal cover as a countermeasure to this expanded legalization of warfare (exemplified by the administration of G. W. Bush). Goldsmith argues that there was a shift from law as a 'political' constraint on political power (in the early twentieth century) to a 'judicial' constraint on political power in the late twentieth/early twenty-first: 'When he [Franklin D. Roosevelt] considered bending the law, he did not worry about being sued or prosecuted . . . He worried instead about the reaction of the press, the Congress, and most of all, the American people' (Goldsmith, 2007: 49). The Bush administration, however, faced 'obstacles' in the form of both domestic and international laws that had come to regulate the conduct of warfare, particularly since the Vietnam War (Goldsmith, 2007: 23). Given this, the Bush administration acted in a context when 'government officials seriously worried that their heat-of-battle judgment calls would result in prosecution by independent counsels, Justice Departments of future administrations, or foreign or international courts' (Goldsmith, 2007: 12).

Goldsmith details what he calls a 'criminalization of war', starting with the War Powers Act of the 1970s, and specific restrictions on the intelligence agencies in the 1970s and 80s, and the Torture Statute of 1994, which 'provides for criminal sanctions, including the death penalty, for perpetrators of torture' (Pfiffner, 2010: 119) passed by the US following the adoption of the UN Convention Against Torture (Goldsmith, 2007: 66). This legalization of warfare was evidenced, and 'reinforced' by 'the swarm of lawyers that rose up in the military and intelligence establishment to interpret multiplying laws and provide cover for those asked to act close to the legal line' (Goldsmith, 2007: 91). Whereas the CIA employed only a small number of lawyers in the 1970s, by 2007 they had over one hundred, while lawyers in the Department of Defense number over ten thousand (Goldsmith, 2007: 91).[20] And this was the scene which set the stage for the Bush administration's response to the attacks of 9/11.

Inside the Pentagon, this situation had begun to be conceptualized as 'lawfare': not just a neutral regulation of war by law, but a vision of law as a tool to be mobilized by the enemy. 'Lawfare', Goldsmith writes,

> is 'the strategy of using or misusing law as a substitute for traditional military means to achieve an operational objective,' according to Air Force Brigadier General Charles Dunlap, who popularized the phrase. Enemies like al Qaeda who cannot match the United States militarily instead criticize it for purported legal violations, especially violations of human rights or the laws of war. (Goldsmith, 2007: 58)

These fears rose with the implementation of 'universal jurisdiction' in the 1980s and 90s, and came to a head with the formation of the International Criminal Court in 2002.[21] The 2005 *National Defense Strategy of the United States* presented lawfare as an official threat, declaring that 'our strength as a nation state will continue to be challenged by those who employ a strategy of the weak using international fora, judicial processes, and terrorism' (Goldsmith, 2007: 53).

These developments led to fears both among individual government officials and the military and intelligence services. Goldsmith reports that former Secretary of State Henry Kissinger became extremely 'rattled' by the extradition of Pinochet and threats that he too would be brought up on human rights charges (Goldsmith, 2007: 57). In 2002, as various groups called for Kissinger to be charged with war crimes, 'he decided to call an old friend from his government days, Gerald Ford's Chief of Staff and the current Secretary of Defense, Donald Rumsfeld' (Goldsmith, 2007: 58). In Goldsmith's view, however, the main impetus for the development of legal infrastructure for torture was not the concerns of senior officials, but rather, 'a paralyzing culture of risk-averse legalism in the military and, especially, intelligence establishments' (Goldsmith, 2007: 94).

Other accounts of the war on terror are also replete with examples of just such demands for cover (eg Pfiffner, 2010). In sum, there is evidence that what I have called the 'legalization' of torture, or the development of an explicit, quasi-open legal infrastructure to defend its use, should be understood as resulting from responses to the rise of a transnational field of human rights. In order to appease the military and intelligence sector, as well as fears of top officials, the Bush administration paved the way for an explicit defence of practices that in the past might have been undertaken covertly, a strategy which while perhaps seeming more rational on its face, opened all those involved to personal retribution should their actions be exposed. The strategy of legalization and quasi-openness, in contrast, provides a pre-emptive defence against such attacks.

On reading the accounts of insiders within the Bush administration writing of their experiences of the first years on the war on terror, what first becomes apparent is the intentionality of what I am calling the 'legalization' of torture – that is, its inscription into legal documents and regulations. Jack Goldsmith describes travelling to Guantanamo on what he terms a 'plane full of lawyers',[22] and his account emphasizes the central role of legal expertise in the war on terror. His memoir of that year emphasizes the extent to which the president and his staff felt *constrained* by the rise of an apparatus of both domestic and international law governing human rights and the government use of force, and yet this constraint did not lead them to bend their actions and rhetoric to comply with international law, but instead, to argue that international law should be redefined to fit with their actions. Goldsmith writes that 'President Bush acted in an era in which many aspects of presidential war power had become encumbered by elaborate criminal restrictions, and in which government officials seriously worried that their heat-of-battle judgment calls would result in prosecution by independent counsels, Justice Departments of future administrations, or foreign or international courts' (2007: 12).

It was thus, in the view of the Bush White House, the very rise of the legal apparatus enforcing human rights and the laws of war that led them to develop an explicit legal apparatus in defence of (what they generally did not refer to, but others did, as) 'torture'. In other words, the relative 'openness' of the state with regard to torture[23] should be seen not as a bizarre aberration, but as a calculated move on the part of a government which chose to use 'forbidden practices', and which saw secrecy and denial as less plausible defences than they had been in the past, as a result of the rise of a moral, legal and institutional apparatus which aimed to root out and punish such hypocrisy. Accounts of those directly involved suggest that they were acting in response to two, related, states of affairs: first, the broader legalization (legal regulation) of warfare which had occurred in the US since the 1970s, and the (subsequent) emergence of 'demands for cover' from the military and intelligence sectors.

Conclusion

This paper began with the puzzle of why the US war on terror has been characterized by a brazen rejection of international human rights norms, rather than, as might be expected, a strategy of either compliance or hypocrisy. I have argued that rather than a paradox, this move should actually be understood as a strategic state response to the rise of an international field of transnational human rights regulation. Within a theoretical framework which situates human rights norms, and practices such as documentation, exposure and prosecution as key practices of human rights advocates within a transnational field, it is possible to understand how and why the forces acting upon states might have shifted so as to make 'brazenness' and legal justification of torture and other human rights violations a strategic move for the United States after 9/11.

A transnational fields framework has greater explanatory power as compared to alternate analytic approaches. Constructivist IR theories, as well as sociological world-society theories both tend to presume that norms will take on greater power over time, and fail to predict that powerful states might choose to openly resist such norms. Realist approaches, meanwhile, tend to ignore the importance of culture and norms overall, finding the cultural realm insignificant. This approach also improves upon earlier constructivist approaches to the study of norms in IR, which tended to lack a theory of agency (Checkel, 1998, cited in Scheipers, 2015).

By conceptualizing states as operating within a transnational field, together with other state and non-state actors, the approach put forth in this paper avoids the teleological assumptions of these alternate frameworks, while allowing us to better analyse the multi-directional impact of transnational actors upon states, and vice versa. Such an approach allows us to better analyse seemingly puzzling developments, such as the 'legalization' of human rights violations, as strategies, which bring together both rhetoric and practice. By conceptualizing state action as strategic moves within a transnational field, we move beyond a conception of such activities as simply 'norm violations' and can understand the *gains* states might obtain from such actions, as well as the broader contexts which make such gains possible.

Acknowledgements

Earlier versions of this paper were presented at the Society for Historians of American Foreign Relations, June 2014, and at a workshop on 'Fielding Transnationalism' at Boston University, October 2014. Thanks to Monika Krause and Julian Go, as well as two anonymous reviewers, for comments.

Notes

1 When I speak of 'openness' here, I do not mean to imply that there was a complete turnaround from total secrecy about government use of torture and other 'forbidden practices' to absolute transparency. Rather, the status of such practices in the war on terror is best characterized as 'quasi-open' – a status that encompassed at times quite complete transparency, at times denial, and at much of the time, rested on a strategy of creating and mobilizing legal and linguistic ambiguity as to whether the practices in question actually did constitute 'torture'. This openness,

whether full or partial, is puzzling because it appears as the dramatic reversal of a norm that had been growing ever stronger over the second half of the twentieth century.

2 Perhaps most notoriously at the 'School of the Americas' where the CIA trained Latin American paramilitary squads in the arts of torture and disappearance.

3 While there is also an important *domestic* legal and human rights field which has been important here, this paper focuses on the role of the transnational human rights field. A fuller analysis elsewhere will be needed to tease out the distinct roles of domestic versus international law in constraining the state and its use of violence. For purposes of this article, the focus will remain on the effects of the transnational field, presuming that developments towards the legalization/legal constraint on use of force within the domestic field can, in this instance, be understood to be in large part responses to the rise of such legal constraints in the transnational arena, and thus should largely be understood as mediating the relation between the transnational field and the state.

4 'Legal black hole' is often attributed to Steyn (2004), although the term has come into increasingly common use, particularly among critics from the legal profession.

5 As I discuss below, the evidence on this question is uncertain.

6 This paper is part of an ongoing, larger research project, which will be engaging with all of these sources.

7 There is also a significant literature tracing the rise of human rights 'norms' and the institutionalization of human rights in laws, treaties and international institutions (eg Keck and Sikkink, 1998; Clark, 2001; Dezalay and Garth, 2006; Levy and Sznaider, 2006; Borgwardt, 2007; Hunt, 2007; Burke, 2010; Sikkink, 2011; Moyn, 2012a, 2012b; Brysk, 2013; Joas, 2013; Keys, 2014), but as this paper is concerned more with the response to human rights, I will mention these only briefly.

8 Although see (Shor, 2008) for an attempt to resolve some of these difficulties.

9 I purposely use the loaded term 'barbarism' here in recognition of the fact that the discourse of human rights presumes a 'civilizing' trajectory from rhetoric and action that are less to more 'enlightened'.

10 These categories were developed inductively in response to the frameworks used in most existing studies of the effects of human rights norms, although the names for the categories are my own.

11 There is, of course, a further complication here, which is that the Bush administration, during the state I am calling 'brazenness' *simultaneously* affirmed the value of 'human rights' and openly affirmed the necessity of violations of human rights; contradictions that cannot be fully explored within the scope of this paper, but which will be analyzed in future research.

12 Katherine Sikkink makes a similar argument in her recent book, *The Justice Cascade* (Sikkink, 2011), writing that, while at first: 'I assumed that U.S. officials *could not* have fully understood the implications of the justice cascade, because *if* they had fully understood, they wouldn't have adopted policies that were criminal under both U.S. and international law. . . I now believe that the very production of these memos was a response to the rise in national and international human rights prosecutions . . . the memos themselves are indications, however perverse, of the impact of the justice cascade' (2011: 190–192). However Sikkink only develops this argument briefly in the form of a speculative explanation, whereas this paper develops the theory more fully and draws on evidence to support it.

13 I use the term 'strategy' here in the Bourdieusian sense (Bourdieu, 1977).

14 'As early as 21 October 2001, a Washington Post article reported FBI agents outlining their frustrations over the refusal of suspects to provide information and suggesting they might have to use pressure to get those details. On 5 November 2001, a Newsweek article appeared entitled "Time to Think About Torture." In January 2003, The Economist published a cover story entitled "Is Torture Ever Justified?"' (Foot, 2006: 133). 'Six weeks after September 11, news articles reported that frustrated FBI interrogators were considering harsh interrogation tactics, and the New York Times reported that torture had become a topic of conversation "in bars, on commuter trains, and at dinner tables"' (Luban, 2006: 35).

15 Most notably through the release of photos from the notorious Abu Ghraib prison in 2004.

16 The treaty entered into force, actually creating the ICC, in 2002.
17 The US after 9/11 is not the *only* case in which the relational mode of brazenness has occurred: earlier cases would include the UK and Israel, at certain points in time. In other work I will explore the *relations* between these cases, although this paper focuses solely on the US case.
18 The concept of 'lawfare' first took hold in American military discourse in 2001, when 'a prominent US military lawyer proposed the neologism "lawfare", which he defined as "the use of law as a weapon of war"' (Jones, 2015).
19 Rumsfeld then notes that after Belgium asserted universal jurisdiction and Franks was named in the lawsuit, he threatened to move NATO's headquarters, and 'the Belgian government repealed their law' (Rumsfeld, 2011: 598).
20 On this 'legalization' of the Department of Defense, see also Ansorge (2012).
21 'The enforcement gap finally began to close with the development of the idea of universal jurisdiction. . . . The idea had been kicking around in human rights circles since World War II but got a big boost with two important events in the 1980s. The first was a 1980 case in New York called *Filartiga*, which allowed a Paraguayan citizen to sue a Paraguayan official who tortured his son in Paraguay . . . The second boost for universal jurisdiction came when Baltasar Garzon, a Spanish magistrate, began to investigate the South American dirty wars of the 1970s . . . The House of Lords, in a landmark decision, ruled that universal jurisdiction was a valid concept, and that England must hand Pinochet over to Spain. ... Sovereign immunity no longer stood as a roadblock to trials of government officials for gross human rights violations' (Goldsmith, 2007: 55–56). (See also Sikkink, 2011.)
22 'Perhaps the oddest thing about my fortieth-birthday trip to GTMO and the naval brigs was that the plane was full of lawyers' (Goldsmith, 2007: 129).
23 And while I have here focused on the justification of torture under the Bush administration, but would argue that while the subsequent Obama administration has moved back from the defense of torture, it has enacted similar strategies with regard to its use, and open defense of, assassination (particularly via drone warfare).

References

Agamben, G., (2005), *State of Exception*, Chicago: University of Chicago Press.

Ansorge, J. T., (2012), 'Between policy and law: an intellectual history of FM 27-1', paper presented at 2012 conference of Social Science History Association, Vancouver BC.

Aradau, C. and van Munster, R., (2009), 'Exceptionalism and the war on terror: criminology meets international relations', *British Journal of Criminology*, 49: 686–701.

Bellamy, A. J., (2006), 'No pain, no gain? Torture and ethics in the war on terror', *International Affairs*, 82: 121–148.

Borgwardt, E., (2007), *A New Deal for the World: America's Vision for Human Rights*, Cambridge, MA: Harvard University Press.

Bourdieu, P., (1977), *Outline of a Theory of Practice*, Cambridge and New York: Cambridge University Press.

Bourdieu, P., (1990), *The Logic of Practice*, Stanford, CA: Stanford University Press.

Bourdieu, P., (1993), *The Field of Cultural Production: Essays on Art and Literature*, New York: Columbia University Press.

Brooks, C. and Manza, J., (2013), *Whose Rights? Counterterrorism and the Dark Side of American Public Opinion*, New York: Russell Sage Foundation.

Brysk, A. (ed.), (2013), *The Politics of the Globalization of Law: Getting from Rights to Justice*, New York: Routledge.

Burke, R., (2010), *Decolonization and the Evolution of International Human Rights*, Philadelphia, PA: University of Pennsylvania Press.

Bush, G. W., (2010), *Decision Points*, New York: Crown Publishers.

Checkel, J. T., (1998), 'The constructivist turn in international relations theory', *Journal of World Politics*, 50 (2): 324–348.

Clark, A. M., (2001), *Diplomacy of Conscience: Amnesty International and Changing Human Rights Norms*, Princeton, NJ: Princeton University Press.
Cole, W., (2012), 'Human rights as myth and ceremony? Reevaluating the effectiveness of human rights treaties, 1981–2007', *American Journal of Sociology*, 117: 1131–1171.
Danner, M., (2005), 'We are all torturers now', *New York Times*, 6 January, at A27.
Dayan, C., (2011), *The Law Is a White Dog: How Legal Rituals Make and Unmake Persons*, Princeton, NJ: Princeton University Press.
Dezalay, Y. and Garth, B. G., (2006), 'From the Cold War to Kosovo: the rise and renewal of the field of international human rights', *Annual Review of Law and Social Science*, 2: 231–255.
Fariss, C. J., (2014), 'Respect for human rights has improved over time: modeling the changing standard of accountability', *American Political Science Review*, 108: 297–318.
Foot, R., (2006), 'Torture: the struggle over a peremptory norm in a counter-terrorist era', *International Relations*, 20: 131–151.
Go, J., (2008), 'Global fields and imperial forms: field theory and the British and American empires', *Sociological Theory*, 26: 201–229.
Gocek, F. M., (2015), *Denial of Violence: Ottoman Past, Turkish Present, and Collective Violence against the Armenians*, 1789–2009, Oxford: Oxford University Press.
Goldsmith, J., (2007), *The Terror Presidency: Law and Judgment inside the Bush Administration*, New York: W. W. Norton & Co.
Gregory, D. and Pred, A. (eds), (2007), *Violent Geographies: Fear, Terror, and Political Violence*, New York: Routledge.
Hafner-Burton, E. M., (2013), *Making Human Rights a Reality*, Princeton, NJ: Princeton University Press.
Hafner-Burton, E. M. and Tsutsui, K., (2013), 'Human rights in a globalizing world: the paradox of empty promises', *American Journal of Sociology*, 110: 1373–1411.
Hafner-Burton, E. M., Tsutsui, K. and Meyer, J. W., (2008), 'International human rights law and the politics of legitimation: repressive states and human rights treaties', *International Sociology*, 23: 115–141.
Hajjar, L., (2010), 'Lawyers, litigation, and the us anti-torture campaign', American Political Science Association Annual Meeting.
Hajjar, L., (2011), 'The legal campaign against American torture', *Jadaliyya*, 5 July.
Hannah, M., (2006), 'Torture and the ticking bomb: the war on terrorism as a geographical imagination of power/ knowledge', *Annals of the Association of American Geographers*, 96: 622–640.
Hunt, L., (2007), *Inventing Human Rights: A History*, New York: W. W. Norton & Co.
Ignatieff, M., (2003), *Human Rights as Politics and Idolatry*, Princeton, NJ: Princeton University Press.
Ip, J., (2009), 'Two narratives of torture', *Northwestern Journal of International Human Rights*, 7: 35–77.
Joas, H., (2013), *The Sacredness of the Person: A New Genealogy of Human Rights*, Washington DC: Georgetown University Press.
Johns, F., (2005), 'Guantanamo Bay and the annihilation of the exception', *European Journal of International Law* 16: 613–614.
Jones, C. A., (2015), 'Lawfare and the juridification of late modern war', *Progress in Human Geography*, 16 March, 1–19.
Keck, M. E. and Sikkink, K., (1998), *Activists Beyond Borders: Advocacy Networks in International Politics*, Ithaca, NY: Cornell University Press.
Kelly, T., (2012), *This Side of Silence: Human Rights, Torture, and the Recognition of Cruelty*, Philadelphia: Univeristy of Pennsylvania Press.
Keys, B., (2014), *Reclaiming American Virtue: The Human Rights Revolution of the 1970s*, Cambridge, MA: Harvard University Press.
Khalili, L., (2008), 'On torture', *Middle East Report*, 249: 32–38.
Kiriakou, J. and Ruby, M., (2009), *The Reluctant Spy: My Secret Life in the Cia's War on Terror*, New York: Bantam Books.

Krause, M., (2014), *The Good Project: Humanitarian Relief Ngos and the Fragmentation of Reason*, Chicago: University of Chicago Press.
Levinson, S. (ed.), (2004), *Torture: A Collection*, Oxford: Oxford University Press.
Levy, D. and Sznaider, N., (2006), 'Sovereignty transformed: a sociology of human rights', *The British Journal of Sociology*, 57: 657–676.
Luban, D., (2006), 'Liberalism, torture, and the ticking bomb', in K. J. Greenberg (ed.), *The Torture Debate in America*, 35–83, Cambridge: Cambridge University Press.
McCoy, A. W., (2006), *A Question of Torture: Cia Interrogation, from the Cold War to the War on Terror*, New York: Metropolitan Books/ Henry Holt and Company.
Mertus, J. A., (2008), *Bait and Switch: Human Rights and U.S. Foreign Policy*, New York: Routledge.
Meyer, J. W., Bromley, P. and Ramirez, F. O., (2010), 'Human rights in social science textbooks: cross-national analyses, 1970–2008', *Sociology of Education*, 83: 111–134.
Moon, C., (2012), 'What one sees and how one files seeing:human rights reporting, representation, and action', *Sociology*, 46: 876–890.
Moyn, S., (2012a), *The Last Utopia: Human Rights in History*, Cambridge, MA: Harvard University Press.
Moyn, S., (2012b), 'Substance, scale, and salience: the recent historiography of human rights', *Annual Review of Law and Social Science*, 8: 123–140.
Mudge, S. L. and Vauchez, A., (2012), 'Building Europe on a weak field: law, economics, and scholarly avatars in transnational politics', *American Journal of Sociology*, 118: 449–492.
Myers, R. B. and McConnell, M., (2009), *Eyes on the Horizon: Serving on the Front Lines of National Security*, New York: Simon and Schuster.
Pfiffner, J. P., (2010), *Torture as Public Policy: Restoring U.S. Credibility on the World Stage*, Boulder, CO: Paradigm.
Press, E., (2003), 'In torture we trust?', *The Nation*, 31 March.
Rumsfeld, D., (2011), *Known and Unknown: A Memoir*, London: Sentinel.
Scheipers, S., (2015), *Unlawful Combatants: A Genealogy of the Irregular Fighter*, Oxford: Oxford University Press.
Shor, E., (2008), 'Conflict, terrorism, and the socialization of human rights norms: the spiral model revisited', *Social Problems*, 55: 117–138.
Sikkink, K., (2011), *The Justice Cascade: How Human Rights Prosecutions Are Changing World Politics*, New York: W. W. Norton & Co.
Steyn, J., (2004), 'Guantanamo Bay: the legal black hole', *The International and Comparative Law Quarterly*, 53: 1–15.
van Munster, R., (2004), 'The war on terrorism: when the exception becomes the rule', *International Journal for the Semiotics of Law*, 17: 141–153.
Yoo, J., (2006), *War by Other Means: An Insiders Account of the War on Terror*, New York: Atlantic Monthly Press.
Zegart, A., (2012), 'Torture creep', *Foreign Policy*, 25 September.

 The Sociological Review Monographs, 64:2, pp. 170–193 (2016), DOI: 10.1111/2059-7932.12007

Appendix: List: of memoirs consulted

Person	Role	Memoir title
Goldsmith, Jack	General counsel of the Department of Defense, 2002–3; US Attorney General, leading the office of legal counsel in the Department of Justice, 2003–4	*The Terror Presidency*
Yoo, John	Deputy Assistant US Attorney General in the Office of Legal, Department of Justice, 2001–3	*War by Other Means*
Rice, Condoleezza	National security adviser, 2001–5; Secretary of State, 2005–9	*No Higher Honor*
Cheney, Richard	Vice President	*In My Time*
Bush, George W.	President	*Decision Points*
Ashcroft, John	Attorney General	*Never Again*
Tenet, George	Director of Central Intelligence (CIA), 1997–2004	*At the Center of the Storm*
Feith, Douglas	Undersecretary of Defense	*War and Decision*
Rizzo, John	CIA Acting General Counsel under	*Company Man*
Rumsfeld, Donald	Secretary of Defense	*Known and Unknown*
Myers, Richard (General)	Chairman of the Joint Chiefs of Staff, 2001–5	*Eyes on the Horizon: Serving on the Front Lines of National Security*
Kiriakou, John	CIA analyst	*The Reluctant Spy*
Bolton, John	Ambassador to the United Nations	*Surrender Is Not an Option*
Gates, Robert M.	Secretary of Defense, 2006–11	*Duty*

‘Western hegemony’ in the social sciences: fields and model systems

Monika Krause

Abstract: This paper discusses the role of privileged research objects (‘model systems’) in producing patterns in transnational knowledge production. In its approach it follows Bourdieu’s call to focus on contexts of production and forces internal to disciplines as well as his insistence on practice. Learning from work in science and technology studies it also considers material objects of knowledge and spaces of knowledge-production. It discusses the case of sociology and argues that conventions surrounding privileged research objects matter relatively independently of authors’ national origin or field-position. Examining model systems, I argue, can contribute to our understanding of how some well-established inequalities are produced and reproduced. This focus adds specific stakes to the debates about global knowledge production: we can discuss the problem of neglected cases in ways that are not always included in current reflections that draw on general political – rather than specifically knowledge-political – categories.

Keywords: transnational fields, sociology of the social sciences, Anglo-American hegemony, Western hegemony, model systems, canons

Introduction

The debate about the ‘global’ and the ‘international’ in the sciences has mirrored the debates about globalization and global civil society in general to some extent. There is, on the one hand, what one might call the ‘happy’ view of the globalization of science: in this line of arguing, science has always been cosmopolitan in its values and orientation and, building on this ethos, it has now been diffused throughout the world, using collegial and educational ties and information technology (Schott, 1991). This view emphasizes science’s foundation in shared values and its benefits to all.

This narrative is juxtaposed by a range of arguments and significant evidence about inequality and power related to the production and dissemination of knowledge across national contexts, both concerning the past and the present (International Social Science Council, 2010; Gingras and Mosbah-Natanson,

The Sociological Review Monographs, 64:2, pp. 194–211 (2016), DOI: 10.1111/2059-7932.12008

Published by John Wiley & Sons Ltd, 9600 Garsington Road, Oxford OX4 2DQ, UK and 350 Main Street, Malden, MA 02148, USA

2013). Commentators use different terms to label these power relationships, including 'imperialism', 'northern dominance', 'hegemony', 'core and periphery' (Altbach, 2002), 'Anglo-American hegemony' (Aalbers, 2004; Aalbers and Rossi, 2006), or 'dependency' (Alatas, 2003).

In these labels, and to some extent in the debate more broadly, commentators clearly borrow from theories that try to understand domination and transnational domination more generally. This borrowing usefully highlights some of the ways in which social scientific production is embedded in broader social and ideological structures and the ways in which it is embedded in a long history of power relations.

But it would be reductive to try to understand the scientific world only as a reflection of broader patterns of domination.[1] I would argue that we cannot understand how inequality is produced and reproduced without also looking at processes internal to scientific disciplines. This paper follows Bourdieu's call to focus on contexts of production and forces internal to disciplines as well as his insistence on practice. Learning from work in science and technology studies it also considers material objects of knowledge and spaces of knowledge-production.

The paper begins by reviewing what we can say about dynamics internal to social scientific communities on different scales from a field-theoretical perspective. It then raises the question about inequality, not among nations or positions, but among topics and objects of research. Focusing on the case of sociology, the paper discusses the role of implicitly privileged research objects in producing and maintaining (unequal) patterns in transnational knowledge production.

Philosophers and sociologists of science have alerted us to the ways in which model systems focus research in biology and some other disciplines (Amann, 1994; Kohler, 1994; Creager *et al.*, 2007; Leonelli, 2008; Ankeny and Leonelli, 2011; Howlett and Morgan, 2010; Sealey, 2011). Scholars in biology address general questions about life and disease by working with specific organisms, called model systems, selected for convenience and by convention. For every type of system biologists are interested in (such as an invertebrate organism, or a mammal), scientists tend to select particular ones for the purposes of research (such as fruit flies, or mice). A model system is thought to limit the variation among objects studied and allows researchers to link observations by different researchers in different sites. The literary canon fulfils a somewhat analogous role in literary studies (Poovey, 2001).

I have argued elsewhere that sociology, like biology and literature, focuses a disproportionate amount of attention on some objects rather than others (Guggenheim and Krause, 2012). Relating this analysis to questions about transnational fields, knowledge and inequality, I argue here that the west has served as the model system for societies, but also that model systems have effects independently of the more general phenomenon of 'euro' or 'metrocentrism' in the social sciences (Wallerstein, 1997; Go, 2013; see also Chakrabarty, 2000). Research has focused on a select number of nations within the West, and on specific cases rather than others in various subfields. The paper reviews the way field-effects and model-system effects intersect before revisiting some of the normative stakes of the debate.

Fields: from critique of ideology to contexts of production

Bourdieu writes:

> between an internal reading of the text which consists in considering the text in itself and for itself, and an external reading which crudely relates the text to society in general, there is a social universe that is always forgotten, that of the producers of the works. To speak of the field is to name this microcosm, which is also a social universe but a social universe freed from a certain number of the constraints that characterise the encompassing social universe, a universe that is somewhat apart, endowed with its own laws, its own nomos, without being completely independent of the external laws. (Bourdieu, 2005: 32–33)

Bourdieu insists here on paying close attention to relevant contexts of production; when we apply these principles to an analysis of social scientific work, Bourdieu invites us to look at the social context of the production of social scientific works, and specifically the context of production constituted by relations among producers. He encourages us to at least initially step out of the conversation among colleagues, which favours conceptual engagement, epistemological critique and epistemological counter-proposals (eg de Souzas Santos, 2014; Rehbein, 2014), in order to engage in a sociology of the social sciences (see, eg, recently Lezaun, 2007; Lezaun *et al.,* 2013; Camic *et al.,* 2011)

Nicolas Guilhot has pointed out that in Bourdieu's most topical essay, 'On the international circulation of ideas' (1999), that context of production is framed as a national context (Guilhot, 2014; see also Keim, 2014). But this focus is not an inherent feature of Bourdieusian analysis, as Gisèle Sapiro (2013) has most recently argued. The starting points of field-analysis are relationships; national fields are only one form that sets of relationships can take.

Starting with relationships rather than national fields means we can look beyond some common narratives of globalization, which are also common in narratives about the globalization of science. If we start with relationships, we can note that science has always been transnational, and even the social sciences – younger than the natural sciences, and more closely tied to the state – have a long transnational history (Gingras, 2002; Zincke, 2014; Heilbron *et al.,* 2008; but see Heilbron, 2014). Of course national fields have played an important role, with pushes in the nineteenth century (Wittrock *et al.,* 2008) and after the Second World War (Steinmetz, 2007). But the nationalization of science has always remained a 'project', and is always incomplete as it co-exists with colonial relations (Bhambra, 2007; Steinmetz, this volume), with fraternization of elites across borders, and with technical specialization.

Rather than as a transition from national to global relations, the transformations of the last 30 or 40 years should be examined as a changing configuration of local, national, regional and global relations. New technologies and new

 The Sociological Review Monographs, 64:2, pp. 194–211 (2016), DOI: 10.1111/2059-7932.12008

networks, intervene into a space that is already fielded on several levels. Arguably in sociology national, regional, such as European or Latin American (Heilbron *et al.*, 2008), and global fields (Heilbron, 2014) coexist today, along with sub-and interdisciplinary spaces (see also Buchholz, this volume). For each of these fields, we could ask a number of questions regarding centralization, kind and type of autonomy, and symbolic structure (Gorski, 2013; Krause, n.d.). We can ask how centralized or not the distribution of field-specific capital is, that is, how hierarchical a field is (eg Bourdieu, 1975). The literature on the social sciences suggests that there is a hierarchy among national fields, positing the US, and perhaps the UK, as the centre of the emerging global field, and Europe, Australia and Latin America as the second-tier (Heilbron, 2014). The status of the US and the UK is bolstered by the dominance of English-speaking journals, which are edited in the US and the UK, draw heavily on UK and US reviewers – often recruiting junior US and UK reviewers before more senior international ones – but are often accepted and indeed privileged by hiring, tenure and grant committees in other countries and continents (eg Beigel, 2014b).

From a field-theoretical perspective, it is worth remembering though that inequalities are not, or at least not only, amongst national fields. Not all American social scientists have more field-specific (or other types of) capital than all non-American social scientists. National fields are symbolically and materially divided in ways that are not superseded by their (partial) integration into a larger space.

The fact that a field is central in an international hierarchy of fields does not mean it is necessarily highly autonomous in every sense of the term. We might find, for example, that American sociology is very autonomous vis-à-vis other national scientific fields – in that it does not cite work from foreigners, does not cite work in other languages, and does not value foreign PhDs (Beigel, 2014b; Gingras, 2002; Kennedy and Centeno, 2007; Kennedy, 2015) but is not necessarily very autonomous vis-à-vis its own political field.[2]

We can ask about the type of symbolic oppositions that structure the differentiation of positions within fields – though much emphasis has been placed on the opposition between one autonomous and one heteronomous pole, these divisions can take varying forms (eg Krause, 2014). Considering the fact that different national fields coexist and fields on different scales coexist, we can note that resources from other scales can be a dimension of symbolic divisions within a field. Indeed, one of the divisions in each national field may be between globalizers and those with more local engagements; and among globalizers between orthodox and heterodox globalizers (see Fourcade, 2006).

In this context utterances celebrating the universality of science and denouncing provincialism are performances that need themselves to be analysed in terms of the positions they express. The same is true for positions denouncing globalization and celebrating local authenticity. Ulrich Best has argued, for example, that the debate about Anglo-American dominance in geography has been launched by European nationals with claims to elite positions within the emerging European field of geography – a field, which is established in opposition at the same time to a global field of geography, and in opposition to several national fields of geography (Best, 2009).

Model systems: asking about research practices and objects

Missing from an analysis of positions and fields sketched so far, are research practices and the actual content of the work published in the social sciences. Even if the mapping of symbolic structures of national fields, regional fields, and global fields were complete and even if it included examples of concrete studies and work being cited in this map, this would still be at some remove from practices involved in the production in social scientific work and at some remove from the content of the work.

Bourdieu calls for an analysis of practice, but in his studies of fields he often does not go very far in that direction. Despite Bourdieu's claim to overcome the false opposition between structure and agency, studies following Bourdieu can tend to be either strong on the analysis of field or on the analysis of practice – compare, for example, Hjellbrekke *et al.* (2007) and Denord *et al.* (2011) on the one hand and Wacquant (2007) on the other hand as works that exemplify the analytic gains of either focus. Some commentators have argued that a focus on fields has replaced the analysis of practice in the course of Bourdieu's work (Warde, 2004).

Here we can draw on work in science and technology studies, which has pioneered ethnographic attention to knowledge-production (Latour and Woolgar, 1986; Knorr-Cetina, 1981). This work has sensitized scholars to new dimensions of description, which close empirical observation makes possible. It has paid specific attention to tools and objects of research and places of knowledge-production. This work also invites closer attention to the question what it is exactly that circulates when 'ideas' circulate (Bourdieu, 1999) or when 'theory' travels (Said, 1983; Clifford, 1989). Texts do not travel by themselves. Not only do they need an infrastructure for travelling, they also carry 'stuff' with them – in the case of empirical studies usually some combination of research object, place, method, writing and perhaps translation.

In addition to asking about inequality among nations, and the field-theoretical inquiry into inequality among positions, we can ask about inequality among research objects. I want to ask how disciplines attribute attention to research objects.

I call a model system in any discipline an object of study that pools resources and is used by convention to stand in for a more general class of epistemic objects (Creager *et al.,* 2007). The knowledge gained through the analysis of model systems is supposed to hold also for other, not clearly specified cases. The analytical notion of model system here subsumes what is also sometimes called 'exemplars' (Kuhn, 1970), 'paradigmatic cases' or 'canonical cases'.

As I draw on research that emphasizes the diversity of practices within even the natural sciences, it is important to point out that a focus on model system is only one of many ways in which disciplines can structure and reward

 The Sociological Review Monographs, 64:2, pp. 194–211 (2016), DOI: 10.1111/2059-7932.12008

attention to concrete research objects. Model systems initially came to the attention of philosophers of science as an alternative to law-seeking physics (Creager *et al.*, 2007). In law-seeking science there is no stand-in, but rather the claim is of direct access to the epistemic object by virtue of a total or a representative sample. Another logic that contrasts with the logic of model systems is the logic of coverage where a focus on a previously unstudied or neglected case is rewarded (see Guggenheim and Krause, 2012).

Model systems in sociology

I have argued elsewhere (Guggenheim and Krause, 2012) that some prominent subfields in sociology do use model systems though to the extent that social science research uses population-level data or representative samples, it does not use model systems and requires a different kind of engagement. In that article, we compiled an initial list of candidates for sociological model systems (Guggenheim and Krause, 2012: 108). We name the model system first and then the type of object it stands in for, followed by an indication of some exemplary and seminal literature that focuses on the model system (or work that analyses the literature on the model system).

1) Doctors (professions) (Abbott, 1988; Becker *et al.*, 1977)
2) Chicago (cities) (Park and Burgess, 1925)
3) African-Americans in cities (race) (DuBois, 1899; Wilson, 1980, 1987)
4) The French Revolution (radical social change) (Skocpol, 1979, 1985; Sewell, 1985).
5) The biological laboratory (the production of scientific knowledge) (Latour and Woolgar, 1986; Knorr-Cetina, 1981).
6) The Scientific Revolution (the relationship of science and society) (Merton, 1938).
7) English working class (class formation in capitalism) (Marx, 2007[1857]; Thompson, 1964; Calhoun, 1982)
8) Car industry (organization, work) (Rot, 2006)
9) Women (gender studies)
10) Juvenile petty criminals (the sociology of law, criminology) (Shaw *et al.*, 1938; Cohen, 1955)
11) Marx, Durkheim, Weber (theory, history of sociology)
12) High art (culture) (White and White, 1993)

Studies about doctors are foundational for the sociology of professions, studies about Chicago are foundational to urban sociology and urban ethnography, and studies of the French Revolution are central to comparative-historical sociology. Criminology has focused intensely on petty criminals and has, as a result, relatively neglected other forms of criminals. Studies of the car industry have had significant influence on the sociology of work. Sociological theory is still prominently shaped by a consideration and reconsideration of the classic texts as model systems for sociological thought.

In each of these subfields, classic works on the model system are central to teaching and to theoretical debate. A reinterpretation of a classic case can garner significant rewards in terms of attention and recognition, while it is more difficult for work on an odd or unrecognizable case to be accepted as theoretically relevant.

I would claim that these patterns are produced on the collective level and are largely unreflected in everyday life, despite the fact that some scholars, particularly in sociology, have developed very sophisticated ways of formalizing how knowledge about specific cases could be contextualized to draw more general conclusions from individual studies (Burawoy, 2009; Ragin and Becker, 1992).

The West as a model system

Connecting the discussion of model systems with the critique of 'euro' or 'metrocentrism' (Wallerstein, 1997; Go, 2013; Chakrabarty, 2000) lends itself to an analysis by analogy. We can restate the critique of Western hegemony in the social sciences by arguing that the West has served as the model system for societies, or more specifically as the model system for 'modern' or 'developed' societies. This means, on the one hand, that those societies and institutions command a large share of attention, and that the analysis of Western societies and institutions implicitly serve as a stand-in for the analysis of societies and institutions in general. The notions of 'modernity' and 'development' have been used to imply that lessons from the model system can be transferred to other cases, even if it may take some time.

In the logic of metrocentrism as in the logic of model systems, other cases have to be justified in relationship to the privileged case. As Chakrabarty notes:

> that Europe works as a silent referent in historical knowledge becomes obvious in a very ordinary way. There are at least two everyday symptoms of the subalternity of non-western, third world histories. Third-world historians feel a need to refer to works in European history; historians of Europe do not feel any need to reciprocate. ... the greats and the models of the historian's enterprise are always at least culturally 'European'. 'They' produce their work in relative ignorance of nonwestern histories and this does not even seem to affect the quality of their work. This is a gesture, however, that we cannot return. We cannot even afford an equality or symmetry of ignorance at this level without taking the risk of appearing 'old-fashioned' or 'outdated'. (Chakrabarty, 2000: 28).

The unsaid privileging of Western countries and Western institutions as reference cases is reinforced via Anglo-American journals, which allow some cases in as the default and ask those writing on other cases to explain themselves in much more details (Stöckelová, 2016; Meriläinen *et al.*, 2008; Johnson (Latour), 1988; see Kennedy, 2015: ch. 5). Scholars report that reviewers question much more thoroughly why a non-standard case might be relevant. They also report that they

 The Sociological Review Monographs, 64:2, pp. 194–211 (2016), DOI: 10.1111/2059-7932.12008

are asked to provide additional context on non-standard cases, as reviewers feel it is legitimate to profess ignorance on non-standard cases, and to posit readers that know nothing about non-standard cases.

Bruno Latour states in a footnote to a paper he published under the pseudonym Jim Johnson in an American journal, 'The reason for this use of pseudonym was the opinion of the editors that no American sociologist is willing to read things that refer to specific places and times which are not American. Thus I inscribed in my text American scenes so as to decrease the gap between the prescribed reader and the pre-inscribed one' (Johnson, 1988).

Modelcentrism

We should distinguish between general ethnocentrism and the role of model systems more specifically in focusing attention and stratifying research objects. We can restate the problem of metrocentrism in terms of model systems but model systems also play a role relatively independently of general ethnocentrism. Analysing these dynamics in terms of model systems leads us to look more closely at case selection within 'the West'. Historically, the West may have been the model for political modernity, as Chakrabarty has argued, but Europe was the model system for the West and particular countries have served as model systems for Europe. The very history of the discipline is based not so much on the West but on the study of a very small set of states (see also Wagner *et al.*, 1991). Those who live in smaller European nations are not the victims of colonization but have a harder time contributing to the seemingly cumulative research on model systems for societies.[3]

Partly because modernity has been defined with reference to classics of sociological theory, the German and French cases have been particularly important. France and Germany are the reference points for discussions of state-formation, citizenship and nationalism. Oskar Negt and Alexander Kluge (2014 [1981]) have argued that for our understanding of industrialization and class-formation, England – rather than, for example, Germany – has been the privileged case. They have argued that this has left us with assumptions about a very rapid and relatively complete separation of people from the land, which are not correct when thinking about Germany (and other places). The theory of modernity might have looked different if it had started from different cases or been able to consistently focus on a variety of cases.

The French revolution has been the model case for revolutions, and with that it has become foundational to the whole subfield of comparative historical sociology. This central place of the French Revolution can be seen when scholars make arguments about the way in which it was embedded in colonial relations (Go, 2013). It is expressed when the French revolution becomes the site of more general debates about culture (Skocpol, 1985; Sewell, 1985). This way of referencing the French Revolution recalls one of the functions of canons in literature: by agreeing to discuss the same books and authors, theoretical differences can be thrown into relief.

The Sociological Review Monographs, 64:2, pp. 194–211 (2016), DOI: 10.1111/2059-7932.12008

Some of the model systems on the list above are not place-specific, such as 'doctors' as a stand-in for 'professions' or 'gangs' as a stand-in for 'crime'. For studies of these objects, it does seem to be an advantage to be located in the West, or more specifically in one of a few 'model nations' within the West. These contexts seem to render studies 'contextless' – beyond that it does not seem to matter what kind of hospital is studied and where they are located – many studies are set in university hospitals, others in major cities, but some studies are of community hospitals and the classic study by Becker *et al.* (1977), for example, is set in Kansas.

Urban sociology, unsurprisingly, is particularly place-specific. Conversations about cities have had different model systems: The first model system may have been Paris, or Berlin. As Thomas Gieryn has shown, in early American sociology, Chicago sociologists managed to turn their field, the city of Chicago, into *the* canonical research setting for urban sociology and the nascent discipline as a whole (Gieryn, 2006). What was explored in Chicago as a specific field site became general knowledge about cities. Chicago was a stand-in for 'city' that was a stand-in for 'modern society', in a way in which, for example, Heidelberg and Freiburg in Germany were not.

Model systems can change and Chicago's status as a model system has been challenged. Chicago was the dense city of the twentieth century that exposed the frantic pace of industrial and financial centres and that drew a massive influx of migrants to the jobs these industries offered. At the end of the century, Chicago was an outdated model and Los Angeles became a new model system (see Dear and Dishman, 2001; Judd and Simpson, 2011). Today, Los Angeles in turn, sees its status as model system questioned and research is beginning to pay attention and to the fast-growing cities of the south.

It is worth noting that as research starts considering non-Western cities, it does not choose a representative sample or a range of cities but focuses on establishing new model systems that are studied at the expense of other cities. Lagos and Mumbai concentrate a large share of the attention (Gandy, 2005). We could argue that Dharavi (Mumbai), and Kibera (Nairobi) function as model systems for the object 'slum'. Many other forms of settlements are comparatively neglected, including what Robinson (2006) calls ordinary cities and Hilgers (2012) studies as middle-sized cities.

This analysis lends intra-scientific specificity to the more general problems of metrocentrism: in scholarly work, the focus on model systems can flirt with notions of inherent aesthetic value underlying the literary or art historical canon, which can very explicitly argue that we need to study the 'best' cases. It also flirts with notions of generalizability, but it does so without engaging in the standardization practices that underpin claims to generalizability in both biology and literary studies.

The charge in post-colonial critique has been that the West hides its particularity and presents itself as universal. In some ways, 'the West' is also hiding behind the particularity of specific objects. The logic of distributing attention to a model system, allows an open acknowledgement of particularity on the level of the

 The Sociological Review Monographs, 64:2, pp. 194–211 (2016), DOI: 10.1111/2059-7932.12008

specific study, with implicit claims for general conclusion and a simple crowding out of other cases or topics.

In sociology, the claims for generalizability of model system research are usually implicit; it is worth noting that while other disciplines that use model systems invest in an infrastructure that is thought to ensure standardization as a precondition for comparability and the control of context, sociology does not. We can distinguish between the specimen, the object in front of the researcher, and model system, the kind of object researchers are trying to study. Both biologists and literary scholars put a lot of efforts into standardizing specimen. Biologists do not all study the same animal – a fruit fly, for example – but they try to control the variation among individual fruit flies studied and they study similar fruit flies. They do not circulate the actual animal, but they circulate genetically identical drosophila so that they know the variation observed is not due to genetic differences of the object of study, or they study genetically different drosophila, but then they know about the differences between the different genotypes. The equivalent of the biological 'specimen' for literary studies is the physical copy of James Joyce's *Ulysses*, for instance, that a scholar is working with. Not all editions of the book are the same and indeed scholars pay much attention to the differences between different editions in order to find out who is studying 'the real' Joyce, but also to make clear which differences of interpretation are owed to different versions of the text (eg Rossman, 1988). Translations add another level of variation and issues of translation are discussed as problems of research. But standard editions of texts go very far in making sure that research objects are identical and deviations can be identified and named.

The specimen of sociological model systems do not travel and are not copied. Because of this, the objects of research are less standardized than in other disciplines and different research projects on different specimens of the same model system are not easily comparable.

The case of theory

'Model systems' or 'canons' have been most explicitly set and most explicitly contested in social theory. Theory syllabi focus on some thinkers, not others; secondary commentary in journals focuses on some authors not others (Connell, 1997; Seidman, 1994; see also Bhambra, 2014).

Considering the materiality of research objects, it is worth pointing out that this is a specific kind of canon for the discipline of sociology. 'Marx', 'Durkheim' and 'Weber' are not technically objects of social research, such as, for example, the family or the state, but authors. In the subfield of sociological theory, the canon thus operates like a literary canon – but without a theory of genre or a theory of how to work with texts.

Theorists are themselves model system in that they concentrate attention and serve as privileged objects of research; it is also worth noting that the process by which a person becomes a theorist promotes a reading that isolates them from their original context and their empirical concerns (Bagheer, 2012); canonization of people focuses attention on specific studies, while obscuring their local origins or even the fact that they were studies of specific objects.

Bourdieu has commented on this process, writing that 'as a rule, non-French interpreters of my work, both anthropological and sociological, have offered a reading of it limited to its purely theoretical dimension. This has often led them to ignore its properly empirical dimension, as well as the contribution that my research brings to our knowledge of French society and, mutatis mutandis, of all modern societies' (Bourdieu, 1993: 270).

We might inquire here into the tension between the analysis Bourdieu provides in the first part of the quote, and the universalizing claim towards the end. Bourdieu on the one hand observes how his reception as a theorist leads to a neglect of the specific context of his work. But he then proceeds to at least flirt with the idea that France can stand in for other 'modern societies'.

Theoretical canonization might interact with the factors discussed in the section on 'The West as a model system' and 'Modelcentrism'. Because of the link between model systems and generalizability, insights derived from model countries and cases may be more readily recognized as 'theoretical'. That may mean it is harder to become a famous theorist from a base in a small European or non-Western country. It may also mean that if one wanted to become a famous theorist based in a small European country, it might be strategically advisable to travel for research or become the kind of theorist whose work is not based on empirical research.

Connell's account of the phenomenon 'X in Australia' (1997: 81) hints at the difficulty of becoming a 'theorist' based on non-model system research. Researchers in Australia, Connell notes, felt compelled to re-do canonical studies in other settings: 'The task of the Australian sociologist was to apply the metropolitan research technique, demonstrate that the phenomenon also existed in Australia, and say empirically what form it took here' (1997: 81).

Critical discussion of the theoretical canon has focused on who is or should be included. Including diverse theorists, whose concerns arise in different contexts, might lead to the inclusion of more diverse local realities. But critics often collude in the personalization of the enterprise 'theory', whereby people and their work become the model system to be studied and argued over. This personalization itself comes with a cost to the representation of diverse geographic contexts.

Fields and model systems

I have suggested that we need to pay attention to the internal dynamics of social scientific disciplines, when trying to understand unequal patterns in global knowledge production. To the analysis of differentiation of and inequality among positions in national, regional and transnational fields, I have proposed to add an analysis of the inequality among research objects and topics. How might the hierarchy of topics and objects interact with the symbolic structure and hierarchy of positions targeted by field-analysis? The following four hypothesis could be investigated further.

The Sociological Review Monographs, 64:2, pp. 194–211 (2016), DOI: 10.1111/2059-7932.12008

Firstly, access to model systems can be a source of field-specific capital. Research on model systems can be assumed to contribute to knowledge of general importance; with that inequality of access to model systems becomes an inequality of access to the opportunity to contribute to knowledge perceived to be of general importance. This matters both within national fields and within transnational fields. Researchers in 'model cities', for example, can work with the assumption that their findings have relevance beyond their immediate context. Researchers in 'model nations' can presuppose that their research can directly contribute to general knowledge. When they study cases of non-located model systems, such as doctors or gangs they do not need to comment in as much depth on how the specificity of their location shapes their findings.

Access is particularly important for original qualitative research. The case for model systems based on textual sources and library research is somewhat different. Access to the sources on the French Revolution or the Holocaust is not equally distributed, but it is somewhat more equally distributed than access to long-term field research in Chicago.

Secondly, though, conventions regarding model systems do not only provide field-specific capital to those who have direct access to model systems and are able to conduct original research. They do not only reinforce a single dimension of centrality, between positions with access to model systems, say, and others. Sociological canons, like other canons, can also be a resource for some in outsider positions because they provide a relatively explicit message about what needs to be known (see Guillory, 1993).

Within national fields or the transnational field, knowledge about sociological canons provide a shortcut to field-specific capital for those in relatively peripheral positions who try to play by the dominant rules of the game – as opposed to those who are distanced by choice or by force. This is particularly true for second-hand uses of model system research, such as in citation and in teaching. Model systems can become a means by which elites in subordinated fields compete with their own colleagues; the reference to model system research becomes a line of symbolic division in such fields.

In an essay published in 1985, Bourdieu has described the dynamic between central and peripheral positions in the field of Francophone literature. Asking, 'Is there a Belgian literature?', he shows that Belgians have a choice of whether to compete in Paris on unequal grounds, or become labelled as local literature (Bourdieu, 1985). Researchers from peripheral countries face a similar choice within the global field; but national academic systems may provide more protection within the transnational field for those 'Belgians' who write in 'Parisian' ways than is provided within the field of francophone literature (see also Christin, this volume).

Thirdly, I would hypothesize that access to other kinds of field-specific capital can supersede the constraints imposed by assumptions about model systems. In extreme cases of this, field-position may trump access to model systems. Considering urban research, the rise of new model systems in the global south has not led to much new power for local researchers. These model systems have arisen at the same time as international travel has become fast and cheap, and outsiders are able to do fly-in research (see Gandy, 2005). We have to remember that in some fields, like mountaineering, archaeology, and to some extent in the history of anthropology, local status is precisely what precludes people from claiming shares in locality-specific achievements. In the history of mountaineering the local guides did not benefit from their easy access to iconic mountains – or indeed their superior skill – they were defined out of the relevant universe of actors (see, eg, Krauss, 2013).

There is another way in which the constraints associated with model systems matter less for those with access to other forms of field-specific capital. There is perhaps more licence for those in central and secure positions to address other cases. If and when the investment on interesting cases pays off intellectually, they can garner the rewards.

Model systems have a certain effect in (transnational) fields. I would also hypothesize, lastly, that fielded transnational exchanges in turn have an effect on the role of model systems in sociology, reinforcing their status. International exchanges may lead to dialogue that questions the status of nationally specific model system and might lead to greater interest in variation among cases of non-located model systems, such as doctors or gangs. But internationalization may at the same time lead to a higher consensus on canons in different sociological sub-fields. Though more studies cross national boundaries, these studies cover only a subset of objects and cases considered in the original context. In this process exemplary cases are taken out of the context of other possible cases, and exemplary studies are deprived of the context of the broader literature that they emerge out of, as discussed by Bourdieu (1999).

Conclusion

I have suggested that in addition to inequality between 'core' and 'periphery', and between different nations, we can consider the differentiation of positions within fields. This alerts us, for example, to the ways in which transnational, national and regional fields overlap and to the ways national fields are shaped by oppositions between 'globalizers' and their opponents. Further, I argued that in addition to the differentiation of positions in fields, we consider inequality among research objects. We can then analyse how the differentiation of positions and the inequality of research objects may intersect.

In closing I would like to return to only one of the normative dimensions of the patterns under discussion: the effects of model systems and the way they function within fields on the quality of knowledge production. It is worth noting that distributing attention among research objects in an unequal way is in itself not only a bad thing in this regard: Model system research has had some benefits for research in biology and literary studies: in contrast to law-oriented research modelled on experimental physics, model system research encourages and rewards attention to specific cases (Creager *et al.,* 2007). Focus on research objects facilitates communication among researchers and particularly among researchers in different subfields and different national settings. It can help clarify theoretical differences by limiting empirical variation; it can help clarify theoretically relevant empirical variation by limiting other kinds of variation. In these ways, a focus on model systems can help create cumulative effects of what would otherwise be isolated pieces of research.

But there are also drawbacks of this kind of focus in terms of the knowledge produced: assumptions derived from research on model systems might be unthinkingly applied to other cases, when results from research on model systems is not easily transferable to other objects. Indeed even translating findings from one study of the 'same' research object to another ('comparability') requires a level of standardization usually absent in the social sciences. By focusing on model systems, researchers are not considering the full range of variation among cases. Some objects that have value in and of themselves may never be studied and understood.

Focusing on processes internal to (social)-scientific disciplines, the question then becomes what kind of mechanisms disciplinary fields, and disciplinary transnational fields in particular, have to reflect on whether and how it makes sense to focus attention on specific cases. How can we exploit the strengths of model system research and how can we mitigate its weaknesses? How can we learn most from different studies of the same research objects, while also reflecting on the fact that specimens are not standardized? How can we train scholars to be literate both regarding canonical cases and what it would mean to think about the full variation of cases? What kind of mechanism would help ensure research as a whole in some way reflects the underlying variety of cases, as well as the variety of national contexts?

These kinds of questions are not only a challenge for transnational fields – it would be misleading, for example, to imply that unequal attention to cases began with Anglo-American centrality in an emerging transnational field – but it is *also* a challenge for transnational fields. We can inquire into what kind of transnational practices and networks serve primarily the exchange and accumulation of field-specific capital within national, regional and transnational fields and what kind of transnational practices and networks have the potential to foster the kind of reflexivity discussed above.

Acknowledgements

I am grateful to Michael Guggenheim and Daniel Menchik for discussions that strengthened this paper. I am also grateful to five anonymous reviewers and to the participants of the 'Fielding Transnationalism' workshop at Boston University in 2014, as well as the series editor Steve Brown, for useful comments on this paper.

Notes

1 Fernanda Beigel has noted that using metaphors from economic development to describe the scientific world system might lead us to confuse the results of symbolic violence – the lack of

international visibility of Argentinian sociology for example – with real deprivation – a lack of productive capacity in Argentina (Beigel, 2014a).

2 See Benson (2005, 2013) and Krause (n.d.) on the different forms of autonomy.

3 But see Fleck and Nowotny (1993) on Austrian sociology and Kennedy (2015) on the influence of Polish sociology and of research on Poland.

References

Aalbers, M. B., (2004), 'Creative destruction through the Anglo-American hegemony: a non-Anglo-American view on publications, referees and language', *Area*, 36 (3): 319–322.

Aalbers, M. B. and Rossi, U., (2006), 'Beyond the Anglo-American hegemony in human geography: a European perspective', *GeoJournal*, 67 (2): 137–147.

Abbott, A. D., (1988), *The System of Professions: An Essay on the Division of Expert Labor*, Chicago: University of Chicago Press.

Alatas, S. F., (2003), 'Academic dependency and the global division of labour in the social sciences', *Current Sociology*, 51 (6): 599–613.

Altbach, P. G., (2002), 'Centers and peripheries in the academic profession: the special challenges of developing countries', in P. G. Altbach (ed.), *The Decline of the Guru: The Academic Profession in Developing and Middle-Income Countries*, 1–22, Chestnut Hill, MA: The Boston College Center for International Higher Education.

Amann, K., (1994), ‚Menschen, Mäuse und Fliegen: Eine wissenssoziologische Analyse der Transformation von Organismen in epistemische Objekte', *Zeitschrift fuer Soziologie*, 23 (1): 22–40.

Ankeny, R. A. and Leonelli, S., (2011), 'What's so special about model organisms?', *Studies in History and Philosophy of Science*, 41 (1): 313–323.

Bagheer, S., (2012), 'The invention of theory: the changing status of Max Weber's Protestant ethic throughout the 20th century', paper presented at the *Junior Theorist Symposium*.

Becker, H. S., Geer, B., Hughes, E. C. and Strauss, A. L., (1977), *Boys in White: Student Culture in Medical School*. New York: Transaction.

Beigel, F., (2014a), 'Current tensions and trends in the World Scientific System', *Current Sociology*, 62: 617–625.

Beigel, F., (2014b), 'Publishing from the periphery: structural heterogeneity and segmented circuits. The evaluation of scientific publications for tenure in Argentina's CONICET', *Current Sociology*, 62: 743–765.

Benson, R., (2005), 'Mapping field variation: journalism in France and the United States', in R. Benson and E. Neveu (eds), *Bourdieu and the Journalistic Field*, 85–112, Cambridge: Polity Press.

Benson, R., (2013), *Shaping Immigration News: A French American Comparison*, Cambridge: Cambridge University Press.

Best, U., (2009), 'The invented periphery: constructing Europe in debates about "Anglo hegemony" in geography', *Social Geography*, 4: 83–91.

Bhambra, G. K., (2007), *Rethinking Modernity: Postcolonialism and the Sociological Imagination, Basingstoke: Palgrave Macmillan.*

Bhambra, G. K., (2014), 'A sociological dilemma: race, segregation, and US sociology', *Current Sociology*, 62 (4): 472–492.

Bourdieu, P., (1975), 'The specificity of the scientific field and the social conditions of the progress of reason', *Social Science Information*, 14: 19–47.

Bourdieu, P., (1985), 'Existe-il une literature belge', *Etudes de Lettres*, 4: 3–6.

Bourdieu, P., (1993), 'Concluding remarks: for a sociogenetic understanding of cultural works', in C. Calhoun, E. LiPuma and M. Postone (eds), *Bourdieu: Critical Perspectives*, 263–275, Cambridge: Polity Press.

Bourdieu, P., (1999), 'On the social conditions of the international circulation of ideas', in R. Shusterman (ed.), *Bourdieu: A Critical Reader*, 220–228, London: Wiley.

Bourdieu, P., (2005), 'The political field, the social science field, and the journalistic field', in R. Benson and E. Neveu (eds), *Pierre Bourdieu and the Journalistic Field*, 29–47, Cambridge: Polity Press.

 The Sociological Review Monographs, 64:2, pp. 194–211 (2016), DOI: 10.1111/2059-7932.12008

Burawoy, M., (2009), *The Extended Case Method. Four Countries, Four Decades, Four Great Transformations, and One Theoretical Tradition*, Berkeley, CA: The University of California Press.

Calhoun, C., (1982), *Questions of Class Struggle*, Chicago: Chicago University Press.

Camic, C., Gross, N. and Lamont, M., (2011), *Social Knowledge in the Making*, Chicago: Chicago University Press.

Chakrabarty, S. D., (2000), *Provincializing Europe: Post-colonial Thought and Historical Difference*, Princeton, NJ: Princeton University Press.

Clifford, J., (1989), 'Notes on Travel and Theory', *Inscriptions*' 5.

Cohen, A., (1955), *Delinquent Boys: The Culture of the Gang*' Glencoe, IL: Free Press.

Connell, R. W., (1997), 'Why is classical theory classical?', *American Journal of Sociology*, 102 (6): 1511–1557.

Creager, A. N. H., Lunbeck, E. and Wise, M. N., (2007), *Science without Laws: Model Systems, Cases, Exemplary Narratives*, Chapel Hill, NC: Duke University Press.

De Souza Santos, B., (2014), *Epistemologies of the South: Justice against Epistemicide*. Boulder, CO: Paradigm.

Dear, M. and Dishman, J. D. (eds), (2001), *From Chicago to L.A.: Making Sense of Urban Theory*, Thousand Oaks, CA: Sage.

Denord, F., Hjellbrekke, J., Korsnes, O., Lebaron, F. and Le Roux, B., (2011), 'Social capital in the field of power: the case of Norway', *The Sociological Review*, 59 (1): 86–108.

DuBois, W. E. B., (1899), *The Philadelphia Negro: A Social Study*. Philadelphia: University of Pennsylvania Press.

Fleck, C. and Nowotny, H., (1993), 'A marginal discipline in the making. Austrian sociology in the making', in B. Nedelmann and P. Sztompka (eds), *Sociology in Europe: Berlin*, 99–119, New York: de Gruyter.

Fourcade, M., (2006), 'The construction of a global profession: the transnationalization of economics', *American Journal of Sociology*, 112 (1): 145–195.

Gandy, M., (2005), 'Learning from Lagos', *New Left Review*, 33: 37–53.

Gieryn, T. F., (2006), 'City as truth-spot: laboratories and field-sites in urban studies', *Social Studies of Science*, 36 (1): 5–38.

Gingras, Y., (2002), 'Les formes spécifiques de l'internationalité du champ scientifique', *Actes de la recherche en sciences sociales*, 141-142 (March): 31–45.

Gingras, Y. and Mosbah-Natanson, S., (2010), 'Where are social sciences produced?', *Europe*, 47 (43.8): 46–51.

Go, J., (2013), 'For a postcolonial sociology', *Theory and Society*, 42 (1): 25–55.

Gorski, P. S., (2013), 'Bourdieusian theory and historical analysis: maps, mechanisms, and methods', in P. S. Gorski (ed.), *Bourdieu and Historical Analysis*. 327–367, Chapel Hill: Duke University Press.

Guggenheim, M. and Krause, M., (2012), 'How facts travel. the model systems of sociology', *Poetics*, 40: 101–117.

Guilhot, N., (2014), 'The international circulation of international relations theory', in W. Keim, E. Çelik, C. Ersche and V. Wöhrer (eds), *Global Knowledge Production in the Social Sciences. Made in Circulation*, 63–87, London: Ashgate.

Guillory, J., (1993), *Cultural Capital: The Problem of Literary Canon Formation*, Chicago: University of Chicago Press.

Heilbron, J., (2014), 'The social sciences as an emerging global field', *Current Sociology*, 62 (5): 685–703.

Heilbron, J., Guilhot, N. and Jeanpierre, L., (2008), 'Toward a transnational history of the social sciences', *Journal of the History of the Behavioral Sciences*, 44 (2): 146–160.

Hilgers, M., (2012), 'Contribution à une anthropologie des villes secondaires', *Cahiers d'Etudes africaines*, LII (1), 205: 29–55.

Hjellbrekke, J., Le Roux, B., Korsnes, O., Lebaron, F., Rouanet, H. and Rosenlund, E., (2007), 'The Norwegian field of power anno 2000', *European Societies*, 9 (2): 245–273.

Howlett, P. and Morgan, M. S., (2010), *How Well Do Facts Travel? The Dissemination of Reliable Knowledge*, Cambridge: Cambridge University Press.

International Social Science Council, (2010), *World Social Science Report: Knowledge Divides*, Paris: International Social Science Council.
Johnson, J. (Bruno Latour), (1988), 'Mixing humans and nonhumans together: the sociology of a door-closer', *Social Problems*, 35.
Judd, D. R. and Simpson D. (eds), (2011), *The City, Revisited: Urban Theory from Chicago, Los Angeles, and New York*, Minneapolis: University of Minnesota Press.
Keim, W., (2014), 'Conceptualising circulation of knowledge in the social sciences', in W. Keim, E. Çelik, E. Ersche and V. Wöhrer (eds), *Global Knowledge Production in the Social Sciences: Made in Circulation*, 87–117, London: Ashgate.
Kennedy, M. and Centeno, M., (2007), 'Internationalism and global transformations in American sociology', in C. Calhoun (ed.), *Sociology in America: A History*, Chicago: Chicago University Press.
Kennedy, M., (2015), *Globalizing Knowledge: Intellectuals, Universities, and Publics in Transformation*, Stanford, CA: Stanford University Press.
Knorr-Cetina, K., (1981), *The Manufacture of Knowledge: An Essay on the Constructivist and Contextual Nature of Science*, Oxford: Pergamon Press.
Kohler, R., (1994), *Lords of the Fly: Drosophila Genetics and the Experimental Life*, Chicago: University of Chicago Press.
Krauss, M., (2013), *Der Traeger war immer schon vorher da*. Berlin: Nagel and Kimchi.
Krause, M., (2014), *The Good Project: Humanitarian NGOs and the Fragmentation of Reason*, Chicago: University of Chicago Press.
Krause, M., (n.d.), 'How fields vary', unpublished manuscript.
Kuhn, T. S., (1970), *The Structure of Scientific Revolutions*, 2nd edn, Chicago: University of Chicago Press.
Latour, B. and Woolgar, S., (1986), *Laboratory Life: The Construction of Scientific Facts*, Princeton, NJ: Princeton University Press.
Leonelli, S., (2008), 'Circulating evidence across research contexts: the locality of data and claims in model organism biology', LSE Working Papers on the Nature of Evidence: How Well Do 'Facts' Travel?, no. 25.
Lezaun, J., (2007), 'A market of opinions: the political epistemology of focus groups', *Sociological Review*, 55 (2): 130–151.
Lezaun, J., Muniesa, F. and Vikkelsø, S., (2013), 'Provocative containment and the drift of social-scientific realism', *Journal of Cultural Economy*, 6 (4): 278–293.
Marx, K., (2007 [1857]), *Capital: A Critique of Political Economy, Volume I, Part I: The Process of Capitalist Production*. New York: Cosimo Inc.
Meriläinen, S., Tienari, J., Thomas, R. and Davies, A., (2008), 'Hegemonic academic practices: experiences of publishing from the periphery', *Organization*, 15: 584–597.
Merton, R. K., (1938), *Science, Technology and Society in 17th Century England*, Bruges: St Catherine Press.
Negt, O. and Kluge, A., (2014 [1981]), *History and Obstinacy*, Cambridge, MA: MIT Press.
Park, R. and Burgess, E. W., (1925), *The City*, Chicago: Chicago University Press.
Poovey, M., (2001), 'The model system of contemporary literary criticism', *Critical Inquiry*, 27: 408–438.
Ragin, C. C. and Becker, H. S., (1992), *What Is a Case? Exploring the Foundations of Social Inquiry*. Cambridge: Cambridge University Press.
Rehbein, B., (2014), 'Epistemology in a multi-centred world', in W. Keim, E. Çelik, E. Ersche and V. Wöhrer (eds), *Global Knowledge Production in the Social Sciences: Made in Circulation*, 217–223, London: Ashgate.
Robinson, J., (2006), *Ordinary Cities: Between Modernity and Development*, London: Routledge.
Rossman, C., (1988), 'New "Ulysses": the hidden controversy. *The New York Review of Books*, 35: 53–58.
Rot, G., (2006), *Sociologie de l'atelier : Renault, le travail ouvrier et le sociologue. Octarès*, Toulouse, France.

 The Sociological Review Monographs, 64:2, pp. 194–211 (2016), DOI: 10.1111/2059-7932.12008

Said, E., (1983), 'Traveling theory', in E. Said (ed), *The World, the Text, and the Critic*, 226–247, Cambridge, MA: Harvard University Press.

Sapiro, G., (2013), 'Le Champ est-il national?' La theorie de la differenciation sociale au prisme de l'histoire globale. *Actes de la Recherche en Sciences Sociales*, 200 (December): 70–86.

Schott, T., (1991), 'The world scientific community: globality and globalisation', *Minerva*, 29 (4): 440–62.

Sealey, A., (2011), 'The strange case of the Freudian case history: the role of long case histories in the development of psychoanalysis', *History of the Human Sciences*, 24 (1): 36–50.

Seidman, S., (1994), *The Postmodern Turn: New Perspectives on Social Theory*, Cambridge: Cambridge University Press.

Sewell, W. H., (1985), 'Ideologies and social revolutions: reflections on the French case', *Journal of Modern History*, 57 (1): 57–85.

Shaw, C., McKay, H. D., McDonald, J. E., McDonald, J. F., Hanson, H. B. and Burgess, E. W., (1938), *Brothers in Crime*, Chicago: University of Chicago Press.

Skocpol, T., (1979), *States and Social Revolutions: A Comparative Analysis of France, Russia, and China*, Cambridge: Cambridge University Press.

Skocpol, T., (1985), 'Cultural idioms and political ideologies in the revolutionary reconstruction of state power: a rejoinder to Sewell', *Journal of Modern History*, 57 (1): 86–96.

Steinmetz, G., (2007), 'American sociology before and after World War II: the (temporary) settling of a disciplinary field', in C. Calhoun (ed.), *Sociology in America: A History*, 314–367, Chicago: Chicago University Press.

Stöckelová, T., (2016), 'Frame against the grain: asymmetries, interference and the politics of EU comparison', in J. Deville, M. Guggenheim, Z. Hrdlickova (eds), *Practising Comparison: Logics, Relations, Collaboration*, Manchester: Mattering Press, forthcoming.

Thompson, E. P., (1964), *The Making of the English Working Class*, New York: Pantheon Books.

Wacquant, L., (2007), *Body and Soul: Notebooks of an Apprentice Boxer*, New York: Oxford University Press.

Wagner, P., Wittrock, B. and Whitley, R. (eds), (1991), *Discourses on Society. The Shaping of the Social Science Disciplines*, Dordrecht: Kluwer Academic.

Wallerstein, I., (1997), 'Eurocentrism and its avatars: the dilemmas of social science', *New Left Review*, 226: 93–108.

Warde, A., (2004), 'Practice and field: revising Bourdieusian concepts', Centre for Research on Innovation and Competition, Discussion Paper No. 64. Manchester: University of Manchester.

White, H. C. and White, C. A., (1993), *Canvases and Careers: Institutional Change in the French Painting World*, Chicago: University of Chicago Press.

Wilson, W. J., (1980), *The Declining Significance of Race: Blacks and Changing American Institutions*, Chicago: University of Chicago Press.

Wilson, W. J., (1987), *The Truly Disadvantaged: The Inner City, the Underclass, and Public Policy*, Chicago: University of Chicago Press.

Wittrock, B., Heilbron, J. and Magnusson, L., (2008), *The Rise of the Social Sciences and the Formation of Modernity: Conceptual Change in Context, 1750–1850*. Dordrecht: Kluwer.

Zincke, C. R., (2014), 'Local and global communication in Chilean social science. inequality and relative autonomy', *Current Sociology*, 62 (September): 704–722.

Is journalism a transnational field? Asymmetrical relations and symbolic domination in online news

Angèle Christin

Abstract: Are all transnational exchanges 'fielded'? This article explores the limits of the concept of transnational field by focusing on the case of journalism. At first glance, journalism might seem to be the perfect example of a transnational field. The frequency, speed and extent of international exchanges between media outlets has increased dramatically with the development of online news, leading media scholars to develop the concept of 'global news'. Yet I argue that such international exchanges do not necessarily constitute a field. Using ethnographic methods, I analyse the circulation of online news between the United States and France, two countries with strikingly different journalistic traditions. Specifically, I compare two editorial partnerships between US and French websites, one linking prestigious online magazines across the Atlantic and the other connecting tabloid-oriented news sites. I find that editorial content does not circulate seamlessly between the two countries. Based on this study, the article proposes three criteria that must be met for transnational fields to exist: competition over the legitimate definition of the field, reciprocal field effects, and the existence of common stakes. More broadly, the article contributes to defining the limits of the concept of 'transnational field' for the study of international exchanges.

Keywords: field, transnationalism, journalism, online news, France, United States

Introduction

Over the past decades, transnational exchanges have become a major subject of sociological inquiry. Field theory plays a growing role in this research program. Cultural, political and economic phenomena taking place at the transnational or global level have been reconceptualized as social fields, drawing on Bourdieu's definition (Bourdieu, 1971, 1996a; Bourdieu and Wacquant, 1992; Sapiro, 2013). For instance, researchers have analysed the internationalization of cultural fields, including the field of television (Kuipers, 2011) and the literary field (Sapiro, 2008). They have studied the transnational production and reception of the social sciences (Heilbron *et al.*, 2008), hard sciences (Gingras, 2002), economics

The Sociological Review Monographs, 64:2, pp. 212–234 (2016), DOI: 10.1111/2059-7932.12009

Published by John Wiley & Sons Ltd, 9600 Garsington Road, Oxford OX4 2DQ, UK and 350 Main Street, Malden, MA 02148, USA

(Dezalay and Garth, 2002; Fourcade, 2006), philosophy (Hauchecorne, 2009), and law (Dezalay and Garth, 1998, 2002). In the political arena, sociologists and political scientists have relied on the concept of field to examine a broad range of transnational phenomena, including colonial empires (Go, 2008; Steinmetz, 2008) and European integration (Mudge and Vauchez, 2012; Wagner, 2005). Existing research demonstrates the benefits of applying the concept of field to phenomena reaching beyond national borders, as well as the limits of 'methodological nationalism' (Wimmer and Schiller, 2003).

Yet there has been relatively little research to date focusing on the possible *limits* of the concept of transnational field. Are all transnational exchanges 'fielded'? What are the criteria associated with different degrees of 'fieldness'? What can we learn about the usefulness of the concept of 'transnational field' by studying a limit case? The article explores these questions by focusing on the example of journalism, specifically the circulation of online news between news sites located in the United States and France. At first glance, journalism might seem to be an emblematic example of a transnational field. Breaking news occurring in Sierra Leone, Scotland and Syria make the headlines of the websites of *The New York Times*, *Le Monde* and *Al Jazeera*. Every day, millions of readers around the world scroll through the online versions of newspapers both local and distant. Over the past decade, the frequency, speed and extent of international exchanges between news websites has increased dramatically, leading media scholars to describe our time as an age of globalized news.

Yet the multiplication of international exchanges between news outlets should not mask the national and even local character of news-making. Thus, it is essential to examine the different features of national fields in order to understand the distinct sets of constraints – both material and symbolic – that shape the production of information. National journalistic fields may indeed differ in important ways. This is the case in the United States and France: the media structures and journalistic cultures of the two countries are often described as polar opposites in terms of market forces, role of the state and form of the news (Benson, 2013; Benson and Saguy, 2005; Chalaby, 1996; Padioleau, 1985). Because of these structural and cultural differences between the United States and France, examining the circulation of online media content between the two countries provides a limit case for studying whether journalism is indeed a transnational field.

The analysis proceeds in three steps. First, I introduce journalism and online news in the United States and France. Second, drawing on a multi-sited ethnographic study of online news organizations, I analyse two partnerships between French and American news sites: one linking two publications specializing in political analysis (*TheNotebook* in the United States and *LaPlace* in France) (the publications' names, as well as those of interviewees, have been changed), the second between two sites more oriented toward tabloid news and celebrity gossip (*AmericanMag* in the United States and *FrenchMag* in France). In both cases, problems arose when editors sought to share articles between the two countries: editorial content did not travel smoothly across the Atlantic. Third, drawing on Bourdieu's definition of the concept of field, I examine whether online news in the United States and France is a transnational field. I delineate three criteria that must be met for a transnational journalistic field to exist: first, a struggle for the legitimate definition of 'good journalism'; second, the presence of reciprocal field effects; and third, the existence of common stakes (eg audiences, awards and jobs). Based on these three criteria, I argue that the exchanges taking place between US and French news sites constitute a weak transatlantic field. The article concludes by discussing the range of application and potential limits of the concept of transnational field.

Online news as a global or national field? Comparing the United States and France

Contemporary journalism has a double nature. On the one hand, the production of information is a deeply transnational type of activity: journalists routinely collect, process and disseminate news across borders. The Internet has amplified these international exchanges of information, leading media scholars to craft the concept of 'global news' to characterize the current media system. On the other hand, journalism is a decidedly national activity shaped by the specific structures and rules of the game of domestic journalistic fields, as exemplified by the comparison of the United States and France.

From news agencies to 'global journalism'

News has always travelled across national borders: a large mass of trade news, diplomatic secrets, and political gossip circulated across Europe as early as the fifteenth and sixteenth centuries (Pettegree, 2014). It was mostly over the course of the nineteenth century, however, that news-making became an organized field of activity routinely crossing national borders.

The first major news actors at the global level were news agencies, including Agence France-Presse (AFP, formerly Havas, created in France in 1835), The Associated Press (AP, created in the United States in 1846), and Reuters (created in the United Kingdom in 1851). Over time, news agencies developed highly formalized procedures for gathering, translating, verifying, and disseminating information coming from around the world. In so doing, they became the primary producers of the global commodity called 'news' (Bielsa and Bassnett, 2009; Boyd-Barrett and Rantanen, 1998; Palmer, 1983).

In the nineteenth century, newspapers also started to rely on foreign correspondents in order to report international news. The position of foreign correspondent was traditionally one of the most high-profile roles within newspapers. Foreign correspondents were described as 'cosmopolitans among cosmopolitans, [men] in gray flannels who rank very high in the hierarchy of reporters' (Hamilton and Jenner, 2004: 301). Foreign correspondents typically acted as anthropologists in a foreign place: they translated and reframed exotic news for a national audience (Hannerz, 2012; Willnat and Weaver, 2003). Because of financial constraints and a perceived lack of interest among readers and viewers, the number

The Sociological Review Monographs, 64:2, pp. 212–234 (2016), DOI: 10.1111/2059-7932.12009

of foreign correspondents decreased starkly over the past twenty years, leading observers to worry about the future of international news (Hamilton and Jenner, 2004; Utley, 1997).

Yet new forms of international circulations have emerged. Existing research focuses on three concurrent trends. First, the news media have become deterritorialized in many ways by the Internet. Bloggers in different countries can upload real-time updates about local events. Social networking sites such as Twitter and Facebook have become increasingly important communication channels for citizens, bloggers and journalists around the world (Lasorsa *et al.*, 2012; Reese *et al.*, 2007). On the reception side, news websites are readily accessible from everywhere, provided that one has an Internet connection and that the Internet is not subject to government censorship (van Dijk, 2006). Consequently, prestigious English-language news outlets with a strong online presence such as *The New York Times*, CNN, and the BBC have become increasingly important in assessing newsworthiness at the global level (Usher, 2014; Thurman, 2007).

A second trend is the transformation of the journalistic workforce around the world. Journalists have become more educated, multilingual and cosmopolitan over time (Reese, 2010). In many countries, the number of journalism degree programmes increased rapidly between the 1970s and the 2000s (Frőhlich and Holtz-Bacha, 2003; Lafarge and Marchetti, 2011; Ruellan, 1993). This contributed to a relative standardization of journalistic training. In most journalism schools' core curriculum, the US or broadly 'liberal' model of presenting 'facts' in an objective, impartial way is presented as an example to follow (Hallin and Mancini, 2004). Journalists are usually expected to be fluent in English in order to be accepted in these top journalism programmes.

The third trend stems from the first two and consists of the emergence of a 'global news style' (Berglez, 2008). This results in journalists in web newsrooms across the globe using increasingly similar narrative forms and angles to cover topics of worldwide interest (Gurevitch and Levy, 1990). Writing styles have become more informal in online news compared to print publications, which contributes to a relative convergence of news styles. In part, this is said to be due to the blurring of the boundary between different formats such as hard news, stories, blog posts, and tweets (Schudson, 2011). In addition, what is deemed 'newsworthy' usually mirrors existing power relations at the global level. Thus, media outlets around the world have increased the proportion of their coverage of events in the United States (Benson and Saguy, 2005; Janssen *et al.*, 2008). Consequently, media experts increasingly rely on the concept of 'global journalism' in order to describe the transnational circulation of information in the digital age (Berglez, 2008; Deuze, 2006; Herbert, 2000; Loeffelhoz *et al.*, 2009; Reese, 2010).

Based on this line of analysis, one might characterize journalism as a global arena in which editors, staff writers, freelancers, bloggers and whistleblowers rely on each other in order to gather, verify and publish relevant information regardless of national borders. In this view, media content would circulate seamlessly across borders. Yet a closer examination of journalism in the United States and France reveals enduring differences in news production between the two national contexts. The next section outlines the current situation of online news in the United States and France before mapping the journalistic fields to which they belong.

Enduring national differences: online news in the United States and France

The Internet has dramatically transformed the media landscape over the past twenty years. The first news websites were created in the United States in the mid-1990s. The number of news websites increased rapidly. In 2010, for the first time, more Americans read news online than in print (American Society of News Editors, 2013; Pew Research Center, 2014). Online news followed the same path in many Western countries, though not always at the same time. In France, there was a delay in the mass availability of broadband Internet compared to the United States: with the exception of *LeMonde.fr*, which was created in December 1995, French news websites and news blogs only started developing in the mid-2000s.

In the United States as well as in France, two main types of online news organizations emerged over time. The first category includes the online sites of legacy media companies (ie, newspapers, magazines, television and radio networks). These sites typically draw their prestige and some of their revenues from the legacy media supporting them. For instance, the online sites of *The New York Times* and *Le Monde* have large amounts of both cultural and economic capital, like their print counterpart, whereas the online versions of the *New York Post* and *Le Parisien* have high amounts of economic capital but little cultural capital.

The second category of actors consists of 'digital native' or 'pure-play' sites, that is, web-only publications without a print or television counterpart. Most of them enjoyed an exponential increase in traffic, revenue and number of employees over the past five years. The positions of these new entrants may be more or less autonomous or heteronomous. For instance, sites such as *ProPublica* in the United States or *Mediapart* in France were founded by high-status print journalists and offer in-depth investigative reporting, whereas sites such as *BuzzFeed* and *TMZ* seek out tabloid news and celebrity gossip, have high levels of economic capital, but are not prestigious among the journalistic occupation.

Yet these similarities between US and French online news should not mask important differences between the two countries. Take the role of market forces: the amount of capital invested in news websites is much higher in the United States than France, consistent with the stronger role of corporate money in US media (Benson, 2013; Krause, 2011). In the United States, major companies such as AOL, Time Warner, Comcast and Microsoft, as well as venture capital funds, have invested massively in the online news business. In France, to the contrary, there are few venture capitalists and media companies willing to invest in new media startups. More generally, the amount of capital managed by venture capitalists in France is 33 times smaller than in the United States, relative to a GDP only six times smaller (Filloux, 2014). As a result, French news sites typically have modest financial means.

 The Sociological Review Monographs, 64:2, pp. 212–234 (2016), DOI: 10.1111/2059-7932.12009

Similarly, the role of the state in shaping the development of online media differs significantly between the two countries. In the United States, there is no system of public support for online news. This is consistent with the dominant interpretation of the First Amendment according to which any type of public interference encroaches on the freedom of the press. In France, the wide-ranging system of public aid to the press has been extended to include online news. A special public budget line ('*Fonds d'aide au développement des services de presse en ligne*') was created in 2010 to support the development of news websites in France (Charon and Le Floch, 2011). In 2014, the parliament voted a law that lowered the Value Added Tax to 2.1 per cent for news websites instead of the general rate of 20 per cent, thus granting them the same tax privileges as print publications.

These distinctive features of online news in the United States and France are in line with the findings of existing research examining the differences between the two countries' journalistic traditions (Benson, 2013; Benson and Neveu, 2005). In his comparative study of news coverage about immigration in US and French media, Benson argues in favour of using Bourdieu's concept of field to analyse journalistic production at the national level: 'Journalism is a field in most if not all Western democratic nation-states, in that it has developed some limited amount of autonomy from the state and the capitalist market and that it is an arena of contestation and struggle operating according to "rules of the game" consciously or unconsciously enacted by actors in the field' (Benson, 2013: 12). In addition, Benson argues that the US and French journalistic fields 'represent opposite "ideal types"' (Benson, 2013: 15): the influence of market forces on the media is much stronger in the United States, whereas the state plays a more important role in the media sector in France. According to Benson, this has important consequences on the form of the news in the two countries: in the United States, immigration news tends to be based on personalized narratives, whereas in France it is usually framed in more abstract terms.

Benson's analysis primarily focuses on newspapers, magazines and television networks, but US and French news websites present similar characteristics. Thus the framework of national journalistic fields is helpful for understanding the differences between US and French online news. In many ways, the overall cohesion of national journalistic fields has increased with the emergence of online media. Not only are radio and television networks now in direct competition for the same online audience with newspapers and magazines through their respective websites, but journalistic careers also increasingly unfold across news sites associated with these different types of media (radio, television, printed press, etc.).

In other words, contrary to the 'global journalism' narrative of the seamless circulation of news across borders, the 'national journalistic fields' perspective indicates that enduring national differences might affect the circulation of online media between countries.

Angèle Christin

Seamless circulations? A comparison of two editorial partnerships between US and French news sites

In the media world, partnerships are more or less formalized agreements between news organizations allowing them to exchange and translate content published on each other's site. Such partnerships are prevalent in online news. Over the past decade, several partnerships were created between US and French news websites. The first partnership studied in this analysis took place between 2007 and 2009 between *TheNotebook* (New York) and *LaPlace* (Paris). Both sites were created by well-known print journalists and specialize in political news, opinions and analysis. The second partnership connects *AmericanMag* (New York) and *FrenchMag* (Paris), two sites created by journalists with little prior experience in print media; these two sites feature a more tabloid-oriented editorial line.

This section draws on a multi-sited ethnographic study (Hine, 2007) conducted between 2011 and 2013 at these four websites (Christin, 2014a, 2014b). I interviewed 36 journalists working for *LaPlace* and conducted several months of observations at the French newsroom. I also conducted a week of ethnographic observation at *FrenchMag* and interviewed eight journalists and bloggers there. In New York, I interviewed 28 journalists working for *TheNotebook* and spent several weeks observing the American newsroom; I also interviewed nine people working for *AmericanMag*.

Most online publications are secretive about their craft: owners and editors fear that external observers will steal their formulas for maximizing the visibility of their content on Google, Facebook and Twitter. They are also adamant about protecting the 'culture' of their newsroom, which they believe contributes in a crucial way to the alchemy of the publication's success. Hence, it took significant time – between three months and a year – and efforts to receive permission to spend time in each of the newsrooms studied in this project. In each case, I had to win the trust of the editors-in-chief and the section editors before being allowed to spend time with the journalists, who themselves asked me many questions about my project, researched my previous work, and often required thorough anonymization, before agreeing to spend time with me.

Once I had gained the trust of the editors and journalists, I organized my days of observation in a similar way in each newsroom. I shadowed web journalists and followed them in their daily work routines, from editorial meetings where they pitched their ideas to coffee breaks when they engaged in heated arguments about the quality of articles, writers, and other publications. I asked journalists questions about their work and their careers, both informally and during semi-structured interviews. Following these discussions and interviews, I often asked journalists and editors to provide me with emails, articles or archival material they had mentioned during our conversation.

Based on this ethnographic material, I find that, despite important differences between the two partnerships, the journalists in charge of creating and implementing the partnerships faced similar issues.

 The Sociological Review Monographs, 64:2, pp. 212–234 (2016), DOI: 10.1111/2059-7932.12009

Four sites with different characteristics

Before turning to the findings, however, it is essential to provide additional information about the different news organizations under consideration.

TheNotebook is the oldest of the news websites under examination. It was founded in the mid-1990s by a famous journalist of the New York magazine world, under the patronage of a leading US company. The site does not charge for access, instead relying on advertising revenue as its main source of income. In 2004, *TheNotebook* was acquired by a large media group for about $15 million. In 2012, the website attracted about ten million unique visitors per month. During my years of fieldwork, the website had not reached financial equilibrium, but, according to its managers and editors, it was close to making a profit. In 2013, *TheNotebook*'s editorial team was composed of 46 journalists and editors.

The other US site under consideration, *AmericanMag*, though created more recently than *TheNotebook*, is a much larger enterprise. It was founded in the mid-2000s by several people with experience in technology startups and television networks. *AmericanMag* rapidly specialized in news aggregation and tabloid content; it expanded exponentially over the years. The site was acquired by a large technology company in 2011 for more than $300 million. In 2012, *AmericanMag* attracted about 45 million unique visitors per month, published more than 500 stories per day, and had its own streaming video network. It now employs several hundred staffers, though no precise employee count is available.

On the French side, *LaPlace.com* was created in Paris in the mid-2000s by several journalists formerly employed by a leading national newspaper. In 2011, the website was still not profitable. The founders hence decided to sell the company to a larger media group for about $8 million. In 2013, *LaPlace* had slightly more than two million unique visitors each month but was still not profitable; the organization had 25 employees, including 15 journalists.

Finally, *FrenchMag* was created more recently, in the early 2010s. *AmericanMag* owns 51 per cent of its shares and provides all the technological support, as well as a large proportion of the content translated and featured on the French site. The amount of capital invested in the creation of the website was kept secret. In 2013, *FrenchMag* attracted about the same traffic as *LaPlace*, around two millions unique visitors per month. The website employs 19 journalists.

As this summary makes clear, the French news organizations are more recent creations than their US counterparts. They are also far smaller, both in terms of economic capital and with respect to the size of their editorial staff. With these elements in minds, we can turn to the partnerships, first between *TheNotebook* and *LaPlace* and second between *AmericanMag* and *FrenchMag*.

TheNotebook and LaPlace

In the mid-2000s, shortly after its creation, the Parisian website *LaPlace* proudly announced its partnership with *TheNotebook*. At the time, the editors and journalists of the French site lauded this as an opportunity for the French public to read the most up-to-date American articles translated into French on their favourite news site. Two years later, however, the partnership ended. By then, *LaPlace* had translated and published about fifty articles from *TheNotebook*. Yet the arrangement was hardly symmetrical: *TheNotebook* never translated any articles from *LaPlace*.

How was this partnership negotiated? Philippe, one of *LaPlace*'s founders and its editor-in-chief, explained that it was all due to the connections he made when he was foreign correspondent in the United States. Philippe, who graduated from the Institut d'Etudes Politiques de Paris ('Sciences Po'), an elite institution of higher education, before receiving a Master's from a top journalism school in France, started as an economic journalist at a leading French daily national newspaper, eventually becoming their Washington correspondent. Philippe remembers his excitement during his time on the East Coast:

> *Philippe* (founder and editor-in-chief, *LaPlace*): When I arrived in the United States ... I really discovered the Internet there. Of course I was using it before, but there I started surfing a lot, I saw what was going on, websites such as *TheNotebook* or *Talking Points Memo* [...] Everything new, interesting, everything counter-intuitive was there. And the blogosphere is very rich in the U.S., they even have conservative blogs... It was very lively, people talked to each other... In France it was less the case.

At that time, *TheNotebook* was one of the most prestigious online news sites. It was staffed with journalists who had worked previously at prestigious publications such as *The New Republic* or *The New Yorker*. The site offered analysis and commentary about politics, news, and culture with an editorial line expressing a witty and conversational take on current events.

When Philippe came back to Paris, he started talking with two colleagues – also foreign correspondents at the same newspaper – about launching a news website. Their project explicitly sought to replicate and improve on some of the innovations that they had witnessed in the United States. *TheNotebook* was a particular source of inspiration. After six months of discussions and negotiations, the founders had amassed enough money to start the project. Philippe then travelled to New York to negotiate an editorial partnership with *TheNotebook*. He took advantage of his visit to videotape *TheNotebook*'s newsroom and an editorial meeting in order to show to his staff the daily functioning of a 'modern' American web newsroom.

> *Philippe*: We had a partnership with *TheNotebook* for a while, because I knew the editor-in-chief, Sam. I even went to visit their newsroom! I have a video of it ... I had a tiny video camera, I entered their newsroom during the editorial meeting. I wanted to show their newsroom to the staff here at *LaPlace*. At the beginning we had an agreement, we could translate some of their articles and put them on our website ... and they could do the same. They never did it. We did it quite a lot. But ... translating American articles for a French audience is not easy. They are too long ... And it didn't work well in French, their pieces had to be completely re-written.

During my days of observation at *LaPlace*, I noted that most staff writers took pride in this proximity with *TheNotebook*: many of them read *TheNotebook* every morning, they knew the names of several prominent journalists working there,

 The Sociological Review Monographs, 64:2, pp. 212–234 (2016), DOI: 10.1111/2059-7932.12009

and they emphasized strong feelings of affinity and admiration for *TheNotebook*. This respect for and conscious imitation of *TheNotebook* exemplifies the symbolic domination of US media in Europe. It also resonates with Bourdieu's insight that 'the economic-technical, and especially, symbolic dominance of American [media], serves a good many [non-American] journalists as both a model and a source of ideas, formulas and tactics' (Bourdieu, 1999: 41; see also Benson and Saguy, 2005; Kuipers, 2011).

The situation in New York was rather different. When I started conducting fieldwork at *TheNotebook* in 2012, I soon realized that the US staff writers and editors barely knew about *LaPlace*. This was made clear when I interviewed Sam, the editor-in-chief of *TheNotebook*:

> *Sam* (editor-in-chief, *TheNotebook*): I met Philippe through a friend. He said he was starting *LaPlace* and we set this kind of casual partnership, it was probably during the first year that the site was up. I don't even remember what it was, it was very casual, we let them run our stories, they would tell us when they had something ... There was no money, no investment or anything. [...] My French is much worse than it used to be 20 years ago. Once in a while I go to their website and check, 'oh, what's going on.' But it's not ... I don't follow what they do closely. I don't know if they're successful, I don't know if they're popular, I have no idea.

This asymmetry in the relationship between the editors of *TheNotebook* and *LaPlace* is mirrored by the unequal circulation of journalistic content between the two sites during the partnership. Whereas *LaPlace* translated and published many articles from *TheNotebook*, *TheNotebook* never published a single article from *LaPlace*, probably because no one in their newsroom spoke French fluently or was particularly interested in French domestic news.

Even on the French side, translating content from *TheNotebook* and packaging it for a French audience was not a straightforward process. Philippe explains that it is 'not easy' to publish American articles for a French audience. He points out that US pieces tend to be 'too long', do not 'work well', and often have to be 'completely rewritten'. During my days of fieldwork at *LaPlace*, I witnessed many conversations among French staff writers who held similar views: they usually found US news articles interesting, funny and stimulating, but also noted that they would not be easily comprehensible to an average French reader. For example, even though *TheNotebook* has a centre-left editorial line in the US media landscape, *LaPlace*'s journalists often criticized *TheNotebook*'s articles for being too right-wing, especially regarding the financial crisis, health care policies, or the Israeli–Palestinian conflict. Similarly, the Parisian journalists often explained that *TheNotebook*'s humour would not make sense to a French audience: the contrarian headlines that made the reputation of the US web magazine were too different from the French tradition regarding newspaper humour, which tends to rely more on irony, sarcasm, and witty 'puns' in the headlines. According to the French writers, the only US articles that 'worked' well for a French audience were snarky pieces about hipsters in New York, opinionated articles about net neutrality, and descriptions of the latest US debates about Beyoncé's feminist ideology. Notably, the only US articles that could easily be translated and adapted for a French audience were not articles about international news or politics, but rather opinion pieces about American urban, tech and pop culture.

AmericanMag and FrenchMag

In October 2011, the New-York based site *AmericanMag* announced that it would launch an affiliate site in France in early 2012. The new website would be called *FrenchMag* and its French editor-in-chief would be a famous and controversial television journalist.

Many French media experts reacted to this announcement negatively. They expressed concern about the intrusion of tabloid-style Anglo-American media into the French landscape. Since its creation in the mid-2000s, *AmericanMag*'s trademark has been to mix political opinions, fast-paced breaking news, and tabloid news. Claire, the new editor-in-chief of *FrenchMag*, explained that she intended to replicate this mix of political opinions and celebrity gossip. She also pointed out that she would invite prominent political figures to contribute to the website. This mix of 'high' political opinion and 'low' celebrity gossip was unheard of in France.

Both the French and the American editors were highly conscious of the necessity to adapt the editorial line of *AmericanMag* for a French audience. Josh, *AmericanMag*'s international editor, explains:

> *Josh* (international editor, *AmericanMag*): With *FrenchMag* ... We did the hiring and we gave them our technology. It's important for us to keep the same platform and the same philosophy, but in a new market: we try to take the spirit of the American website and apply it in France. We don't want them to be an exact copy of the American site, we want them to be as successful in France as we are in the U.S. ... It's a site for experimentation. For example, we capitalize our headlines, in France they don't. It's true that it looks a little weird with small letters ... That's okay, we're not hegemonic. But they have to have the same mix of serious news and shallow news. In France, there is not the same tabloid culture. So the website is not really 'low.' When the French journalists took a look at our 'side boobs' pages, they were, like, 'What is this?!!' They don't have the same puritanical American culture.

Josh is well aware of the challenges associated with international expansion. On the one hand, he repeatedly emphasizes that *FrenchMag* needs to keep the 'same philosophy' as *AmericanMag*, exporting its mix of political opinions and tabloid news and more broadly its 'spirit'. Yet he also explains that *AmericanMag* is 'not hegemonic': *FrenchMag* should adapt to its national market. Thus, some formatting issues like the capitalization of headlines adhere to national tradition. Similarly, the content of the 'tabloid' section varies, since French readers are less interested in sensationalistic tabloid news than their American counterparts. In other words, Josh, one of the main actors in the transnational diffusion of online news, behaves as a careful observer of foreign media cultures (Hannerz, 2012), drawing fine-grained distinctions between the national preferences of the readers.

This close monitoring of audience preferences also takes place among the editors and staff writers of *FrenchMag*. Edouard, *FrenchMag*'s managing editor, describes the complex ways in which they distinguish themselves from *AmericanMag*:

> *Edouard* (Managing Editor, *FrenchMag*): Our editorial line is very much inspired by *AmericanMag* ... But at the same time we have total freedom. We don't mimic the line of *AmericanMag*. Actually, we do the same kind of journalism we've always done and we look at *AmericanMag* at the same time. I mean, we're clearly more French than they are, in the sense that we provide more background information and more analysis in our articles. Often they put a flashy headline and then a news wire and that's it. We're reluctant to do this. We don't like to post stupid news wires. And we publish a lot of political analysis and opinions, this is something we try to promote. [...] Compared to *AmericanMag*, we always try to have a good reason to post something, it has to be breaking news or important in some way ... For example we don't do 'side boobs' or actresses in mini-bikinis ... We don't want to post something without a good reason. Maybe it's a cultural difference?

Later in the interview, Edouard argued that he was particularly sensitive to these cultural differences because of his own 'atypical' background (in his own words): his mother was American and he grew up in Switzerland before moving to Paris. Based on Josh and Edouard's quotes, it seems that journalists at *FrenchMag* are trying to do two opposite things at once: they draw heavily on the editorial line of *AmericanMag*, while at the same trying to do something completely different. Though *FrenchMag* is a subsidiary of *AmericanMag*, the French journalists and editors carefully distinguish themselves from the American company. They argue that they provide more in-depth analysis, refusing merely to cut-and-paste news wires and pictures of 'mini-bikinis'.

Editorial prestige and distinction in the US and French fields of online news

To conclude this analysis of the relations between *TheNotebook*, *LaPlace*, *AmericanMag* and *FrenchMag*, it is essential to note that within each country, the relationship between the higher status site and the lower status site is strikingly similar.

In the United States, editors and journalists working for *TheNotebook* strongly distinguish what they do from what *AmericanMag* does. They repeatedly explain that their editorial line is deeper, more interesting, and more original than the mere aggregation of news wires and celebrity gossip provided by *AmericanMag*, while also acknowledging the success of *AmericanMag* in terms of traffic. At *TheNotebook*, Sam explains:

> *Sam* (editor-in-chief, *TheNotebook*): *AmericanMag* is in a completely different business, they're doing something completely different ... I'm sure that they have advertising that we would love to have and they have readers that we would love to have ... but we're not in the same set. What they're trying to do ... they do create good journalism, I'm not saying that everything they do is bad, but their basic business is this

> quick aggregation, quick recapitulation of the news, and that's not our business. Our business is analysis, understanding, it's something richer than that.

In France, Philippe holds a similar opinion about *FrenchMag*:

> *Philippe* (editor-in-chief, *LaPlace*): *FrenchMag* relies on a well-known brand and they're using well-known recipes that worked in the United States. But is it also going to work in France? Are they going to do serious journalism? I don't know. If they only publish stupid blog posts and steal information from other people… the added value is not great. Same for gossip. I mean … The first piece ever published on *FrenchMag* is about a supposed affair between [*a famous actor and the then-Minister of Justice*]… We don't do that. We don't write about celebrities just to write about them.

Thus, despite the journalists' constant efforts to distinguish themselves from *AmericanMag*, *FrenchMag* is still perceived as the Trojan horse of American tabloid news infiltrating the French media landscape, especially by journalists writing from more prestigious sites such as *LaPlace*. This impression was confirmed by an incident that I observed during my ethnographic fieldwork.

Ethnographic observation
***FrenchMag*, 17 April 2013**

During a day of ethnographic observation in the newsroom of *FrenchMag,* I witnessed a curt exchange on Twitter between Edouard, the managing editor of *FrenchMag*, and Gael, the managing editor of *LaPlace*.

FrenchMag had just translated and posted an article from *AmericanMag* about one of Beyoncé's revealing costumes at a show. The headline was a pun based on an old-fashioned word in French used to describe women's breasts. Half an hour after the article was published, Edouard sneered and said out loud, with an ironic tone and added emphasis: 'Gael [from *LaPlace*] just tweeted that our Beyoncé article is "*degrading*" … That this is not "*his* vision of journalism…"' [*his emphasis*].

All the staff writers in the newsroom took a couple of seconds to look at the incriminating tweet. One of them commented: 'What a hypocrite … It means that he clicked on the article! Such bad faith!' Another writer concurred: 'They always pick the wrong battle at *LaPlace* … I mean, I never check their website, I don't find it relevant, so why do they keep checking our site?'

Approaching transnational fields

Based on the study of these exchanges between US and French news sites, what can we say about the existence of a transatlantic journalistic field? Based on the two cases of editorial partnerships examined above, this final section analyses the criteria needed for such a transnational field to exist.

According to Bourdieu, fields are relatively autonomous configurations of relations between social positions (Bourdieu and Wacquant, 1992; see also Go and Krause, this volume). Bourdieu uses the metaphor of the 'game', in which players

 The Sociological Review Monographs, 64:2, pp. 212–234 (2016), DOI: 10.1111/2059-7932.12009

who have stakes in the game (*illusio*) compete for the monopoly to define what the field is about. Such strategies are determined by people's relative position in the field, which in turn stems from their overall amount of capital and its structure (eg the respective importance of economic, cultural and social capital). Individual strategies also depend on the actor's *habitus*, the incorporated system of dispositions and representations that is mostly shaped by primary socialization but may evolve depending on one's social trajectory. According to Bourdieu, fields of cultural production are typically organized around two conflicting orders of legitimacy: an autonomous logic, based on the degree of specific consecration ('art for art's sake'), and a heteronomous logic that relies either on various measures of market success or on political approval by the dominant figures of the field of power (Bourdieu, 1994; Bourdieu, 1996a).[1]

Drawing on this definition, I now examine the extent to which the transnational exchanges between US and French journalists are 'fielded' and focus on three criteria: competition between journalists to define 'good journalism', the presence of reciprocal field effects, and the existence of common stakes for US and French journalists and news organizations.

What is 'good journalism'? Competition and distinction in the US and France

As we saw earlier, a large number of exchanges take place between US and French online media: journalists routinely translate and publish US articles into French and frequently travel between the two countries. These transnational exchanges involve intense competition between different actors to define what journalism – and more specifically web journalism – should be. Thus, Edouard from *FrenchMag* explicitly criticizes *AmericanMag* for its 'stupid news wires' whereas Josh from *AmericanMag* characterizes *FrenchMag* as 'not having the same tabloid culture' and describes its homepage display as 'weird'. Similarly, journalists from *LaPlace* distinguish what they do from what *TheNotebook* does: they criticize the US site's articles as being 'too long' and not politically engaged. Last, Sam in New York and Philippe in Paris respectively criticize the editorial line of *AmericanMag* and *Frenchmag* as 'not serious' and 'degrading'.

These disputes about what constitutes good journalism in online news are interesting in several respects. First, they indicate that French and US web journalists are engaged in an intense symbolic struggle to define the norms of journalistic excellence in a period of rapid economic and technological transformations. Second, national patterns of distinction and domination emerge in these disputes. French journalists both admire and criticize US journalism: they explain that the articles published on US websites are exciting and well written but also emphasize that they tend to be shallow and ignore important political questions. Last, these debates show that the exchanges taking place between US and French online media are structured in ways that mirror the internal structure of each national journalistic field. In Bourdieusian terms, one partnership connects sites located at the autonomous end of the US and French fields of online news, whereas the other partnership takes place between sites

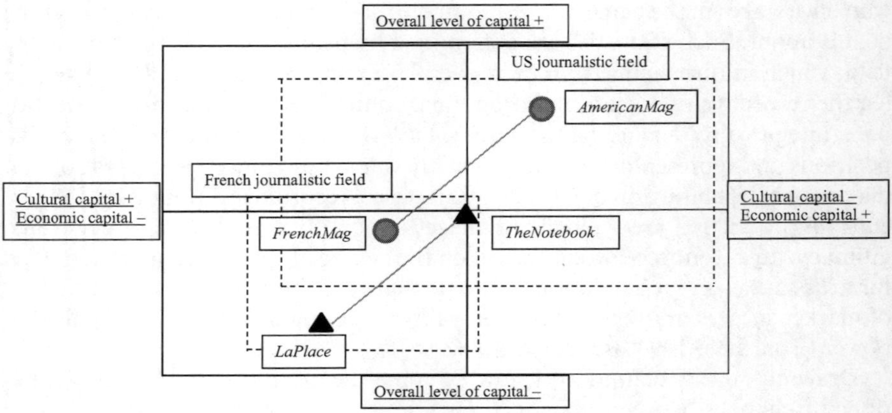

Figure 1 *The transatlantic journalistic field*

located at the heteronomous end of their respective national field: *TheNotebook* and *LaPlace* both have high amounts of cultural capital and relatively little economic capital, whereas *AmericanMag* and *FrenchMag* have a tabloid-oriented editorial line and high amounts of economic capital.

In other words, the journalistic exchanges between the United States and France appear to have the structure of a transnational cultural field, in the sense that they are organized around an autonomous and a heteronomous pole. Following Bourdieu's analysis of the literary field (Bourdieu, 1996a) and the field of aesthetic taste (Bourdieu, 1994), Figure 1 summarizes the respective positions of the four websites in the US and French fields of online news and sketches the structure of this transatlantic journalistic field.

As can be seen in Figure 1, the transatlantic journalistic field seems structured around two axes: the vertical axis is determined by the overall amount of capital whereas the horizontal axis is determined by the structure of capital, that is, by the relative amounts of economic and cultural capital. News organizations in the United States overall have a higher amount of capital than French news organizations; they also have more economic capital than cultural capital compared to French organizations. Therefore, the US journalistic field is located on the upper right corner of the transatlantic field, whereas the French journalistic field is located on the lower left corner. In addition, the US journalistic field is larger than the French journalistic field (in terms of overall number of news organizations, journalist workforce and size of the audience), which appears in the graph. Within each national field, the four websites under consideration occupy distinct positions. In France, *LaPlace* has low amounts of economic capital and high amounts of cultural capital. *TheNotebook* also has more cultural capital than economic capital, but, simply by virtue of belonging to the US journalistic field, it has more revenues than *LaPlace*. *FrenchMag* occupies a heteronomous position in the French journalistic field and has more economic capital than cultural

 The Sociological Review Monographs, 64:2, pp. 212–234 (2016), DOI: 10.1111/2059-7932.12009

capital, which makes it closer to the US journalistic field. Finally, *AmericanMag* has high amounts of economic capital and little cultural capital within the US journalistic field, which explains its position on the upper right side of the graph. The two partnerships are represented by parallel lines between the different websites.

Two comments – or notes of caution – should be added at this point. First, do the partnerships represented in this graph constitute 'relations' or 'interactions' between news organizations? This distinction matters because, whereas Bourdieu defines fields as structures of *objective relations* between sets of positions, other approaches such as symbolic interactionism and the study of 'art worlds' (Becker, 1982) focus instead on *actual interactions* between social actors. At first glance, the ethnographic method and specific partnerships analysed in this project seem to be closer to the latter approach than the former, since studying such partnerships brings our attention to cases of actual interactions between web journalists and news organizations. Yet one should not draw too strong a distinction between interactions and relations in this case. As the graph makes clear, the partnerships between French and US journalists could only take place in a context of structural similarity between the different sites (thus the parallel lines between the four websites). In other words, it is *because* of the similarities between the amount and the structure of their capitals and the proximity between their objective positions in the field that *TheNotebook* and *LaPlace*, as well as *FrenchMag* and *AmericanMag,* were able to develop editorial partnerships.

Second, the analysis so far interpreted Figure 1 as representing a transatlantic journalistic field. Yet an alternative approach would be to analyse the similarities between the positions of the different websites as structural homologies between two national fields, independently of their internationalization. In other words, the criterion of symbolic struggles at the international level might not be sufficient to assess whether a transatlantic journalistic field does in fact exist.

Field effects and the problem of asymmetry

A second important criterion regards the form and direction of field effects. According to Bourdieu, the boundaries of a field can be delineated by looking at the 'effects' of the field on social agents. For example, when writing about the field of 'grandes écoles' (French elite institutions of higher education), Bourdieu points out that 'the existence of field effects … is one of the chief indicators of the fact that a set of agents and institutions functions as a field, as well as one of the reliable instruments for empirically determining the limits of this field, which are simply the point at which these effects are no longer found' (Bourdieu, 1996b: 132).

What are the effects, then, of the transnational field of online news? French web journalists strongly feel the influence and symbolic domination of American journalism, but the opposite is hardly true. French web journalists are all able to read fluently in English; they follow English-language websites, know the names of famous US bloggers and journalists, and follow US domestic news;

they regularly translate and adapt US news articles for a French audience. The French sites that have partnerships with US sites also compete for the definition of who is more 'cosmopolitan' and 'knows' the US media better, which in turn translates into symbolic and material benefits within the French journalistic field. But the effects of this transnational field of online news are much less clear in the United States. The American journalists and editors only rarely read or speak French. They neither follow French websites nor pay attention to French domestic news. In the cases of the partnerships that I studied, the two US sites never translated or published a single French article.

In sum, the effects of transnational exchanges are strongly asymmetrical in the case of journalism. As in other cases of symbolic and economic domination at the international level (Dezalay and Garth, 2002), peripheral actors pay attention to and draw legitimacy from the dominant actor, but the dominant actor does not reciprocate. Following Bourdieu's definition, this calls for a reconceptualization of the transnational exchanges between US and French news sites as being weakly 'fielded' at best.

The stakes of the game

Finally, the concept of transnational fields raises the question of the stakes of the game. According to Bourdieu, all the participants in a given field share at least one thing in common: an interest in the specific stakes of the field (*illusio*). It is possible to further distinguish between symbolic stakes (ie, defining what the field is about) and concrete or institutionalized stakes (ie, streams of revenue, awards or jobs). In order for a transnational field to exist, actors need to share at least some common stakes. As we saw earlier, web journalists in France certainly share with their American counterparts a belief in the importance of journalism; they engage in a constant struggle to define what 'good journalism' in the digital age should be. But do they also share more concrete types of stakes? I examine three types of stakes in turn: audiences (and advertising revenues), awards and jobs.

As far as audiences are concerned, French and American journalists have very little in common, for two main reasons. First, because of the language difference, the number of people in France who read US news sites is low; the number of people in the United States reading French news is probably even lower. There are no available figures about the exact number of people engaging in news readership in other languages, but one might note that in 2014 all of the 100 most-visited websites in the United States and France are respectively US and French sites.[2] Second, even when international readers access a given website, the news organization is typically unable to get advertising revenue for these readers. Not only are most websites unable to collect sufficient socio-demographic information about their international readers, but advertisers themselves are reluctant to engage in international marketing campaigns and still predominantly focus on national audiences (Sternberg, 2013). As a result, many news sites do not take their international audience into account in their negotiations with advertisers (Thurman, 2007).

Journalistic awards are also overwhelmingly national in character. For the Pulitzer Prize, only articles 'coming from a United States newspaper or news site' can enter the competition, thus excluding international publications;[3] the eligibility criteria are similar for the Prix Albert Londres, the most prestigious journalistic award in France (Gatien, 2013). A notable exception are the awards of the Online News Association (ONA), the Online Journalism Awards, which are 'open to work published in any language worldwide'.[4] Yet an overwhelming majority of the ONA judges are affiliated with US and British publications and most of the Online Journalism Awards go each year to English-language publications.[5]

Finally, language differences complicate job mobility between the United States and France. As the previous sections showed, journalists always write in a specific language and style, with a specific audience in mind, and using specific formats and angles designed for their national audience. This makes it difficult for web journalists to start writing in another language for another audience. During the three years of fieldwork that I conducted at online news sites in New York and Paris, almost all of my French interviewees read English and spoke it fluently. Yet I only met one journalist who was able to write in both English and French: she was 24 years old, had just graduated from a joint journalism programme between Columbia and Sciences-Po, and grew up in a bilingual family. When I interviewed her in early 2012, she was planning to go back to Paris, where she grew up and did most of her training, because she felt more at ease writing for French news outlets. She also thought that she had a 'competitive advantage' (her words) in France because of her American training and her knowledge of the New York media world.

Hence, US and French journalists do not compete for the same jobs, news organizations in the two countries do not compete for similar audiences, and the most prestigious journalistic awards are restricted to national publications. In other words, the two fields do not appear to have concrete stakes in common.

A weak transnational field?

Let me now return to the original question motivating this article: based on this study of online news in the United States and France, is it possible to reach a conclusion about the existence of a transatlantic journalistic field?

The findings are mixed. If one relies on the idea of a struggle for the legitimate definition of journalism, then US and French web journalists do belong to a common, transnational journalistic field. Conversely, if one focuses on the question of reciprocal field effects and mutual awareness, then US and French web journalists do not belong to the same transnational field, since US journalists are barely aware of the existence of French media, while French journalists follow US news obsessively. Finally, if one takes into account the criterion of concrete stakes in common, once again US and French news organizations and web journalists do not seem to belong to the same field.

Interestingly, this situation resembles the 'weak field' of European studies analysed by Mudge and Vauchez (2012). As the authors explain, 'one marker of the field's weakness is that the orienting stakes of scholarly production about Europe are often external: scholars of Europe are rarely oriented toward the pursuit of a career as strictly 'European' scholars, partly because there are few professional avenues that allow it' (Mudge and Vauchez, 2012: 451). Scholars who study the European Union might engage in constant negotiations at the international level over the legitimate course of action for European integration, but most careers still take place at the national level. The case of online news is even more complicated due to the absence of common material stakes and the issue of asymmetrical field effects. This makes the transatlantic journalistic space an even weaker field than the 'weak field' of European studies.

Conclusion

This article focused on a limit case to explore what is needed for transnational exchanges to be characterized as a field. At first glance, journalism might seem to be an emblematic example of a global field. Yet I showed that the existence of frequent transnational exchanges between news organizations does not necessarily mean that they are 'fielded'. Specifically, this article examines how online news travels between two countries with strikingly different journalistic traditions. Drawing on an ethnographic study of two editorial partnerships between US and French news sites, I argue that one characteristic of Bourdieusian fields is indeed met: journalists share symbolic stakes and compete for the legitimate definition of 'good journalism'. Nonetheless, two other features indicate that these exchanges are, in fact, only weakly 'fielded': the flow of media content between the two countries is deeply asymmetrical and news organizations and individual journalists do not share concrete stakes. Hence, the exchanges taking place between US and French news sites are still strongly mediated by the structure and culture of their respective national fields, indicating that this transnational space only weakly qualifies as an autonomous cultural field with strong 'vertical' differentiation from the national level (Sapiro, 2013; see also Buchholz, this volume).

In other words, based on the cases presented in this article, it appears that 'news' still does not mean the same thing in the United States and France. Far from being a neutral medium, 'language' here stands for the broader and elusive sets of meanings and expectations elaborated over time within each country's journalistic field. National writing styles incorporate highly specific and complex skills, habits, and informal know-how that together constitute a national media culture. Thus, journalists emphasize how most articles written in another language become irrelevant when they are translated into their mother tongue. 'Texts without contexts' (Bourdieu, 2002), these articles lose a significant part of their interest when they are extracted from their national field of production and presented to another audience with different dispositions and expectations. The example of online journalism illustrates that, in some cases, despite strong technological and economic pressure towards internationalization and convergence, national fields can retain most of their influence in shaping the production and

 The Sociological Review Monographs, 64:2, pp. 212–234 (2016), DOI: 10.1111/2059-7932.12009

reception of symbolic goods. One could expand these findings by exploring other cases of transnational journalistic exchanges. What happens when news travels between countries sharing the same language (for example, the United States and the United Kingdom) or drawing on similar traditions of news production (for example, Germany and Scandinavian countries) (Hallin and Mancini, 2004)? Further empirical research is needed in order to explore the fine-grained manifestations of globalization on the production of information in the digital age.

Last, and more broadly, this article demonstrated the range of application and potential limits of the concept of 'transnational field' in making sense of international and global phenomena. Not all social spaces are fielded: the transnational level is no exception. The conclusions of this article raise three promising paths for future research. First, we need more studies of cases in which language differences hinder international exchanges. Second, it is important to develop a diverse set of methods for examining different facets of the emergence and institutionalization of transnational fields. Though historical methods, interviews and correspondence analysis are obvious choices for studying fields, this article showed that multi-sited ethnographies can also shed light on the fine-grained modalities associated with transnational exchanges, thus challenging taken-for-granted claims about how 'global' a given social space really is. Third, we need to be more specific about the range of application and limits of the concept of transnational field. The article makes a first step in that direction by identifying three criteria that need to be met for transnational exchanges to qualify as 'fielded'.

Acknowledgements

I would like thank Monika Krause, Julian Go, Kim Lane Scheppele, Marianne Blanchard, two anonymous reviewers, as well as the participants of the workshop on 'Fielding Transnationalism' (Boston University, October 2014) and the session on 'Global and Transnational Sociology: Alternative Perspectives' (American Sociological Association Annual Meeting, Chicago, August 2015) for their helpful comments on earlier versions of this article.

Notes

1 This 'heteronomous' logic is sometimes analysed as consisting of two different logics: the political logic and the economic logic, which are not necessarily correlated. Journalism is thus seen as being characterized by a 'double dependency' on these different logics (Benson and Neveu, 2005).
2 http://www.alexa.com/topsites/countries (updated on 1 March 2015; accessed on 6 March 2015).
3 http://www.pulitzer.org/how_to_enter (updated on 12 December 2014; accessed on 6 March 2015)
4 http://journalists.org/awards/online-journalism-awards-rules-eligibility/ (updated on 8 October 2014; accessed on 5 March 2015).
5 For instance, in 2014, only one ONA award out of 34 went to a non-English language article (only four non-English outlets were among the many finalists). Out of the 12 judges involved in the final round of evaluation, two were affiliated to non-English language news organizations (*Zeit Online* and *La Nación*).

References

American Society of News Editors, (2013), 'ASNE newsroom census', available at: http://asne.org/content.asp?contentid=121 (accessed 9 May 2014).
Becker, H. S., (1982), *Art Worlds*, Berkeley, CA: University of California Press.
Benson, R., (2013), *Shaping Immigration News: A French-American Comparison*, New York: Cambridge University Press.
Benson, R. and Neveu, E. (eds), (2005), *Bourdieu and the Journalistic Field*, Cambridge: Polity Press.
Benson, R. and Saguy, A. C., (2005), 'Constructing social problems in an age of globalization: a French-American comparison', *American Sociological Review*, 70 (2): 233–259.
Berglez, P., (2008), 'What is global journalism?', *Journalism Studies*, 9 (6): 845–858.
Bielsa, E. and Bassnett, S., (2009), *Translation in Global News*, New York: Routledge.
Bourdieu, P., (1971), 'Genèse et structure du champ religieux', *Revue Française de Sociologie*, 12 (3): 295–334.
Bourdieu, P., (1994), 'L'emprise du journalisme', *Actes de la Recherche en Sciences Sociales*, 101: 3–9.
Bourdieu, P., (1996a), *The Rules of Art: Genesis and Structure of the Literary Field*, Stanford, CA: Stanford University Press.
Bourdieu, P., (1996b), *The State Nobility: Elite Schools in the Field of Power*, Stanford, CA: Stanford University Press.
Bourdieu, P., (1999), *On Television*. New York: The New Press.
Bourdieu, P., (2002), 'Les conditions sociales de la circulation internationale des idées', *Actes de la recherche en sciences sociales*, 145 (5): 3–8.
Bourdieu, P. and Wacquant, L. J. D., (1992), *An Invitation to Reflexive Sociology*, Chicago: University of Chicago Press.
Boyd-Barrett, O. and Rantanen, T., (1998), *The Globlization of News*, London: SAGE.
Chalaby, J. K., (1996), 'Journalism as an Anglo-American invention: a comparison of the development of French and Anglo-American journalism, 1830s–1920s', *European Journal of Communication*, 11 (3): 303–326.
Charon, J.-M. and Le Floch, P., (2011), *La Presse en Ligne*, Paris: La Découverte.
Christin, A., (2014a), 'Clicks or Pulitzers? Web journalists and their work in the United States and France', PhD dissertation, Department of Sociology, Princeton University / Ecole des hautes études en sciences sociales.
Christin, A., (2014b), 'When it comes to counting clicks, journalists say one thing but feel pressure to do another', *Nieman Journalism Lab*, August issue.
Deuze, M., (2006), 'Global journalism education: a conceptual approach', *Journalism Studies*, 7(1): 20–34.
Dezalay, Y. and Garth, B. G., (1998), *Dealing in Virtue: International Commercial Arbitration and the Construction of a Transnational Legal Order*, Chicago: University of Chicago Press.
Dezalay, Y. and Garth, B. G., (2002), *The Internationalization of Palace Wars: Lawyers, Economists, and the Contest to Transform Latin American States*, Chicago: University of Chicago Press.
Filloux, F., (2014), 'BuzzFeed: An Open Letter to Ben Horowitz', *Monday Note*, 334, September 7.
Fourcade, M., (2006), 'The construction of a global profession: the transnationalization of economics', *American Journal of Sociology*, 112 (1): 145–194.
Fröhlich, R. and Holtz-Bacha, C., (2003), *Journalism Education in Europe and North America: An International Comparison*, New York: Hampton Press.
Gatien, E., (2013), *Prétendre à l'excellence. Prix Albert Londres, prix journalistiques et transformations du journalisme*, Paris: Fondation Varenne.
Gingras, Y., (2002), 'Les formes spécifiques de l'internationalité du champ scientifique', *Actes de la recherche en sciences sociales*, 141–142 (1): 31–45.
Go, J., (2008), 'Global fields and imperial forms: field theory and the British and American Empires', *Sociological Theory*, 26 (3): 201–229.
Gurevitch, M. and Levy, M., (1990), 'The global newsroom', *British Journalism Review*, 2 (1): 27–37.

 The Sociological Review Monographs, 64:2, pp. 212–234 (2016), DOI: 10.1111/2059-7932.12009

Hallin, D. C. and Mancini, P., (2004), *Comparing Media Systems: Three Models of Media and Politics*, Cambridge: Cambridge University Press.
Hamilton, J. M. and Jenner, E., (2004), 'Redefining foreign correspondence', *Journalism* 5 (3): 301–321.
Hannerz, U., (2012), *Foreign News: Exploring the World of Foreign Correspondents*, Chicago: University of Chicago Press.
Hauchecorne, M., (2009), 'Le "professeur Rawls" et le "Nobel des pauvres"', *Actes de la recherche en sciences sociales*, 176–177 (1): 94–113.
Heilbron, J., Guilhot, N., and Jeanpierre, L., (2008), 'Toward a transnational history of the social sciences', *Journal of the History of the Behavioral Sciences*, 44 (2): 146–160.
Herbert, J., (2000), *Practising Global Journalism: Exploring Reporting Issues Worldwide*, Burlington, MA: Focal Press.
Hine, C., (2007), 'Multi-sited ethnography as a middle-range methodology for contemporary STS', *Science, Technology, & Human Values*, 32 (6): 652–671.
Janssen, S., Kuipers, G. and Verboord, M., (2008), 'Cultural globalization and arts journalism: the international orientation of arts and culture coverage in Dutch, French, German, and U.S. newspapers, 1955 to 2005', *American Sociological Review*, 73 (5): 719–740.
Krause, M., (2011), 'Reporting and the transformations of the journalistic field: US news media, 1890–000', *Media, Culture & Society*, 33 (1): 89–104.
Kuipers, G., (2011), 'Cultural globalization as the emergence of a transnational cultural field: transnational television and national media landscapes in four European countries'. *American Behavioral Scientist*, 55(5): 541–557.
Lafarge, G. and Marchetti, D., (2011), 'Les portes fermées du journalisme', *Actes de la recherche en sciences sociales*, 189 (4): 72–99.
Lasorsa, D. L., Lewis, S. C. and Holton, A. E., (2012). 'Normalizing Twitter', *Journalism Studies*, 13 (1): 19–36.
Loeffelholz, M., Weaver, D. and Schwarz, A., (2008), *Global Journalism Research: Theories, Methods, Findings, Future*, Malden, MA: Wiley-Blackwell.
Mudge, S. L. and Vauchez, A., (2012), 'Building Europe on a weak field: law, economics, and scholarly avatars in transnational politics', *American Journal of Sociology*, 118 (2): 449–492.
Padioleau, J. G., (1985), *Le Monde et le Washington Post: Précepteurs et Mousquetaires*, Paris: Presses Universitaires de France.
Palmer, M., (1983), *Des petits journaux aux grandes agences: naissance du journalisme moderne, 1863–1914*, Paris: Aubier.
Pettegree, A., (2014), *The Invention of News: How the World Came to Know about Itself*, New Haven and London: Yale University Press.
Pew Research Center's Project for Excellence in Journalism, (2014), 'The State of the News Media 2014', available at: http://www.journalism.org/packages/state-of-the-news-media-2014/
Reese, S. D., (2010), 'Journalism and globalization', *Sociology Compass*, 4 (6): 344–353.
Reese, S. D., Rutigliano, L., Hyun, K. and Jeong, J., (2007), 'Mapping the blogosphere: professional and citizen-based media in the global news arena', *Journalism*, 8 (3): 235–261.
Ruellan, D., (1993), *Le Professionnalisme du Flou: Identité et Savoir-faire des Journalistes Français*, Grenoble: Presses Universitaires de Grenoble.
Sapiro, G., (2013), 'Le champ est-il national?', *Actes de la recherche en sciences sociales*, 200 (5): 70–85.
Sapiro, G. (eds), (2008), *Translatio : Le marché de la traduction en France à l'heure de la mondialisation*, Paris: CNRS.
Schudson, M., (2011), *The Sociology of News*, New York: Norton.
Steinmetz, G., (2008), 'The colonial state as a social field: ethnographic capital and native policy in the German Overseas Empire before 1914', *American Sociological Review*, 73 (4): 589–612.
Sternberg, J., (2013), 'Global audiences: better in theory than reality', article published in *Digiday* on February 6. Available at: http://digiday.com/publishers/global-audiences-better-in-theory-than-reality/ (accessed 15 March 2015).

Thurman, N., (2007), 'The globalization of journalism online. a transatlantic study of news websites and their international readers', *Journalism*, 8 (3): 285–307.
Usher, N., (2014), *Making News at The New York Times*, Ann Arbor, MI: University of Michigan Press.
Utley, G., (1997), 'The shrinking of foreign news: from broadcast to narrowcast', *Foreign Affairs*, 76 (2): 2–10.
Van Dijk, J.A.G., (2006), 'Digital divide research: achievements and shortcomings', *Poetics*, 34 (4-5): 221–235.
Wagner, A.-C., (2005), *Vers une Europe syndicale : Une enquête sur la Confédération européenne des syndicats*, Bellecombe-en-Bauges: Editions du Croquant.
Willnat, L. and Weaver, D., (2003), 'Through their eyes: the work of foreign correspondents in the United States', *Journalism*, 4 (4): 403–422.
Wimmer, A. and Schiller, N. G., (2003), 'Methodological nationalism, the social sciences, and the study of migration: an essay in historical epistemology', *International Migration Review*, 37 (3): 576–610.

Please quote the article DOI when citing SR content, including monographs. Article DOIs and "How to Cite" information can be found alongside the online version of each article within Wiley Online Library. All articles published within the SR (including monograph content) are included within the ISI Journal Citation Reports® Social Science Citation Index.

Notes on contributors

Larissa Buchholz is a Junior Fellow at the Harvard Society of Fellows. She earned an MA in interdisciplinary Cultural Sciences in Germany and a PhD in Sociology at Columbia University. She specializes in the sociology of culture and knowledge, sociological theory and transnational-global sociology. She has published on global fields, the uses of ethnography for studying embodiment, culture and networks, the international circulation of social-scientific ideas, and the sociology of intellectuals. Her most recent research project, 'The Global Rules of Art', has won numerous awards and is under contract with Princeton University Press. E-mail: lbuchholz@fas.harvard.edu

Angèle Christin is a postdoctoral fellow at the Data and Society Research Institute and the New School for Social Research in New York. She studies web journalism, algorithms, and work practices in the digital age. She published two books to date, in French. Her work was also published in *Poetics*, *Nieman Lab*, *Réseaux*, etc. She defended her dissertation in sociology in 2014 at Princeton University and the Ecole des Hautes Etudes en Sciences Sociales (Paris). E-mail: christa@newschool.edu

Shai M. Dromi is a doctoral candidate in sociology at Yale University. He is a comparative-historical sociologist interested in political culture, humanitarian movement, and collective memory. His current research focuses on the emergence of the humanitarian NGO sector. He has previously worked and published on attitudes towards urban poverty and on the effects of cultural trauma on Middle East politics. His recent articles appeared in *Sociological Forum, Sociological Inquiry* and *New Literary History*. E-mail: shai.dromi@yale.edu

Julian Go is Professor of Sociology at Boston University. His most recent books include *Postcolonial Thought and Social Theory* (Oxford University Press, 2016) and Global Historical Sociology, co-edited with George Lawson (Cambridge University Press, 2016). E-mail: juliango@bu.edu

Monika Krause is a Senior Lecturer in Sociology at Goldsmiths, University of London. Her work focuses on specialized fields of practice from a comparative

The Sociological Review Monographs, 64:2, pp. 235–237 (2016), DOI: 10.1111/2059-7932.12030

Published by John Wiley & Sons Ltd, 9600 Garsington Road, Oxford OX4 2DQ, UK and 350 Main Street, Malden, MA 02148, USA

perspective. She is the author of *The Good Project. Humanitarian Relief NGOs and the Fragmentation of Reason* (Chicago University Press, 2014), which was awarded the British Sociological Association's Philip Abrams Memorial Prize of the British Sociological Association and the Association for Research on Non-profits and the Voluntary Sector's Hodgkinson Book Award. She is currently directing an ESRC-funded project on triage in churches, human rights organizations and environmental conservation agencies. E-mail: bored.marxist@gmail.com

Stephanie Mudge is an Assistant Professor of Sociology at the University of California, Davis. She has authored or co-authored articles in the *American Journal of* Sociology, the *Annual Review of Sociology,* the *European Journal of Sociology, Socio-economic Review,* and *Social Science History*. Her book manuscript, *Reinventing Leftism,* explores how Western left political parties in Sweden, Germany, the UK and the US reinvented themselves twice over the past hundred years, with an emphasis on the role of experts and academics. She is a past recipient of fellowships from the Fulbright Association, the European University Institute's Max Weber Programme, the Max Planck Institute for the Study of Societies, and the Sheffield Political Economy Research Institute. She is also a member of the editorial board of *Sociological Theory.* Her ongoing projects focus on party-expert configurations, political party organizational formation, and the development of progressive politics in Western Europe and the USA since the late 1990s. E-mail: mudge@ucdavis.edu

Martin Petzke is Lecturer in Sociology at the University of Lucerne, Switzerland. He has written on prejudice and group conformity, the theory of Pierre Bourdieu, the sociology of Georg Simmel, religion and globalization, and religious organizations. His current research interests include sociological theory, world society studies, religion, migration, and the sociology of knowledge. Among his recent publications is a book on global evangelicalism: *Weltbekehrungen. Zur Konstruktion globaler Religion im pfingstlich-evangelikalen Christentum* [World Conversions. On the Construction of Global Religion in Evangelical Christianity] (Bielefeld, 2013). E-mail: Martin.Petzke@unilu.ch

Lisa Stampnitzky is Lecturer in Politics at the University of Sheffield, and completed her PhD in Sociology at the University of California, Berkeley. Her research interests lie at the intersection of knowledge, violence, and power, with a particular focus on the production of popular and expert knowledge about war, terrorism, and human rights. She is the author of *Disciplining Terror: How Experts Invented 'Terrorism'* (Cambridge University Press, 2013), winner of the Francesco Guicciardini Prize for Best Book in Historical International Relations and the International Political Sociology Book Award (both from the International Studies Association), and the Social Science History Association President's Book Award. This article draws on her current book project, *How Torture Became Speakable*, which analyses why the post-9/11 war on terror has been

The Sociological Review Monographs, 64:2, pp. 235–237 (2016), DOI: 10.1111/2059-7932.12030

characterized by the open justification of practices that violate human rights norms. E-mail: lisastampnitzky@gmail.com

George Steinmetz is the Charles Tilly Collegiate Professor of Sociology at the University of Michigan and a Corresponding Member of the Centre de Sociologie européenne, Paris. He is a social theorist and a historical sociologist of states, empires, and social science. He is the author of *The Devil's Handwriting: Precoloniality and the German Colonial State in Qingdao, Samoa, and Southwest Africa* (Chicago University Press, 2007) and *Regulating the Social: The Welfare State and Local Politics in Imperial Germany* (Princeton University Press, 1993). He is the editor of State/Culture. State Formation after the Cultural Turn (Cornell University Press, 1999), *The Politics of Method in the Human Sciences: Positivism and its Epistemological Others* (Duke University Press, 2005) and *Sociology and Empire* (Duke University Press, 2013). His forthcoming book examines the formation of French and British sociology between the 1930s and the 1960s in the context of late colonial empire. E-mail: geostein@umich.edu

Antoine Vauchez is a CNRS Research Professor (*Directeur de recherche*) at the Centre européen de sociologie et de science politique (Université Paris 1-Sorbonne). Over the years, he has been a postdoctoral fellow at the American Bar Foundation (Northwestern University, 2000), a Senior Emile Noël fellow at New York University (2014), and a Visiting Professor at Columbia University (2013). His research engages in historical and political sociology, researching extensively the interactions between forms of expertise, transnational knowledge communities and transnational politics with a particular emphasis on law, economics and on the European Union. Among other journals, he has published his work in the *American Journal of Sociology, International Political Sociology,* the *Berliner Journal für Soziologie, European Political Science Research,* etc. Recently, he has authored a monograph providing a renewed narrative of Europe's political and legal integration (*Brokering Europe. Euro-lawyers and the Making of a Transnational Polity,* Cambridge University Press), and an essay *Democratizing Europe* (Palgrave, 2015). E-mail: vauchez@hotmail.com

Nicholas Hoover Wilson is an Assistant Professor of Sociology at Stony Brook University in New York. His interests lie at the intersection of the organization of imperial administrations, how territories are incorporated or differentiated from political units, and the historical transformation of moral categories. He is working on a book manuscript about how the category of 'corruption' transformed over the course of the English East India Company's presence in India. E-mail: nicholas.wilson@stonybrook.edu

Index

The Sociological Review Monographs, 64:2, pp. 238–241 (2016), DOI: 10.1111/2059-7932.12029

Published by John Wiley & Sons Ltd, 9600 Garsington Road, Oxford OX4 2DQ, UK and 350 Main Street, Malden, MA 02148, USA

The Sociological Review Monographs, 64:2, pp. 238–241 (2016), DOI: 10.1111/2059-7932.12029

The Sociological Review Monographs, 64:2, pp. 238–241 (2016), DOI: 10.1111/2059-7932.12029

The Sociological Review Monographs, 64:2, pp. 238–241 (2016), DOI: 10.1111/2059-7932.12029